RIA's Complete Analysis of the Tax Increase Prevention and Reconciliation Act

With Code Sections as Amended and Committee Reports

Here's your copy of RIA's industry-leading "Complete Analysis of the Tax Increase Prevention and Reconciliation Act". We appreciate your patronage.

Here's a list of handy reference numbers:

1-800-950-1216—To place an order for this or other publications
1-800-431-9025—If you have questions about a previously placed order or a customer service issue
1-800-742-3348—If you have a question about product content

395 Hudson Street
New York, N.Y. 10014

ria.thomson.com

RIA's Complete Analysis of the Tax Increase Prevention and Reconciliation Act

THOMSON RIA™

Sydney Pokorny
Xiomara Tejeda

Sue Ellen Sobel, *Supervisor*
Alexis Brown
Adel Faltas
Jennifer Huber
Denise Marshall

Data Analysts

Young Sone
Lisa Alcock

Citator Data Managers

Janie Davis
Ivette Terry

Paralegals

Joann Casanova
Catherine Daleo
Monica Grier
Danny Wang

Indexing

David Thompson, *Manager*
Janet Mazefsky, *Assistant Manager*
Tom Adewolu
Oslin Busby
George Flynn
Linda Lao
Andrea Leal
Irene Richards
Arlene Verderber

Legal Resource Center

Peter Durham, *Manager*
Agueda Boone
Pierre Calixte
Sandra Crowder
Patricia Link
Ed Mack
Theresa Scherne
Bernadette Stanton
Michael Stanton
Holly Yue

Velma Goodwine-McDermon, *Supervisor*
Charyn Johnson
William Lesesne

Product Development

Todd Gordon, *Director*

Kim Chirls, *Lead Project Manager*

End-User Technical Services

Jose Fiol, *Team Lead*

Steven McGill, *Design Lead*
Eric Bauer
Jay Loyola
Tanya McDonald
Joseph Oliveri
Raymond Santiago
Valencia Singleton
Dominic Smith

Product Technology

Perry Townes, *Senior Director*

Tim Bills, *Manager*

Jay Liu, *Manager*

John Melazzo, *Manager*

Laurie Mitchell, *Manager*

Gene Wojna, *Manager*

Eileen Wood, *Information Manager*

Daryl Alexander
Ron Bergeron
Tom Bontrager
Geoff Braine
Janice Cheung
Resa Cirrincione
Sharon Coon
Tracey Cruz
Olga Davidov
Chris DiGanci
Andy Dreistadt
Tatyana Fersht
Janine Francesca
Sammy Francois
Peggy Frank
Terri Ganssley
Lee Gingello
Anthony Guglielmo
Michelle Harmon
Jay Kwon
Terry LaGoy
Cynthia Lewis
Jackie Lynott
Chris Macano
David McInerney
Linda Ni
Ejelonu Onukogu
Pamela J. Otruba
Michelle Paulin
Genevie Peters
Dan Pirro
Steve Pitamber
Jason Rapaccuiolo
Patricia Reilly
Ruth Russell
Becky Sears
Alfred Sehayek
Jason Shen
Esme Smartt
Pisa Sone
Margaret Taylor
Torrod Taylor
Alana Trafford
Vivian Turner
Dmitriy Viner
Rhonda Waller
Jieping Wang
Dennis Wendell
Ava Williams
Steve Wisniewski
Hongtu Zhang
Teresa Zhang

Content Technology

Brian McNamara, *Director*

Gale Metz, *Director*

Alanna Dixon, *Manager*

David Levine, *Manager*

Nicole Kardos, *Project Manager*

Sergey Arutchev
David Bantel
Bob Bridier
Mary Jo Catlett
Karen de Luna
Nadine Graham
Steven Haber
Chris Jungheim
Stephen Karg
Julie Lu
Darren McNelis
Scott Murphy
William Peake
Tasso Quidera
Luc Quirion
Irina Resnikoff
Derek Sanders
Linda Wiseman
Chris Yourch

Manufacturing & Fulfillment Services

Rick Bivona, *Director*

Anthony Scribano, *Scheduling and Fulfillment Manager*

Gail Gneiding, *Manufacturing and Outside Composition Manager*

Rachel Hassenbein, *Associate Fulfillment Manager*

John Disposti, *Senior Manufacturing Coordinator*

Greg Miller, *Associate Production Manager*

Enid Skolnik, *Associate Fulfillment Manager*

Anthony Lovari, *Inventory Manager*

Bryan Gardner, *Senior Manufacturing Coordinator*

Linda Gottlieb
Chris Harrington
Jennifer Kalison
Allison Richmond

Table of Contents

¶ 1. Organization of the Book

Organization of RIA's Complete Analysis of the Tax Increase Prevention and Reconciliation Act

This book contains RIA's Complete Analysis of H.R. 4297, the Tax Increase Prevention and Reconciliation Act of 2005 (generally referred to in the Analysis as the "Tax Increase Prevention Act"), which was signed into law by the President on May 17, 2006.

The Tax Increase Prevention Act began life as a tax reconciliation bill designed primarily to retroactively extend a number of popular tax breaks that expired at the end of 2005, and extend a number of tax breaks due to expire in future years. Months of partisan debate produced short-term alternative minimum tax (AMT) relief, the extension of certain tax breaks, such as favorably-taxed capital gains and dividends that were due to expire after 2008, and a number of revenue raisers.

The Tax Increase Prevention Act features the following extenders and new tax breaks:

- For 2006, the AMT exemption amount for married taxpayers increases to $62,550 and for unmarried individuals to $42,500 (instead of dropping to $45,000 and $33,750 respectively), and nonrefundable personal tax credits may be claimed to the full extent of an individual's regular tax and AMT (instead of being limited to the excess of regular tax liability over tentative minimum tax).
- Pre-Tax Increase Prevention Act law's favorable tax rates for capital gains and qualified dividend income remain in place through 2010 (instead of sunsetting after 2008).
- Pre-Tax Increase Prevention Act law's favorable Code Sec. 179 expensing provisions remain in place through the end of 2009 (instead of through the end of 2007).
- The exception under subpart F for active financing and insurance income is extended for two years, to tax years of foreign corporations beginning before Jan. 1, 2009, and for any tax year of a U.S. shareholder with or within which the tax year of the foreign corporation ends.
- Until 2009, there's a new temporary exception from subpart F for dividends, interest, rents and royalties received by one CFC (controlled foreign corporation) from a related CFC to the extent attributable to non-subpart F income of the payor.
- The active business test for tax-free corporate spin-offs is simplified by looking at all corporations in the distributing corporation's and the spun-off subsidiary's respective affiliated group to determine if the active business test

is satisfied (applies for distributions after May 17, 2006 and before Jan. 1, 2011).

• A taxpayer may elect to treat the sale or exchange of musical compositions or copyrights in musical works created by his personal efforts as the sale or exchange of a capital asset (applies for sales or exchanges before Jan. 1, 2011, in tax years beginning after May 17, 2006).

The Tax Increase Prevention Act pays for the extended and new tax breaks highlighted above with a number of revenue-raising provisions, including the following:

• The $100,000 modified AGI limit on conversions of traditional IRAs to Roth IRAs is eliminated for tax years beginning after Dec. 31, 2009. For 2010 conversions, unless a taxpayer elects otherwise, the amount includible in gross income because of the conversion is included ratably in 2011 and 2012. Special rules apply if converted amounts are distributed before 2012.

• For purposes of the 50% W-2 wage limit on the Code Sec. 199 domestic production deduction, taxpayers may only include amounts which are properly allocable to domestic production gross receipts; and the special limit on wages treated as allocated to partners or shareholders of pass-through entities is repealed (both effective for tax years beginning after May 17, 2006).

• For tax years beginning after 2005, the age at which the kiddie tax applies is changed from under 14 to under 18 years of age. An exception to the tax would apply for a child who is married and files a joint return for the tax year, and for distributions from certain qualified disability trusts.

• Information reporting is required for interest paid on tax-exempt bonds after Dec. 31, 2005.

• For offers-in-compromise submitted on and after the date that is 60 days after May 17, 2006, taxpayers must make partial payments to IRS while their offer is being considered by IRS.

• For tax years beginning on or after May 17, 2006, the Tax Increase Prevention Act codifies proposed regs which provide that, for purposes of applying the earnings stripping rules to a corporation that owns, directly or indirectly, an interest in a partnership, the corporation's share of partnership liabilities, interest income, and interest expense is treated as those of the corporation.

• For amounts paid or incurred after May 17, 2006, the amortization period for geological and geophysical (G&G) costs paid or incurred by certain major integrated oil companies is 5 years instead of the more favorable 24-month amortization period that applies to other taxpayers.

Contents. A complete list of topics discussed, arranged by paragraph title and number . . . . ¶ 2

Analysis of the Tax Provisions. This section includes the Analysis of the Tax Increase Prevention Act arranged in topical order. Each analysis paragraph starts with a boldface title. That is followed by a list of the Code sections substantively affected by the change, the Tax Increase Prevention Act section that caused the change, and the generally effective date for the change. Each analysis paragraph discusses the background for the change, the new law change, and the effective date for that change. Analysis paragraphs may include (1) illustrations and observations providing practical insight into the effects of the change, (2) recommendations explaining how to take advantage of opportunities presented by the law change, (3) cautions explaining how to avoid pitfalls created by the law change, and (4) client letters alerting taxpayers to significant new law changes. The Analysis of the Tax Increase Prevention Act is reproduced at ¶ 100 *et seq.* . . . . p. 1

Client Letters. Client letters are included on the following topics:

- Extension of relief from the AMT;
- Beginning in 2010, income limitations on Roth IRA conversions are eliminated;
- Kiddie tax age limit raised from under 14 to under 18;
- Tax provisions affecting individuals; and
- Business and corporate changes.

The Client Letters begin at ¶ 1000 *et seq.* . . . . p. 151

Code as Amended. All Code sections that were amended, added, repealed, or redesignated by the tax provisions of the Tax Increase Prevention Act, appear in Code section order as amended, added, repealed, or redesignated. New matter is shown in italics. Deleted material and effective dates are shown in footnotes. The Code as Amended is reproduced at ¶ 3000 *et seq.* . . . . p. 201

Act Sections Not Amending Code. This section reproduces in Act section order, all Tax Increase Prevention Act sections, or portions thereof that are tax related but do not amend specific Code sections. The Tax Increase Prevention Act Sections Not Amending Code are reproduced at ¶ 4000 *et seq.* . . . . p. 301

Committee Reports. This section reproduces all relevant parts of the Conference Report (Conf Rept No. 109-455) and the House Report (H Rept No. 109-304) relating to the Tax Increase Prevention Act. Also reproduced are any relevant parts of the Joint Committee on Taxation Explanation (JCX-77-05) relating to S. 2020, a predecessor Senate bill to the Tax Increase Prevention Act.

The relevant Committee Reports for the Tax Increase Prevention Act (in this case, Conf Rept No. 109-455, H Rept No. 109-304, and JCX-77-05) are reproduced at ¶ 5001 *et seq.* . . . . p. 401

¶ 2. Contents

¶ 100. Extension of Reduced Capital Gain and Dividend Rates

¶ 101. 5% and 15% tax rates on adjusted net capital gain are extended for two years

Code Sec. 1(h)(1)(B), Tax Increase Prevention Act § 102
Code Sec. 1(h)(1)(C), Tax Increase Prevention Act § 102
Code Sec. None, Tax Increase Prevention Act § 102
Generally effective: Tax years beginning after Dec. 31, 2008 and before Jan. 1, 2011
Committee Reports, see ¶ 5002

A noncorporate taxpayer's adjusted net capital gain is taxed at a maximum rate of 15%, or, to the extent it would have been taxed at a 10% or 15% rate if it had been ordinary income, at a maximum rate of 5% (0% for tax years beginning after 2007, see ¶ 102). Adjusted net capital gain is net capital gain for the tax year (i.e., the excess of net long-term capital gains over net short-term capital losses for a tax year):

. . . less the sum of specified types of long-term capital gain that are taxed at a maximum rate of 28% (gain on the sale of most collectibles and gain on the unexcluded part of Code Sec. 1202 small business stock) or 25% (unrecaptured section 1250 gain, i.e., gain attributable to real estate depreciation),

. . . plus qualified dividend income (see ¶ 107 *et seq.*).

However, under section 303 of the 2003 Jobs and Growth Act, the 5% and 15% maximum rates on adjusted net capital gain were due to expire at the end of 2008, and the rates in effect before passage of that Act (ranging from 8% to 20%) were due to come back into effect. (For post-2007 0% rate, see ¶ 102.)

(FTC 2d/FIN ¶ I-5110 *et seq.*, ¶ I-5110.10; USTR ¶ 14.08; TaxDesk ¶ 223,309 *et seq.*, ¶ 223,320)

New Law. The Tax Increase Prevention Act extends the 5% and 15% rates on adjusted net capital gain through tax years beginning before Jan. 1, 2011. (2003 Jobs and Growth Act § 303 as amended by Tax Increase Prevention Act § 102)

☐ **Effective:** Tax years beginning after Dec. 31, 2008 (Com Rept, see ¶ 5002) and before Jan. 1, 2011. (Tax Increase Prevention Act §102)

FTC 2d References are to Federal Tax Coordinator 2d
FIN References are to RIA's Analysis of Federal Taxes: Income
USTR References are to United States Tax Reporter: Income, Estate & Gift, and Excise
PCA References are to Pension Analysis (print & electronic)
PE References are to the Pension Explanations (print & electronic)

¶ 102. Post-2007 0% tax rate on adjusted net capital gains is extended for two years

Code Sec. 1(h)(1)(B), Tax Increase Prevention Act § 102
Code Sec. None, Tax Increase Prevention Act § 102
Generally effective: Tax years beginning after Dec. 31, 2008 and before Jan. 1, 2011
Committee Reports, see ¶ 5002

For tax years beginning after 2007, a noncorporate taxpayer's adjusted net capital gain (see ¶ 101) that would otherwise be taxed at the regular 10% or 15% rates if it were ordinary income will be taxed at a 0% rate for regular tax purposes. However, under section 303 of the 2003 Jobs and Growth Act, this rate was due to expire at the end of 2008, and the 10%/8% rates on adjusted net capital gain that would otherwise be taxed at the 10% or 15% rates if it were ordinary income, which were in effect before passage of that Act, were due to come back into effect. (FTC 2d/FIN ¶ I-5110.1; USTR ¶ 14.08; TaxDesk ¶ 223,310)

> ***observation:*** In other words, under the 2003 Jobs and Growth Act as originally enacted, the 0% rate was scheduled to be in effect only for tax years beginning in 2008.

New Law. The Tax Increase Prevention Act extends the 0% rate on adjusted net capital gain that would otherwise be taxed at the regular 10% or 15% rates if it were ordinary income through tax years beginning before Jan. 1, 2011. (2003 Jobs and Growth Act § 303 as amended by Tax Increase Prevention Act § 102)

> ***observation:*** As a result of the above extension, the 0% rate on adjusted net capital gain will be available for tax years beginning in 2008, 2009, and 2010.

> ***observation:*** The above change applies for regular tax purposes. For parallel change for alternative minimum tax (AMT) purposes, see ¶ 103.

☐ **Effective:** Tax years beginning after Dec. 31, 2008 (Com Rept, see ¶ 5002) and before Jan. 1, 2011. (Tax Increase Prevention Act §102)

¶ 103. 5% (0% in 2008) and 15% maximum AMT rates on adjusted net capital gain are extended for two years

Code Sec. 55(b)(3)(B), Tax Increase Prevention Act § 102
Code Sec. 55(b)(3)(C), Tax Increase Prevention Act § 102
Code Sec. None, Tax Increase Prevention Act § 102
Generally effective: Tax years beginning after Dec. 31, 2008 and before Jan. 1, 2011
Committee Reports, see ¶ 5002

The starting point for the computation of the alternative minimum tax (AMT) is taxable income. Various adjustments and preferences are added or subtracted to arrive at alternative minimum taxable income (AMTI). For noncorporate taxpayers, the taxable excess, determined after subtraction of an exemption amount, is subject to a tentative minimum tax of 26% or 28% (subject to reduction for any AMT foreign tax credit).

However, a noncorporate taxpayer's tentative minimum tax is subject to a limit which is intended to insure that the 5% and 15% maximum tax rates on adjusted net capital gain that apply for regular tax purposes (see ¶ 101) also apply for AMT purposes. This limit, set forth by Code Sec. 55(b)(3), is the sum of various amounts, which include:

(1) 5% (0% for tax years beginning after 2007) of so much of the taxpayer's adjusted net capital gain (or, if less, taxable excess) as did not exceed the amount on which a 10% or 15% regular tax rate was imposed under Code Sec. 1(h)(1)(B), and

(2) 15% of the adjusted net capital gain (or, if less, taxable excess) in excess of the amount on which tax was determined under paragraph (1) above.

Under section 303 of the 2003 Jobs and Growth Act, these 5%/0%/15% rates were due to expire at the end of 2008, and the rates on adjusted net capital gain in effect before passage of that Act (ranging from 8% to 20%) were due to come back into effect. (FTC 2d/FIN ¶ A-8102; USTR ¶ 554.01; TaxDesk ¶ 691,002).

New Law. The Tax Increase Prevention Act extends the 5% (0% for tax years beginning after 2007) and 15% AMT rates on adjusted net capital gain through tax years beginning before Jan. 1, 2011. (2003 Jobs and Growth Act § 303 as amended by Tax Increase Prevention Act § 102)

FTC 2d References are to Federal Tax Coordinator 2d
FIN References are to RIA's Analysis of Federal Taxes: Income
USTR References are to United States Tax Reporter: Income, Estate & Gift, and Excise
PCA References are to Pension Analysis (print & electronic)
PE References are to the Pension Explanations (print & electronic)

☐ **Effective:** Tax years beginning after Dec. 31, 2008 (Com Rept, see ¶ 5002) and before Jan. 1, 2011. (Tax Increase Prevention Act §102)

¶ 104. 7% AMT preference percentage for excluded gain on sale of qualified small business stock is extended for two years

Code Sec. 57(a)(7), Tax Increase Prevention Act § 102
Code Sec. None, Tax Increase Prevention Act § 102
Generally effective: Tax years beginning after Dec. 31, 2008 and before Jan. 1, 2011
Committee Reports, see ¶ 5002

Under Code Sec. 1202, a taxpayer who satisfies certain requirements may exclude from gross income 50% of the gain that he realizes on the disposition of "qualified small business stock" (60% in the case of certain stock in empowerment zone businesses). However, 7% of the amount excluded from gross income under this rule (i.e., 14% of the total gain) is treated as a preference item for alternative minimum tax (AMT) purposes.

Under section 303 of the 2003 Jobs and Growth Act, this preference percentage was due to expire at the end of 2008, and the 28% and 42% preference percentages in effect before passage of that Act were due to come back into effect. (FTC 2d/FIN ¶ A-8304; USTR ¶ 574; TaxDesk ¶ 697,004)

New Law. The Tax Increase Prevention Act extends the 7% preference percentage through tax years beginning before Jan. 1, 2011. (2003 Jobs and Growth Act § 303 as amended by Tax Increase Prevention Act § 102)

> ***observation:*** For qualifying stock that meets the holding period requirements, where a taxpayer qualifies for the full 50% exclusion for regular tax purposes, 3.5% (7% of 50%) of the total gain on the sale or exchange will be an AMT preference.
>
> ***observation:*** Thus, for stock qualifying under this rule, the maximum rate under the AMT will be 14.98% (53.5% × 28%), compared to a maximum effective regular tax rate of 14%. These maximum effective tax rates can be explained as follows:
>
> Where a taxpayer qualifies for the full 50% exclusion for regular tax purposes, 50% of the gain is included in gross income and therefore in alternative minimum taxable income (AMTI)—the amount on which AMT is computed—as well. To this amount is added the preference item described above—i.e., 7% of the excluded amount, which equals 3.5% of the total amount of gain qualifying for the exclusion (i.e., 7% of the 50% exclusion). Thus, 53.5% (50% + 3.5%) of the gain is in-

cluded in AMTI. Under the AMT rules, this amount is subject to a maximum rate of tax of 28% (see FTC 2d/FIN ¶ A-8101; USTR ¶ 554; TaxDesk ¶ 691,001). Therefore, the maximum rate under the AMT is 14.98% (53.5% × 28%).

This contrasts with the 14% maximum effective rate on these gains for regular tax purposes (the 50% of the gain included in gross income multiplied by the 28% capital gains rate to which the included Code Sec. 1202 gain is subject, under the rules explained at FTC 2d/FIN ¶ I-5110.11 *et seq.*; USTR ¶ 14.08; TaxDesk ¶ 223,321).

observation: The percentages mentioned in the above *RIA observations* must be appropriately increased in cases involving empowerment zone businesses where the exclusion is 60% rather than 50%.

☐ **Effective:** Tax years beginning after Dec. 31, 2008 (Com Rept, see ¶ 5002) and before Jan. 1, 2011. (Tax Increase Prevention Act §102)

¶ 105. 15% withholding rate that IRS may impose on USRPI gains passed through to foreign persons by U.S. partnerships, trusts or estates is extended for two years

Code Sec. 1445(e)(1), Tax Increase Prevention Act § 102
Code Sec. None, Tax Increase Prevention Act § 102
Generally effective: Tax years beginning after Dec. 31, 2008 and before Jan. 1, 2011
Committee Reports, see ¶ 5002

A U.S. partnership, the trustee of a U.S. trust, or the executor of a U.S. estate is required to deduct and withhold tax on any gain realized on the disposition of a United States real property interest (USRPI) to the extent that gain is includable in the income of a foreign partner or foreign beneficiary of the entity, or, in the case of a trust, of a foreign person under the grantor trust rules. The deduction/withholding rate may be 15% to the extent provided by IRS regs. Congress expected that IRS would authorize the 15% rate when the person who was taxable on the gain was an individual.

However, under section 303 of the 2003 Jobs and Growth Act, this 15% rate was due to expire at the end of 2008, and the 20% rate in effect before passage

FTC 2d References are to Federal Tax Coordinator 2d
FIN References are to RIA's Analysis of Federal Taxes: Income
USTR References are to United States Tax Reporter: Income, Estate & Gift, and Excise
PCA References are to Pension Analysis (print & electronic)
PE References are to the Pension Explanations (print & electronic)

of that Act was due to come back into effect. (FTC 2d/FIN ¶ O-13035; USTR ¶ 14,454.02; TaxDesk ¶ 644,019)

New Law. The Tax Increase Prevention Act extends the 15% rate through tax years beginning before Jan. 1, 2011. (2003 Jobs and Growth Act § 303 as amended by Tax Increase Prevention Act § 102)

> ***observation:*** The above extension parallels the Tax Increase Prevention Act's extension of the 15% maximum rate that may be imposed on adjusted net capital gain (see ¶ 101).

☐ **Effective:** Tax years beginning after Dec. 31, 2008 (Com Rept, see ¶ 5002) and before Jan. 1, 2011. (Tax Increase Prevention Act §102)

¶ 106. 15% maximum tax rate on individuals' nonqualifying withdrawals from Merchant Marine capital gain accounts of capital construction funds (CCFs) is extended for two years

Code Sec. 7518(g)(6)(A), Tax Increase Prevention Act § 102
Code Sec. None, Tax Increase Prevention Act § 102
Generally effective: Tax years beginning after Dec. 31, 2008 and before Jan. 1, 2011
Committee Reports, see ¶ 5002

Taxable income is reduced by certain amounts deposited for the tax year in a capital construction fund (CCF)—for the construction or reconstruction in the U.S. of American vessels—established by agreement with the Secretary of Transportation or the Secretary of Commerce. "Nonqualifying withdrawals" from a CCF are taxable, but are taxed separately from the taxpayer's other income or losses. For individuals' nonqualifying withdrawals from the capital gain account that is a required part of a CCF, the tax rate may not exceed 15%.

However, under section 303 of the 2003 Jobs and Growth Act, that rate was due to expire at the end of 2008, and the 20% rate in effect before passage of that Act was due to come back into effect. (FTC 2d/FIN ¶ J-1360; USTR ¶ 75,184).

New Law. The Tax Increase Prevention Act extends the 15% rate through tax years beginning before Jan. 1, 2011. (2003 Jobs and Growth Act § 303 as amended by Tax Increase Prevention Act § 102)

> ***observation:*** The above extension parallels the Act's extension of the 15% maximum rate that may be imposed on adjusted net capital gain (see ¶ 101).

☐ **Effective:** Tax years beginning after Dec. 31, 2008 (Com Rept, see ¶ 5002) and before Jan. 1, 2011. (Tax Increase Prevention Act §102)

¶ 107. 5% and 15% adjusted capital gains rates on noncorporate taxpayers' qualified dividend income are extended for two years

Code Sec. 1(h)(3)(B), Tax Increase Prevention Act § 102
Code Sec. 1(h)(11), Tax Increase Prevention Act § 102
Code Sec. None, Tax Increase Prevention Act § 102
Generally effective: Tax years beginning after Dec. 31, 2008 and before Jan. 1, 2011
Committee Reports, see ¶ 5002

"Qualified dividend income"—generally, dividends received during the tax year from domestic corporations and "qualified foreign corporations," subject to holding period requirements and specified exceptions—is effectively treated as adjusted net capital gain, and therefore taxed at the same 5% and 15% maximum rates that apply to adjusted net capital gain, see ¶ 101.

However, under section 303 of the 2003 Jobs and Growth Act, this treatment was due to expire at the end of 2008, and qualified dividend income was then to be taxed at ordinary income rates. (FTC 2d/FIN ¶ I-5115 *et seq.*; USTR ¶ 14.085; TaxDesk ¶ 223,345 *et seq.*)

New Law. The Tax Increase Prevention Act extends the treatment of qualified dividend income as adjusted net capital gain, taxable at the same 5% and 15% maximum rates that otherwise apply to adjusted net capital gain, through tax years beginning before Jan. 1, 2011. (2003 Jobs and Growth Act § 303 as amended by Tax Increase Prevention Act § 102)

☐ **Effective:** Tax years beginning after Dec. 31, 2008 (Com Rept, see ¶ 5002) and before Jan. 1, 2011. (Tax Increase Prevention Act §102)

FTC 2d References are to Federal Tax Coordinator 2d
FIN References are to RIA's Analysis of Federal Taxes: Income
USTR References are to United States Tax Reporter: Income, Estate & Gift, and Excise
PCA References are to Pension Analysis (print & electronic)
PE References are to the Pension Explanations (print & electronic)

¶ 108. Long-term capital loss treatment for individuals' losses on stock to the extent extraordinary dividends were taxed as capital gains is extended for two years

Code Sec. 1(h)(11)(D)(ii), Tax Increase Prevention Act § 102
Code Sec. None, Tax Increase Prevention Act § 102
Generally effective: Tax years beginning after Dec. 31, 2008 and before Jan. 1, 2011
Committee Reports, see ¶ 5002

If an individual receives, with respect to any share of stock, qualified dividend income (dividends taxed at the 5% and 15% maximum rates applicable to adjusted net capital gain, see ¶ 107), from one or more dividends that are extraordinary dividends—defined generally by Code Sec. 1059(c) as any dividend that's more than 10% (5% in the case of preferred stock) of the holder's adjusted basis in the underlying stock—any loss on the sale or exchange of that share of stock must, to the extent of the extraordinary dividends, be treated as long-term capital loss. In other words, if, with respect to any share of stock, an individual receives an extraordinary dividend that's eligible for treatment as qualified dividend income, any loss on the sale of the stock must be treated as a long-term capital loss to the extent of the dividend.

> ***observation:*** If an individual receives an extraordinary dividend with respect to stock, and the dividend is also qualified dividend income, the individual must treat any loss on the sale of the stock as long-term capital loss, to the extent of the extraordinary dividend, regardless of whether the stock has actually been held for the long-term holding period. Thus, if, with respect to the same stock, an individual realizes both qualifying dividend income (taxed at long-term capital gain rates) and a loss, the individual will be required to use the loss to reduce his long-term gain.
>
> This rule is not restricted to situations where the individual taxpayer realizes qualifying dividend income and a loss on the underlying stock in the same tax year. Long-term capital loss treatment for a loss on "extraordinary dividend" stock applies, even if the extraordinary dividend, taxed as qualified dividend income, was received in an earlier tax year.

Under section 303 of the 2003 Jobs and Growth Act, the above rule was due to expire at the end of 2008 (along with the rules taxing qualified dividend income at the 5% or 15% maximum adjusted net capital gain rates, see ¶ 107).

(FTC 2d/FIN ¶ I-5104.1; USTR ¶ 14.087; TaxDesk ¶ 223,304.1)

New Law. The Tax Increase Prevention Act extends the above rule through tax years beginning before Jan. 1, 2011. (2003 Jobs and Growth Act § 303 as amended by Tax Increase Prevention Act § 102)

> ***observation:*** This extension parallels the extension of the rules taxing qualified dividend income at the 5% or 15% maximum rates applicable to adjusted net capital gain, see ¶ 107.

☐ **Effective:** Tax years beginning after Dec. 31, 2008 (Com Rept, see ¶ 5002) and before Jan. 1, 2011. (Tax Increase Prevention Act §102)

¶ 109. Exclusion of qualified dividend income from investment income for investment interest deduction limit purposes (unless taxpayer elects to include it) is extended for two years

Code Sec. 163(d)(4)(B), Tax Increase Prevention Act § 102
Code Sec. None, Tax Increase Prevention Act § 102
Generally effective: Tax years beginning after Dec. 31, 2008 and before Jan. 1, 2011
Committee Reports, see ¶ 5002

A noncorporate taxpayer's deduction for investment interest expense is limited to the amount of the taxpayer's net investment income, i.e., the excess of investment income over investment expenses for the year. (FTC 2d/FIN ¶ K-5311; USTR ¶ 1634.053; TaxDesk ¶ 315,011) Any investment interest that is disallowed because it exceeds this limit is carried over to the next tax year and treated as investment interest paid or accrued in that year. (FTC 2d/FIN ¶ K-5321; USTR ¶ 1634.053; TaxDesk ¶ 315,021)

"Investment income" for this purpose includes, among other items, qualified dividend income (dividends taxed at the 5% or 15% maximum adjusted net capital gain rates, see ¶ 107), but only to the extent the taxpayer elects to treat the qualified dividend income as investment income for purposes of the limitation on the investment interest deduction. And any amount that the taxpayer elects to treat as investment income in this fashion is excluded from qualified dividend income treatment. Thus, to the extent the taxpayer elects to treat dividends as investment income for purposes of determining the amount of deductible investment interest, those dividends aren't eligible to be taxed at the maximum 5% or 15% maximum adjusted net capital gain rates.

FTC 2d References are to Federal Tax Coordinator 2d
FIN References are to RIA's Analysis of Federal Taxes: Income
USTR References are to United States Tax Reporter: Income, Estate & Gift, and Excise
PCA References are to Pension Analysis (print & electronic)
PE References are to the Pension Explanations (print & electronic)

> ***observation:*** This means that a taxpayer whose investment interest deduction is limited because the interest exceeds the amount of his net investment income can increase the deduction by electing to include all or part of qualified dividend income in investment income. The cost of making the election is that the dividends will be taxed as ordinary income rather than capital gain. Thus, if the taxpayer's investment interest would be fully deductible even without the election, the election should not be made.

However, under section 303 of the 2003 Jobs and Growth Act, the above rule was due to expire at the end of 2008 (along with the rules taxing qualified dividend income at the 5% or 15% maximum adjusted net capital gain rates, see ¶ 107). (FTC 2d/FIN ¶ I-5115.1, ¶ K-5318.1; USTR ¶ 14.085, ¶ 1634.053; TaxDesk ¶ 223,346, ¶ 315,018.1)

New Law. The Tax Increase Prevention Act extends the above rule regarding the treatment of qualified dividend income as investment income through tax years beginning before Jan. 1, 2011. (2003 Jobs and Growth Act § 303 as amended by Tax Increase Prevention Act § 102)

> ***observation:*** This extension parallels the extension of the rules taxing qualified dividend income at the 5% or 15% maximum rates applicable to adjusted net capital gain, see ¶ 107.

☐ **Effective:** Tax years beginning after Dec. 31, 2008 (Com Rept, see ¶ 5002) and before Jan. 1, 2011. (Tax Increase Prevention Act §102)

¶ 110. Passthrough of qualified dividend income by RICs and REITs is extended for two years

Code Sec. 854(a), Tax Increase Prevention Act § 102
Code Sec. 854(b)(1)(B), Tax Increase Prevention Act § 102
Code Sec. 854(b)(1)(C), Tax Increase Prevention Act § 102
Code Sec. 854(b)(2), Tax Increase Prevention Act § 102
Code Sec. 854(b)(5), Tax Increase Prevention Act § 102
Code Sec. 857(c)(2), Tax Increase Prevention Act § 102
Code Sec. None, Tax Increase Prevention Act § 102
Generally effective: Tax years beginning after Dec. 31, 2008 and before Jan. 1, 2011
Committee Reports, see ¶ 5002

RICs. If the qualified dividend income (i.e., dividends taxed at the 5% or 15% maximum adjusted net capital gain rates, see ¶ 107) received by a regulated investment company (RIC) during any tax year is less than 95% of its gross income, then, in computing the amount of the qualified dividend income paid by the RIC, passthrough limitation rules similar to those that apply for purposes of passing through the dividends-received deduction (see FTC 2d/FIN ¶ E-6151 *et seq.*; USTR ¶ 8524.02; TaxDesk ¶ 173,001) apply. Thus, where the aggregate qualified dividend income received by a RIC during the tax year is less than 95% of its gross income, the dividends paid by the RIC that are eligible for qualified dividend income treatment are limited to the aggregate qualified dividend income received by the RIC. The amount treated as qualified dividend income under this rule is limited to the amount designated as qualified dividend income by the RIC in a notice that must be mailed to shareholders within 60 days of the close of the RIC's tax year.

However, under section 303 of the 2003 Jobs and Growth Act, the above rules were due to expire at the end of 2008 (along with the rules taxing qualified dividend income at the 5% or 15% maximum adjusted net capital gain rates, see ¶ 107). (FTC 2d/FIN ¶ E-6163.1; USTR ¶ 8524.02; TaxDesk ¶ 173,002.1)

REITs. Rules similar to the RIC rules discussed above apply to allow a passthrough of qualified dividend income by real estate investment trusts (REITs).

As in the case of the RIC rules, under section 303 of the 2003 Jobs and Growth Act, the rules allowing the passthrough of qualified dividend income by REITs were due to expire at the end of 2008 (along with the rules taxing qualified dividend income at the 5% or 15% adjusted net capital gain rates, see ¶ 107). (FTC 2d/FIN ¶ E-6619.1; USTR ¶ 8574.02; TaxDesk ¶ 173,009)

New Law. The Tax Increase Prevention Act extends the rules allowing the passthrough of qualified dividend income by RICs and REITs through tax years beginning before Jan. 1, 2011. (2003 Jobs and Growth Act § 303 as amended by Tax Increase Prevention Act § 102)

> ***observation:*** This extension parallels the extension of the rules taxing qualified dividend income at the 5% or 15% maximum rates applicable to adjusted net capital gain, see ¶ 107.

☐ **Effective:** Tax years beginning after Dec. 31, 2008 (Com Rept, see ¶ 5002) and before Jan. 1, 2011. (Tax Increase Prevention Act §102)

FTC 2d References are to Federal Tax Coordinator 2d
FIN References are to RIA's Analysis of Federal Taxes: Income
USTR References are to United States Tax Reporter: Income, Estate & Gift, and Excise
PCA References are to Pension Analysis (print & electronic)
PE References are to the Pension Explanations (print & electronic)

¶ 111. Passthrough of qualified dividend income by common trust funds is extended for two years

Code Sec. 584(c), Tax Increase Prevention Act § 102
Code Sec. None, Tax Increase Prevention Act § 102
Generally effective: Tax years beginning after Dec. 31, 2008 and before Jan. 1, 2011
Committee Reports, see ¶ 5002

A Code Sec. 584 common trust fund maintained by a bank isn't subject to tax. Instead, each trust participant includes in income its proportionate share of the common trust fund's short term capital gain or loss, long-term capital gain or loss, and ordinary income, regardless of whether the trust distributes these amounts. Each common trust fund participant's proportionate share of the qualified dividend income (i.e., dividends taxed at the 5% or 15% maximum adjusted net capital gain rates, see ¶ 107) received by the fund is treated as qualified dividend income.

> ***observation:*** Thus, the qualified character of the dividends passes through to the common trust fund participants, and their share of the qualified dividend income is taxed at the 5% or 15% maximum adjusted net capital gain rates.

However, under section 303 of the 2003 Jobs and Growth Act, this qualified dividend income passthrough rule was due to expire at the end of 2008 (along with the rules taxing qualified dividend income at the 5% or 15% maximum adjusted net capital gain rates, see ¶ 107). (FTC 2d/FIN ¶ E-3602; USTR ¶ 5844; TaxDesk ¶ 657,304)

New Law. The Tax Increase Prevention Act extends the qualified dividend income passthrough rule for common trust funds through tax years beginning before Jan. 1, 2011. (2003 Jobs and Growth Act § 303 as amended by Tax Increase Prevention Act § 102)

> ***observation:*** This extension parallels the extension of the rules taxing qualified dividend income at the 5% or 15% maximum rates applicable to adjusted net capital gain, see ¶ 107.

☐ **Effective:** Tax years beginning after Dec. 31, 2008 (Com Rept, see ¶ 5002) and before Jan. 1, 2011. (Tax Increase Prevention Act §102)

¶ 112. Passthrough of qualified dividend income by partnerships is extended for two years

Code Sec. 702(a)(5), Tax Increase Prevention Act § 102
Code Sec. None, Tax Increase Prevention Act § 102
Generally effective: Tax years beginning after Dec. 31, 2008 and before Jan. 1, 2011
Committee Reports, see ¶ 5002

Qualified dividend income received by noncorporate shareholders is taxed at the 5% or 15% maximum rates applicable to adjusted net capital gain, see ¶ 107. For a partnership, each partner's distributive share of qualified dividend income received by the partnership is treated as qualified dividend income in the partner's hands.

> ***observation:*** Thus, the qualified character of the dividends passes through to the partners, and the partners' distributive shares of the partnership's qualified dividend income is taxed at the maximum 5% or 15% maximum rates applicable to adjusted net capital gain.

However, under section 303 of the 2003 Jobs and Growth Act, the passthrough rule for partnership qualified dividend income was due to expire at the end of 2008 (along with the rules taxing qualified dividend income at the 5% or 15% maximum adjusted net capital gain rates, see ¶ 107). (FTC 2d/FIN ¶ B-1903; USTR ¶ 7024.01; TaxDesk ¶ 584,003)

New Law. The Tax Increase Prevention Act extends the above passthrough rule for partnership qualified dividend income through tax years beginning before Jan. 1, 2011. (2003 Jobs and Growth Act § 303 as amended by Tax Increase Prevention Act § 102)

> ***observation:*** This extension parallels the extension of the rules taxing qualified dividend income at the 5% or 15% maximum rates applicable to adjusted net capital gain, see ¶ 107.

☐ **Effective:** Tax years beginning after Dec. 31, 2008 (Com Rept, see ¶ 5002) and before Jan. 1, 2011. (Tax Increase Prevention Act §102)

FTC 2d References are to Federal Tax Coordinator 2d
FIN References are to RIA's Analysis of Federal Taxes: Income
USTR References are to United States Tax Reporter: Income, Estate & Gift, and Excise
PCA References are to Pension Analysis (print & electronic)
PE References are to the Pension Explanations (print & electronic)

¶ 113. Qualified dividend income treatment for ordinary income on disposition of Code Sec. 306 stock extended for two years

Code Sec. 306(a)(1)(D), Tax Increase Prevention Act § 102
Code Sec. None, Tax Increase Prevention Act § 102
Generally effective: Tax years beginning after Dec. 31, 2008 and before Jan. 1, 2011
Committee Reports, see ¶ 5002

If Code Sec. 306 stock (stock, other than common stock, whose sale, redemption, or other taxable disposition gives rise to ordinary income rather than capital gain) is disposed of, other than in a redemption, the amount realized is treated as ordinary income up to the stock's pro rata share of the amount that would have been a dividend if the corporation had made a cash distribution equal to the fair market value of the stock disposed. Amounts treated as ordinary income under this rule are treated as qualified dividend income (taxable at the 5% or 15% maximum rates applicable to adjusted net capital gain, see ¶ 107).

> ***observation:*** Thus, to the extent a shareholder recognizes ordinary income on the disposition of Code Sec. 306 stock, that income is taxed at the 5% or 15% maximum rates applicable to adjusted net capital gain.

However, under section 303 of the 2003 Jobs and Growth Act, the above rule was due to expire at the end of 2008 (along with the rules taxing qualified dividend income at the 5% or 15% maximum adjusted net capital gain rates, see ¶ 107). (FTC 2d/FIN ¶ F-12101; USTR ¶ 3064.02; TaxDesk ¶ 244,401)

New Law. The Tax Increase Prevention Act extends the above rule through tax years beginning before Jan. 1, 2011. (2003 Jobs and Growth Act § 303 as amended by Tax Increase Prevention Act § 102)

> ***observation:*** This extension parallels the extension of the rules taxing qualified dividend income at the 5% or 15% maximum rates applicable to adjusted net capital gain, see ¶ 107.

☐ **Effective:** Tax years beginning after Dec. 31, 2008 (Com Rept, see ¶ 5002) and before Jan. 1, 2011. (Tax Increase Prevention Act §102)

¶ 200. Provisions Affecting Individuals

¶ 201. AMT exemption amounts for 2006 are increased to $42,500 (from $33,750) for unmarrieds, to $62,550 (from $45,000) for joint filers, and to $31,275 (from $22,500) for marrieds filing separately

Code Sec. 55(d)(1)(A), as amended by Tax Increase Prevention Act § 301(a)(1)
Code Sec. 55(d)(1)(B), as amended by Tax Increase Prevention Act § 301(a)(2)
Generally effective: Tax years beginning in 2006
Committee Reports, see ¶ 5015

In computing the alternative minimum tax (AMT) for individuals, the AMT tax rate is applied against the taxpayer's alternative minimum taxable income (AMTI), as reduced by the taxpayer's exemption amount (which phases out for AMTI above certain threshold levels). Pre-Tax Increase Prevention Act law provided the following AMT exemption amounts for tax years beginning in 2006: $33,750 for unmarried individuals who aren't surviving spouses; $45,000 for married couples filing jointly and surviving spouses; and $22,500 (technically, 50% of the joint return/surviving spouse amount) for married individuals filing separately.

For tax years beginning in 2005, the AMT exemption amounts were: $40,250 for unmarried individuals who weren't surviving spouses; $58,000 for married couples filing jointly and surviving spouses; and $29,000 for marrieds filing separately. The higher amounts reflected the temporary increase provided by 2001 Economic Growth and Tax Relief Reconciliation Act § 701 (Sec. 701, PL 107-16, 6/7/2001), as amended by 2003 Jobs and Growth Act § 106 (Sec. 106, PL 108-27, 5/28/2003) and 2004 Working Families Act § 103 (Sec. 103, PL 108-311, 10/4/2004), for 2001 through 2005, to reduce the number of individuals who otherwise would be subject to the AMT. Under pre-Tax Increase Prevention Act law, the temporary increase expired after 2005. (FTC 2d/FIN ¶ A-8162; USTR ¶ 554.01; TaxDesk ¶ 691,302)

New Law. The AMT exemption amounts are increased as follows (instead of dropping) for tax years beginning in 2006:

FTC 2d References are to Federal Tax Coordinator 2d
FIN References are to RIA's Analysis of Federal Taxes: Income
USTR References are to United States Tax Reporter: Income, Estate & Gift, and Excise
PCA References are to Pension Analysis (print & electronic)
PE References are to the Pension Explanations (print & electronic)

. . . to $62,550 (up from $58,000 in 2005)—instead of dropping to $45,000—for married couples filing a joint return and surviving spouses (Code Sec. 55(d)(1)(A) as amended by Tax Increase Prevention Act §301(a)(1));

. . . to $42,500 (up from $40,250 in 2005)—instead of dropping to $33,750—for an individual who isn't married or a surviving spouse. (Code Sec. 55(d)(1)(B) as amended by Tax Increase Prevention Act §301(a)(2))

> ***observation:*** The Tax Increase Prevention Act doesn't change the rule that the AMT exemption amount for married individuals filing separately is 50% of the AMT exemption amount for married individuals filing jointly and surviving spouses (see FTC 2d/FIN ¶ A-8162; USTR ¶ 554.01; TaxDesk ¶ 691,302). Thus, although the Tax Increase Prevention Act doesn't specifically provide an increased AMT exemption amount for married individuals filing separately in 2006, the exemption amount for those individuals is effectively increased for 2006 (up from $29,000 in 2005), because the married/surviving spouse exemption amount was specifically increased to $62,550. That is, the AMT exemption amount for married individuals filing separately is $31,275 (50% × $62,550) for tax years beginning in 2006. Under pre-Tax Increase Prevention Act law, their AMT exemption amount would have dropped to $22,500 in 2006.

> ***observation:*** In addition to increasing the individual AMT exemption amounts for 2006, Tax Increase Prevention Act § 301 also has the effect of postponing for one year the reductions that, under pre-Tax Increase Prevention Act law, were scheduled to go into effect for tax years beginning after 2005.

> ***observation:*** In other words, Tax Increase Prevention Act § 301 provides a one-year "patch" for the individual AMT exemption amounts, to hold additional families harmless from the AMT for 2006. Congress thus adopted the Senate proposal to give taxpayers some current AMT relief—i.e., before any extensive overhaul of the AMT system as part of a more fundamental tax reform. The House proposal would have extended the 2005 AMT exemption levels and indexed them for inflation.

> ***viewpoint:*** Professor Daniel J. Lathrope, the Director of the LL.M. Program at the University of California, Hastings College of the Law, and the author of WG&L's *Alternative Minimum Tax,* notes that the changes made by Tax Increase Prevention Act § 301 for 2006 continue the practice of providing year-by-year stopgaps to limit the reach of the AMT. This legislation simply delays the day when there will be an even bigger jump in the number of taxpayers subject to the AMT. Taxpayers will continue to see this type of piecemeal legislation until Con-

gress either indexes the AMT exemption amount and rates for inflation or reforms the tax.

For the one-year extension of the rule allowing nonrefundable personal credits to offset AMT (as well as regular tax), see ¶ 202.

The impact of Tax Increase Prevention Act § 301 can be seen in the following table:

AMT Exemption Amount

	Tax Increase Prevention Act			Pre-Tax Increase Prevention Act		
	Unmarried	Joint	Married Filing Separate	Unmarried	Joint	Married Filing Separate
2005	$40,250	$58,000	$29,000	$40,250	$58,000	$29,000
2006	$42,500	$62,550	$31,275	$33,750	$45,000	$22,500
2007	$33,750	$45,000	$22,500	$33,750	$45,000	$22,500

observation: The AMT exemption amounts for 2006 are only slightly higher than the exemption amounts that were in effect for 2005. As a result, individuals who owed only a small amount of AMT in 2005 may find themselves not owing AMT in 2006, assuming their financial situation remains the same. On the other hand, the fact that regular income tax rate schedules are adjusted annually for inflation reduces the regular tax liability of someone whose financial situation remains unchanged from 2005 to 2006. So the increase in the AMT exemption amounts for 2006 might not be enough to protect the taxpayer from the AMT in 2006.

Kiddie tax AMT exemption amount. For a child subject to the "kiddie tax" (i.e., a child under age 18 with unearned income over $1,700 for 2006, see ¶ 204), the AMT exemption amount can't exceed the sum of the child's earned income plus $6,050 in 2006. In addition, the kiddie tax AMT exemption can't be more than the child's regular AMT exemption (the unmarried individual's exemption amount, discussed above). (FTC 2d/FIN ¶ A-8163; USTR ¶ 594; TaxDesk ¶ 691,303)

observation: As stated above, the unmarried individual's exemption amount is $42,500 for tax years beginning in 2006. Thus, the child's exemption amount for 2006 is $42,500. This means that in 2006, a child subject to the kiddie tax may have up to $36,450 of earned in-

FTC 2d References are to Federal Tax Coordinator 2d
FIN References are to RIA's Analysis of Federal Taxes: Income
USTR References are to United States Tax Reporter: Income, Estate & Gift, and Excise
PCA References are to Pension Analysis (print & electronic)
PE References are to the Pension Explanations (print & electronic)

come (earned income + \$6,050 = \$42,500 or \$42,500 − \$6,050 = \$36,450).

AMT exemption amount for estates and trusts.

observation: The Tax Increase Prevention Act doesn't change the \$22,500 exemption amount for an estate or trust (see FTC 2d/FIN ¶ A-8164; USTR ¶ 554.01; TaxDesk ¶ 691,304).

Phase-out of AMT exemption amount.

observation: The Tax Increase Prevention Act doesn't change the phase-out rules for the AMT exemption amount. Under those rules, the AMT exemption amount is reduced by an amount equal to 25% of the amount by which the individual's AMTI (FTC 2d/FIN ¶ A-8101; USTR ¶ 554.01; TaxDesk ¶ 691,301) exceeds the following threshold amounts: \$112,500 for unmarried individuals, \$150,000 for married individuals filing a joint return and surviving spouses, and \$75,000 for married individuals filing separate returns. (FTC 2d/FIN ¶ A-8162; USTR ¶ 554.01; TaxDesk ¶ 691,302) Thus, the exemption is completely phased-out at an AMTI dollar amount equal to:

Applicable phase-out threshold + (4 × applicable exemption amount).

observation: Thus, the AMT exemption for 2006 completely phases-out (i.e., the taxpayer is subject to AMT on *all* of his AMTI), at the following AMTI levels:

- \$282,500 (\$112,500 + \$170,000 [4 × \$42,500]) for an individual who isn't married and isn't a surviving spouse,
- \$400,200 (\$150,000 + \$250,200 [4 × \$62,550]) for married individuals filing jointly or for a surviving spouse, and
- \$200,100 (\$75,000 + \$125,100 [4 × \$31,275]) for a married individual filing separately.

Post-2006 AMT exemption amounts.

observation: Absent future legislation (e.g., an extension of the one-year AMT patch), the reduction in the AMT exemption amounts that, under pre-Tax Increase Prevention Act law, was scheduled for tax years beginning after 2005, will apply for tax years beginning after 2006. This means that in 2007, the AMT exemption amounts will drop to \$33,750 for unmarried individuals who aren't surviving spouses; to \$45,000 for married couples filing jointly and surviving spouses; and to \$22,500 for marrieds filing separately.

☐ **Effective:** Tax years beginning in 2006. ((Code Sec. 55(d)(1))) ((Tax Increase Prevention Act §301(b)))

> ***observation:*** Although (Tax Increase Prevention Act §301(b)) provides that the increased AMT exemption amounts apply for "tax years beginning after Dec. 31, 2005," Act § 301(a) amends Code Sec. 55(d)(1) so that the increased exemptions apply only for 2006. That is, the AMT exemption amounts prescribed by the Tax Increase Prevention Act for 2006 don't apply in tax years beginning after 2006.

> ***observation:*** Tax Increase Prevention Act § 301 increases the AMT exemption amounts for 2006, and so applies retroactively to Jan. 1, 2006.

> ***recommendation:*** Individuals subject to estimated tax in 2006 may have already used the lower AMT exemption amounts that were in effect under pre-Tax Increase Prevention Act law to compute their first installment of estimated tax for 2006 (i.e., the installment due on Apr. 17, 2006 [Apr. 18, 2006, for individuals in certain states]). That is, unmarried individuals may have used $33,750 (rather than $42,500), married couples filing jointly and surviving spouses may have used $45,000 (rather than $62,550), and marrieds filing separately may have used $22,500 (rather than $31,175), as their AMT exemption amount for 2006. Individuals in this situation should recompute their required payments for the second, third and fourth installments for 2006, to account for the retroactive increases in the AMT exemption amounts for 2006. (See FTC 2d/FIN ¶ S-5200 *et seq.*; USTR ¶ 66,544; TaxDesk ¶ 571,300 *et seq.*)

FTC 2d References are to Federal Tax Coordinator 2d
FIN References are to RIA's Analysis of Federal Taxes: Income
USTR References are to United States Tax Reporter: Income, Estate & Gift, and Excise
PCA References are to Pension Analysis (print & electronic)
PE References are to the Pension Explanations (print & electronic)

¶ 202. Nonrefundable personal credits may offset AMT through 2006 (instead of 2005)

Code Sec. 26(a)(2), as amended by Tax Increase Prevention Act § 302(a)(2)
Code Sec. 23(b)(4), Tax Increase Prevention Act § 302(a)(2)
Code Sec. 24(b)(3), Tax Increase Prevention Act § 302(a)(2)
Code Sec. 25B(g), Tax Increase Prevention Act § 302(a)(2)
Code Sec. 25(e)(1)(C), Tax Increase Prevention Act § 302(a)(2)
Code Sec. 25D(c)(2), Tax Increase Prevention Act § 302(a)(2)
Code Sec. 1400C(d), Tax Increase Prevention Act § 302(a)(2)
Code Sec. 904(h), Tax Increase Prevention Act § 302(a)(2)
Generally effective: Tax years beginning after Dec. 31, 2005 and before Jan. 1, 2007
Committee Reports, see ¶ 5016

The amount of nonrefundable personal credits (e.g., the dependent care credit, credit for the elderly and permanently and totally disabled, mortgage credit certificate (MCC) credit, child tax credit, HOPE and Lifetime Learning credits, adoption credit, pre-2007 saver's credit, nonbusiness energy property credit, and residential energy efficient property credit) allowed in a tax year is subject to limitations based on tax liability.

A special limitation in effect for 2000 through 2005 allowed all the nonrefundable personal credits to offset both regular tax and alternative minimum tax (AMT). Under pre-Tax Increase Prevention Act law, this special limitation—under Code Sec. 26(a)(2)—didn't apply after 2005. Under the limitations that were in effect for tax years beginning in 2006 (i.e., the limitation under Code Sec. 26(a)(1)), the nonrefundable personal credits (other than the adoption credit, child tax credit, and pre-2007 saver's credit) could offset regular tax, but not AMT. An individual's total combined credits for 2006 were limited to the excess of his regular tax liability over his tentative minimum tax (without regard to the AMT foreign tax credit). (FTC 2d/FIN ¶ L-18101, ¶ L-18102; USTR ¶ 264; TaxDesk ¶ 398,000, ¶ 398,001) Under the separate limitations that apply to the adoption credit, child tax credit, and pre-2007 saver's credit in years when Code Sec. 26(a)(2) doesn't apply, those credits could offset both regular tax and AMT in 2006. (FTC 2d/FIN ¶ A-4405, ¶ A-4054, ¶ A-4455; USTR ¶ 234, ¶ 244.01, ¶ 25B4; TaxDesk ¶ 569,505, ¶ 569,104, ¶ 569,205)

New Law. The Tax Increase Prevention Act provides that for tax years beginning in 2006, the nonrefundable personal credits may offset AMT as well as regular tax. (Com Rept, see ¶ 5016)

Specifically, for tax years beginning in 2006 (as well as in 2000 through 2005), the aggregate amount of personal nonrefundable credits may not exceed the sum of:

. . . the taxpayer's regular tax liability reduced by the foreign tax credit allowable under Code Sec. 27(a), and

. . . the tax imposed by Code Sec. 55(a) (Code Sec. 26(a)(2) as amended by Tax Increase Prevention Act §302(a)(2))—i.e., the AMT (see FTC 2d/FIN ¶ A-8101; USTR ¶ 554.01; TaxDesk ¶ 691,002).

The Tax Increase Prevention Act thus extends the rule allowing the nonrefundable personal credits to the full extent of the regular tax and the AMT for one year, so that it applies for tax years beginning on or before Dec. 31, 2006. (Com Rept, see ¶ 5016)

> ***observation:*** In other words, Tax Increase Prevention Act § 302(a)(2) provides a one-year postponement of the effective date for the limitations that, under pre-Tax Increase Prevention Act law, applied after 2005. Those postponed limitations will apply after 2006 (see "Tax liability limitations on nonrefundable personal credits after 2006," below).

> ***observation:*** This means that in 2006 (as was the case in 2005), all of the otherwise allowable nonrefundable personal credits—i.e., not just the adoption credit, child tax credit, and pre-2007 saver's credit—may be used to reduce AMT (as well as regular tax). This is because the maximum amount of total nonrefundable personal credits that a taxpayer will be able to claim in 2006 can't exceed the sum of: (1) his regular tax liability (reduced by the foreign tax credit) for 2006, plus (2) his AMT liability for 2006. Under this rule, the taxpayer will be able to claim up to the amount of that sum (i.e., regular tax plus AMT) as nonrefundable personal credits.

> ***observation:*** A taxpayer is subject to the AMT if his "tentative minimum tax liability" for the tax year is greater than his regular tax liability for the tax year. The AMT equals the amount of that excess, if any (see FTC 2d/FIN ¶ A-8101; USTR ¶ 554.01; TaxDesk ¶ 691,002).

> ***illustration (1):*** In 2006, the Greens' regular tax is $8,000, and their tentative minimum tax is $7,200. Thus, they pay only the regular tax of $8,000. The Greens can claim up to $8,000 of nonrefundable personal credits for 2006. Under pre-Tax Increase Prevention Act law, the amount of nonrefundable personal credits the Greens could claim for 2006 was limited to $800—i.e., the excess of $8,000 regular tax over $7,200 tentative minimum tax.

FTC 2d References are to Federal Tax Coordinator 2d
FIN References are to RIA's Analysis of Federal Taxes: Income
USTR References are to United States Tax Reporter: Income, Estate & Gift, and Excise
PCA References are to Pension Analysis (print & electronic)
PE References are to the Pension Explanations (print & electronic)

illustration (2): In 2006, the Whites' regular tax is $5,000, and their tentative minimum tax is $5,500. Thus, they must pay a regular tax of $5,000, plus an AMT of $500 (excess of $5,500 tentative minimum tax over $5,000 regular tax). The Whites can claim up to $5,500 of nonrefundable personal credits for 2006 (the sum of their $5,000 regular tax and $500 AMT). Under pre-Tax Increase Prevention Act law, the Whites couldn't have claimed any nonrefundable personal credits for 2006, because their regular tax ($5,000) didn't exceed their tentative minimum tax ($5,500).

viewpoint: Experts at Practitioners Publishing Company (Thomson-PPC) comment that under pre-Tax Increase Prevention Act law, the personal energy credits (the Code Sec. 25C nonbusiness energy property credit and the Code Sec. 25D residential energy efficient property credit, both of which came into effect in 2006) available in 2006 and 2007 were limited to the taxpayer's regular tax liability over the tentative minimum tax for the year. By extending the application of Code Sec. 26(a)(2) through 2006, the Tax Increase Prevention Act allows these credits to offset both the AMT and regular tax in 2006. Thus, taxpayers should consider making residential improvements qualifying for these credits in 2006 versus waiting until 2007.

observation: The rule allowing the nonrefundable personal credits to reduce the AMT (as well as regular tax) benefits middle income individuals who:

. . . have low taxable income (and thus a low regular tax), e.g., because of a large number of personal exemptions;

. . . are subject to the AMT because personal exemptions (as well as the standard deduction and certain itemized deductions) are not allowed in computing the AMT (see FTC 2d/FIN ¶s A-8305, A-8315; USTR ¶ 564,02; TaxDesk ¶s 697,005, 697,015); and

. . . have substantial nonrefundable personal credits such as the child tax credit and HOPE and Lifetime Learning credits.

For the Tax Increase Prevention Act provision that increases the AMT exemption amounts for 2006, see ¶ 201.

How extension of Code Sec. 26(a)(2) through 2006 affects other credit limitations and carryover rules.

observation: The 2005 Gulf Opportunity Zone Act (Sec. 403(i)(3), PL 109-135, 12/21/2005) redrafted the rules relating to the carryover of certain unused personal credits, and the foreign tax credit, so as to include in the Code rules for both the tax years in which the personal credits are allowed against the AMT—i.e., tax years when Code Sec. 26(a)(2) applies, and the tax years in which the credits are not so allowed—i.e., tax years when Code Sec. 26(a)(1) applies. Thus, the one-year extension of the AMT offset resulting from extending the period in which Code Sec. 26(a)(2) applies through 2006 also affects the limitations and carryover rules for certain credits in 2006.

Adoption credit. The adoption credit is subject to the tax liability limitation prescribed by Code Sec. 23(b)(4) in tax years when Code Sec. 26(a)(2) doesn't apply (see FTC 2d/FIN ¶ A-4405; USTR ¶ 234; TaxDesk ¶ 569,505).

observation: The Tax Increase Prevention Act extends Code Sec. 26(a)(2) so that it applies to tax years beginning in 2006. This means that the adoption credit is subject to the Code Sec. 26(a)(2) limitation, rather than the separate limitation under Code Sec. 23(b)(4), in 2006. As noted above, the separate tax liability limitation on the adoption credit lets taxpayers use the credit to offset AMT as well as regular tax. Thus, the one-year extension of the Code Sec. 26(a)(2) limitation (which lets *all* the nonrefundable personal credits offset AMT as well as regular tax) for an additional year doesn't affect the AMT offset allowance for the adoption credit in 2006. However, Code Sec. 23(b)(4) has specific ordering rules which may reduce the amount of the allowable adoption credit.

Child tax credit. The child tax credit is subject to the tax liability limitation prescribed by Code Sec. 24(b)(3) in tax years when Code Sec. 26(a)(2) doesn't apply (see FTC 2d/FIN ¶ A-4054; USTR ¶ 244.01; TaxDesk ¶ 569,104).

observation: The Tax Increase Prevention Act extends Code Sec. 26(a)(2) so that it applies to tax years beginning in 2006. This means that the child tax credit is subject to the Code Sec. 26(a)(2) limitation, rather than the separate limitation under Code Sec. 24(b)(3), in 2006. As noted above, the separate tax liability limitation on the child tax credit lets taxpayers use the credit to offset AMT as well as regular tax. Thus, the one-year extension of the Code Sec. 26(a)(2) limitation (which lets *all* the nonrefundable personal credits offset AMT as well as regular tax) for an additional year doesn't affect the AMT offset allowance for the child tax credit in 2006. However, Code Sec. 24(b)(3) has specific ordering rules which may reduce the amount of the allowable child tax credit.

FTC 2d References are to Federal Tax Coordinator 2d
FIN References are to RIA's Analysis of Federal Taxes: Income
USTR References are to United States Tax Reporter: Income, Estate & Gift, and Excise
PCA References are to Pension Analysis (print & electronic)
PE References are to the Pension Explanations (print & electronic)

Pre-2007 saver's credit. The pre-2007 saver's credit (so-called because it is scheduled to expire after 2006) is subject to the tax liability limitation prescribed by Code Sec. 25B(g) in tax years when Code Sec. 26(a)(2) doesn't apply (see FTC 2d/FIN ¶ A-4455; USTR ¶ 25B4; TaxDesk ¶ 569,205).

> ***observation:*** The Tax Increase Prevention Act extends Code Sec. 26(a)(2) so that it applies to tax years beginning in 2006. This means that the pre-2007 saver's credit is subject to the Code Sec. 26(a)(2) limitation, rather than the separate limitation under Code Sec. 25B(g), in 2006. As noted above, the separate tax liability limitation on the pre-2007 saver's credit lets taxpayers use the credit to offset AMT as well as regular tax. Thus, the one-year extension of the Code Sec. 26(a)(2) limitation (which lets *all* the nonrefundable personal credits offset AMT as well as regular tax) for an additional year doesn't change the AMT offset allowance for the saver's credit in 2006. However, Code Sec. 25B(g) has specific ordering rules which may reduce the amount of the allowable pre-2007 saver's credit.

MCC credit. If the MCC credit for any tax year exceeds the limitation under Code Sec. 26(a)(2) (or under Code Sec. 26(a)(1), if Code Sec. 26(a)(2) doesn't apply) for the tax year, reduced by the sum of the nonrefundable personal credits (other than the MCC credit, adoption credit, residential energy efficient property credit, and D.C. first-time homebuyer credit) for the year, the excess is carried over to each of the next three years. (FTC 2d/FIN ¶ A-4010; USTR ¶ 254.01; TaxDesk ¶ 380,502)

> ***observation:*** The Tax Increase Prevention Act extends Code Sec. 26(a)(2) so that it applies to tax years beginning in 2006. This means that the Code Sec. 26(a)(2) limitation is the starting point for determining the MCC credit carryover for 2006.

Residential energy efficient property credit. If the residential energy efficient property credit exceeds the limitation under Code Sec. 26(a)(2) (or under Code Sec. 26(a)(1), if Code Sec. 26(a)(2) doesn't apply) for the tax year, reduced by the sum of the other nonrefundable personal credits, the excess is carried over to the next tax year and added to the residential energy efficient property credit for that year. (FTC 2d/FIN ¶ A-4781; USTR ¶ 25D4; TaxDesk ¶ 569,551)

> ***observation:*** The Tax Increase Prevention Act extends Code Sec. 26(a)(2) so that it applies to tax years beginning in 2006. This means that the Code Sec. 26(a)(2) limitation is the starting point for determining the residential energy efficient property credit carryover for 2006.

D.C. first-time homebuyer credit. If the D.C. first-time homebuyer credit exceeds the limitation under Code Sec. 26(a)(2) (or under Code Sec. 26(a)(1), if Code Sec. 26(a)(2) doesn't apply) for the tax year, reduced by the nonrefundable personal credits (other than the D.C. first-time homebuyer credit and the residential energy efficient property credit), the excess is carried over to the next tax year and added to the D.C. first-time homebuyer credit allowable for that year. (FTC 2d/FIN ¶ A-4255; USTR ¶ 14,00C4; TaxDesk ¶ 568,805)

> ***observation:*** The Tax Increase Prevention Act extends Code Sec. 26(a)(2) so that it applies to tax years beginning in 2006. This means that the Code Sec. 26(a)(2) limitation is the starting point for determining the D.C. first-time homebuyer credit carryover for 2006. Although the D.C. first-time homebuyer credit isn't available for property purchased after 2005 (see FTC 2d/FIN ¶ A-4258; USTR ¶ 14,00C4; TaxDesk ¶ 568,801), an individual still may be able to claim the credit in 2006 (and later years) under the carryover provisions. For example, if the individual's D.C. first-time homebuyer credit for 2005 exceeded the limitation in effect for 2005, the excess may be carried over and claimed in 2006, subject to the limitation in effect for 2006.

Foreign tax credit. For tax years to which Code Sec. 26(a)(2) doesn't apply, the U.S. tax liability against which an individual's foreign tax credit is taken is reduced by the sum of the nonrefundable personal credits (other than the adoption credit, child tax credit, and pre-2007 saver's credit) allowable for the year. (FTC 2d/FIN ¶ O-4401; USTR ¶ 9044.01; TaxDesk ¶ 393,001)

> ***observation:*** The Tax Increase Prevention Act extends Code Sec. 26(a)(2) so that it applies in 2006. The above-described reduction isn't made in computing the foreign tax credit for a tax year in which Code Sec. 26(a)(2) applies. Thus, in computing the foreign tax credit for 2006, an individual doesn't reduce his U.S. tax liability by the allowable nonrefundable personal credits (other than the adoption credit, child tax credit, and pre-2007 saver's credit). This, in turn, results in a larger foreign tax credit for 2006.

Alternative motor vehicle credit/qualified alternative vehicle fuel refueling credit.

> ***observation:*** Tax Increase Prevention Act § 302 applies only to the nonrefundable personal credits allowed (or treated as allowed) under Code Sec. 21 through Code Sec. 26. There is no reference to the Code

FTC 2d References are to Federal Tax Coordinator 2d
FIN References are to RIA's Analysis of Federal Taxes: Income
USTR References are to United States Tax Reporter: Income, Estate & Gift, and Excise
PCA References are to Pension Analysis (print & electronic)
PE References are to the Pension Explanations (print & electronic)

Sec. 30B alternative motor vehicle (AMV) credit (see FTC 2d/FIN ¶ L-18020 *et seq.*; USTR ¶ 30B4; TaxDesk ¶ 397,100 *et seq.*) or the Code Sec. 30C qualified alternative vehicle fuel refueling (QAVFR) credit (see FTC 2d/FIN ¶ L-18040 *et seq.*; USTR ¶ 30C4; TaxDesk ¶ 397,200 *et seq.*), which were added by the 2005 Energy Tax Act, effective for 2006. For both credits, the nonbusiness portion of the credit—i.e., any portion that doesn't relate to depreciable property—is subject to a specific tax liability limitation. The specific limitations for these credits don't permit use of the nonbusiness portion of either credit as an offset against AMT in 2006. (See FTC 2d/FIN ¶ L-18022; L-18042; USTR ¶ 30B4; 30C4; TaxDesk ¶ 397,102; 397,202.) The Tax Increase Prevention Act doesn't make any changes to those separate limitations, or otherwise provide for those credits to be used to offset AMT in 2006 (e.g., by making them subject to the general Code Sec. 26(a) limitation).

viewpoint: Experts at Practitioners Publishing Company (Thomson-PPC) comment that the increased 2006 AMT exemption amounts under the Tax Increase Prevention Act (see ¶ 201) will allow some previously ineligible taxpayers to claim the AMV credit or a portion thereof in 2006.

Tax liability limitations on the nonrefundable personal credits after 2006. As discussed above, Tax Increase Prevention Act § 302(a)(2) extends the rule permitting nonrefundable personal credits to offset AMT (as well as regular tax) so that it applies through 2006 (instead of through 2005).

observation: Absent another extension, for tax years beginning after 2006, the *nonrefundable personal credits other than the adoption credit and the child tax credit* will be subject to the limitation under Code Sec. 26(a)(1). The aggregate amount of those credits can't exceed the excess of: (a) the individual's regular tax liability, over (b) the individual's tentative minimum tax, determined without regard to the AMT foreign tax credit (see FTC 2d/FIN ¶ L-18101; USTR ¶ 264; TaxDesk ¶ 398,000).

illustration (3): In 2007, the Greens' regular tax is $7,400, and their tentative minimum tax is $6,500. They have $1,200 in HOPE and Lifetime Learning credits and no other credits. Although they don't owe AMT, they are able to claim only $900 of the credits ($7,400 regular tax liability minus $6,500 tentative minimum tax).

observation: Absent another extension, for tax years beginning after 2006, the *adoption credit* and the *child tax credit* will be limited as follows:

(1) The *adoption credit* can't exceed the excess of: (a) the sum of regular tax liability plus AMT liability, over (b) the sum of nonrefundable personal credits other than the adoption credit, plus the foreign tax credit (see FTC 2d/FIN ¶ A-4405; USTR ¶ 234; TaxDesk ¶ 569,505).

(2) The *child tax credit* can't exceed the excess of: (a) the sum of regular tax liability plus AMT liability, over (b) the sum of nonrefundable personal credits other than the child tax credit and the adoption credit, plus the foreign tax credit (see FTC 2d/FIN ¶ A-4054; USTR ¶ 244.01; TaxDesk ¶ 569,104).

illustration (4): For 2007, H and W, married taxpayers, have a regular tax liability of $2,100 and no AMT liability. Without taking into account any credit limitations, they are entitled to a $1,200 child tax credit and a $1,000 HOPE credit. The sum of their regular tax plus AMT exceeds the sum of their nonrefundable personal credits other than the child credit by $1,100 ($2,100 – $1,000). They are thus entitled to claim only $1,100 of the child tax credit. They may claim the full $1,000 HOPE credit.

observation: The adoption credit and the child tax credit are the only nonrefundable personal credits that may reduce AMT liability in tax years beginning after 2006. The saver's credit is scheduled to expire after 2006.

illustration (5): In 2007, the Browns' regular tax is $4,000, and their tentative minimum tax is $4,500. They have a $1,000 HOPE credit and a $1,000 child credit. Because their tentative minimum tax exceeds their regular tax liability, they can't claim any HOPE credit for the year. However, they can use the full $1,000 child credit. Thus, their total tax after the child credit is $3,500 ($4,000 regular tax, plus $500 AMT, reduced by the $1,000 child credit).

observation: The limitations that will be in effect after 2006 may reduce a taxpayer's nonrefundable personal tax credits even if the taxpayer has no AMT liability.

observation: The specific limitations on the adoption credit and the child tax credit that will apply after 2006 are similar to those that apply through 2006. Each of the specific limitations allows individuals to use the specific credit to offset their AMT liability. However, the post-2006 limitations have specific ordering rules which may reduce the amount allowable for these credits.

☐ **Effective:** Tax years beginning after Dec. 31, 2005 (Tax Increase Prevention Act §302(b)) and before Jan. 1, 2007. (Com Rept, see ¶ 5016)

¶ 203. AGI limit on conversion of non-Roth IRAs to Roth IRAs is eliminated; income from conversion can be deferred and spread over two years—after 2009

Code Sec. 408A(c)(3)(B), as amended by Tax Increase Prevention Act § 512(a)(1)
Code Sec. 408A(d)(3)(A)(iii), as amended by Tax Increase Prevention Act § 512(b)(1)
Code Sec. 408A(d)(3)(E)(i), as amended by Tax Increase Prevention Act § 512(b)(2)(A)
Generally effective: For tax years beginning after Dec. 31, 2009
Committee Reports, see ¶ 5030

The total amount that an individual may contribute to an IRA or a Roth IRA for a year is generally limited to the lesser of: (1) a dollar amount ($4,000 for 2006), and (2) the amount of the individual's compensation that is includible in gross income for the year. For an individual who will have reached age 50 by the end of the year, the dollar amount is increased by an additional amount ($1,000 for 2006). For a married couple, contributions can be made up to the dollar limit for each spouse if the combined compensation of the spouses that is includible in gross income is at least equal to the contributed amount. (FTC 2d/FIN ¶ H-12290.6 *et seq.*; USTR ¶ 408A4; TaxDesk ¶ 283,306 *et seq.*; PCA ¶ 35,207 *et seq.*; PE ¶ 408A-4)

The extent to which contributions to an individual's traditional IRA are deductible depends on whether he (or his spouse) is an active participant in an employer-sponsored retirement plan, and his adjusted gross income (AGI). If neither the individual nor his spouse is an active plan participant, then IRA contributions are deductible (subject to the limits above). If the individual or his spouse is an *active plan participant*, then the deduction for an IRA contribution is phased out for individuals with AGI over certain levels. To the extent an individual does not or cannot make deductible IRA contributions, he may make *nondeductible* contributions to a traditional IRA. Distributions from a traditional IRA are includible in gross income to the extent not attributable to a return of nondeductible contributions. Thus, a distribution of earnings on contributions to a traditional IRA is includible in gross income. (FTC 2d/FIN ¶ H-12215 *et seq.*; H-12253 *et seq.*; USTR ¶ 2194.01 *et seq.*; 4084.03; TaxDesk ¶ 283,001 *et seq.*; 143,001 *et seq.*; PCA ¶ 35,116 *et seq.*; 35,154 *et seq.*; PE ¶ 219-4.01 *et seq.*; 408-4.03)

Individuals with AGI of below certain levels may make contributions to a Roth IRA (up to the maximum IRA contribution limit). The maximum Roth IRA contribution is phased out between $150,000 to $160,000 of AGI, for married individuals filing a joint return, and between $95,000 and $105,000 for all other returns (except a married individual filing a separate return).

Contributions to a Roth IRA are not deductible. Qualified distributions from a Roth IRA (including distributions of earnings on Roth IRA contributions) are excludable from gross income. In general, a qualified distribution is a distribution that is made on or after the individual reaches age 59-1/2, dies, or is disabled, or which is a qualified special purpose distribution. A distribution from a Roth IRA is not a qualified distribution if it is made within the 5-tax-year period beginning with the tax year for which the individual first made a contribution to a Roth IRA. (FTC 2d/FIN ¶ H-12290.6 *et seq.* H-12290.29; USTR ¶ 408A4; TaxDesk ¶ 283,306 *et seq.*; 283,337; PCA ¶ 35,207 *et seq.*; 35,230 ; PE ¶ 408A-4)

Distributions from a Roth IRA that are not qualified distributions are includible in gross income to the extent they are attributable to earnings. A distribution that is not a qualified distribution is treated as made in the following order: (1) generally, regular Roth IRA contributions; (2) the taxable portion of traditional IRA-to-Roth IRA rollovers (including conversions), (3) the nontaxable portion of rollovers and conversions described in item (2); and (4) earnings on contributions. Aggregation rules also apply. (FTC 2d/FIN ¶ H-12290.34 *et seq.*; USTR ¶ 408A4; TaxDesk ¶ 283,342 *et seq.*; PCA ¶ 35,235 *et seq.*; PE ¶ 408A-4)

Conversion of traditional IRAs to Roth IRAs. An individual with modified AGI of not more than $100,000 for a tax year may convert a traditional IRA into a Roth IRA at any time. The conversion of a traditional IRA into a Roth IRA is treated as a distribution from the traditional IRA and a contribution to the Roth IRA. The taxable portion of the amount converted (were it not part of a qualified rollover contribution) is includible in income for the year of the distribution. But the 10% Code Sec. 72(t) early distribution tax doesn't apply to the conversion income.

For purposes of the $100,000 limitation, an individual's AGI is modified by not taking into account: (a) the amount includible in gross income from the rollover of a non-Roth IRA to a Roth IRA, and (b) required minimum distributions. (FTC 2d/FIN ¶ H-12290.11, ¶ H-12290.16, ¶ H-12290.20; USTR ¶ 408A4; TaxDesk ¶ 283,312, ¶ 283,316, ¶ 283,326; PE ¶ 408A-4)

For '98 conversions of an individual's traditional IRA to a Roth IRA in a qualified rollover contribution, the otherwise-taxable amount converted was in-

---

FTC 2d References are to Federal Tax Coordinator 2d
FIN References are to RIA's Analysis of Federal Taxes: Income
USTR References are to United States Tax Reporter: Income, Estate & Gift, and Excise
PCA References are to Pension Analysis (print & electronic)
PE References are to the Pension Explanations (print & electronic)

cludible in income ratably over the 4-year period beginning with the '98 tax year, unless the individual elected out of the 4-year spread.

A taxpayer who in '98 converted a traditional IRA into a Roth IRA, and then withdrew amounts from the Roth IRA before the last year of the 4-year spread (over which the conversion income was taxable) had to include in income for each of the first 3 tax years in the 4-year period: (1) the amount otherwise includible in income under the 4-year rule for that year, plus (2) the lesser of: (a) the taxable portion of the aggregate distributions from Roth IRAs for the tax year which were allocable to the conversion, and (b) (i) the amount required to be included in income from the conversion for all four tax years in the 4-year spread, reduced by (ii) the '98 conversion amounts included in income for all preceding years. (FTC 2d/FIN ¶ H-12290.21; H-12290.40; USTR ¶ 408A4; TaxDesk ¶ 283,327; 283,348; PCA ¶ 35,222; 35,241; PE ¶ 408A-4)

Although qualified rollover contributions of a traditional IRA to a Roth IRA (including conversions) are not subject to the 10% Code Sec. 72(t) tax on early withdrawals, the 10% additional tax does apply to Roth IRA distributions of amounts properly allocable to a qualified rollover contribution of a traditional IRA to a Roth IRA that is made within the 5-tax-year period beginning with the tax year in which the rollover contribution was made, to the extent of the amount includible in income from the rollover. (FTC 2d/FIN ¶ H-12290.38; USTR ¶ 408A4; TaxDesk ¶ 283,346; PCA ¶ 35,239; PE ¶ 408A-4)

If an individual who converted a regular IRA into a Roth IRA in '98 dies before all of the conversion income has been included in his income under the four-year rule, the remaining conversion income is included in his income for the tax year in which he dies. But a special rule applies for a surviving spouse who acquires the decedent's entire interest in any Roth IRA that was converted. (FTC 2d/FIN ¶ H-12290.41; USTR ¶ 408A4; TaxDesk ¶ 283,349; PCA ¶ 35,242; PE ¶ 408A-4)

New Law. For tax years beginning after 2009 (see effective date, below), the Tax Increase Prevention Act eliminates the income limitation that currently prevents some taxpayers from converting traditional IRAs to Roth IRAs. Specifically, for any tax year, including a tax year in which a taxpayer (i) has an adjusted gross income (with certain modifications) of over $100,000, or (ii) is married and files a separate return, a taxpayer will be allowed to make a "qualified rollover contribution" to a Roth IRA from an individual retirement plan other than a Roth IRA. (Code Sec. 408A(c)(3)(B) as amended by Tax Increase Prevention Act §512(a)(1))

> ***observation:*** An individual who has an interest in a qualified retirement plan and can receive an eligible rollover distribution of his interest and roll it over into an IRA in 2010, can then convert the amount to a Roth IRA. Although he'd have to include in income the taxable por-

tion of the distribution on conversion to the Roth IRA, he'd avoid tax on the earnings permanently.

observation: By eliminating the AGI limitation on rollovers of traditional IRAs into Roth IRAs, the Tax Increase Prevention Act allows most taxpayers to circumvent the AGI limitation for making regular contributions to a Roth IRA. That's because taxpayers can make a contribution to a traditional IRA regardless of the amount of their AGI. Even if the AGI limit on deductible contributions to a traditional IRA for individuals who were active participants in certain retirement plans applied to prevent them from making deductible contributions, those individuals would be entitled to make nondeductible contributions to an IRA. These contributions could then be rolled over to a Roth IRA without any AGI limitation.

observation: Converting a traditional IRA to a Roth IRA may be particularly advantageous to individuals:

- who expect to be in a higher tax bracket during retirement (perhaps due to future tax rate increases, such as if the reductions in the tax rate made by the Economic Growth and Tax Relief Reconciliation Act of 2001 (EGTRRA), which are due to expire after 2010, are not extended, or due to a large anticipated investment yield), because sheltering future income on funds by placing them in a Roth IRA—by currently paying the tax on the IRA funds—makes less sense if the funds will be withdrawn when the individual is in a lower tax bracket;

- whose IRAs contain predominantly after-tax amounts; or

- who want to avoid (a) the lifetime Code Sec. 401(a)(9)(A) required minimum distribution (RMD) rules, and (b) the Code Sec. 401(a) incidental death benefit requirements, both of which apply to traditional IRAs, but not Roth IRAs. Avoiding the lifetime RMD rules allows tax-free earnings to continue to accumulate for the ultimate benefit of the Roth-IRA owner's heirs. Also, unlike earnings and deductible contributions in a traditional IRA, amounts received by Roth IRA beneficiaries won't have to be included in the beneficiaries' income, because only taxable income (e.g., as in traditional IRAs) in the beneficiaries' hands is Code Sec. 691 income in respect of a decedent.

2-year period for including 2010 conversion income in gross income. Under the Tax Increase Prevention Act, the amount that is includible in a taxpayer's gross income from a 2010 conversion of a traditional IRA to a Roth IRA can be included in income over a 2-tax-year period beginning in the year after the conversion. Specifically, any amount that would otherwise have to be included in gross income for any tax year beginning in 2010 by reason of a qualified rollover contribution to a Roth IRA of an amount distributed from an individual retirement plan other than a Roth IRA, must be included ratably over the 2-tax-year period beginning with the first tax year, *beginning in 2011.* (Code Sec. 408A(d)(3)(A)(iii) as repealed by Tax Increase Prevention Act §512(b)(1))

> ***observation:*** Thus, the amount of taxable income from a 2010 conversion is not includible in gross income until 2011 and 2012. This tax break is available for 2010 conversions only.

As an alternative, a taxpayer may elect to not have the 2-tax-year spread apply, and to include the taxable portion of a traditional IRA-to-Roth IRA rollover or conversion in gross income in 2010 (i.e., the year of distribution). But the 2-year spread will apply if the taxpayer does not make the election. (Code Sec. 408A(d)(3)(A)(iii))

> ***observation:*** Unless IRS provides a form and/or a procedure for making the election, presumably a taxpayer would elect to not have the 2-tax-year spread apply by simply including in gross income on his 2010 tax return the entire amount of the taxable income from a 2010 IRA-to-Roth-IRA conversion.

Acceleration of conversion income inclusion for premature distributions. The Tax Increase Prevention Act prevents taxpayers from receiving premature distributions from a Roth IRA that received amounts from a converted traditional IRA while retaining the benefit of the 2-year income inclusion spread. Thus, for premature distributions of converted amounts, the Act provides for acceleration of income inclusion, and law which remains unchanged after the Tax Increase Prevention Act subjects premature distributions of rolled over amounts to the 10% Code Sec. 72(t) early distribution tax.

Specifically, under an income inclusion rule, the amount that will have to be included in an individual's gross income for any tax year beginning in 2010, or the first tax year in the 2-year conversion income spread period (i.e., 2011), is:

(1) the aggregate distributions from the individual's Roth IRAs for the tax year which are allocable, under law which remains unchanged after the Tax Increase Prevention Act, to the portion of the qualified rollover contribution (including conversions) required to be included in gross income (under Code Sec. 408A(d)(3)(A)(i)), plus

(2) the lesser of:

(a) half of the amount includible in income as a result of the traditional IRA-to-Roth-IRA rollover (e.g., a conversion), and

(b) the aggregate amount that must be included in gross income as a result of the traditional IRA-to-Roth-IRA rollover for all tax years in the 2-year period (without regard to the amount of the premature distribution of rolled over amounts, in item (1)), reduced by amounts included in gross income for all preceding tax years. (Code Sec. 408A(d)(3)(E)(i) as amended by Tax Increase Prevention Act §512(b)(2)(A))

> ***illustration:*** Taxpayer T has a traditional IRA with a value of $10,000, consisting of deductible contributions and earnings, but T has no Roth IRA. T converts the traditional IRA to a Roth IRA in Jan. of 2010. As a result of the conversion, $10,000 is includible in gross income. Unless T elects otherwise, $5,000 of the income resulting from the conversion normally would be included in income in 2011, and $5,000 in 2012. Assume, however, that in May of 2010, T takes a $2,000 distribution from the Roth IRA, which is not a qualified distribution. Under the ordering rules, which continue unchanged after the Tax Increase Prevention Act, all of the $2,000 distribution is attributable to amounts includible in income as a result of the conversion.
>
> Under the income inclusion rule (above), the amount of the taxable conversion distribution, $2,000 is included in income in 2010. No amount includible in 2011 or 2012 is involved, and no conversion income was included in income for a year prior to 2010.
>
> In 2011, under the Tax Increase Prevention Act, the amount included in income is $5,000: $0 distribution in 2011 + the lesser of (a) $5,000 (half of the income resulting from the conversion), and (b) $8,000 (i.e., $10,000 taxable conversion income – $2,000 previously included in income).
>
> In 2012, the amount included in income is $3,000: $0 distribution in 2012 + the lesser of (a) $5,000 half of the income resulting from the conversion, and (b) $3,000, i.e., $10,000 – ($2,000 included in income in 2010 + $5,000 included in income in 2011).

Amounts of conversion income withdrawn before the 5-tax-year holding period for qualified distributions are subject to the 10% Code Sec. 72(t) tax on early distributions. (FTC 2d/FIN ¶ H-12290.38; USTR ¶ 408A4; TaxDesk ¶ 283,346; PCA ¶ 35,239; PE ¶ 408A-4)

FTC 2d References are to Federal Tax Coordinator 2d
FIN References are to RIA's Analysis of Federal Taxes: Income
USTR References are to United States Tax Reporter: Income, Estate & Gift, and Excise
PCA References are to Pension Analysis (print & electronic)
PE References are to the Pension Explanations (print & electronic)

observation: Thus, amounts withdrawn within the 2-year income spread for 2010 conversions will be subject to the 10% Code Sec. 72(t) tax on early distributions, unless an exception applies (e.g., the taxpayer has reached age 59-1/2).

If an individual who converted a traditional IRA into a Roth IRA in 2010 dies before 2012 (when all of the conversion income will have been included in his income under the 2-year rule), the remaining conversion income is included in his income for the tax year in which he dies.

However, if the individual's surviving spouse acquires the individual's entire interest in any Roth IRA into which the traditional IRA was converted in 2010, the spouse may elect to continue the 2-year income spread by including in income the remaining amounts of the conversion income over the remainder of the 2-year period. The amounts would be includible in the spouse's gross income in the tax years ending with (or within) the tax years of the deceased individual in which the amounts would have been includible. This election cannot be made or changed after the due date for filing the tax return for the spouse's tax year which includes the date of death. (Code Sec. 408A(d)(3)(E)(ii))

observation: Although Code Sec. 408A(d)(3)(E)(ii) (above) was not changed by the Tax Increase Prevention Act, the Act changed the effect of Code Sec. 408A(d)(3)(E)(ii) by amending Code Sec. 408A(d)(3)(A)(iii), which is referenced in Code Sec. 408A(d)(3)(E)(ii).

☐ **Effective:** For tax years beginning after Dec. 31, 2009. (Tax Increase Prevention Act §512(c))

¶ 204. Unearned income of children under age 18 (instead of under age 14) is subject to kiddie tax

Code Sec. 1(g)(2)(A), as amended by Tax Increase Prevention Act § 510(a)
Code Sec. 1(g)(2)(C), as amended by Tax Increase Prevention Act § 510(c)
Generally effective: Tax years beginning after Dec. 31, 2005
Committee Reports, see ¶ 5028

Under the so-called "kiddie tax," the unearned income of certain minor children that exceeds $1,700 (for 2006) is taxed at the parents' highest marginal tax rate if taxing the income at that rate results in a higher tax. Under pre-Tax Increase Prevention Act law, the kiddie tax applied to a child who hadn't attained the age of 14 at the close of the tax year and who had a living parent at the close of the tax year.

(FTC 2d/FIN ¶ A-1301; USTR ¶ 14.09; TaxDesk ¶ 568,301)

New Law. The Tax Increase Prevention Act increases the age to which the kiddie tax rules apply from under age 14 to under age 18. (Com Rept, see ¶ 5028) That is, the kiddie tax rules apply to a child who has not yet attained age 18 before the close of the tax year (Code Sec. 1(g)(2)(A) as amended by Tax Increase Prevention Act §510(a)) and who has at least one living parent at the close of the tax year. However, the Tax Increase Prevention Act also adds the requirement for application of the kiddie tax rules, that the child not file a joint return for the tax year. (Code Sec. 1(g)(2)(C) as amended by Tax Increase Prevention Act §510(c)) That is, the kiddie tax doesn't apply to a child who is married and who files a joint return for the tax year. (Com Rept, see ¶ 5028)

> ***observation:*** The Code Sec. 1(g)(2)(C) exception to the kiddie tax rules above won't apply to an under-age-18-year-old child who is married, but who files as married-filing-separately (instead of jointly) for the tax year, and that child will be subject to kiddie tax where the other requirements for application of the tax apply.

> ***observation:*** Thus, under the Tax Increase Prevention Act rules above, for 2006 (see the effective date below), the kiddie tax applies to a child who has not reached his or her 18th birthday by December 31, 2006, who has more than $1,700 of unearned income, who has at least one living parent at the close of the tax year, and who doesn't file a joint return for 2006.

> ***viewpoint:*** Experts at Practitioners Publishing Company (Thomson-PPC) comment that because of the Tax Increase Prevention Act changes above, the transfer of income-generating stocks, bonds, and other investments to children under age 18 should be reconsidered or postponed to eliminate or decrease the child's unearned income.

> ***observation:*** Although the opportunity to lower taxes by transferring income-producing assets to children under 18 is curtailed by the kiddie tax, investing a child's funds in investments that produce little or no current taxable income can help avoid the kiddie tax. These investments include, for example: stocks and mutual funds oriented toward capital growth that produce little or no current income; vacant land expected to appreciate; stock in a closely-held family business that pays little or no cash dividends; tax-exempt municipal bonds and bond funds (although the interest on some specialized types of bonds may be subject to the alternative minimum tax); and U.S. series EE savings bonds for which interest reporting may be deferred.

Investments that produce no taxable income, and that are therefore not subject to the kiddie tax, also include tax-advantaged savings vehicles such as: traditional and Roth IRAs (which can be established or contributed to if the child has earned income); qualified tuition programs ("529 plans"); and Coverdell education savings accounts ("CESAs").

recommendation: Because *earned income*, regardless of amount, is taxed under the kiddie tax rules at the child's tax rates—and not at the parent's—one way of providing a child with income without triggering increased tax liability under the kiddie tax rules is to employ the child (at reasonable compensation) in, for example, a trade or business owned by the parent. The child's earnings won't be subject to the kiddie tax and will generate a deduction for the family business (assuming the wages are reasonable for the work actually performed). This strategy may be particularly appropriate for older children (i.e., the 15 to 17 year-olds) whose unearned income, under the Tax Increase Prevention Act, is now subject to the kiddie tax rules.

For treatment of distributions from certain qualified disability trusts as *earned income* under another change in the kiddie tax rules made by the Tax Increase Prevention Act, see ¶ 205.

observation: Under the kiddie tax rules, a parent can elect (on Form 8814) to include in the parent's gross income for the tax year the child's gross income in excess of $1,700 (for 2006) if certain requirements are met (see FTC 2d/FIN ¶ A-1326 *et seq.*; USTR ¶ 14.11; TaxDesk ¶ 568,401 *et seq.*). This avoids the need to file a separate return for the child, and except where the child can claim certain deductions the electing parent can't (see below), the tax on the child's income will generally be the same whether the parent elects to report the income or the child files a separate return. However, whenever the election is made, it's important to consider that the addition of the child's income to the parent's adjusted gross income may affect the various floors, ceilings and/or income-based phase-out limitations on, and thus the amount of, the parent's deductions.

In addition, an electing parent can't take certain deductions that could be taken on the child's return absent the parent's election—for example, the child's itemized deductions such as the child's investment expenses or charitable contributions (see FTC 2d/FIN ¶ A-1330; TaxDesk ¶ 568,405). Thus, where a child can claim any of these deductions, it's important to determine whether there will be a tax savings from having the child file a separate return. Where the child files the return, the kiddie tax is computed on Form 8615, which must be attached to the child's return (see FTC 2d/FIN ¶ A-1301; TaxDesk ¶ 568,301).

☐ **Effective:** Tax years beginning after Dec. 31, 2005. (Tax Increase Prevention Act §510(d))

> ***observation:*** Because the changes to the kiddie tax rules above take effect as of 2006, affected individuals may need to make, or increase, estimated tax payments for 2006.

¶ 205. Distributions from certain qualified disability trusts are excepted from kiddie tax

Code Sec. 1(g)(4)(C), as amended by Tax Increase Prevention Act § 510(b)
Generally effective: Tax years beginning after Dec. 31, 2005
Committee Reports, see ¶ 5028

Under the "kiddie tax" rules (as modified by another Tax Increase Prevention Act provision, see ¶ 204), generally, an under-age-18-year-old child's net unearned ("investment") income that exceeds $1,700 (for 2006) is taxed at the parents' (higher) tax rate. The child's earned income, however, regardless of the amount, is taxed at the child's tax rates, and not at the parents' rate. Earned income for this purpose is, generally, wages, salaries, professional fees, or other amounts received as compensation for personal services actually performed. (FTC 2d/FIN ¶ A-1307; USTR ¶ 14.09; TaxDesk ¶ 568,307) Under pre-Tax Increase Prevention Act law, if a child was the beneficiary of a trust, trust income that was included in the child's gross income for the year would be unearned (investment) income for kiddie tax purposes (FTC 2d/FIN ¶ A-1309; USTR ¶ 14.09; TaxDesk ¶ 568,309) and, thus, potentially taxable at the parents' higher tax rate.

New Law. The Tax Increase Prevention provides an exception to the kiddie tax for distributions from certain qualified disability trusts. (Com Rept, see ¶ 5028) Specifically, for purposes of the kiddie tax rules, in the case of any child who is a beneficiary of a qualified disability trust (as defined in Code Sec. 642(b)(2)(C)(ii), see second observation below), any amount included in the child's income under Code Sec. 652 (applicable to simple trusts) and Code Sec. 662 (applicable to complex trusts) during a tax year is treated as *earned income* of the child for the tax year. (Code Sec. 1(g)(4)(C) as amended by Tax Increase Prevention Act §510(b))

> ***observation:*** That is, if an under-age-18 child is a beneficiary of a qualified disability trust, distributions from the trust of taxable interest, dividends, capital gains, or other investment income from the trust (see

---

FTC 2d References are to Federal Tax Coordinator 2d
FIN References are to RIA's Analysis of Federal Taxes: Income
USTR References are to United States Tax Reporter: Income, Estate & Gift, and Excise
PCA References are to Pension Analysis (print & electronic)
PE References are to the Pension Explanations (print & electronic)

FTC 2d/FIN ¶s C-3001, C-3006; USTR ¶s 6524, 6624; TaxDesk ¶s 655,001, 655,006) are considered earned income for kiddie tax purposes, and thus are taxed at the child's tax rate.

observation: Under Code Sec. 642(b)(2)(C)(ii) relating to the personal exemption deduction for trusts (see FTC 2d/FIN ¶ C-2206.1; USTR ¶ 6424.01; TaxDesk ¶ 653,004.1), a "qualified disability trust" is defined as any trust that:

. . . is a disability trust described in Section 1917(c)(2)(B)(iv) of the Social Security Act (SSA) (42 U.S.C. 1396p) (relating to determining eligibility for medical assistance under the SSA, of assets transferred to a trust established solely for the benefit of a disabled individual under age 65); and

. . . all of the beneficiaries of which as of the close of the tax year are determined by the Commissioner of Social Security to have been disabled (within the meaning of section 1614(a)(3) of the SSA, 42 U.S.C. 1382c(a)(3)) for some portion of that year. A trust doesn't fail to meet this requirement merely because the trust corpus may revert to a person who isn't so disabled after the trust ceases to have any beneficiary who is so disabled.

☐ **Effective:** For tax years beginning after Dec. 31, 2005. (Tax Increase Prevention Act §510(d))

¶ 206. Foreign earned income exclusion amended

Code Sec. 911(b)(2)(D)(ii), as amended by Tax Increase Prevention Act § 515(a)
Code Sec. 911(c)(1)(B)(i), as amended by Tax Increase Prevention Act § 515(b)(1)
Code Sec. 911(c)(1)(A), as amended by Tax Increase Prevention Act § 515(b)(2)(A)
Code Sec. 911(c)(2), as amended by Tax Increase Prevention Act § 515(b)(2)(B)
Code Sec. 911(f), as amended by Tax Increase Prevention Act § 515(c)
Generally effective: Tax years beginning after Dec. 31, 2005
Committee Reports, see ¶ 5033

The U.S. generally taxes its citizens and residents on their worldwide income. An election applies to exclude earned income of a qualified individual who has his tax home in a foreign country and is either (i) a U.S. citizen who is a bona fide resident of a foreign country or countries for an uninterrupted period that includes an entire tax year, or (ii) a U.S. citizen or resident present in a foreign country or countries for at least 330 full days in any 12 consecutive month period. Under pre-Tax Increase Prevention Act law, the maximum exclusion amount for any calendar year was $80,000 in 2002 through 2007 and was indexed for inflation after 2007 using 2006 as the base year. (FTC 2d/FIN ¶ O-1101, ¶ O-1201; USTR ¶ 9114.01, ¶ 9114.12; TaxDesk ¶ 191,002, ¶ 191,004)

A qualified individual is also allowed an exclusion from gross income for certain foreign housing costs paid or incurred by or on his behalf (or a deduction where the costs are not paid by the employer). Under pre-Tax Increase Prevention Act law, the amount of the housing cost exclusion was equal to the excess of a taxpayer's housing expenses over a base housing cost amount. Housing expenses include the reasonable expenses paid or incurred during the taxable year for a taxpayer's housing (and a spouse's and dependents' housing if they live with the taxpayer) in a foreign country, including expenses attributable to housing such as utilities and insurance, but not interest and taxes. If the taxpayer maintains a second household outside the U.S. for a spouse or dependents who do not reside with the taxpayer because of dangerous, unhealthful, or otherwise adverse living conditions, the housing expenses of the second household also are eligible for exclusion. Under pre-Tax Increase Prevention Act law, the base housing cost amount above which costs were eligible for exclusion in a tax year was 16% of the annual salary (computed on a daily basis) of a grade GS-14, step 1, U.S. government employee, multiplied by the number of days of foreign residence or presence in the tax year. For 2006 this salary was $77,793, with the result that the 2006 amount was $12,447 for a taxpayer entitled to the exclusion for the entire year. (FTC 2d/FIN ¶ O-1161, ¶ O-1162, ¶ O-1164, ¶ O-1166, ¶ O-1167, ¶ O-1171; USTR ¶ 9114.02; TaxDesk ¶ 191,028, ¶ 191,033, ¶ 191,034, ¶ 191,500)

The combined foreign earned income exclusion and housing cost exclusion cannot exceed the taxpayer's total foreign earned income. In addition, the taxpayer's foreign tax credit is reduced by the amount of the credit attributable to the exclusion. (FTC 2d/FIN ¶ O-1102, ¶ O-1114; USTR ¶ 9114.01, ¶ 9114.11; TaxDesk ¶ 191,004, ¶ 191,500)

New Law. The Tax Increase Prevention Act amends the foreign earned income exclusion so that the $80,000 amount is adjusted for inflation after 2005 (instead of after 2007) using 2004 (instead of 2006) as the base year. (Code Sec. 911(b)(2)(D)(ii) as amended by Tax Increase Prevention Act §515(a)) Thus, the maximum that can be excluded in 2006 is $82,400. (Com Rept, see ¶ 5033)

FTC 2d References are to Federal Tax Coordinator 2d
FIN References are to RIA's Analysis of Federal Taxes: Income
USTR References are to United States Tax Reporter: Income, Estate & Gift, and Excise
PCA References are to Pension Analysis (print & electronic)
PE References are to the Pension Explanations (print & electronic)

> ***observation:*** Adjusting the foreign earned income exclusion for inflation two years earlier than under pre-Tax Prevention Increase Act law increases the total amount that may be excluded by higher-income individuals. Whether this increase will actually save taxes depends on how much taxable income an individual has after the exclusion is taken into account since the non-excluded income may now be taxed at a higher tax rate than under pre-Tax Prevention Increase Act law, see the discussion below of the application of higher rates to taxpayers entitled to foreign exclusions.

The Tax Increase Prevention Act also amends the housing cost amount so that the base housing cost amount is 16% (computed on a daily basis) of the maximum foreign earned income exclusion (the $80,000 amount adjusted for post-2005 inflation) for the calendar year in which the tax year begins (Code Sec. 911(c)(1)(B)(i) as amended by Tax Increase Prevention Act §515(b)(1)) multiplied by the number of days of bona fide residence or presence for which the qualified individual is eligible for the exclusion.

> ***observation:*** Thus, the base housing cost amount is $13,184 ($82,400 x 16%) for 2006.

The Tax Increase Prevention Act also places a limit on the housing cost exclusion. (Code Sec. 911(c)(1)(A) as amended by Tax Increase Prevention Act §515(b)(2)(A)) The limit is equal to 30% (subject to adjustment as described below) of the maximum foreign earned income exclusion (computed on a daily basis) for the calendar year in which the tax year begins (Code Sec. 911(c)(2)(A)(i) as amended by Tax Increase Prevention Act §515(b)(2)(B)) multiplied by the number of days of bona fide residence or presence for which the qualified individual is eligible for the exclusion. (Code Sec. 911(c)(1)(A)(ii))

Thus, reasonable foreign housing expenses in excess of the base housing amount may be excluded from gross income (or, if paid by the taxpayer, may be deducted), but the amount of the exclusion is limited to 30% of the maximum amount of a taxpayer's foreign earned income exclusion minus the base housing cost amount of 16% of the maximum amount of the taxpayer's foreign earned income exclusion. For 2006, the maximum amount of the foreign housing cost exclusion is $11,536 ($24,720 ($82,400 x 30%)) - $13,184 for a taxpayer entitled to the exclusion for the entire year. (Com Rept, see ¶ 5033)

> ***observation:*** In effect, the maximum foreign housing cost exclusion is 14% of the maximum foreign earned income exclusion. The actual foreign housing cost exclusion will be less than 14% of the foreign earned income exclusion whenever total foreign housing costs are less than 30% of the maximum foreign earned income exclusion.

IRS may issue regs or other guidance providing for the adjustment of the 30% limit on the basis of geographic differences in housing costs relative to housing costs in the U.S. (Code Sec. 911(c)(2)(B)) IRS may use publicly available data, such as the Quarterly Report Indexes published by the U.S. State Department or any other information deemed reliable by IRS, in making adjustments. IRS may also adjust the 30% upward or downward. Any adjustments should be made on an annual basis. (Com Rept, see ¶ 5033)

Application of higher rates to taxpayers entitled to foreign exclusions. Where a taxpayer excludes income under the foreign earned income exclusion or the housing cost exclusion for any tax year, then, notwithstanding the regular income tax or alternative minimum tax rules, the following rules apply. The taxpayer's regular tax is equal to the excess (if any) of:

- the regular tax that would be imposed for the tax year if the taxpayer's taxable income were increased by the amount of these exclusions for the tax year (Code Sec. 911(f)(1)(A) as amended by Tax Increase Prevention Act §515(c)) over
- the tax which would be imposed for the tax year if the taxpayer's taxable income were equal to the amount of these exclusions for the tax year. (Code Sec. 911(f)(1)(B))

> ***illustration (1):*** For 2006, A, a single taxpayer, is entitled to the foreign earned income exclusion and the foreign housing cost exclusion for the entire year. A is entitled to the maximum foreign earned income exclusion of $82,400 and to a foreign housing cost exclusion of $10,000. (A has actual housing cost expenses of $23,184 which is $10,000 more than the base housing cost amount of $13,184.) A has taxable income of $17,600 after taking the exclusions into account. Without the exclusions, A's taxable income would be $110,000 ($17,600 + $82,400 + $10,000).
>
> A's income tax for 2006 equals the excess of $25,132 (the tax on total taxable income of $110,000) over $20,204 (the tax on the total exclusion of $92,400). Thus, A's total tax for 2006 is $4,928.
>
> Under pre-Tax Prevention Act Increase law, A would have been entitled to a foreign earned income exclusion of $80,000, and a foreign housing exclusion of $10,737 (housing cost expenses of $23,184 less the base housing cost amount of $12,447 available under prior law). A's taxable income would have been $19,263 ($110,000 less the total foreign exclusions of $90,737). The tax on $19,263 would have been

only $2,520, or $2,408 less than it would be under Tax Prevention Act Increase law. This is so even though the total exclusions would have been only $90,737 under pre-Tax Prevention Increase law compared to the $92,400 of exclusions available under Tax Prevention Increase Act law.

Similarly, the tentative minimum tax (see FTC 2d/FIN ¶ A-8101; USTR ¶ 554.01; TaxDesk ¶ 691,001) for the tax year is equal to the excess (if any) of:

- the amount that would be the tentative minimum tax for the tax year if the taxpayer's taxable excess (generally, the alternative minimum taxable income minus the exemption amount) were increased by the amount of these exclusions for the tax year (Code Sec. 911(f)(2)(A)), over
- the amount that would be the tentative minimum tax for the tax year if the taxpayer's taxable excess were equal to the amount of these exclusions for the tax year. (Code Sec. 911(f)(2)(B))

observation: By adding the excluded amounts to the taxable excess instead of to alternative minimum taxable income before reduction by the exemption means that the taxable excess is not increased further by a reduction in the allowable exemption that results when alternative minimum taxable income is above a specified amount.

The amount of the exclusions taken into account for this purpose is determined by reducing the total amount of any deductions or exclusions disallowed under the Code Sec. 911(d)(6) rule that prevents double benefits from excluded amounts (see FTC 2d/FIN ¶ O-1112; USTR ¶ 9114.11; TaxDesk ¶ 191,016) (Code Sec. 911(f))

Under this rule, the tax rates applied to the taxpayer's income in excess of the exclusion amount is taxed under the regular tax and alternative minimum tax by applying to the remaining income the tax rates that would have been applicable had the individual not elected the exclusion. (Com Rept, see ¶ 5033)

Illustration (2): An individual has $80,000 of foreign earned income that is excluded and $20,000 in other taxable income (after deductions). The individual is subject to tax on the $20,000 at the rate or rates applicable to taxable income in the range of $80,000 to $100,000. (Com Rept, see ¶ 5033)

☐ **Effective:** Tax years beginning after Dec. 31, 2005. (Tax Increase Prevention Act §515(d))

¶ 207. Dollar cap on below-market loans made to qualified continuing care facilities temporarily eliminated, and other rules temporarily eased, for years 2006 through 2010

Code Sec. 7872(h), as amended by Tax Increase Prevention Act § 209(a)
Code Sec. 7872(g)(6), as amended by Tax Increase Prevention Act § 209(b)(1)
Generally effective: Calendar years beginning after 2005
Committee Reports, see ¶ 5013

A below-market loan is a loan that has an interest rate below the applicable Federal rate (AFR), or has no interest rate at all. Under the so-called below-market loan rules, loans that lack interest rates or have rates that don't reflect market conditions are recharacterized to reflect the reality of the underlying transaction, by imputing a higher rate of interest. The result of this imputation is that the lender has to include the imputed interest in income, and the borrower, subject to the deduction limits, gets a deduction for the imputed interest. (FTC 2d ¶ J-2901; USTR ¶ 78,724.02; TaxDesk ¶ 155,001)

Under pre-Tax Increase Prevention Act law, loans to *qualified* continuing care facilities were subject to the below-market loan rules. (FTC 2d ¶ J-2917; TaxDesk ¶ 155,020)

A special exception existed, however, under which the below-market loan rules didn't apply to (i) any below-market loan made by a lender to a qualified continuing care facility pursuant to a continuing care contract, and (ii) the lender (or the lender's spouse) attained age 65 before the close of the year. (FTC 2d ¶ J-2988; USTR ¶ 78,724.20; TaxDesk ¶ 155,056)

For the special exception to apply, the aggregate outstanding amount of these loans couldn't exceed $90,000, as adjusted for inflation (scheduled to be $163,300 for 2006). If the exception applied, the individual had no imputed interest attributed to him for the below-market loan. (FTC 2d ¶ J-2989; USTR ¶ 78,724.20; TaxDesk ¶ 155,057)

> ***observation:*** Thus, this exception provided a tax break by allowing lenders to make up to $163,300 (for 2006) in below-market loans to qualified continuing care facilities, without incurring imputed interest.

FTC 2d References are to Federal Tax Coordinator 2d
FIN References are to RIA's Analysis of Federal Taxes: Income
USTR References are to United States Tax Reporter: Income, Estate & Gift, and Excise
PCA References are to Pension Analysis (print & electronic)
PE References are to the Pension Explanations (print & electronic)

Qualified continuing care facility. Under pre-Tax Increase Prevention Act law, a qualified continuing-care facility was designed to provide services under continuing care contracts, and had to meet the following conditions: (i) substantially all of the residents of the facility had to be covered by continuing-care contracts; and (ii) substantially all of the facilities used to provide services under a continuing-care contract had to be owned or operated by the borrower (i.e., the continuing-care facility). A qualified continuing-care facility did not include any facility of a type traditionally considered a nursing home. (FTC 2d ¶ J-2990, ¶ J-2991; TaxDesk ¶ 155,058, ¶ 155,059)

Continuing care contract. Under pre-Tax Increase Prevention Act law, a "continuing care contract" was defined as a written contract between an individual and a qualified continuing care facility under which:

(A) the individual or individual's spouse may use a qualified continuing care facility for their life or lives,

(B) the individual or individual's spouse—

(i) would first (i) reside in a separate, independent living unit with additional facilities outside the unit for providing meals and other personal care, and (ii) would not require long-term nursing care, and

(ii) would later be provided long-term and skilled nursing care as the health of the individual or individual's spouse required, and

(C) no additional substantial payment was required if the individual or individual's spouse required increased personal care services or long-term and skilled nursing care. (FTC 2d/FIN ¶ J-2991; TaxDesk ¶ 155,059)

New Law. The Tax Increase Prevention Act temporarily modifies the rules governing the application of the below-market loans rules to qualified continuing care facilities. (Code Sec. 7872(h) as amended by Tax Increase Prevention Act §209(a))

Dollar cap on outstanding loans eliminated. The Tax Increase Prevention Act removes the prior-law statutory limit (scheduled to be $163,300 for 2006) on outstanding below-market loans. (Com Rept, see ¶ 5013)

> ***observation:*** There is no statutory provision explicitly repealing the dollar cap on outstanding loans—new Code Sec. 7872(h) simply does not have a provision establishing a cap. The dollar cap is scheduled to return, however, when the new rules sunset, and pre-Tax Increase Prevention Act Code Sec. 7872(g)(2) again takes effect.

The changes made to the rules governing the application of the below-market loan rules to qualified continuing care facilities by the Tax Increase Prevention Act apply only for a five-year period (2006 through 2010). In effect, the new rules and definitions provided under new Code Sec. 7872(h) replace those of pre-Tax Increase Prevention Act Code Sec. 7872(g) for this five-year period. Beginning in 2011, new Code Sec. 7872(h) is scheduled to sunset, and the rules under Code Sec. 7872(g) will again apply (see below). (Com Rept, see ¶ 5013)

The Tax Increase Prevention Act provides that the below-market loan rules do not apply for any calendar year to (i) any below-market loan owed by a facility that, on the last day of the year, is a "qualified continuing care facility," if (ii) the loan was made pursuant to a continuing care contract, and if (iii) the lender (or the lender's spouse) reaches age 62 before the end of the year. (Code Sec. 7872(h)(1))

> ***observation:*** Thus, the minimum age (for the lender or the lender's spouse) at which the exception from the below-market loan rules for loans to (the re-defined) qualified continuing care facilities can apply is reduced to 62 from 65, until 2011.

Qualified continuing care facility. The Tax Increase Prevention Act redefines a "qualified continuing care facility" as one or more facilities:

(i) which are designed to provide services under continuing care contracts,

(ii) which include an independent living unit, along with an assisted living or nursing facility, or both, and

(iii) substantially all of the independent living unit residents of which are covered by continuing care contracts. (Code Sec. 7872(h)(3)(A))

Nursing homes excluded. The Tax Increase Prevention Act further provides that the term "qualified continuing care facility" does not include any facility which is traditionally considered a nursing home. (Code Sec. 7872(h)(3)(B))

Continuing care contract. The Tax Increase Prevention Act also modifies the definition of "continuing care contract." Specifically, a "continuing care contract" is a written contract between an individual and a qualified continuing care facility under which:

(A) the individual or individual's spouse may use a qualified continuing care facility for their life or lives,

(B) the individual or individual's spouse will be provided with housing, as appropriate for the individual's or spouse's health—

(i) in an independent living unit (with additional available facilities outside the unit for providing meals and other personal care), and

---

(ii) in an "assisted living facility" or a "nursing facility," as is available in the continuing care facility, and

(C) the individual or individual's spouse will be provided assisted living or nursing care as the health of the individual or spouse requires, and as is available in the continuing care facility.

> ***observation:*** Thus, the pre-Tax Increase Prevention Act requirement that a continuing care contract provide that no additional substantial payment is required if the individual or individual's spouse requires increased personal care services or long-term and skilled nursing care does not apply for years 2006 through 2010. Presumably, this change allows continuing care facilities to assess individuals for "additional substantial payments" for increased personal care services or long-term and skilled nursing care.

The Tax Increase Prevention Act also requires that IRS issue guidance limiting the definition of continuing care contract to contracts that provide, to an individual or spouse, only those facilities, care, and services described above. (Code Sec. 7872(h)(2))

> ***observation:*** Thus, the pre-Tax Increase Prevention Act rule that a continuing care contract require that an individual and spouse be healthy enough to first reside in "a separate, independent living unit" does not apply for years 2006 through 2010. Presumably, this will allow individuals not capable of residing in a "separate, independent living unit" (e.g., those requiring skilled nursing care) to enter into continuing care contracts nonetheless.

"Assisted living facility" and "nursing facility" defined. In defining the terms "continuing care contract" and "qualified continuing care facility" (above), the term "assisted living facility" means a facility providing assistance (1) with activities of daily living (such as eating, toileting, transferring, bathing, dressing, and continence), or (2) in cases of cognitive impairment, to protect the health or safety of an individual.

The term "nursing facility" means a facility that offers care requiring the use of licensed nursing staff. (Com Rept, see ¶ 5013)

New rules sunset in 2011. The Tax Increase Prevention Act provides that Code Sec. 7872(h) will not apply to any calendar year after 2010. (Code Sec. 7872(h)(4))

Suspension of Code Sec. 7872(g). To ensure that there is no conflict in applying Code Sec. 7872(h), the Tax Increase Prevention Act amends Code Sec. 7872(g) to provide that Code Sec. 7872(g) does not apply to any calendar year to which Code Sec. 7872(h) applies (i.e., 2006 through 2010). (Code Sec. 7872(g)(6) as amended by Tax Increase Prevention Act §209(b)(1))

☐ **Effective:** For calendar years beginning after Dec. 31, 2005—for loans made before, on, or after Dec. 31, 2005. (Tax Increase Prevention Act §209(c))

¶ 208. Capital gain treatment is permitted for certain self-created musical works sold or exchanged before Jan. 1, 2011

Code Sec. 1221(b)(3), as amended by Tax Increase Prevention Act § 204(a)
Code Sec. 170(e)(1)(A), as amended by Tax Increase Prevention Act § 204(b)
Generally effective: Sales and exchanges in tax years beginning after May 17, 2006 and before Jan. 1, 2011
Committee Reports, see ¶ 5008

The maximum tax rate on the net capital gain income of an individual for tax years beginning in 2006 is 15 percent, see FTC 2d/FIN ¶ I-5110.3; USTR ¶ 14.085; TaxDesk ¶ 223,312. The maximum tax rate on ordinary income of an individual for 2006, however, is 35 percent, see FTC 2d/FIN ¶ A-1102; USTR ¶ 14.08; TaxDesk ¶ 568,202. (Com Rept, see ¶ 5008)

Code Sec. 1221(a)(3) provides that copyrights or literary, musical, or artistic compositions, a letter or memorandum or similar property are not capital assets and also are not capital gain/ordinary loss assets if the taxpayer:

(1) created the copyrights, etc., through his or her own personal efforts, or

(2) in the case of a letter, memorandum, or similar property, was the one for whom the property was prepared or produced, or

(3) owns any property described in (1) or (2), above, whose basis is determined in whole or in part by reference to the basis of the property in the hands of a person who created the property through his personal efforts. (FTC 2d/FIN ¶ I-6601; USTR ¶ 12,214.45; TaxDesk ¶ 252,501)

Another exclusion from the definition of a capital asset is inventory property or property a taxpayer holds primarily for sale in the ordinary course of the taxpayer's trade or business. (FTC 2d/FIN ¶ I-6100; USTR ¶ 12,214.01; TaxDesk ¶ 249,500) (Com Rept, see ¶ 5008)

Under pre-Tax Increase Prevention Act law, when a taxpayer who owned copyrights in, for example, books, songs, or paintings that the taxpayer created (or when a taxpayer to which the copyrights had been transferred by the works' creator in a substituted basis transaction) sold the property, gain from the sale was treated as ordinary income, not capital gain. (Com Rept, see ¶ 5008)

If "ordinary income property" (property any portion of the gain on which wouldn't have been long-term capital gain if the property had been sold by the taxpayer at its fair market value on the date it was contributed) is contributed to a charitable organization, the amount treated as contributed must be reduced by the amount (referred to as ordinary income) which would have been recognized as gain other than long-term capital gain if the property had been sold by the donor at its fair market value at the time of its contribution to the charitable organization, see FTC 2d/FIN ¶ K-3160; USTR ¶ 1704.42; TaxDesk ¶ 331,609. That is, a taxpayer is generally allowed a deduction for the fair market value of property contributed to a charity, except that, if a taxpayer contributes property that would have generated ordinary income (or short-term capital gain), the taxpayer's charitable contribution deduction is limited to the adjusted basis of the property. (Com Rept, see ¶ 5008)

New Law. The Tax Increase Prevention Act provides that, at the election of the taxpayer, Code Sec. 1221(a)(1) (which excludes from the definition of a capital asset, inventory or property held by the taxpayer primarily for sale to customers in the ordinary course of the taxpayer's trade or business) and Code Sec. 1221(a)(3) (which excludes from the definition of a capital asset, a copyright, literary, musical, or artistic composition, as further defined above) do not apply to musical compositions or copyrights in musical works sold or exchanged before Jan. 1, 2011, by a taxpayer described in Code Sec. 1221(a)(3). (Code Sec. 1221(b)(3) as amended by Tax Increase Prevention Act §204(a)) That is, at the election of a taxpayer, the sale or exchange before Jan. 1, 2011 of musical compositions or copyrights in musical works created by the taxpayer's personal efforts (or having a basis determined by reference to the basis in the hands of the taxpayer whose personal efforts created the compositions or copyrights) is treated as the sale or exchange of a capital asset. (Com Rept, see ¶ 5008)

> ***observation:*** Thus, for example, a composer who sells his or her copyrighted composition in a sale in a tax year beginning after May 17, 2006 and before Jan. 1, 2011 will pay tax at the lower rates that apply to capital gain. A painter or author, however, will not be eligible for that tax advantage.

> ***viewpoint:*** Robert P. Rothman, Of Counsel to DLA Piper Rudnick Gray Cary US LLP in New York, with thanks to Monica McCabe, Esq. for her contribution on matters of copyright law, comments as follows: The statutory language is not entirely clear as to the meaning of "musical composition" and "musical work." In particular, in the case of a song, for example, does the new rule provide relief only for the portion

of income attributable to the music, or does it include the lyrics? Further, does the answer to this depend on whether the lyrics and the music were written by the same person or different persons?

In this connection, it is instructive to note that, as a matter of copyright law, generally the music and lyrics of a song are covered by a single copyright. This is the case even if the composer and the lyricist are different (in which case they jointly own the copyright on the entire work). This suggests that the better interpretation of the statute is that the music and lyrics should not be bifurcated, and that (provided there is a "sale or exchange"), the portion of the income attributable to the entire song should qualify for capital gain treatment. However, it might be possible to draw a contrary conclusion based on the fact that the amendments made by Tax Increase Prevention Act §207 (see ¶ 405) specifically include lyrics in the definition of "applicable musical property," whereas lyrics are not mentioned in the changes made by Tax Increase Prevention Act §204.

observation: IRS will have to issue guidance on the manner and time for making the election.

However, the Tax Increase Prevention Act preserves the pre-Tax Increase Prevention Act limitation on a taxpayer's charitable deduction for the contribution of these musical compositions or copyrights (Com Rept, see ¶ 5008) by providing that the amount of any charitable contribution otherwise taken into account as a deduction must be reduced by the amount of gain that would not have been long term capital gain *(determined without regard to Code Sec. 1221(b)(3))* if the taxpayer had sold the contributed property at fair market value. (Code Sec. 170(e)(1)(A) as amended by Tax Increase Prevention Act §204(b))

observation: Thus, by adding the phrase "determined without regard to Code Sec. 1221(b)(3)" to Code Sec. 170(e)(1)(A), the Tax Increase Prevention Act ensures that a taxpayer's charitable contribution deduction for a contribution of musical compositions or copyrights in musical works is limited to the adjusted basis of the property whether or not it is property described in Code Sec. 1221(b)(3) for which the capital gain treatment election would be available.

Redesignation. Pre-Tax Increase Prevention Act Code Sec. 1221(b)(3) has been redesignated by the Tax Increase Prevention Act as Code Sec. 1221(b)(4). (Tax Increase Prevention Act §204(a))

☐ **Effective:** Sales and exchanges in tax years beginning after May 17, 2006 (Tax Increase Prevention Act §204(c)) and before Jan. 1, 2011. (Code Sec. 1221(b)(3))

¶ 300. Provisions Affecting Businesses

¶ 301. Only wages allocable to domestic production gross receipts may be taken into account in determining 50%-of-W-2-wages limitation on U.S. production activities deduction

Code Sec. 199(b)(2)(B), as amended by Tax Increase Prevention Act § 514(a)
Generally effective: Tax years beginning after May 17, 2006
Committee Reports, see ¶ 5032

Subject to various limits, taxpayers are allowed a deduction—the U.S. production activities deduction—equal to a specified percentage (3% for 2006, 6% for 2007 – 2009, 9% for 2010 and thereafter) of the taxpayer's "qualified production activities income" for the tax year. See FTC 2d/FIN ¶ L-4326 *et seq.*; USTR ¶ 1994 *et seq.*; TaxDesk ¶ 307,801 *et seq.* Qualified production activities income is the taxpayer's "domestic production gross receipts," net of cost of goods sold, expenses, losses, and deductions allocable to those receipts. See FTC 2d/FIN ¶ L-4367; USTR ¶ 1994.02; TaxDesk ¶ 307,804. (For allocation rules, see FTC 2d/FIN ¶ L-4368 *et seq.*; USTR ¶ 1994.02; TaxDesk ¶ 307,804.) Domestic production gross receipts are the taxpayer's gross receipts from:

(1) the manufacture, production, growth, or extraction in the U.S. of qualifying production property (i.e., tangible personal property, computer software, and certain sound recordings);

(2) the production of qualified films;

(3) the production in the U.S. of electricity, natural gas, or potable water ("utilities");

(4) real property construction in the U.S., and

(5) engineering or architectural services performed in connection with U.S. real property construction.

See FTC 2d/FIN ¶ L-4340; USTR ¶ 1994.03; TaxDesk ¶ 307,805.

Among the limits to which the U.S. production activities deduction is subject is the "50%-of-W-2-wages" limitation. Under this limitation, the amount of the U.S. production activities deduction for any tax year may not exceed 50% of the taxpayer's W-2 wages for that tax year. For purposes of this rule, the term "W-2 wages" means, with respect to any person for any tax year of that person,

FTC 2d References are to Federal Tax Coordinator 2d
FIN References are to RIA's Analysis of Federal Taxes: Income
USTR References are to United States Tax Reporter: Income, Estate & Gift, and Excise
PCA References are to Pension Analysis (print & electronic)
PE References are to the Pension Explanations (print & electronic)

the sum of the amounts described in the following Code sections that are paid by that person with respect to employment of employees by that person during the calendar year ending during that tax year:

(1) Code Sec. 6051(a)(3), i.e., the total amount of wages subject to Code Sec. 3401(a) income tax withholding, see FTC 2d/FIN ¶ S-3152; USTR ¶ 60,514; TaxDesk ¶ 812,002; and

(2) Code Sec. 6051(a)(8), requiring W-2 reporting, see FTC 2d/FIN ¶ S-3152; USTR ¶ 60,514; TaxDesk ¶ 812,002, of—

(a) the total amount of elective deferrals to a cash or deferred arrangement (CODA) under Code Sec. 402(g)(3), see FTC 2d/FIN ¶ H-9152; USTR ¶ 4024; TaxDesk ¶ 284,026),

(b) the total amount of compensation deferred under Code Sec. 457 (deferred compensation plans of state and local governments and tax-exempt organizations), see FTC 2d/FIN ¶ H-3300.1 *et seq.*; USTR ¶ 4574; TaxDesk ¶ 135,701 *et seq.*, and

(c) the amount of the employee's "designated Roth contributions," see FTC 2d/FIN ¶ H-12295.5; USTR ¶ 402A4; TaxDesk ¶ 283,405.

Moreover, W-2 wages include only amounts that are reported on a Form W-2 filed with the Social Security Administration not later than 60 days after the extended due date for the Form W-2.

> ***observation:*** In order to be taken into account in determining a taxpayer's qualified production activities income, a deduction or expense—including wage expenses—must be allocable to domestic production gross receipts. See FTC 2d/FIN ¶ L-4367 *et seq.*; USTR ¶ 1994.02; TaxDesk ¶ 307,804. However, under pre-Tax Increase Prevention Act law, the W-2 wages taken into account for purposes of determining the 50%-of-W-2-wages limitation on a taxpayer's U.S. production activities deduction generally didn't have to be allocable to domestic production gross receipts or attributable to the "production" activities that gave rise to the deduction. Therefore, under pre-Tax Increase Prevention Act law, if the taxpayer engaged some employees in activities that generated the deduction, and other employees in activities that did not, the wages of all of those employees could be treated as W-2 wages for purposes of the 50%-of-W-2-wages limitation if they otherwise satisfied the requirements discussed above.

(FTC 2d/FIN ¶ L-4385 *et seq.*; USTR ¶ 1994.01; TaxDesk ¶ 307,803)

New Law. Under the Tax Increase Prevention Act, for purposes of the 50%-of-W-2-wages limitation on the U.S. production activities deduction, the term "W-2 wages" doesn't include any amount that is not properly allocable to domestic production gross receipts in determining qualified production activities income. (Code Sec. 199(b)(2)(B) as amended by Tax Increase Prevention Act §514(a)) In other words, the Act modifies the 50%-of-W-2-wages limitation so that taxpayers may include as wages only amounts that are properly allocable to domestic production gross receipts—i.e., wages that are deducted in arriving at qualified production activities income under the allocation rules discussed at FTC 2d/FIN ¶ L-4368 *et seq.*; USTR ¶ 1994.02; TaxDesk ¶ 307,804. (Com Rept, see ¶ 5032)

> ***viewpoint:*** Experts at Practitioners Publishing Company (Thomson-PPC) comment that, until enactment of the Tax Increase Prevention Act, W-2 wages for purposes of the 50%-of-W-2-wages limitation on the U.S. production activities deduction equaled the sum of the aggregate amounts included on the Forms W-2 of the taxpayer's employees. Because W-2 wages for purposes of this limitation are now limited to wages allocable to domestic production gross receipts, employers will have to design and implement recordkeeping systems to capture the portion of employees' time and thus pay that is devoted to qualifying activities. Furthermore, taxpayers should consider using separate general ledger accounts to separate wages allocable to domestic production gross receipts from other wages.
>
> Because payments to independent contractors are not considered to be W-2 wages for purposes of the 50%-of-W-2-wages limitation (see FTC 2d/FIN ¶ L-4385; USTR ¶ 1994.01), taxpayers may want to bring qualifying activities in-house that were previously sub-contracted out. However, before doing so, they should perform a cost-benefit analysis to determine whether the deduction gained from including the workers' W-2 wages in the computation of the 50%-of-W-2-wages limitation outweighs the additional expense (and administrative burden) of carrying these workers on the payroll.

For special rules for computing the 50%-of-W-2-wages limitation for partners and S corporation shareholders, see ¶ 302.

☐ **Effective:** Tax years beginning after May 17, 2006. (Tax Increase Prevention Act §514(c))

FTC 2d References are to Federal Tax Coordinator 2d
FIN References are to RIA's Analysis of Federal Taxes: Income
USTR References are to United States Tax Reporter: Income, Estate & Gift, and Excise
PCA References are to Pension Analysis (print & electronic)
PE References are to the Pension Explanations (print & electronic)

¶ 302. Special rule for computing a partner's or S corporation shareholder's W-2 wages for purposes of the 50%-of-W-2-wages limitation on U.S. production activities deduction is repealed

Code Sec. 199(d)(1)(A)(iii), as amended by Tax Increase Prevention Act § 514(b)(1)
Generally effective: Tax years beginning after May 17, 2006
Committee Reports, see ¶ 5032

Subject to various limits, taxpayers are allowed a deduction—the U.S. production activities deduction—for specified domestic manufacturing, production (including production of electricity, natural gas, potable water, and "qualified films"), growth, extraction, real property construction, architectural, and engineering activities. The deduction is equal to a specified percentage (3% for 2006, 6% for 2007 – 2009, 9% for 2010 and thereafter) of the taxpayer's "qualified production activities income" (the basis for computing the deduction, see FTC 2d/FIN ¶ L-4367; USTR ¶ 1994.02; TaxDesk ¶ 307,804) for the tax year. Among these limits is the "50%-of-W-2-wages" limitation. Under this limitation, the amount of the U.S. production activities deduction for any tax year may not exceed 50% of the taxpayer's W-2 wages for that tax year. For full discussion of this limit, see ¶ 301.

Under pre-Tax Increase Prevention Act law, in the case of a partnership or S corporation, each partner or S corporation shareholder was treated as having W-2 wages for the tax year in an amount equal to the *lesser* of:

(1) that person's allocable share of the W-2 wages of the partnership or S corporation for the tax year, as determined under regs, or

(2) two times the specified percentage of the qualified production activities income allocated by the partnership or S corporation to that person for the tax year.

(FTC 2d/FIN ¶ L-4386 *et seq.*; USTR ¶ 1994.01)

New Law. Under the Tax Increase Prevention Act, for purposes of determining the 50%-of-W-2-wages limitation on the U.S. production activities deduction, in the case of a partnership or S corporation, each partner or S corporation shareholder is treated as having W-2 wages for the tax year in an amount equal to that person's allocable share of the W-2 wages of the partnership or S corporation for the tax year, as determined under regs. (Code Sec. 199(d)(1)(A)(iii) as amended by Tax Increase Prevention Act §514(b)(1)) In other words, the Act repeals the special limitation on wages treated as allocated to partners or S corporation shareholders described at (2) above. As a result, for purposes of the 50%-of-W-2-wages limitation, a partner or S corporation shareholder is treated as having been allocated wages from a partnership or S corporation in an amount equal to that person's allocable share of the wages paid by the partnership or S corporation, as determined under regs, even if that amount is more than twice the specified percentage of qualified production activities income allocated to that person for the tax year. (Com Rept, see ¶ 5032)

> ***viewpoint:*** Experts at Practitioners Publishing Company (Thomson-PPC) comment that, until enactment of the Tax Increase Prevention Act, the 50%-of-W-2 wages limitation for partners and S corporation shareholders equaled the *lesser* of the partner's or shareholder's allocable share of the W-2 wages of the entity, or two times the specified percentage (3% in 2006) of qualified production activities income allocated to that person for the tax year. As a simplification measure, the Tax Increase Prevention Act repeals the special limitation on wages treated as allocated to partners or shareholders. Because this limitation could only serve to reduce the amount of a partner's or S corporation shareholder's U.S. production activities deduction, its repeal is a favorable development.

For the Tax Increase Prevention Act's restriction of W-2 wages (for purposes of the 50%-of-W-2-wages limitation) to wages allocable to the activities that give rise to the U.S. production activities deduction, see ¶ 301.

☐ **Effective:** Tax years beginning after May 17, 2006. (Tax Increase Prevention Act §514(c))

¶ 303. Certain CERCLA environmental settlement funds established before Jan. 1, 2011 are treated as not subject to federal income tax

Code Sec. 468B(g), as amended by Tax Increase Prevention Act § 201(a)
Generally effective: Accounts and funds established after May 17, 2006
Committee Reports, see ¶ 5005

A designated settlement fund is any fund (1) which is established under a court order; (2) which completely extinguishes the taxpayer's tort liability with respect to a class of claimants; (3) which is managed and controlled by persons independent of the taxpayer; (4) in which neither the taxpayer nor any person related to the taxpayer has a beneficial interest in the fund's income or corpus; and (5) to which no amount may be transferred other than qualified payments. A fund established before Aug. 17, '86 cannot qualify as a designated settle-

FTC 2d References are to Federal Tax Coordinator 2d
FIN References are to RIA's Analysis of Federal Taxes: Income
USTR References are to United States Tax Reporter: Income, Estate & Gift, and Excise
PCA References are to Pension Analysis (print & electronic)
PE References are to the Pension Explanations (print & electronic)

ment fund. (See FTC 2d/FIN ¶s G-2789, G-2790; USTR ¶ 468B4; TaxDesk ¶ 442,025.) A designated settlement fund is established for the principal purpose of resolving and satisfying present and future claims against the taxpayer (or any related or formerly related person) that arises out of personal injury, death or property damage. The taxpayer must elect to establish a designated fund (see FTC 2d/FIN ¶ G-2793; USTR ¶ 468B4; TaxDesk ¶ 442,025). If a taxpayer makes a payment to a designated settlement fund under a court order, the deduction timing rules that require economic performance are considered to be met as the payments are made by the taxpayer to the fund. (See FTC 2d/FIN ¶ G-2788; USTR ¶ 468B4; TaxDesk ¶ 442,025.)

The cleanup of hazardous waste sites is sometimes funded by environmental "settlement funds" or escrow accounts. These escrow accounts are established in consent decrees between the Environmental Protection Agency (EPA) and the settling parties under the jurisdiction of a federal district court. The EPA uses these accounts to resolve claims against private parties under the Comprehensive Environmental Response, Compensation and Liability Act of '80 (CERCLA). See FTC 2d/FIN ¶ G-2808; USTR ¶ 468B4. (Com Rept, see ¶ 5005)

Under pre-Tax Increase Prevention Act law, no escrow account, settlement fund or similar fund was exempt from current income tax. (FTC 2d/FIN ¶ G-2791; USTR ¶ 468B4)

New Law. The Tax Increase Prevention Act provides that certain settlement funds established in consent decrees for the sole purpose of resolving claims under CERCLA are to be treated as beneficially owned by the U.S. government and therefore not subject to federal income tax. (Com Rept, see ¶ 5005) Specifically, certain escrow accounts, settlement funds or similar funds are treated as beneficially owned by the U.S. and exempt from income tax if all of the following conditions are met: (Code Sec. 468B(g)(2) as amended by Tax Increase Prevention Act §201(a))

- The escrow account, settlement fund or other similar fund is established under a consent decree entered by a U.S. District Court judge. (Code Sec. 468B(g)(2)(A))
- The account or fund is created for the receipt of settlement payments as directed by a government entity (defined below) for the sole purpose of resolving or satisfying one or more claims asserting liability under CERCLA. (Code Sec. 468B(g)(2)(B))
- The authority and control over the expenditure of the funds in the account, or settlement fund, or similar fund (including expenditure of contributions to the account or fund and any net earnings on those contributions) is with the government entity. (Code Sec. 468B(g)(2)(C))
- On termination, any remaining funds will be disbursed to the government entity for use in accordance with applicable law. (Code Sec. 468B(g)(2)(D))

Except for the settlement funds described in Code Sec. 468B(g)(2) above, nothing in any provision of law is to be construed as providing that an escrow account, settlement fund, or similar fund is not subject to current income tax. IRS will prescribe regs providing for the taxation of such an account or fund, whether as a grantor trust or otherwise. (Code Sec. 468B(g)(1))

Government entity defined. The term "government entity," for purposes of the above conditions, means the U.S., any state or political subdivision of the U.S., the District of Columbia, any U.S. possession, and any agency or instrumentality of the U.S., any state or political subdivision of a state, the District of Columbia, or any U.S. possession. (Code Sec. 468B(g)(2))

When accounts or funds have to be established. The exemption from tax under Code Sec. 468B(g)(2) above doesn't apply to accounts and funds established after Dec. 31, 2010. (Code Sec. 468B(g)(3))

☐ **Effective:** Accounts and funds established after May 17, 2006.
(Tax Increase Prevention Act §201(b))

¶ 304. FSC and ETI binding contract transition rules repealed

Code Sec. None, Tax Increase Prevention Act § 513
Generally effective: Tax years beginning after May 17, 2006
Committee Reports, see ¶ 5031

In 1999, the World Trade Organization (WTO) ruled that the foreign sales corporation (FSC) provisions of the Code were an illegal export subsidy. As a result, in 2000 Congress repealed the FSC provisions and replaced them with an extraterritorial income (ETI) tax regime. However, under a binding contract transition rule, the repeal didn't apply to transactions in the ordinary course of business involving a FSC which occurred after Dec. 31, 2001 under a binding contract that was in effect on Sept. 30, 2000, and at all times thereafter.

Under the ETI regime, gross income didn't include ETI that was qualifying foreign trade income. Qualifying foreign trade income was determined by taking the greatest of three computed amounts based on foreign trading gross receipts, foreign trade income, and foreign sale and leasing income. In 2002, the WTO held that the ETI regime was also a prohibited export subsidy. As a result, in 2004 Congress repealed the ETI provisions. However, under a general transition rule taxpayers could receive 80% of their otherwise applicable ETI benefits for transactions in 2005, and 60% of their otherwise applicable ETI benefits for transactions in 2006. In addition, under a binding contract transition rule, the ETI provisions continued to apply to transactions in the ordinary course of business that occurred under a binding contract in effect on Sept. 17, 2003, and at all times thereafter.

> ***observation:*** The FSC binding contract transition rule is found in the 2000 FSC Repeal Act. (Sec. 5(c)(1), PL 106-519, 11/15/2000) The ETI binding contract transition rule is found in the 2004 Jobs Act. (Sec. 101(f), PL 108-357, 10/22/2004)

In early 2006, the WTO held that the ETI general transition rule and the FSC and ETI binding contract transition rules were prohibited export subsidies. (FTC 2d/FIN ¶ O-1652, ¶ O-1657, ¶ O-1658, ¶ O-1660.1; USTR ¶ 1114, ¶ 9214; TaxDesk ¶ 191,701, ¶ 191,711, ¶ 191,712)

New Law. The Tax Increase Prevention Act repeals both the FSC binding contract transition rule (2000 FSC Repeal Act §5(c)(1) as amended by Tax Increase Prevention Act §513(a)) and the ETI binding contract transition rule. (2004 Jobs Act §101(f) as amended by Tax Increase Prevention Act §513(b))

> ***observation:*** Thus, taxpayers who had entered into long term contracts before the FSC and ETI rules were repealed and who had planned on benefitting from those rules well into the future under the binding contract transition rules won't be able to do so.

> ***viewpoint:*** Linda Carlisle, a tax partner at White & Case, Washington, D.C., offers the following comment: In a letter to Chairman Thomas dated May 2, 2006, the European Union (EU) had threatened to reintroduce sanctions on a number of U.S. products if the grandfathering provisions as enacted remained in place. The letter notes, however, that a "negotiated solution" to the dispute could involve repealing the grandfathering of sales contacts (e.g., long term contracts for the sales of airplanes yet to be built), while leaving the grandfather for leasing transactions (e.g., purchase options at the end of a lease). The Conference Committee chose to repeal the grandfather provisions entirely. Retroactive repeal of the transition rules that were not required to avoid retaliation is very unusual.

> ***observation:*** The EU has indicated that it's satisfied with the repeal of the binding contract transition rules. Thus, the EU will not impose sanctions that were scheduled to go into effect on May 16, 2006.

☐ **Effective:** Tax years beginning after May 17, 2006. (Tax Increase Prevention Act §513(c))

¶ 305. Weight limit for qualifying vessels in alternative tonnage tax regime lowered for 2006 through 2010

Code Sec. 1355(a)(4), as amended by Tax Increase Prevention Act § 205(a)
Generally effective: Tax years beginning after Dec. 31, 2005
Committee Reports, see ¶ 5009

Corporations may elect a tonnage tax in lieu of the U.S. corporate income tax on taxable income from international shipping activities. Under this tonnage tax regime, an electing corporation's gross income doesn't include its income from "qualifying shipping activities," which include operating qualifying vessels in U.S. foreign trade. Instead, an electing corporation is subject to tax on qualifying shipping activities only at the maximum corporate income tax rate on its notional shipping income, which is based on the net tonnage of the corporation's qualifying vessels. (FTC 2d/FIN ¶s O-11550, O-11551, O-11552; USTR ¶s 13,524, 13,534, 13,544; TaxDesk ¶s 644,600, 644,601)

Under pre-Tax Increase Prevention Act law, the weight of a qualifying vessel had to be at least 10,000 deadweight tons. (FTC 2d/FIN ¶ O-11554; USTR ¶ 13,554; TaxDesk ¶ 644,602)

New Law. The Tax Increase Prevention Act reduces the minimum tonnage for a qualifying vessel from 10,000 deadweight tons to 6,000 deadweight tons for tax years beginning after Dec. 31, 2005, and ending before Jan. 1, 2011. (Code Sec. 1355(a)(4) as amended by Tax Increase Prevention Act §205(a))

Deadweight measures the lifting capacity of a ship expressed in long tons (2,240 lbs.), including cargo, crew, and consumables such as fuel, lube oil, drinking water, and stores. It is the difference between the number of tons of water a vessel displaces without such items on board and the number of tons it displaces when fully loaded. (Com Rept, see ¶ 5009)

> ***observation:*** This change should allow operators of smaller U.S.-flag vessels to be more competitive with operators of larger U.S.-flag vessels and with operators of foreign vessels.

☐ **Effective:** For tax years beginning after Dec. 31, 2005. (Tax Increase Prevention Act §205(b))

FTC 2d References are to Federal Tax Coordinator 2d
FIN References are to RIA's Analysis of Federal Taxes: Income
USTR References are to United States Tax Reporter: Income, Estate & Gift, and Excise
PCA References are to Pension Analysis (print & electronic)
PE References are to the Pension Explanations (print & electronic)

¶ 400. Expensing & Amortization

¶ 401. The $100,000 Code Sec. 179 expense election limit, $400,000 phaseout threshold, and inflation adjustments are extended for two years to tax years beginning before Jan. 1, 2010

Code Sec. 179(b)(1), as amended by Tax Increase Prevention Act § 101
Code Sec. 179(b)(2), as amended by Tax Increase Prevention Act § 101
Code Sec. 179(b)(5)(A), as amended by Tax Increase Prevention Act § 101
Generally effective: Tax years beginning after 2007 and before 2010
Committee Reports, see ¶ 5001

A taxpayer, other than an estate, trust, and certain noncorporate lessors, can elect under Code Sec. 179 to deduct as an expense, rather than to depreciate, up to a specified amount of the cost of new or used tangible personal property placed in service during the tax year in the taxpayer's trade or business (Code Sec. 179 property), see FTC 2d/FIN ¶ L-9901; USTR ¶ 1794; TaxDesk ¶ 268,411. Under pre-Tax Increase Prevention Act law, a taxpayer can expense up to $100,000 for tax years beginning after Dec. 31, 2002 and before Jan. 1, 2008, and up to $25,000 for tax years beginning after Dec. 31, 2007. Also, under pre-Tax Increase Prevention Act law, the annual expense limit was reduced (but not below zero) by the amount by which the cost of qualifying property placed in service during the tax year exceeded $400,000 for tax years beginning after Dec. 31, 2002 and before Jan. 1, 2008 and exceeded $200,000 for tax years beginning after Dec. 31, 2007, see FTC 2d/FIN ¶ L-9907; USTR ¶ 1794.01; TaxDesk ¶ 268,411.

The $100,000 and $400,000 amounts are each increased by a cost of living adjustment determined under Code Sec. 1(f)(3) (dealing with inflation adjustments for tax rate brackets, see FTC 2d/FIN ¶ A-1103; USTR ¶ 15.08(5); TaxDesk ¶ 568,203), but substituting "calendar year 2002" (as the base year) for "calendar year 1992". For 2006, after adjustment for inflation, the $100,000 amount is $108,000, and the $400,000 amount is $430,000. Under pre-Tax Increase Prevention Act law, the inflation adjustment applied for tax years beginning in a calendar year after Dec. 31, 2003 and before Jan. 1, 2008, see FTC 2d/FIN ¶ L-9907.1; USTR ¶ 1794.01; TaxDesk ¶ 268,411.

observation: Under the expensing election, a taxpayer can deduct costs immediately, rather than depreciating them over several years.

FTC 2d References are to Federal Tax Coordinator 2d
FIN References are to RIA's Analysis of Federal Taxes: Income
USTR References are to United States Tax Reporter: Income, Estate & Gift, and Excise
PCA References are to Pension Analysis (print & electronic)
PE References are to the Pension Explanations (print & electronic)

And, unlike depreciation subject to the mid-quarter or half-year conventions, a full expense deduction is allowed no matter when in the tax year the qualifying property is placed in service, even on the last day of the year, see FTC 2d/FIN ¶ L-9902; USTR ¶ 1794.01; TaxDesk ¶ 268,403. In addition, the Code Sec. 179 expensing election can yield other benefits. For example, by lowering the adjusted gross income (AGI) of a taxpayer who is unincorporated (or operates his business through a pass-through entity), the taxpayer may be able to benefit from itemized deductions or personal exemptions that would otherwise be limited or phased-out by the taxpayer's AGI.

New Law. Congress believes that Code Sec. 179 expensing will continue to provide important benefits if extended. Accordingly, the Tax Increase Prevention Act continues in effect, for an additional two years, the increased $100,000 amount that a taxpayer can deduct as a Code Sec. 179 expense (see "**Increased amount that can be expensed**" below) and the increased $400,000 phaseout threshold amount (see "**Increased phaseout threshold**" below). The Tax Increase Prevention Act also extends, through 2009 (from 2007), the indexing for inflation of both the $100,000 maximum dollar amount that can be deducted and the $400,000 phaseout amount (see "**Extended inflation adjustment**" below). (Com Rept, see ¶ 5001)

observation: Under the expensing election, a taxpayer can deduct costs immediately, rather than depreciating them over several years. And, unlike depreciation subject to the mid-quarter or half-year conventions, a full expense deduction is allowed no matter when in the tax year the qualifying property is placed in service, even on the last day of the year, see FTC 2d/FIN ¶ L-9902; USTR ¶ 1794.01; TaxDesk ¶ 268,403. In addition, the Code Sec. 179 expensing election can yield other benefits. For example, by lowering the adjusted gross income (AGI) of a taxpayer who is unincorporated (or operates his business through a pass-through entity), the taxpayer may be able to benefit from itemized deductions or personal exemptions that would otherwise be limited or phased-out by the taxpayer's AGI.

For an extension of the inclusion of off-the-shelf computer software in the definition of Code Sec. 179 property, see ¶ 403.

For an extension of the right to revoke the Code Sec. 179 expense election without IRS consent, see ¶ 402.

caution: The Code Sec. 179(b)(3) rule limiting the amount of the expensing deduction (after application of the phaseout rule) to the amount of taxable income from any of the taxpayer's active trades or businesses has not been changed by the Tax Increase Prevention Act. An amount that can't be deducted because of this taxable income limit can be carried over indefinitely until it can be deducted, see FTC 2d/FIN ¶ L-9911; USTR ¶ 1794.01; TaxDesk ¶ 268,415.

observation: The carryover applies only to amounts not deducted, in the year in which property is placed in service, because of the taxable income limitation under Code Sec. 179(b)(3). Thus, the carryover isn't available for amounts not deducted, in the year property is placed in service, because of: (1) the annual dollar limitation on the amount that can be expensed, (2) the phaseout dollar limitation based on the amount of qualifying property placed in service by the taxpayer, or (3) the taxpayer's decision not to make the Code Sec. 179 election or to make an election in an amount that is less than the maximum allowable, see FTC 2d/FIN ¶ L-9917; TaxDesk ¶ 268,420.

Increased amount that can be expensed. The Tax Increase Prevention Act increases the amount allowed for Code Sec. 179 expensing for tax years beginning after Dec. 31, 2007 and before Jan. 1, 2010 from $25,000 to $100,000. (Code Sec. 179(b)(1) as amended by Tax Increase Prevention Act §101)

observation: The $100,000 cap for tax years beginning in 2008 and 2009 is before adjustment for inflation. For 2006, after adjustment for inflation, the $100,000 amount is $108,000 (see FTC 2d/FIN ¶ L-9907.1; USTR ¶ 1794.01; TaxDesk ¶ 268,411). Thus, for 2007, 2008, and 2009, the $100,000 statutory amount after adjustment for inflation will be at least $108,000.

observation: Thus, under the Tax Increase Prevention Act, the maximum dollar amount that can be deducted under Code Sec. 179 is $100,000 (before inflation adjustment) for property placed in service in tax years beginning before Jan. 1, 2010.

observation: The extension provided by the Tax Increase Prevention Act diminishes the tax incentive for accelerating into 2007 equipment purchases that exceed $25,000.

recommendation: Small businesses that engage in long-term planning for their equipment acquisitions should review their plans.

observation: Unless Code Sec. 179 is further extended, the expensing ceiling for tax years beginning in 2010 and later will revert back to $25,000.

FTC 2d References are to Federal Tax Coordinator 2d
FIN References are to RIA's Analysis of Federal Taxes: Income
USTR References are to United States Tax Reporter: Income, Estate & Gift, and Excise
PCA References are to Pension Analysis (print & electronic)
PE References are to the Pension Explanations (print & electronic)

illustration (1): In each of its tax years beginning in 2005 through 2010, Taxpayer X places in service $40,000 of qualifying property. X's annual expense election is limited to $40,000 for 2005 through 2009, and $25,000 for 2010.

illustration (2): Assume that in Illustration (1) X places $120,000 of qualifying property in service in its tax year beginning in 2008. Assuming that the same inflation adjustments that applied for 2006 apply for 2008, X's expense election for that year is limited to $108,000.

Increased phaseout threshold. The Tax Increase Prevention Act also increases the phaseout threshold for tax years beginning after Dec. 31, 2007 and before Jan. 1, 2010 from $200,000 to $400,000. (Code Sec. 179(b)(2) as amended by Tax Increase Prevention Act §101)

observation: The $400,000 cap for tax years beginning in 2008 and 2009 is before adjustment for inflation. For 2006, after adjustment for inflation, the $400,000 is $430,000 (see FTC 2d/FIN ¶ L-9907.1; USTR ¶ 1794.01; TaxDesk ¶ 268,411). Thus, for 2007, 2008, and 2009, the $400,000 statutory amount after adjustment for inflation will be at least $430,000.

observation: Thus, under the Tax Increase Prevention Act, the $400,000 amount (before inflation adjustment) applies for property placed in service for tax years beginning before Jan. 1, 2010.

observation: Unless Code Sec. 179 is further extended, the starting point for reduction of the expensing ceiling for tax years beginning after Dec. 31, 2009 will revert back to $200,000.

illustration (3): In each of its tax years beginning in 2006 through 2010, Taxpayer Y places in service $215,000 of qualifying property. Assuming that the same inflation adjustments that applied for 2006 apply for 2007 through 2009 (no inflation adjustment applies in 2010, see below), Y can expense $108,000 each year for 2006 through 2009. Since the $215,000 cost of property placed in service for each of these years doesn't exceed the $430,000 threshold, no limitation applies. For 2010 (when the pre-Tax Increase Prevention Act rules are restored), Y's expense election is limited to $10,000 ($25,000 – [$215,000 – $200,000]).

illustration (4): Assume that Y in Illustration (3) placed $440,000 of qualifying property in service in its tax year beginning in 2008. Assuming that the same inflation adjustments that applied for 2006 apply for

2008, Y's expense election for that year would be limited to $98,000 ($108,000 – [$440,000 – $430,000]).

observation: Under Tax Increase Prevention Act law, assuming that the same inflation adjustments that applied for 2006 apply for 2008 and 2009, the expensing election is phased out completely (i.e., reduced to zero) for a tax year beginning in 2008 or 2009 when a taxpayer's investment in qualified property for that year reaches $538,000 ($108,000 – [$538,000 – $430,000]). Under pre-Tax Increase Prevention Act law, the expensing election would have phased out completely for 2008 (a year in which no inflation adjustment applied under pre-Tax Increase Prevention Act law) when a taxpayer's investment in qualified property for that year reached $225,000 ($25,000 – [$225,000 – $200,000]).

observation: Under Tax Increase Prevention Act law, the expensing election is phased out completely (i.e., reduced to zero) for a tax year beginning after 2009 (years in which no inflation adjustment applies, see below) when a taxpayer's investment in qualified property for that year reaches $225,000 ($25,000 – [$225,000 – $200,000]).

observation: In applying the Code Sec. 179(b)(2) phaseout to qualified property that is qualified zone property under Code Sec. 1397A(a)(2) (see FTC 2d/FIN ¶ L-9952; USTR ¶ 13,97A4; TaxDesk ¶ 268,413), qualified renewal property under Code Sec. 1400J(b) (see FTC 2d/FIN ¶ L-9988; USTR ¶ 14,00J4; TaxDesk ¶ 268,704), and New York Liberty Zone property under Code Sec. 1400L(f)(1)(b) (see FTC 2d/FIN ¶ L-9992; USTR ¶ 14,00L4.15; TaxDesk ¶ 268,502), only 50% of the cost of the property is taken into account for purposes of the limitation.

Extended inflation adjustment. The Tax Increase Prevention Act also extends the inflation adjustment for the $100,000 maximum expensing amount and the $400,000 phaseout threshold to any tax year beginning in a calendar year after Dec. 31, 2007 and before Jan. 1, 2010. Specifically, for any tax year beginning in a calendar year after 2005 and before Jan. 1, 2010, the $100,000 and $400,000 amounts are each increased by a cost of living adjustment determined under Code Sec. 1(f)(3), but substituting "calendar year 2002" (as the base year) for "calendar year 1992". (Code Sec. 179(b)(5)(A) as amended by Tax Increase Prevention Act §101)

observation: The inflation adjustments to the dollar amounts only apply to tax years that begin in calendar years 2004 through 2009.

observation: Any increase in the $100,000 amount by an inflation adjustment that doesn't result in a multiple of $1,000 is rounded to the nearest multiple of $1,000. Any increase in the $400,000 amount by an inflation adjustment that doesn't result in a multiple of $10,000 is rounded to the nearest multiple of $10,000, see FTC 2d/FIN ¶ L-9907.1; USTR ¶ 1794.01.

☐ **Effective:** Tax years beginning after 2007 and before 2010. (Com Rept, see ¶ 5001)

¶ 402. Right to revoke or change the Code Sec. 179 expense election without IRS consent is extended for two years to tax years beginning before Jan. 1, 2010

Code Sec. 179(c)(2), as amended by Tax Increase Prevention Act § 101
Generally effective: Tax years beginning after 2007 and before 2010
Committee Reports, see ¶ 5001

A taxpayer, other than an estate, trust, and certain noncorporate lessors, may elect under Code Sec. 179 to deduct as an expense, rather than to depreciate, up to a specified amount of the cost of new or used tangible personal property placed in service during the tax year in the taxpayer's trade or business (Code Sec. 179 property), see FTC 2d/FIN ¶ L-9901; USTR ¶ 1794; TaxDesk ¶ 268,411. Under pre-Tax Increase Prevention Act law, any Code Sec. 179 expense election, and any specification contained in the election, could be revoked by the taxpayer with respect to any property for any tax year beginning after Dec. 31, 2002 and before Jan. 1, 2008. Under Reg §1.179-5(c)(1), an expense election can be revoked without IRS's consent on an amended return for that tax year. Once made, the revocation is irrevocable. Under pre-Tax Increase Prevention Act law, for tax years beginning after Dec. 31, 2007, the Code Sec. 179 expense election, and any specification made in it, could be revoked only with IRS's consent. (FTC 2d/FIN ¶ L-9933; USTR ¶ 1794.04; TaxDesk ¶ 268,410)

observation: A specification contained in the Code Sec. 179 expense election is, for example, the selection of the particular property that is subject to the expensing election. Thus, a taxpayer that wished to substitute one type of equipment that he had originally selected for the expensing election for another type of equipment would be changing a specification contained in the Code Sec. 179 expense election. Under pre-Tax Increase Prevention Act law, for tax years beginning after Dec. 31, 2007, this specification could not have been changed unless IRS consented, even though the change didn't alter the amount of the election.

A taxpayer requesting IRS's consent must set forth in detail the reasons for the request, and the request would be granted only in extraordinary circumstances, see FTC 2d/FIN ¶ L-9933; USTR ¶ 1794.04; TaxDesk ¶ 268,410.

New Law. Congress believes that the Code Sec. 179 expensing rules will continue to provide important benefits if extended. (Com Rept, see ¶ 5001) Accordingly, the Tax Increase Prevention Act extends a taxpayer's ability to revoke a Code Sec. 179 expense election, and any specification contained in the election, for two additional years, to any tax year beginning before Jan. 1, 2010. Specifically, any Code Sec. 179 expense election, and any specification contained in the election, can be revoked by the taxpayer with respect to any property for any tax year beginning after Dec. 31, 2002 and before Jan. 1, 2010. (Code Sec. 179(c)(2) as amended by Tax Increase Prevention Act §101)

> ***observation:*** Thus, the Tax Increase Prevention Act continues the pre-Tax Increase Prevention Act rule in Reg §1.179-5(c)(1) with respect to revoking or changing an expensing election on amended returns without IRS's consent with respect to a tax year beginning before Jan. 1, 2010.

> ***observation:*** The rule in Code Sec. 179(c)(2) that provides that once made, the revocation is irrevocable, applies both under pre-Tax Increase Prevention Act law, and under the Tax Increase Prevention Act.

> ***observation:*** Unless Code Sec. 179(c)(2) is further amended, taxpayers will need IRS consent to revoke a Code Sec. 179 election made on a return for a tax year beginning after Dec. 31, 2009.

For an increase in the maximum amount of Code Sec. 179 property that can be expensed annually and increased phaseout thresholds, see ¶ 401.

For an extension of the inclusion of off-the-shelf computer software in the definition of Code Sec. 179 property, see ¶ 403.

☐ **Effective:** Tax years beginning after 2007 and before 2010. (Com Rept, see ¶ 5001)

FTC 2d References are to Federal Tax Coordinator 2d
FIN References are to RIA's Analysis of Federal Taxes: Income
USTR References are to United States Tax Reporter: Income, Estate & Gift, and Excise
PCA References are to Pension Analysis (print & electronic)
PE References are to the Pension Explanations (print & electronic)

¶ 403. Inclusion of off-the-shelf computer software as "section 179 property" eligible for the expensing election is extended for two years to tax years beginning before Jan. 1, 2010

Code Sec. 179(d)(1)(A)(ii), as amended by Tax Increase Prevention Act § 101
Generally effective: Tax years beginning after 2007 and before 2010
Committee Reports, see ¶ 5001

A taxpayer, other than an estate, trust, and certain noncorporate lessors, may elect to deduct as an expense (rather than depreciating) the cost of "section 179 property" placed in service during the tax year in the taxpayer's trade or business, see FTC 2d/FIN ¶ L-9901; USTR ¶ 1794; TaxDesk ¶ 268,411. "Section 179 property" is defined as section 1245 property which is acquired by purchase for use in the active conduct of a trade or business, and which is either: (1) tangible MACRS property, or (2) certain computer software. "Section 179 property" includes computer software (as defined in Code Sec. 197(e)(3)(B), i.e., any program designed to cause a computer to perform a desired function, see FTC 2d/FIN ¶ L-7958.5; USTR ¶ 1974; TaxDesk ¶ 269,014) which is described in Code Sec. 197(e)(3)(A)(i) (i.e., which is readily available for purchase by the general public, is subject to a nonexclusive license, and has not been substantially modified, see FTC 2d/FIN ¶ L-7958; USTR ¶ 1974; TaxDesk ¶ 269,014), to which the depreciation rules of Code Sec. 167 apply. Under pre-Tax Increase Prevention Act law, this computer software had to be placed in service in a tax year beginning after Dec. 31, 2002 and before Jan. 1, 2008. (FTC 2d/FIN ¶ L-9922; USTR ¶ 1794.02; TaxDesk ¶ 268,424)

> ***observation:*** Alternately, if an expensing election isn't elected for the computer software, or can't be elected (for example, for tax years beginning after Dec. 31, 2007 under pre-Tax Increase Prevention Act law), the taxpayer can depreciate the software by using the straight-line method and a useful life of 36 months, see FTC 2d/FIN ¶ L-7935; USTR ¶ 1674.033; TaxDesk ¶ 265,434.

The definition of "section 179 property" specifically excludes air conditioning or heating units, as well as property used for lodging, property used outside the U.S., and property used by governmental units, foreign persons or entities, and certain tax-exempt organizations, see FTC 2d/FIN ¶ L-9922; USTR ¶ 1794.02; TaxDesk ¶ 268,424.

New Law. Congress believes that the Code Sec. 179 expensing rules will continue to provide important benefits if extended. (Com Rept, see ¶ 5001) Accordingly, the Tax Increase Prevention Act extends the inclusion of off-the-shelf computer software in the definition of "section 179 property" for two additional years; i.e., for software that is placed in service in a tax year beginning before Jan. 1, 2010. Specifically, "section 179 property" includes computer software (as defined in Code Sec. 197(e)(3)(B)) which is described in Code Sec. 197(e)(3)(A)(i), to which the depreciation rules of Code Sec. 167 apply, and which is placed in service in a tax year beginning after Dec. 31, 2002 and before Jan. 1, 2010. (Code Sec. 179(d)(1)(A)(ii) as amended by Tax Increase Prevention Act §101)

> ***observation:*** Thus, under the Tax Increase Prevention Act, off-the-shelf computer software (as described in Code Sec. 179(d)(1)(A)(ii)) that is placed in service after Dec. 31, 2002 and before Jan. 1, 2010 is "section 179 property" eligible for the expensing election if it is section 1245 property that is acquired by purchase for use in the active conduct of a trade or business.

> ***observation:*** Unless Code Sec. 179(d)(1) is further extended, off-the-shelf computer software placed in service in tax years beginning after Dec. 31, 2009 will not be eligible for expensing as section 179 property. Since computer software is, in general, intangible property, without a specific exception as in Code Sec. 179(d)(1) (that includes this property in the definition of section 179 property), computer software fails the requirement that section 179 property must be tangible property.

For an increase in the maximum amount of Code Sec. 179 property that can be expensed annually and increased phaseout thresholds, see ¶ 401.

For an extension of the revocation of the Code Sec. 179 expense election without IRS consent, see ¶ 402.

☐ **Effective:** Tax years beginning after 2007 and before 2010. (Com Rept, see ¶ 5001)

¶ 404. Major integrated oil companies must use 5-year amortization for geological and geophysical expenditures

Code Sec. 167(h)(5), as amended by Tax Increase Prevention Act § 503(a)
Generally effective: Amounts paid or incurred after May 17, 2006
Committee Reports, see ¶ 5022

FTC 2d References are to Federal Tax Coordinator 2d
FIN References are to RIA's Analysis of Federal Taxes: Income
USTR References are to United States Tax Reporter: Income, Estate & Gift, and Excise
PCA References are to Pension Analysis (print & electronic)
PE References are to the Pension Explanations (print & electronic)

Under pre-Tax Increase Prevention Act law, any geological and geophysical ("G & G") expenses paid or incurred in connection with the exploration for, or development of, oil or gas "within the U.S." (as defined in Code Sec. 638, see FTC 2d/FIN ¶ O-10980; USTR ¶ 6384.01) are allowed as a deduction ratably over the 24-month period beginning on the date that the expenses were paid or incurred. (FTC 2d/FIN ¶ N-3201; USTR ¶ 1674.126; TaxDesk ¶ 271,701)

> ***observation:*** The 24-month amortization rule, under pre-Tax Increase Prevention Act law, rendered inapplicable to all taxpayers earlier court decisions such as *Schermerhorn Oil Corp.,* (1942) 46 BTA 151 and *Louisiana Land and Exploration Co.,* (1946) 7 TC 507 and IRS's position in Rev Rul 77-188, 1977-1 CB 76, as amplified by Rev Rul 83-105, 1983-2 CB 51 (see FTC 2d/FIN ¶ N-3201; USTR ¶ 6125.011(5)) that held that geological and geophysical costs incurred in connection with oil and gas properties are capital expenditures and, as such, are allocable to the cost of the acquired or retained property. (FTC 2d/FIN ¶ N-3201; USTR ¶ 6145.01(20)) The term "property," as defined in Code Sec. 614(a), means each separate interest in depletable property owned by the taxpayer in each mineral deposit in each separate tract or parcel of land, see FTC 2d/FIN ¶ N-2013; USTR ¶ 6144; TaxDesk ¶ 271,029.

For purposes of the 24-month amortization of geological and geophysical expenditures, any amount paid or incurred during the tax year is treated as paid or incurred at the mid-point of that tax year. Thus, the half-year convention applies to amortization over a 24-month period of geological or geophysical expenses paid or incurred. Except for the 24-month amortization provision, no depreciation or amortization deduction is allowed with respect to payments of geological and geophysical expenditures. (FTC 2d/FIN ¶ N-3201; USTR ¶ 1674.126; TaxDesk ¶ 271,701)

> ***observation:*** Thus, under pre-Tax Increase Prevention Act law, the 24-month amortization was the exclusive method of writing off geological or geophysical expenditures for all taxpayers.

If a taxpayer retires or abandons any property with respect to which geological or geophysical expenditures are paid or incurred during the 24-month amortization period, the taxpayer can't take a deduction at the time of the retirement or abandonment. Instead, the amortization over 24 months continues with respect to the payment. Thus, in the case of abandoned property, remaining basis cannot be recovered in the year of abandonment of the property, since all basis is recovered over the two-year amortization period discussed above. (FTC 2d/FIN ¶ N-3201; USTR ¶ 1674.126; TaxDesk ¶ 271,701)

> ***observation:*** The 24-month amortization rule under pre-Tax Increase Prevention Act law overturned the rule under Rev Rul 77-188, 1977-1

CB 76, in which IRS allowed a loss deduction for geological or geophysical costs under Code Sec. 165 where no area of interest is located and identified within the original project area and the project area is abandoned as a potential source of mineral production, see FTC 2d/FIN ¶ N-3201; USTR ¶ 1654.156; TaxDesk ¶ 376,001.

Also the uniform capitalization (UNICAP) rules (that generally deny a deduction for certain costs) don't apply to any costs allowable as a deduction under the 24-month amortization rules, see FTC 2d/FIN ¶ G-5518; USTR ¶ 263A4.05; TaxDesk ¶ 456,013.

New Law. The Tax Increase Prevention Act extends the amortization period for geological and geophysical costs to 5 years for certain major integrated oil companies. (Com Rept, see ¶ 5022) Specifically, the Tax Increase Prevention Act provides that, in the case of a "major integrated oil company" (defined below), Code Sec. 167(h)(1) (allowing any geological or geophysical expenses paid or incurred in connection with the exploration for or development of oil and gas to be deducted ratably over a 24-month period, (FTC 2d/FIN ¶ N-3201; USTR ¶ 1674.126; TaxDesk ¶ 271,701)) and Code Sec. 167(h)(4) (treatment of amortization expenses upon abandonment, (FTC 2d/FIN ¶ N-3201; USTR ¶ 1674.126; TaxDesk ¶ 271,701)) are applied by substituting "5-year" period for "24-month" period. (Code Sec. 167(h)(5)(A) as amended by Tax Increase Prevention Act §503(a))

observation: Thus, major integrated oil companies, which were permitted, under pre-Tax Increase Prevention Act law, to amortize geological and geophysical expenditures over the 24-month period beginning on the date that the expenses were paid or incurred, now must amortize any of those expenditures paid or incurred after May 17, 2006 over the 5-year period beginning on the date that the expenses are paid or incurred. Also, if a major integrated oil company retires or abandons any property with respect to which geological or geophysical expenditures are paid or incurred during that 5-year amortization period, it will not be able to take a deduction at the time of the retirement or abandonment. Instead, the amortization over 5 years will continue with respect to the payment. Thus, in the case of abandoned property, remaining basis won't be recovered in the year of abandonment of the property, since all basis will be recovered over the 5-year period.

observation: Expenses paid or incurred during the tax year are treated as made in the middle of the year for purposes of the 24-month amortization provision. Presumably, the same half-year convention also applies to 5-year amortization of geological or geophysical expenses paid or incurred by major integrated oil companies after May 17, 2006.

observation: In addition, except for the 5-year amortization that is allowed to major integrated oil companies for post-May 17, 2006 geological and geophysical expenditures, no depreciation or amortization deduction is allowed for those payments.

observation: Since Code Sec. 263A(c)(3) provides that the UNICAP rules don't apply to any cost allowable as a deduction under Code Sec. 167(h), the UNICAP rules do not apply to major integrated oil companies' post-May 17, 2006 geological and geophysical costs for which 5-year amortization is allowable.

For purposes of the 5-year amortization rule, a major integrated oil company is, with respect to any tax year, a producer of crude oil: (Code Sec. 167(h)(5)(B))

(1) that has an average daily worldwide production of crude oil of at least 500,000 barrels for the tax year, (Code Sec. 167(h)(5)(B)(i))

(2) that had gross receipts in excess of $1 billion for its last tax year ending during calendar year 2005, (Code Sec. 167(h)(5)(B)(ii)) and

(3) to which Code Sec. 613A(c) (exemption from limitation on percentage depletion for independent producers and royalty owners, also called the small producer exemption, see FTC 2d/FIN ¶ N-2401; USTR ¶ 613A4; TaxDesk ¶ 271,014) does not apply by reason of Code Sec. 613A(d)(4) (which excludes from the exemption under Code Sec. 613A(c) certain refiners that have average daily refinery runs of more than 75,000 barrels during the tax year, see FTC 2d/FIN ¶ N-2413; USTR ¶ 613A4; TaxDesk ¶ 271,015), determined (Code Sec. 167(h)(5)(B)(iii)) (A) by substituting 15 percent for 5 percent each place it occurs in Code Sec. 613A(d)(3), see FTC 2d/FIN ¶ N-2405; USTR ¶ 613A4 (which defines who is a related person for purposes of Code Sec. 613A(d), which in turn defines which producers are excluded from the small producer exemption described above) (Code Sec. 167(h)(5)(B)(iii)(I)), and (B) without regard to whether Code Sec. 613A(c) does not apply by reason of Code Sec. 613A(d)(2) (which excludes retailers from the small producer exemption described above, see FTC 2d/FIN ¶ N-2405; USTR ¶ 613A4; TaxDesk ¶ 271,015). (Code Sec. 167(h)(5)(B)(iii)(II))

Thus, the five-year amortization rule for geological and geophysical costs applies only to integrated oil companies that have an average daily worldwide production of crude oil of at least 500,000 barrels for the tax year, gross receipts in excess of $1 billion in the last tax year ending during calendar year 2005, and an ownership interest in a crude oil refiner of 15 percent or more. (Com Rept, see ¶ 5022)

For purposes of Code Sec. 167(h)(5)(B)(i) (average daily worldwide production of oil, see (1) above) and Code Sec. 167(h)(5)(B)(ii) (gross receipts in excess of $1 billion, see (2), above), all persons treated as a single employer under Code Sec. 52(a) and Code Sec. 52(b) are treated as one person and, in the case of a short tax year, the rule under Code Sec. 448(c)(3)(B) will apply. (Code Sec. 167(h)(5)(B))

> ***observation:*** Code Sec. 52(a) provides that, for purposes of the work opportunity credit, all employees of all corporations that are members of the same controlled group of corporations are treated as employed by a single employer. Code Sec. 52(b) provides a similar rule for employees of unincorporated businesses that are under common control. See FTC 2d/FIN ¶ L-17787; USTR ¶ 514; TaxDesk ¶ 380,719.

> ***observation:*** The rule under Code Sec. 448(c)(3)(B) requires corporations that are calculating their gross receipts to determine whether they qualify for cash basis accounting to determine the gross receipts for any tax year of less than 12 months by multiplying the gross receipts of the short period by 12 and dividing the result by the number of months in the short period, see FTC 2d/FIN ¶ G-2069; USTR ¶ 4484; TaxDesk ¶ 440,807.

☐ **Effective:** Amounts paid or incurred after May 17, 2006. (Tax Increase Prevention Act §503(b))

¶ 405. Five-year amortization election for expenses of creating or acquiring musical compositions or music copyrights for property placed in service in tax years beginning after Dec. 31, 2005, and before Jan. 1, 2011

Code Sec. 167(g)(8), as amended by Tax Increase Prevention Act § 207(a)
Generally effective: Expenses paid or incurred for property placed in service in tax years beginning after Dec. 31, 2005, and before Jan. 1, 2011
Committee Reports, see ¶ 5011

The income forecast method of depreciation can be used only for motion picture films, video tapes, sound recordings, copyrights, books, patents, and other property specified in regs. (See FTC 2d/FIN ¶ L-10704A; USTR ¶ 1674.100;

FTC 2d References are to Federal Tax Coordinator 2d
FIN References are to RIA's Analysis of Federal Taxes: Income
USTR References are to United States Tax Reporter: Income, Estate & Gift, and Excise
PCA References are to Pension Analysis (print & electronic)
PE References are to the Pension Explanations (print & electronic)

TaxDesk ¶ 268,004) Under proposed regs, the income forecast method would be made on a property-by-property basis. (See FTC 2d/FIN ¶ L-10704; USTR ¶ 1674.100; TaxDesk ¶ 268,004)

Under the income forecast method, each year's depreciation deduction equals the cost of the property, multiplied by a fraction whose numerator is the current year's net income from the property, and whose denominator is the total income the taxpayer expects to derive from the property. (FTC 2d/FIN ¶ L-10704; USTR ¶ 1674.100; TaxDesk ¶ 268,004)

Only income earned before the close of the tenth tax year after the tax year in which the property was placed in service is taken into account under the income forecast method. (FTC 2d/FIN ¶ L-10705.1; USTR ¶ 1674.100; TaxDesk ¶ 268,007) The taxpayer's entire remaining basis in the property is deducted in the tenth tax year. (FTC 2d/FIN ¶ L-10707.15; USTR ¶ 1674.100; TaxDesk ¶ 268,012)

IRS had provided special rules for certain authors and other taxpayers, with respect to their capitalization of costs under Code Sec. 263A and with respect to the recovery or amortization of the costs. Specifically, Notice 88-62, 1988-1 CB 548 provides an elective safe harbor under which eligible taxpayers can capitalize qualified created costs incurred during the tax year and amortize 50% of the costs in the tax year incurred, and 25% in each of the two successive tax years. Under the safe harbor, qualified creative costs generally are those incurred by a self-employed individual in the production of creative properties (such as films, sound recordings, musical and dance compositions including accompanying words, and other similar properties), provided the personal efforts of the individual predominantly create the properties. An eligible taxpayer is an individual, and also a corporation or partnership, substantially all of which is owned by one qualified employee owner (an individual and family members). (Com Rept, see ¶ 5011)

New Law. The Tax Increase Prevention Act provides an elective five-year amortization period for musical works and copyrights. (Com Rept, see ¶ 5011) If an election is in effect for any tax year, then, notwithstanding the income forecast rules, any expense that: (Code Sec. 167(g)(8)(A) as amended by Tax Increase Prevention Act §207(a)) is paid or incurred by the taxpayer in creating or acquiring any applicable musical property (defined below) placed in service during the tax year, and (Code Sec. 167(g)(8)(A)(i)) is otherwise properly chargeable to capital account (Code Sec. 167(g)(8)(A)(ii)), is amortized ratably over the five-year period beginning with the month in which the property is placed in service. This five-year amortization rule does not apply to any expense which, without regard to the election, would not be allowable as a deduction. (Code Sec. 167(g)(8)(A))

observation: The five-year amortization election applies to expenses paid or incurred by songwriters and composers who *create* any applicable musical property, as well as to expenses paid or incurred by music publishers, performers, producers, and recording companies who *acquire* any applicable musical property. The election could also permit employers whose employees create applicable musical property to amortize the expenses paid or incurred in the creation of that property.

Presumably, five-year amortization will be more advantageous to taxpayers *acquiring* applicable musical property because the amount paid to *acquire* (and thus, the basis for computing any five-year amortization) generally would be a larger amount than the expenses paid or incurred by a songwriter or composer in creating applicable musical property. Also, taxpayers who *create* applicable musical property may qualify for more favorable treatment under Code Sec. 263A(h) (allowing a current deduction of the costs, see below) or Notice 88-62, 1988-1 CB 548 (allowing three-year amortization of qualified creative costs, see above).

illustration (1): On Jan. 2, Year 1, P, a music publisher, acquires applicable musical property for $1,000,000 and places that property in service on Jan. 31, Year 1. If P makes the five-year amortization election for the expenses paid or incurred for the applicable musical property, P's amortization deduction for the property in Year 1 is $200,000.

observation: In some cases, a taxpayer's deduction under the income forecast method might be larger in the tax years immediately after the property is placed in service than the deduction under the five-year amortization election. For example, if the taxpayer expects to derive substantially all of the income from the property in the tax year in which the property is placed in service or the following tax year, then the taxpayer's deduction under the income forecast method might be larger than the taxpayer's deduction under a five-year amortization election.

illustration (2): The facts are the same as in illustration (1) except that P decides to use the income forecast method to determine his depreciation deduction for the expenses paid or incurred for the applicable musical composition instead of electing five-year amortization for those expenses. P anticipates that the total income from the applicable musical property will be $5,000,000. The net income from the property in Year 1 is $4,000,000. P's Year 1 deduction is computed as follows:

$$\$1{,}000{,}000 \text{ (cost of the property)} \times \frac{\begin{array}{c}\$4{,}000{,}000\\ \text{(net income for current year)}\end{array}}{\begin{array}{c}\$5{,}000{,}000\\ \text{(total expected income)}\end{array}} = \$800{,}000$$

In this case, P's deduction under the income forecast method ($800,000) is greater than the deduction under the five-year amortization election ($200,000, see illustration (1) above).

observation: In determining whether to elect five-year amortization or the income forecast method in illustration (2), one of the factors that P should consider is the effect of the election on all of his applicable musical properties placed in service in that tax year, because the five-year amortization election, unlike the income forecast method (see FTC 2d/FIN ¶ L-10704; USTR ¶ 1674.100; TaxDesk ¶ 268,004), can't be made on a property-by-property basis (see below).

observation: The Senate Finance Committee's Summary of the Tax Increase Prevention Act indicates that the election allows music publishers to amortize over a period of five years the advances made to songwriters.

observation: Since the amortization period begins in the month that an applicable musical property is placed in service, the five-year amortization period may occur over six tax years.

Except for the amortization discussed above, no depreciation or amortization deduction is allowed for any expense to which the five-year amortization election applies. (Code Sec. 167(g)(8)(B))

An eligible taxpayer that does *not* make the five-year amortization election may recover the costs under any allowable method, including the income forecast method. (Com Rept, see ¶ 5011)

Applicable musical property defined. An "applicable musical property" is any musical composition (including any accompanying words), or any copyright with respect to a musical composition, that is property that is depreciable under the income forecast method. (Code Sec. 167(g)(8)(C)(i))

observation: The phrase "musical composition (including any accompanying words)" is also used in Code Sec. 263A(h)(3)(A), defining the term "writer" for purposes of the exception to the uniform capitalization (UNICAP) rules for qualified creative expenses, see FTC 2d/FIN ¶ G-5804; USTR ¶ 263A4.13; TaxDesk ¶ 456,014. In IRS Letter Ruling 9643003, IRS privately ruled that a sound recording of a musical composition wasn't considered to be a musical composition for purposes of Code Sec. 263A(h)(3)(A), see FTC 2d/FIN ¶ G-5804; USTR

> ¶ 263A5.01(80). Presumably, IRS would take a similar position for purposes of the five-year amortization election.

However, applicable musical property *doesn't* include any property: (Code Sec. 167(g)(8)(C)(ii))

. . . for which expenses are treated as qualified creative expenses to which Code Sec. 263A(h) (concerning whether the UNICAP rules apply to the expenses of freelance authors, photographers, and artists) applies. (Code Sec. 167(g)(8)(C)(ii)(I))

> ***observation:*** A "qualified creative expense" is any deductible expense paid or incurred in an individual's trade or business (other than as an employee) of being a writer, photographer, or artist, see FTC 2d/FIN ¶ G-5801; USTR ¶ 263A4.13; TaxDesk ¶ 456,014.

. . . to which a simplified procedure established under Code Sec. 263A(j)(2) applies. (Code Sec. 167(g)(8)(C)(ii)(II)).

> ***observation:*** The reference to Code Sec. 263A(j)(2) in Code Sec. 167(g)(8)(C)(ii)(II) is incorrect because Code Sec. 263A(j)(2) does not exist. Presumably, Congress meant to refer to Code Sec. 263A(i)(2) which authorizes IRS to issue regs providing for simplified procedures for the application of the UNICAP for property acquired for resale (i.e., property described in Code Sec. 263A(b)(2), see FTC 2d/FIN ¶s G-5464, G-5479; USTR ¶s 263A4, 263A4.13). In that case, Congress may have intended to refer to the elective safe harbor provided in Notice 88-62, 1988-1 CB 548, for qualified creative costs, see above.

. . . that is an amortizable section 197 intangible (as defined in Code Sec. 197(c), see FTC 2d/FIN ¶ L-7951.1; USTR ¶ 1974; TaxDesk ¶ 269,002). (Code Sec. 167(g)(8)(C)(ii)(III))

> ***observation:*** Copyrights are section 197 intangibles only if acquired in a transaction involving the acquisition of a trade or business or a substantial portion of a trade or business, see FTC 2d/FIN ¶ L-7951; USTR ¶ 1974; TaxDesk ¶ 269,005. The deduction for any amortizable section 197 intangible is determined by amortizing the intangible's basis ratably over the 15-year period beginning with the month in which it was acquired. See FTC 2d/FIN ¶ L-7960; USTR ¶ 1974; TaxDesk ¶ 269,002.

How the five-year amortization election is made. A five-year amortization election has to be made at the time and in the form as IRS may prescribe and applies to all applicable musical property placed in service during the tax year for which the election applies. (Code Sec. 167(g)(8)(D))

> ***observation:*** Since Code Sec. 167(g)(8)(D) provides that the election applies to *all* applicable musical property placed in service during the tax year, a taxpayer can't make the five-year amortization election on a property-by-property basis.

Termination of election after 2010. A five-year amortization election cannot be made for any tax year beginning after Dec. 31, 2010. (Code Sec. 167(g)(8)(E))

☐ **Effective:** Expenses paid or incurred for property placed in service in tax years beginning after Dec. 31, 2005 (Tax Increase Prevention Act §207(b)) and before Jan. 1, 2011. (Com Rept, see ¶ 5011)

¶ 500. Corporate Provisions

¶ 501. Code Section 355 definition of active conduct of a trade or business made less restrictive for certain controlled groups—pre-Jan. 1, 2011 distributions

Code Sec. 355(b)(3), as amended by Tax Increase Prevention Act § 202
Generally effective: Distributions made after May 17, 2006 and before Jan. 1, 2011
Committee Reports, see ¶ 5006

One of the requirements for a Code Sec. 355 tax-free corporate division (e.g., a spin-off) is that the distributing corporation (D) and any controlled corporation that it distributes (C) must be engaged in the active conduct of a trade or business. This requires either that:

(1) immediately after the distribution D and C are engaged in the active conduct of a trade or business, or

(2) immediately before the distribution, D had no assets other than stock or securities of controlled corporations and, immediately after the distribution, each of the controlled corporations is engaged in the active conduct of a trade or business (referred to below as the Code Sec. 355(b)(1) list).

Under pre-Tax Increase Prevention Act law, a corporation satisfied the above active conduct of a trade or business test, if:

(a) it was directly engaged in the active conduct of a trade or business, or

(b) substantially all of its assets consisted of stock and securities of a corporation (or corporations) it controlled immediately after the distribution and the controlled corporation(s) were engaged in the active conduct of a trade or business (referred to below as the Code Sec. 355(b)(2) list).

> ***illustration (1):*** D was a holding company whose sole asset was 100% of the stock of C1 and C2. C1's and C2's sole assets consisted of stock of controlled subsidiaries, which were engaged in the active conduct of a trade or business. C1 and C2 were engaged in the active conduct of a trade or business under item (b) of the Code Sec. 355(b)(2) list above. As a result, D satisfied item (2) of the Code Sec. 355(b)(1) list above.

FTC 2d References are to Federal Tax Coordinator 2d
FIN References are to RIA's Analysis of Federal Taxes: Income
USTR References are to United States Tax Reporter: Income, Estate & Gift, and Excise
PCA References are to Pension Analysis (print & electronic)
PE References are to the Pension Explanations (print & electronic)

Under the guidelines IRS used when it regularly issued rulings on whether the active trade or business test was satisfied, the fair market value of the gross assets of a trade or business being relied on had to equal at least 5% of the total fair market value of the corporation's gross assets. Also, under item (b) in the Code Sec. 355(b)(2) list above, at least 90% of the corporation's gross assets had to consist of stock and securities of controlled corporations engaged in the active conduct of a trade or business.

The Code also requires that the trade or business must have been actively conducted for five years and must not have been acquired within that period in a transaction in which gain or loss was recognized.

Under pre-Tax Increase Prevention Act law, a corporate group often had to undergo elaborate restructuring to satisfy the active trade or business requirement. This was particularly likely if D was a holding company that did not directly engage in a trade or business, since the test was then more stringent than if D itself engaged in an active business (see illustrations (2) and (3) below). (FTC 2d/FIN ¶ F-4801, ¶ F-4802, ¶ F-4803, ¶ F-4804; USTR ¶ 3554.02; TaxDesk ¶ 237,401, ¶ 237,426, ¶ 237,427)

New Law. Under the Tax Increase Prevention Act, for distributions made before Jan. 1, 2011, a corporation is treated as satisfying the active conduct of a trade or business test (the Code Sec. 355(b)(2) list above) if, and only if, it is engaged in the active conduct of a trade or business. (Code Sec. 355(b)(3)(A) as amended by Tax Increase Prevention Act §202) For these purposes, all members of the corporation's "separate affiliated group" are treated as one corporation. (Code Sec. 355(b)(3)(B))

> ***viewpoint:*** Robert Willens, Managing Director, Lehman Brothers, Inc, NY, observes that under the Tax Increase Prevention Act, the active business test is applied by reference to a relevant affiliated group ("separate affiliated group"). Thus, if at least one member of the separate affiliated group is engaged in the active conduct of a trade or business, each member of the group headed by the distributing corporation (D) or the controlled corporation (C) will be treated as so engaged. This is so because all of the members of the "separate affiliated group," the group determined under Code Sec. 1504(a) if D or C was the common parent, are treated as one corporation. Thus, there will no longer be a need to "relocate" active businesses.

> ***viewpoint:*** Robert P. Rothman, Of Counsel to DLA Piper Rudnick Gray Cary US LLP in New York, comments as follows: The new law represents a sensible change, which has been proposed several times in the past, but has never before made it into a final bill. One of the requirements for a tax-free spin-off is that, in general, each of the distributing corporation and the spun-off corporation must be engaged, immediately after the spin-off, in an active trade or business with a five-year

operating history. Under pre-Tax Increase Prevention Act law, for purposes of this rule, a corporation was considered to be engaged in a business if either (i) it was directly engaged in the business, or (ii) substantially all of its assets consisted of stock or securities of controlled (generally, 80%-owned) subsidiaries, which were so engaged (see Code Sec. 355(b)(2) list above). This odd formulation could result in having to engage in restructurings in order to allow a spin-off to take place.

Example: Assume that Corporation A's assets consist of (1) an operating business that doesn't have the required five-year history (with a value of $1,000), (2) all of the stock of corporation B (with a value of $1,000), and (3) all of the stock of corporation C, with a value of $1,000. Corporation B is directly engaged in an active trade or business with a five-year history. Corporation C (which does not carry on a trade or business) owns all of the stock of Corporations D and E. Corporation D has a five-year active business with a value of $600, and Corporation E has an active business without the required five-year history with a value of $400. Assume that A wishes to spin off the stock of C. In order to do so, both A and C must satisfy the active business test. Under pre-Tax Increase Prevention Act law, neither of these corporations meets the test. Corporation A was not directly engaged in a five-year active business. Although it was indirectly so engaged (through B), it couldn't count B's business because, with such a large percentage of A's assets being held directly, it couldn't be said that substantially all of its assets consisted of stock or securities of controlled corporations. Similarly, Corporation C didn't satisfy the then active business test. It was not directly engaged in an active business, and couldn't count the businesses conducted by D and E because, even though substantially all of its assets consisted of stock of controlled subsidiaries, one of those subsidiaries (E) did not itself meet the five-year active business test.

It was frequently possible to engage in pre-spinoff restructurings to avoid these results, For instance, in the Example (above) Corporation A could be made to satisfy the test either by contributing the directly-operated business to B, or by liquidating B into A (in a Code Sec. 332 liquidation). Similarly, C could be made to satisfy the test either by merging D and E, or by contributing the stock of E to D (but not vice versa), or by liquidating D into C under Code Sec. 332. In the case of more complicated corporate structures, however, the necessity of identifying precisely which assets were where and for how long, and the need to move assets around in the face of possible contractual restrictions, could place unnecessary barriers in the way of a spin-off. The new law (at least until its scheduled sunset) avoids this problem. On the facts of the example, A and B would be tested as though they were a single corporation; as such, the test would be satisfied by virtue of B's business. Similarly, C, D and E would be tested as a single corporation, which would satisfy the test as a result of D's business.

illustration (2): D owns 100% of the stock of C1, C2, and C3, each of which is engaged in the active conduct of a trade or business. D performs headquarters functions for its subsidiaries and is not directly engaged in the active conduct of a trade or business. D's investment assets and its headquarters building represent 25% of its assets. D would like to distribute all its C1 stock. Under pre-Tax Increase Prevention Act law, D would have to assume that it doesn't satisfy the active trade or business requirement (without restructuring) because it wasn't directly engaged in the active conduct of a trade or business and C2 and C3 didn't represent substantially all of its assets. Under the Tax Increase Prevention Act, D is engaged in the active conduct of a trade or business, because this requirement is tested for D by treating D, C2 and C3 as one corporation.

illustration (3): Same facts as illustration 2, except that D has minimal assets apart from its subsidiaries' stock and D also owns all of C4's stock. C4 conducts the investment activities of the D group and is not engaged in a trade or business. Until recently, C4's stock represented less than 5% of D's assets but then one of C4's investments appreciated dramatically and C4's value now exceeds 25% of D's assets. D would have to assume that it doesn't satisfy the active business test under pre-Tax Increase Prevention Act law. However, under the Tax Increase Prevention Act, D satisfies the test.

A corporation's separate affiliated group is the affiliated group that would be described in Code Sec. 1504(a) if the corporation were the common parent and the Code Sec. 1504(b) exclusions did not apply (see FTC 2d/FIN ¶ E-7601; FTC 2d/FIN ¶ E-7606; FTC 2d/FIN ¶ E-7618; USTR ¶ 15,024.17; TaxDesk ¶ 603,300; TaxDesk ¶ 603,301; TaxDesk ¶ 603,303). (Code Sec. 355(b)(3)(B))

observation: Thus, Code Sec. 1504(a), which includes an 80% vote and value requirement and disregards "classic" preferred stock (i.e., preferred stock that is nonvoting, not convertible into another class of stock, limited and preferred as to dividends, does not participate in corporate growth to any significant extent, and has redemption and liquidation rights which don't exceed the issue price of the stock (excepting reasonable premiums)) applies, but Code Sec. 1504(b), which excludes eight types of corporations (such as insurance companies and foreign corporations), doesn't apply.

Congress wanted to make it easier for corporate groups that use a holding company structure to engage in tax-free corporate divisions. The Tax Increase Prevention Act accomplishes this by applying the active trade or business test to a relevant affiliated group. For D, the relevant affiliated group consists of D and corporations affiliated with D (when D is treated as the common parent). The relevant affiliated group for C is determined similarly by treating C as the common parent. (Com Rept, see ¶ 5006)

> ***observation:*** Since the new rule only applies to pre-Jan. 1, 2011, distributions, it is drafted as a separate paragraph (Code Sec. 355(b)(3)), which overrides, but doesn't replace, Code Sec. 355(b)(2) (i.e., the Code Sec. 355(b)(2) list above). Thus, when Code Sec. 355(b)(3) expires, it can be ignored (and eventually removed as deadwood) without a substantive Code amendment. However, this approach results in additional complexity and possible confusion because Code Sec. 355(b)(1) (i.e., the Code Sec. 355(b)(1) list above) and Code Sec. 355(b)(2) remain in effect.

☐ **Effective:** Distributions made after May 17, 2006 and before Jan. 1, 2011. (Code Sec. 355(b)(3)(A))

Under a transition rule, Code Sec. 355(b)(3)(A) doesn't apply to any distribution in a transaction which is:

. . . made under an agreement which was binding on May 17, 2006 and at all times thereafter, (Code Sec. 355(b)(3)(C)(i))

. . . described in a ruling request submitted to IRS on or before May 17, 2006 (Code Sec. 355(b)(3)(C)(ii)), or

. . . described on or before May 17, 2006 in a public announcement or in a filing with the Securities and Exchange Commission. (Code Sec. 355(b)(3)(C)(iii))

The Code Sec. 355(b)(3)(C) transition rule (immediately above) does not apply if the distributing corporation elects not to have it apply to its distributions. Once made, the election is irrevocable. (Code Sec. 355(b)(3)(C))

For purposes of determining the continued qualification under the Code Sec. 355(b)(2) list above of distributions made before May 17, 2006, as a result of an acquisition, disposition, or other restructuring after May 17, 2006 and before Jan. 1, 2011, the distribution is treated as made on the date of the acqui-

---

FTC 2d References are to Federal Tax Coordinator 2d
FIN References are to RIA's Analysis of Federal Taxes: Income
USTR References are to United States Tax Reporter: Income, Estate & Gift, and Excise
PCA References are to Pension Analysis (print & electronic)
PE References are to the Pension Explanations (print & electronic)

sition, disposition or restructuring for purposes of applying the above provisions. (Code Sec. 355(b)(3)(D))

Thus, if D was a holding company that distributed C in a spin-off before May 17, 2006, in which D satisfied the substantially all test of pre-Tax Increase Prevention Act law, D would not be treated as violating any requirement that it continue that same qualified structure after the distribution solely because of a restructuring that occurs after May 17, 2006, that results in a structure that would satisfy the requirements of the Tax Increase Prevention Act active trade or business test. (Com Rept, see ¶ 5006)

> ***illustration (4):*** Same facts as illustration (3). (D owns 100% of the stock of C1, C2, and C3, which are engaged in the active conduct of a trade or business, and 100% of the stock of C4, which holds the group's investments. C4's investments represent more than 25% of D's assets). In 2004, D decides to spin off C1 and merges C4 into C3 so that 90% of D's assets will consist of stock of controlled corporations engaged in the active conduct of a trade or business. After May 17, 2006, C4 is again organized as a separate corporation to protect the investment portfolio from C3 liabilities and to provide a state tax advantage. If the C1 spin-off were governed by the Tax Increase Prevention Act, D would have satisfied the active trade or business test with C4 as a separate corporation. Code Sec. 355(b)(3)(D) bars IRS from asserting that the merger of C4 into C3 was a transitory step that should be ignored and, therefore, D didn't satisfy the active trade or business test under pre-Tax Increase Prevention Act law when it distributed C1.

¶ 502. Distribution can't qualify as a Code Sec. 355 corporate division if the distributing corporation or the controlled corporation is a disqualified investment corporation

Code Sec. 355(g), as amended by Tax Increase Prevention Act § 507(a)
Generally effective: Distributions after May 17, 2006
Committee Reports, see ¶ 5025

Under pre-Tax Increase Prevention Act law, where a corporation (D) distributed the stock of its controlled subsidiary (C) in a transaction intended to qualify as a tax-free corporate division, there were no specific limitations on the investment assets that could be held by D or C. If both D and C were engaged in the active conduct of a trade or business, substantially all their assets could represent passive investments. In fact, under IRS guidelines, the fair market value of the gross assets of a trade or business being relied on could equal as little as 5% of the total fair market value of the corporation's gross assets, see ¶ 501. Although the presence of substantial non-business assets was a factor indicating that the distribution was used principally as a proscribed device to distribute earnings and profits, this could be overcome by a sufficiently strong business purpose; and in a split-off in which a shareholder exchanged its entire interest in D for C stock, by the fact that, if tested as a redemption, the distribution would have qualified for exchange treatment, and thus ordinarily wouldn't be considered a device. (FTC 2d/FIN ¶ F-4715; FTC 2d/FIN ¶ F-4719; USTR ¶ 3554.01; TaxDesk ¶ 237,212; TaxDesk ¶ 237,216) In determining if a corporate division was tax free under pre-Tax Increase Prevention Act law, there were no rules regarding disqualified investment corporations. (FTC 2d/FIN ¶ F-4602; USTR ¶ 3554.01; TaxDesk ¶ 237,002)

New Law. Under the Tax Increase Prevention Act, a distribution which is part of a transaction doesn't qualify as a tax-free Code Sec. 355 corporate division (or a corporate division with boot) if immediately after the transaction:

(1) either the distributing corporation (D) or the controlled corporation (C) is a "disqualified investment corporation" (Code Sec. 355(g)(1)(A) as amended by Tax Increase Prevention Act §507(a)), and

(2) any person holds, a 50% or greater interest (see below) in any disqualified investment corporation, but only if

(3) the person did not hold that interest immediately before the transaction. (Code Sec. 355(g)(1)(B))

> ***observation:*** If the transaction doesn't qualify as a tax-free corporate division, D recognizes gain on its distribution of C, and the D shareholders to whom C is distributed are taxable under Code Sec. 301, as if they had received a regular corporate distribution if the distribution is pro rata; and as if they had sold their stock if their interest in D is significantly reduced.

> ***viewpoint:*** Robert Willens, Managing Director, Lehman Brothers, Inc, NY, notes that this eliminates a device popularly referred to as a "cash-rich split off." This was used where a corporation (D) and a substantial but much less than controlling D shareholder (X) agreed to part ways without X having to recognize gain. D would create a subsidiary, C, to which it would transfer cash as well as the assets of a small active trade or business that it had conducted for at least five years and X would exchange its D stock for all the C stock. Because X's interest in D terminated, the transaction would not be treated as a device and the requirements for a tax-free corporate division would be satisfied, and X would walk away with cash-rich C.

FTC 2d References are to Federal Tax Coordinator 2d
FIN References are to RIA's Analysis of Federal Taxes: Income
USTR References are to United States Tax Reporter: Income, Estate & Gift, and Excise
PCA References are to Pension Analysis (print & electronic)
PE References are to the Pension Explanations (print & electronic)

viewpoint: Robert P. Rothman, Of Counsel to DLA Piper Rudnick Gray Cary US LLP in New York, comments as follows: The active trade or business requirement for tax-free spin-offs requires that both the distributing corporation and the spun-off corporation be engaged in an active trade or business with a five-year history, but does not require that such active trade or business constitute any minimum percentage of the value of each such corporation. Before August, 2003, IRS would not issue a private letter ruling unless the active business assets constituted at least 5% of the gross asset value of the corporation being tested. However, this was not a statutorily imposed standard, and was apparently designed to weed out situations where the active business being relied on was so small as to be almost de minimis.

Regs issued under the device restriction, which operates independently of the active business requirement, provide that, among the factors considered in determining the existence of a device is the ratio of the non-active business assets of each corporation to the active business assets. The smaller the proportion of each corporation's assets that meet the five-year active business test to its total assets, the more likely a device will be found to exist. However, the device restriction, which focuses on shareholder-level tax avoidance, is something of an historical artifact. This is particularly true now that most dividends received from domestic corporations by non-corporate shareholders are entitled to the same favorable tax rate as long-term capital gains. Although the device test remains important, its effectiveness in precluding spin-offs that IRS might view as abusive is less than in the past.

The new law adds an additional tool to IRS's arsenal where either a spun-off company or a distributing company has a large proportion of passive assets. However, several features of this are worthy of note. First, in addition to the test, which looks to the percentage of investment assets, the new restriction only comes into play where any person holds a 50% or greater interest in a disqualified investment corporation after the spin-off and did not hold such an interest (taking into account attribution) before the spin-off. Thus, the restriction will generally not apply to pro rata spin-offs (in which each shareholder receives shares of the spun-off corporation in proportion to his share holdings in the distributing corporation, and also retains his historic holdings in the distributing corporation). Rather, it will only apply where one shareholder receives more (or less) than his pro rata share of the spun-off corporation in exchange for a reduced (or increased) interest in the distributing corporation, so that, with respect to either corporation, he goes from less than 50% ownership to 50% or greater ownership. Second, the class of "bad" assets for purposes of the new restriction is limited to the investment-type assets enumerated in the Code. Thus, there can be assets which themselves do not count as "good" for purposes of the five-year active business test, but are nonetheless not "bad" for purposes of the new disqualified investment corporation rules. For example, an active business that does not have a five-year operating history will not be counted against the taxpayer in applying the new restriction; similarly, assets used in a business that is not sufficiently "active" to satisfy Code Sec. 355(b) are nonetheless likely to avoid being counted as "bad" under the new rules.

Finally, it should be kept in mind that the restrictions imposed by prior law continue to apply in addition to the new restriction. Thus, the requirement that each corporation have at least one business that is sufficiently active and which has a five-year history continues to apply. In addition, the device restriction remains in effect. In this connection, it is worth noting that, in general, a distribution which is sufficiently non-pro rata so as to be potentially subject to the new rules is unlikely to be treated as a device; however, in appropriate cases it is possible that the device restriction may nonetheless apply.

Example: Corporation A has a five-year active business constituting 10% of its value and a non-five year active business constituting 90% of its value. It is not a "disqualified investment corporation" under new Code Sec. 355(g)(2). However, the fact that only 10% of its assets meet the five-year active business requirement is a factor (to be weighed along with other factors) in favor of a conclusion that the transaction constitutes a device.

For purposes of the disqualified investment corporation rules, a transaction includes a series of transactions. (Code Sec. 355(g)(4)) The Committee Report describes this as a series of "related" transactions. (Com Rept, see ¶ 5025)

A "50%-or-greater interest" has the same meaning as under the Code Sec. 355(d)(4) disqualified distribution rules (see FTC 2d/FIN ¶ F-5523; USTR ¶ 3554.04; TaxDesk ¶ 238,423). (Code Sec. 355(g)(3)(A))

observation: Thus, a "50%-or-greater interest" is ownership of either 50% of the total combined voting power of all classes of a corporation's stock or 50% of the total value of its shares.

Items (2) and (3) above will apply (to disqualify a distribution from Code Sec. 355 tax free treatment) if a person directly or indirectly holds 50% or more of either the vote or value of D (the distributing corporation) or C (the controlled corporation) immediately following a distribution, and the person did not

FTC 2d References are to Federal Tax Coordinator 2d
FIN References are to RIA's Analysis of Federal Taxes: Income
USTR References are to United States Tax Reporter: Income, Estate & Gift, and Excise
PCA References are to Pension Analysis (print & electronic)
PE References are to the Pension Explanations (print & electronic)

hold that 50% or greater interest directly or indirectly before the distribution. Thus, items (2) and (3) apply, e.g., if a person held D stock with 50% or more of the vote, but less than 50% of the value immediately before C is distributed and, after the distribution of 100% of C, holds 50% or more of the value of either D or C. (Com Rept, see ¶ 5025)

In determining ownership under the Code Sec. 355(g) disqualified stock rules, Code Sec. 318 attribution rules apply (see FTC 2d/FIN ¶ F-11800; USTR ¶ 3184.02; TaxDesk ¶ 243,600). (Code Sec. 355(g)(3)(B))

observation: Thus the attribution rules apply in determining if there is a 50%-or-greater interest and in applying the exceptions for controlled entities and interests in certain partnerships (below).

illustration (1): L owns 80% of D's stock and D owns 100% of C's stock. There have been no relevant changes in ownership. Both D and C are engaged in the active conduct of a trade or business. D distributes C pro rata to its shareholders and L receives 80% of C's stock. Assume that without regard to the disqualified investment corporation rules this spin-off qualifies as a tax-free corporate division. Immediately after the distribution, 80% of D's assets consist of stock and securities held for investment and D is a disqualified investment corporation. Items (1) and (2) on the above list are satisfied, but item (3) is not satisfied, because immediately after the distribution, L holds the same interest in D that he held before the transaction. Thus, the distribution remains tax free. If C (instead of D) were a disqualified investment corporation, literally read, item (3) is satisfied, since D and not L owned C's stock before the transaction. However, under Code Sec. 318(a)(2)(C), L is treated as owning 80% of C before the transaction, since stock is attributed from a corporation to a 50%-or-greater shareholder. Thus, the distribution remains tax-free.

observation: If the only relevant transaction is one corporate division, it appears that generally only a disproportionate distribution, i.e., a split-off, can trigger gain recognition under the disqualified investment corporation rule, see illustration (2) below. IRS has specific regulatory authority to modify the attribution rules to carry out the purposes of the disqualified investment corporation rules or to prevent their avoidance (see "Regulations" below), but in a straight-forward single-distribution situation with no other possibly related persons or related transactions, regs shouldn't affect this conclusion. If a distribution is combined with a later distribution or with another transaction (e.g., a redemption (see below)) a pro rata distribution can be taxable (see illustrations (3) and (4) below).

illustration (2): K owns (actually and by attribution) 40% of D's only class of stock and D owns 100% of C's stock. There have been no relevant changes in ownership. Both D and C are engaged in the active conduct of a trade or business. D distributes 100% of C's stock to K in exchange for all of her D stock. Assume that immediately after the distribution, C is a disqualified investment corporation so item (1) is satisfied. Items (2) and (3) are also satisfied since K owned less than 50% of C's stock before the distribution (applying the attribution rules) and after the distribution K owns at least 50% of C's stock, i.e., 100%. Thus, the distribution isn't tax free.

observation: Since a transaction is defined to include a series of transactions (see above), the disqualified investment company rule can result in taxing a distribution where the above requirements are not literally met immediately after a distribution, but are met after a second distribution and both distributions are considered to be parts of one "transaction."

illustration (3): In Year 1, D distributes C1 to Y in exchange for his 20% stock interest for a good business reason. This increases shareholder K's interest in D to 55%. C1 and D are not disqualified investment corporations and no income or gain is recognized by D or Y. Seven months later, D distributes appreciated C to K in exchange for her appreciated D stock. C is then a disqualified investment corporation, but K's interest has not increased so as to satisfy item (3) above, since she owns 55% of D immediately before the distribution of C. However, if the distribution of C and the distribution of C1 are treated as one transaction, item (3) is satisfied as to K and the distribution of C is not a a tax-free corporate division. Thus, D and K recognize gain.

illustration (4): In Year 1, D has substantial current earnings and profits. D distributes C which has a $30 million value and in which D has a $1 million basis pro rata to its shareholders, K, with a 40% interest and the Estate of Z with a 60% interest. Immediately after the distribution, D is a disqualified investment corporation, but the distribution is not affected by the above rules and still qualifies as a tax-free corporate division. Eleven months later, in Year 2, D distributes controlled C1 to the Estate of Z in exchange for its D stock and K's interest in D increases from 40% to 100%. D is still a disqualified investment corporation; C1 is not substantially appreciated; D has minimal earnings and profits; and Z has a stepped-up basis for its D stock, so little or no gain is recognized by D or Z on the second distribution. By treating the two distributions as one transaction, K can be treated as a 50% shareholder after the distribution of C, so that distribution is taxable to D and to Z. (The distribution of C1 is also presumably taxable to D and Z.)

observation: There is no statutory restriction on the type of transaction that is included in the series of (related) transactions. IRS might use its specific grant of authority to issue regs (see "Regulations" below) to include transactions such as a redemption, e.g., which increases the shareholder's interest in anticipation of a corporate division, or following a corporate division.

illustration (5): Same facts as illustration (3) except that seven months after D distributes C, D redeems the stock held by the Estate of Z. Under regs, or arguably without regs, the result may be the same.

D or C is a disqualified investment corporation if the fair market value of its "investment assets" (see below) is:

(A) for distributions after the end of the one-year period beginning on May 17, 2006, 2/3 or more of the fair market value of all its assets. (Code Sec. 355(g)(2)(A)(1)(i))

(B) for distributions within one year of May 17, 2006, 75% or more of the fair market value of all its assets. (Code Sec. 355(g)(2)(A)(1)(ii))

observation: Thus, some extra slack is cut for the first year after May 17, 2006.

observation: If regs permit goodwill to be taken into account as an asset, the above 2/3 or 75% test is less likely to be satisfied. However, in a truly abusive transaction (see first viewpoint above), there is unlikely to be significant goodwill.

The following items (with the exceptions discussed below) are Code Sec. 355(g)(2)(B) investment assets:

- cash, (Code Sec. 355(g)(2)(B)(i)(I))
- any stock or securities in a corporation, (Code Sec. 355(g)(2)(B)(i)(II))
- any interest in a partnership, (Code Sec. 355(g)(2)(B)(i)(III))
- any debt instrument or other evidence of indebtedness, (Code Sec. 355(g)(2)(B)(i)(IV))
- any option, forward or futures contract, notional principal contract, or derivative, (Code Sec. 355(g)(2)(B)(i)(V))
- foreign currency, (Code Sec. 355(g)(2)(B)(i)(VI)) or

- any similar asset. (Code Sec. 355(g)(2)(B)(i)(VII))

> ***observation:*** This list does not include real estate held for investment, such as net leased property which isn't used in a trade or business. If the lessee has a top credit rating, such real estate can be the functional equivalent of a security because of the relative ease with which it can be mortgaged or otherwise cashed out.

Four categories of assets are not treated as Code Sec. 355(g)(2)(B) investment assets if they satisfy the specific requirements for an exception (discussed below). Those categories are:

(1) Assets used in the active and regular conduct of the financial (i.e., lending, finance, banking, or insurance) trades or businesses discussed below; (Code Sec. 355(g)(2)(B)(ii))

(2) Securities marked to market (see below); (Code Sec. 355(g)(2)(B)(iii))

(3) Stock or securities in a 20%-controlled entity (see below); (Code Sec. 355(g)(2)(B)(iv)) and

(4) Partnership interests or partnership debt, if a partnership trade or business would be taken into account in determining if D or C meet the active trade or business requirement (see below). (Code Sec. 355(g)(2)(B)(v))

Exception for assets used in active conduct of certain financial trades or businesses. An asset satisfies exception (1) above (and is not a Code Sec. 355(g)(2)(B) investment asset) if it is held for use in the active and regular conduct of:

. . . a lending or finance business (within the meaning of Code Sec. 954(h)(4) (see FTC 2d/FIN ¶ O-2480.9)); (Code Sec. 355(g)(2)(B)(ii)(I))

. . . a banking business through a bank (as defined in Code Sec. 581 (see FTC 2d/FIN ¶ E-3002; USTR ¶ 5814.01)), a domestic building and loan association (within the meaning of Code Sec. 7701(a)(19) (see FTC 2d/FIN ¶ E-3504; USTR ¶ 77,014.52), or any similar institution specified by IRS; (Code Sec. 355(g)(2)(B)(ii)(II)) or

. . . an insurance business if the conduct of the business is licensed, authorized, or regulated by an applicable insurance regulatory body. (Code Sec. 355(g)(2)(B)(ii)(III))

This exception only applies to a business if substantially all its income is from persons who are not related (within the meaning of Code Sec. 267(b) (see

---

FTC 2d References are to Federal Tax Coordinator 2d
FIN References are to RIA's Analysis of Federal Taxes: Income
USTR References are to United States Tax Reporter: Income, Estate & Gift, and Excise
PCA References are to Pension Analysis (print & electronic)
PE References are to the Pension Explanations (print & electronic)

FTC 2d/FIN ¶ G-2707) or Code Sec. 707(b)(1) (see FTC 2d/FIN ¶ B-2016; USTR ¶ 7074.03; TaxDesk ¶ 584,514)) to the person conducting the business. (Code Sec. 355(g)(2)(B)(ii))

Exception for securities marked to market. A security as defined in Code Sec. 475(c)(2) (see FTC 2d/FIN ¶ I-7657; USTR ¶ 4754) satisfies exception (2) above and is not a Code Sec. 355(g)(2)(B) investment asset if it is held by a securities dealer and the Code Sec. 475(a) mark to market rule applies (see FTC 2d/FIN ¶ I-7650; USTR ¶ 4754; TaxDesk ¶ 228,718.1). (Code Sec. 355(g)(2)(B)(iii))

Exception for stock or securities in a 20%-controlled entity. The following assets satisfy the third exception above and are not Code Sec. 355(g)(2)(B) investment assets if they are issued by a corporation which is a 20%-controlled entity as to D or C:

. . . any stock and securities in the corporation,

. . . any debt instrument or other evidence of indebtedness,

. . . any option, forward or futures contract, notional principal contract, or derivative. (Code Sec. 355(g)(2)(B)(iv)(I))

In applying this exception, D or C is treated as owning its ratable share of the assets of any 20%-controlled entity. (Code Sec. 355(g)(2)(B)(iv)(II))

> ***observation:*** For a discussion of applying a ratable share of assets approach in the context of a comparable rule under the partnership exception, see below.

A 20%-controlled entity as to D or C is any corporation in which D or C owns directly or indirectly stock meeting the Code Sec. 1504(a)(2) 80% vote and value test (see FTC 2d/FIN ¶ F-7606) when 20% is substituted for 80%, but without regard to stock described in Code Sec. 1504(a)(4). (Code Sec. 355(g)(2)(B)(iv)(III)) Thus, stock isn't considered in determining whether an entity is a 20%-controlled entity if the stock is preferred stock that is (i) nonvoting, (ii) nonconvertible into another class of stock, (iii) limited and preferred as to dividends, (iv) does not participate in corporate growth to any significant extent, and (v) has redemption and liquidation rights which don't exceed the issue price of the stock (excepting reasonable premiums) (see FTC 2d/FIN ¶ F-7618). (Com Rept, see ¶ 5025)

> ***observation:*** The Code Sec. 318 attribution rules apply in determining ownership (see above).

Exception for interest in a partnership conducting an active trade or business. Any interest in a partnership or any debt instrument or other evidence of indebtedness issued by the partnership satisfies the fourth exception above and is not a Code Sec. 355(g)(2)(B) investment asset if one or more of the partnership's trades or businesses is (or, if not for the Code Sec. 355(b)(2)(B) five-year requirement would be (see third observation below)) taken into account by D or C, as the case may be, in determining if the Code Sec. 355(b) active business test is met by the corporation (see FTC 2d/FIN ¶ F-4811). (Code Sec. 355(g)(2)(B)(v)(I))

observation: Coming within the above exception for a partnership interest just means that the partnership interest is not per se an investment asset. A look-through rule then applies (see discussion below).

observation: Under IRS rulings, a corporation can satisfy the Code Sec. 355(b) active trade or business test by performing active and substantial management activities as the managing general partner (or a joint manager) of a partnership in which it has an interest (see FTC 2d/FIN ¶ F-4811). The Tax Increase Prevention Act incorporates this result. There should also be qualification in the not uncommon situation where a corporation conducts an active business as a joint venturer with an affiliate or an unrelated party.

observation: In applying the above partnership exception, the Code Sec. 355(b)(2)(B) requirement that a business must have been carried on for the five-year period ending on the distribution date (see FTC 2d/FIN ¶ F-4819) doesn't apply under the parenthetical language of Code Sec. 355(g)(2)(B)(v)(l) (above). However, there is an additional five year requirement that does apply; Code Sec. 355(b)(2)(C) requires that the business relied on not have been acquired within the five-year period ending on the date of the distribution in a taxable transaction, i.e., a transaction in which gain or loss was recognized in whole or part (see FTC 2d/FIN ¶ F-4826). This rule, as the statute is currently drafted, is not overridden in testing if the partnership's activities would enable D or C to satisfy the active trade or business requirement. In this connection, it should be noted that IRS ruled that the acquisition of a partnership interest by contributing securities to the partnership was an acquisition in a taxable transaction (even though Code Sec. 721 provides nonrecognition in that situation), see Rev Rul 2002-49, 2002-2 CB 288 (situation 2) (FTC 2d/FIN ¶ F-4826).

If a partnership satisfies the above test, D or C (as the case may be) is treated as owning its ratable share of the partnership's assets. (Code Sec. 355(g)(2)(B)(v)(II))

observation: Applying a look-through rule raises numerous questions and will require regs, which, given the lack of specific guidance, will be quasi-legislative. The provision in some respects appears to be a partly baked loaf, but, the open questions will probably not be outcome-determinative in most situations. First, one of two basic approaches will have to be adopted: (1) Under a literal look-through approach, which is apparently intended, each partnership asset will be tested separately. Thus, cash or foreign currency that is part of the partnership's working capital will typically be included because (A) we have cash after the look-through, (B) cash is listed as an investment asset, and (C) the exclusion for an asset used in a financial trade or business doesn't apply. There are conceptual difficulties with applying such a look-through rule to a partnership, which is required to have an active trade or business, while not providing a blanket exception for the assets used in that business. (2) Thus, under a second alternative which would probably require regs or a technical amendment, a look through rule could be applied broad-brush to treat as Code Sec. 355(g)(2)(B) investment assets only partnership assets that (A) are listed as investment assets, and (B) are not used in the partnership's active trade or business (and, perhaps, not held for future use in the business). The second approach finds support from the significance given to an active partnership trade or business in the statute. To a lesser extent it is supported by the fact that the partnership's indebtedness is not intended to be treated as an investment asset in the hands of D or C, thus suggesting that perhaps (at least under regs) assets such as cash and customer obligations could be excluded if they are an integral part of the partnership's business. Additional difficulties will result in applying a look through approach to a partnership in which there are shifting profit and loss percentages (e.g., depending on profits) and profits interests issued as compensation. (Partnership indebtedness involves a separate issue discussed in the following observation.) The bottom line may be that these issues will usually not be outcome determinative, because, in a typical situation, the partnership's or a 20% owned corporate entity's non-business assets will not be Code Sec. 355(g)(2)(B) investment assets. Thus, for example, the headquarters building of a 20% owned corporation or an active trade or business partnership will not be a Code Sec. 355(g)(2)(B) investment asset. Likewise most of the assets of a business purchased within five years (but held along with a qualifying active trade or business) will not be investment assets. It may be noted that the rules for investment partnerships also use a look-through approach (both pre and post Tax Increase Prevention Act) (see FTC 2d/

FIN ¶ B-3602.5), but in that situation there is no gate-keeper active trade or business requirement.

observation: Another issue is how to apply the exception for partnership indebtedness in a qualifying partnership to which the look through rule applies. It would be possible to attempt to allocate partnership assets to the indebtedness, e.g., by first allocating assets secured by the debt to the debt and then certain designated assets, but this will be terribly complex and arbitrary, particularly if the indebtedness is not held in the same proportion as the underlying interest. Also, the comparable corporate provision, where options, notional principal contracts, etc., held by D or C in a 20%-controlled entity are taken into account as non-investment assets, seems unworkable. One possible approach for regs to take would be to treat the indebtedness (or in the case of a corporation, options and notional principal contracts, etc.) as other than an investment asset if it is directly connected with D's or C's business, or it is made to support the active trade or business activities of a 20%-controlled entity.

Regulations. IRS is to issue regs to carry out, or prevent the avoidance of, the purposes of the disqualified investment corporation rules, including regs:

(1) to carry out, or prevent the avoidance of, the purposes of these rules in cases involving:

(A) the use of related persons, intermediaries, pass-through entities, options, or other arrangements, (Code Sec. 355(g)(5)(A)(i)) and

(B) the treatment of assets unrelated to a corporation's trade or business as Code Sec. 355(g)(2)(B) investment assets if, before the distribution, Code Sec. 355(g)(2)(B) investment assets were used to acquire those unrelated assets, (Code Sec. 355(g)(5)(A)(ii))

(2) which in appropriate cases exclude from the application of the disqualified investment corporation rules a distribution which does not have the character of a redemption which would be treated as a sale or exchange under Code Sec. 302, (Code Sec. 355(g)(5)(B)) and

observation: Thus, the transaction is not a split-off in which a cash-rich subsidiary is used as a substitute for a sale.

FTC 2d References are to Federal Tax Coordinator 2d
FIN References are to RIA's Analysis of Federal Taxes: Income
USTR References are to United States Tax Reporter: Income, Estate & Gift, and Excise
PCA References are to Pension Analysis (print & electronic)
PE References are to the Pension Explanations (print & electronic)

(3) which modify application of the attribution rules that are applied for purposes of these disqualified investment corporation rules. (Code Sec. 355(g)(5)(C))

The enumeration of the above situations that regs may address is not intended to restrict or limit the situations that regs may address under the above authority. (Com Rept, see ¶ 5025)

> ***observation:*** Item (1)(B) could apply if investment securities are sold and the proceeds invested in a triple net leased property.

☐ **Effective:** Distributions after May 17, 2006. (Tax Increase Prevention Act §507(b)(1))

The above rules do not apply to any distribution pursuant to a transaction which is:

. . . made pursuant to an agreement which was binding on May 17, 2006 and at all times thereafter, (Tax Increase Prevention Act §507(b)(2)(A))

. . . described in a ruling request submitted to IRS on or before that date, (Tax Increase Prevention Act §507(b)(2)(B)) or

. . . described on or before that date in a public announcement or in a filing with the Securities and Exchange Commission. (Tax Increase Prevention Act §507(b)(2)(C))

¶ 503. Earnings-stripping rules are applied to corporate partners

Code Sec. 163(j)(8), as amended by Tax Increase Prevention Act § 501(a)
Code Sec. 163(j)(9)(D), as amended by Tax Increase Prevention Act § 501(b)
Generally effective: Tax years beginning on or after May 17, 2006
Committee Reports, see ¶ 5020

A corporation's payment of deductible interest to a related person who isn't subject to U.S. tax on the corresponding income is known as "earnings stripping." To limit tax avoidance through earnings stripping, a corporation is denied an interest deduction for disqualified interest (defined below) to the extent of the corporation's excess interest expense (defined below) in any year that the corporation is thinly capitalized—i.e., it has a debt-to-equity ratio greater than 1.5 to 1. (FTC 2d/FIN ¶ K-5361; USTR ¶ 1634.058)

"Disqualified interest" is generally (1) interest paid or accrued to a related person, if the interest isn't subject to U.S. tax in the recipient's hands, and (2) interest paid to unrelated parties in certain cases in which a related party guarantees the debt. (FTC 2d/FIN ¶ K-5361; USTR ¶ 1634.058)

"Excess interest expense" is the excess, if any, of the corporation's net interest expense over the sum of (a) 50% of its adjusted taxable income (ATI) and (b) any excess limitation carryforward. (FTC 2d/FIN ¶ K-5361; USTR ¶ 1634.058) ATI is taxable income less allowable deductions for net interest expense, net operating losses (NOLs), U.S. production activities, depreciation, amortization, and depletion. (FTC 2d/FIN ¶ K-5381; USTR ¶ 1634.058)

For purposes of applying the earnings-stripping limitation to interest payments by a corporate partner of a partnership, proposed regs would treat a partner's proportionate share of partnership liabilities as liabilities incurred directly by the partner. (Prop Reg § 1.163(j)-3(b)(3)) Under the proposed regs:

. . . Interest paid or accrued to a partnership would be treated as paid or accrued to the partners of the partnership in proportion to each partner's distributive share of the partnership's interest income for the tax year. (Prop Reg § 1.163(j)-2(e)(4))

. . . Interest expense paid or accrued by a partnership would be treated as paid or accrued by the partners of the partnership in proportion to each partner's distributive share of the partnership's interest expense for the tax year. (Prop Reg § 1.163(j)-2(e)(5)) (Com Rept, see ¶ 5020)

New Law. The Tax Increase Prevention Act codifies the approach of these proposed regs. (Com Rept, see ¶ 5020) Under the Tax Increase Prevention Act, except to the extent provided by regs, in applying the earnings-stripping rules to a corporation that owns, directly or indirectly, an interest in a partnership (Code Sec. 163(j)(8) as amended by Tax Increase Prevention Act §501(a)):

- the corporation's share of the liabilities of the partnership will be treated as liabilities of the corporation (Code Sec. 163(j)(8)(C));
- the corporation's distributive share of interest income paid or accrued to the partnership will be treated as interest income paid or accrued to the corporation (Code Sec. 163(j)(8)(A)); and
- the corporation's distributive share of interest paid or accrued by the partnership will be treated as interest paid or accrued by the corporation. (Code Sec. 163(j)(8)(B))

> ***observation:*** This rule prevents a corporation from avoiding the earnings-stripping rules by issuing debt through a partnership in which it holds an interest.

FTC 2d References are to Federal Tax Coordinator 2d
FIN References are to RIA's Analysis of Federal Taxes: Income
USTR References are to United States Tax Reporter: Income, Estate & Gift, and Excise
PCA References are to Pension Analysis (print & electronic)
PE References are to the Pension Explanations (print & electronic)

The Tax Increase Prevention Act gives IRS regulatory authority to reallocate (A) shares of partnership indebtedness or (B) distributive shares of the partnership's interest income or interest expense. (Code Sec. 163(j)(9)(D) as amended by Tax Increase Prevention Act §501(b)) For example, Congress intends that the regs prevent corporations with direct or indirect interests in partnerships from circumventing the earnings-stripping rules by allocating partnership interest income or expense (or partnership liabilities) to or away from partners. (Com Rept, see ¶ 5020)

☐ **Effective:** Tax years beginning on or after May 17, 2006. (Tax Increase Prevention Act §501(c))

¶ 600. Foreign Provisions

¶ 601. Exceptions under Subpart F for active banking, financing and insurance income expiring in 2007 extended through tax years beginning before 2009

Code Sec. 953(e)(10), as amended by Tax Increase Prevention Act § 103(a)(1)
Code Sec. 954(h)(9), as amended by Tax Increase Prevention Act § 103(a)(2)
Generally effective: May 17, 2006
Committee Reports, see ¶ 5003

Under Subpart F, U.S. persons who are 10% shareholders of a controlled foreign corporation (CFC) are required to include in income their pro rata share of the CFC's insurance income and adjusted net foreign base company income (FBCI) whether or not this income is distributed to the shareholders. Insurance income generally includes income of a CFC attributable to the issuing and reinsuring of any insurance or annuity contract in connection with risks located in a country other than the CFC's country of organization. FBCI includes foreign personal holding income (FPHCI) and foreign base company services income (FBCSI). FPHCI includes dividends, interest, income equivalent to interest, rents, royalties, and annuities. FBCSI income generally includes income from technical, managerial, engineering, architectural, scientific, skilled, industrial, commercial or similar services performed outside the country of incorporation of the CFC. (FTC 2d/FIN ¶s O-2401, O-2425, O-2432, O-2448, O-2494; USTR ¶s 9534.01, 9544.02)

Under pre-Tax Increase Prevention Act law, certain income from the active conduct of a banking, financing or similar business, or from the conduct of an insurance business (collectively referred to as "active financing income") was temporarily excluded from the definition of Subpart F income, but only for tax years of foreign corporations beginning before Jan. 1, 2007, and for tax years of U.S. shareholders with or within which any such tax year of the foreign corporation ended. (FTC 2d/FIN ¶ O-2404, ¶ O-2423.1, ¶ O-2423.2 *et seq.*, ¶ O-2448.2, ¶ O-2480.3 *et seq.*, ¶ O-2494; USTR ¶ 9534.01, ¶ 9544.02)

New Law. The Tax Increase Prevention Act extends the temporary exclusions for active financing income for two years. Thus, the above rules will apply to tax years of a foreign corporation beginning after Dec. 31, 2006 and

---

FTC 2d References are to Federal Tax Coordinator 2d
FIN References are to RIA's Analysis of Federal Taxes: Income
USTR References are to United States Tax Reporter: Income, Estate & Gift, and Excise
PCA References are to Pension Analysis (print & electronic)
PE References are to the Pension Explanations (print & electronic)

before Jan. 1, 2009 and tax years of U.S. shareholders with or within which such tax years of foreign corporations end. (Code Sec. 953(e)(10) as amended by Tax Increase Prevention Act §103(a)(1)) and (Code Sec. 954(h)(9) as amended by Tax Increase Prevention Act §103(a)(2))

> ***observation:*** This change will allow banks, finance, insurance and similar companies to defer active financing income offshore for tax years beginning before Jan. 1, 2009.

☐ **Effective:** May 17, 2006. The change affects tax years of a foreign corporation beginning after Dec. 31, 2006 and before Jan. 1, 2009 and tax years of U.S. shareholders with or within which such tax years of foreign corporations end. (Com Rept, see ¶ 5003)

¶ 602. Payments between related controlled foreign corporations under foreign personal holding company income rules subject to look-through treatment for tax years beginning before 2009

Code Sec. 954(c)(6), as added by Tax Increase Prevention Act § 103(b)
Generally effective: Tax years of foreign corporations beginning after Dec. 31, 2005 and before Jan. 1, 2009 and tax years of U.S. shareholders with or within which such tax years of foreign corporations end
Committee Reports, see ¶ 5004

Under Subpart F, U.S. persons who are 10% shareholders (U.S. shareholders) of a controlled foreign corporation (CFC) are required to include in income their pro rata share of the CFC's subpart F income whether or not this income is distributed to the shareholders.

Subpart F income includes foreign base company income (FBCI), which in turn includes foreign personal holding income (FPHCI). For subpart F purposes, FPHCI includes dividends, interest, income equivalent to interest, rents and royalties. However, FPHCI does not include dividends and interest from a related corporation organized and operating in the same foreign country in which the CFC is organized, or rents and royalties received by a CFC from a related corporation for the use of property within the country in which the CFC is organized. Interest, rent, and royalty payments do not qualify for this exclusion to the extent that such payments reduce the subpart F income of the payor. (FTC 2d/FIN ¶s O-2303, O-2401, O-2424, O-2424.1, O-2432, O-2433, O-2439, O-2445; USTR ¶s 9544, 9544.02)

New Law. Under the Tax Increase Prevention Act, dividends, interest, rent, and royalties received or accrued from a CFC which is a related person will not be treated as FPHCI to the extent attributable or properly allocable to income of the related person which is not subpart F income. (Code Sec. 954(c)(6)(A) as amended by Tax Increase Prevention Act §103(b)(1)) Thus, dividends, interest, rents, and royalties received by one CFC from a related CFC (described below) are not treated as FPHCI to the extent attributable or properly allocable to non-subpart-F income of the payor. (Com Rept, see ¶ 5004) In making this determination, look-through rules similar to those that a U.S. shareholder uses to allocate interest, rent, royalty and dividend income received from a CFC to separate foreign tax credit baskets will apply (see FTC 2d/FIN ¶s O-4346, O-4347, O-4348; USTR ¶ 9044.01). (Code Sec. 954(c)(6)(A)) Interest will include factoring income which is treated as income equivalent to interest for purposes of determining FPHCI. (Code Sec. 954(c)(6)(A)) For these purposes, a related CFC is a CFC that controls or is controlled by the other CFC, or a CFC that is controlled by the same person or persons that control the other CFC. Ownership of more than 50% of the CFC's stock (by vote or value) is control for these purposes. (Com Rept, see ¶ 5004)

Congress believes that most countries allow their multinational companies to redeploy active foreign earnings with no additional tax burden. Thus, the above changes are designed to make U.S. companies and workers more competitive vis a vis those countries. Allowing U.S. companies to reinvest their active foreign earnings where they are most needed without any immediate additional U.S. tax will allow U.S. companies to make more overseas sales and produce more goods in the U.S. (Com Rept, see ¶ 5004)

> ***observation:*** Thus, the above changes are designed to allow U.S. multinationals to transfer active income between related CFCs in different countries without triggering subpart F income.

> ***viewpoint:*** Joseph Calianno, the International Technical Tax Practice Leader and Partner in the National Tax Office of Grant Thornton LLP, notes that this legislation represents a significant development in the subpart F area and may impact how some taxpayers structure their foreign operations. Subject to certain exceptions (e.g., the same country exceptions under Code Sec. 954(c)(3), the high tax exception under Code Sec. 954(b)(4), etc., dividends, interest, rents and royalties received by one CFC from another CFC normally result in subpart F FPHCI. To avoid the generally negative subpart F implications of such payments, taxpayers frequently structure their foreign operations so that a CFC owns several foreign disregarded entities. The CFC generally will enter into transactions (loan, rental and licensing arrangements) with its wholly owned foreign disregarded entities. Alternatively, the foreign disregarded entities owned by the CFC may enter into transac-

FTC 2d References are to Federal Tax Coordinator 2d
FIN References are to RIA's Analysis of Federal Taxes: Income
USTR References are to United States Tax Reporter: Income, Estate & Gift, and Excise
PCA References are to Pension Analysis (print & electronic)
PE References are to the Pension Explanations (print & electronic)

tions with one another. The dividend, interest, rental and royalty payments under these arrangements generally do not result in FPHCI because, subject to certain exceptions (e.g., Code Sec. 987), such payments generally are disregarded for U.S. federal tax purposes. However, this new legislation may permit taxpayers to achieve results similar to the CFC/foreign disregarded entity structure to avoid subpart F FPHCI when a CFC enters into such an arrangement with a related CFC, if the payment by the related CFC is properly allocable to non-subpart F income of the related CFC. Moreover, taxpayers should compare each type of structure from a foreign tax credit perspective. Under the CFC/foreign disregarded entity structure described above, the earnings and profits (E&P) and foreign taxes of the foreign disregarded entities generally are combined at the CFC level. However, under the separate CFC structure, E&P and foreign taxes generally remain at the separate CFC level until certain events occur (e.g., a dividend paid by one CFC to another CFC that qualifies under Code Sec. 902(b). Thus, because there may be advantages of not combining the E&P and foreign taxes of certain entities, taxpayers should fully evaluate each structure or consider a combination of the two structures to achieve the best overall tax planning result.

IRS is authorized to issue regs to prevent abuse of these rules. (Code Sec. 954(c)(6)(A))

☐ **Effective:** Tax years of foreign corporations beginning after Dec. 31, 2005 and before Jan. 1, 2009, and tax years of U.S. shareholders with or within which such tax years of foreign corporations end. (Code Sec. 954(c)(6)(B)); (Tax Increase Prevention Act §103(b)(2))

¶ 603. Qualified investment entity FIRPTA exclusion is amended

Code Sec. 897(h)(1), as amended by Tax Increase Prevention Act § 505(a)(1)
Code Sec. 897(h)(4)(A)(ii), as amended by Tax Increase Prevention Act § 505(a)(2)
Code Sec. 1445(e)(6), as amended by Tax Increase Prevention Act § 505(b)
Code Sec. 852(b)(3)(E), as amended by Tax Increase Prevention Act § 505(c)(1)
Code Sec. 871(k)(2)(E), as amended by Tax Increase Prevention Act § 505(c)(2)
Code Sec. 897(h)(4)(A)(i)(II), as amended by Tax Increase Prevention Act § 504(a)
Generally effective: Tax years of qualified investment entities beginning after Dec. 31, 2005
Committee Reports, see ¶ 5023, 5024

Under the Code Sec. 897 FIRPTA rules, a nonresident alien or a foreign corporation is taxed on the gain or loss on the disposition of a U.S. real property interest (USRPI) as if it were effectively connected with the conduct of a U.S. trade or business. In addition to real property interests in the U.S. or the Virgin Islands, USRPIs include interests in a domestic corporation unless the taxpayer establishes that the corporation was not, during the 5-year period ending on the disposition date, a U.S. real property holding corporation (USRPHC), generally, a corporation in which the fair market value of its USRPIs is at least 50% of the fair market values of the sum of its USRPIs, non-U.S. real property interests, and other assets used or held for use in a trade or business. An exception applies under which the sale of stock of a regularly-traded corporation is not treated as a sale of a USRPI if the shareholder did not hold more than 5% of the corporation's regularly-traded class of stock. Foreign persons selling interests in USRPIs are generally subject to a 10% withholding tax on the sale proceeds under Code Sec. 1445. (FTC 2d/FIN ¶ O-10701, ¶ O-10735, ¶ O-10771, ¶ O-13000; USTR ¶ 8974, ¶ 14,454; TaxDesk ¶ 643,001, ¶ 643,016, ¶ 643,022, ¶ 644,000)

Another exception applies under which an interest in a domestically controlled qualified investment entity (generally, less than 50% of the stock is held by foreign persons for a five-year period) is not a USRPI. Under pre-Tax Increase Prevention Act law, distributions by a qualified investment entity to a

FTC 2d References are to Federal Tax Coordinator 2d
FIN References are to RIA's Analysis of Federal Taxes: Income
USTR References are to United States Tax Reporter: Income, Estate & Gift, and Excise
PCA References are to Pension Analysis (print & electronic)
PE References are to the Pension Explanations (print & electronic)

nonresident alien or a foreign corporation were looked through so that the recipient was treated as recognizing gain on the recipient's portion of the distribution attributable to the gain on the sale or exchange of USRPIs. However, look-through treatment did not apply to distributions by REITs on a class of shares that was regularly traded on a U.S. established securities market to shareholders that held not more than 5% of the regularly-traded class of stock during the tax year of the distribution. Where look-through treatment did not apply, the distribution was treated as an ordinary dividend that was subject to 30% (unless reduced by treaty) Code Sec. 1441 or Code Sec. 1442 withholding. A qualified investment entity meant any real estate investment trust (REIT) and any regulated investment company (RIC) with the inclusion of RICs terminating after Dec. 31, 2007. (FTC 2d/FIN ¶ E-6617, ¶ O-10734, ¶ O-10753; USTR ¶ 8974.02; TaxDesk ¶ 643,015, ¶ 643,016)

New Law. The Tax Increase Prevention Act amends the rules applicable to qualified investment entities so that the look-through of distributions to the entity applies to distributions to other qualified investment entities, rather than just nonresident aliens and foreign corporations. Thus, distributions to nonresident aliens, foreign corporations, and other qualified entities result in gain recognition by the recipient to the extent of the recipient's portion of the distribution attributable to the gain on the sale or exchange of USRPIs. (Code Sec. 897(h)(1) as amended by Tax Increase Prevention Act §505(a)(1)(A)); (Code Sec. 897(h)(1) as amended by Tax Increase Prevention Act §505(a)(1)(B))

For purposes of applying the look-through rule and the Code Sec. 1445 withholding rules to a distribution from a RIC which is attributable directly or indirectly to a distribution to the RIC from a REIT, a RIC is treated as a qualified investment entity even after Dec. 31, 2007. Thus, distributions from a RIC that receives a distribution from a REIT will be subject to look-through treatment and Code Sec. 1445 withholding after Dec. 31, 2007. (Code Sec. 897(h)(4)(A)(ii) as amended by Tax Increase Prevention Act §505(a)(2))

For limitation of RIC look-through treatment to USRPHC RICs, see below.

> RIA ***viewpoint:*** Robert P. Rothman, Of Counsel to DLA Piper Rudnick Gray Cary US LLP in New York, comments as follows: This amendment precludes taxpayers from using tiered REITs or RICs to avoid FIRPTA treatment on distributions attributable to dispositions of U.S. real property interests. Under prior law, a distribution by a qualified investment entity which was attributable to gain on disposition of a U.S. real property interest retained the character of such gain, but only if such distribution was made to a nonresident alien individual or foreign corporation. Therefore, under a technical reading of the statute, the FIRPTA taint could be effectively purged simply by running the distribution through a second REIT or RIC.

> ***Example:*** R, a REIT, owns a parcel of land located in the U.S. S, also a REIT, owns stock of R. F, a non-resident alien individual, owns stock of S (which is not publicly traded). R sells the land and distributes the proceeds to S, which then distributes them to F. Under prior law, under a literal reading of the Code the distribution received by S from R was not treated as gain from the sale or exchange of a U.S. real property interest (because S is neither a nonresident alien individual nor a foreign corporation), and accordingly the distribution by S to F was not subject to FIRPTA.

The exception from look-through treatment for distributions by REITs that are regularly traded on a U.S. established securities market to shareholders that hold not more than 5% of the corporation's stock is amended so that it applies to distributions by any qualified entity to nonresident aliens or foreign corporations on a regularly-traded class of stock, but only if the shareholder did not hold more than 5% of the regularly-traded class of stock at any time during the one-year period ending on the date of the distribution. (Code Sec. 897(h)(1) as amended by Tax Increase Prevention Act §505(a)(1)(C))

This exception does not apply to distributions to other RICs or REITs. Instead, the character of the distribution as FIRPTA gain is retained and must be tracked by the recipient RIC or REIT. Since the distribution is treated as FIRPTA gain, rather than ordinary income, distributions from the recipient RIC or REIT out of amounts attributable to the distribution are treated as capital gain by its U.S. shareholders, but as FIRPTA gain (or dividend income, if the regularly-traded exception applies). (Com Rept, see ¶ 5024)

Whether a class is regularly traded on a U.S. established securities market is determined under existing authority under FIRPTA, see FTC 2d/FIN ¶ O-10802. (Com Rept, see ¶ 5024)

The Code Sec. 1445 withholding rules are amended so that withholding applies to portions of distributions by qualified entities that are treated under the look-through rule as gain from the sale or exchange of a USRPI. The withholding rate is 35% unless IRS provides for a 15% rate (20% for tax years beginning after Dec. 31, 2010) in regs. (Code Sec. 1445(e)(6) as amended by Tax Increase Prevention Act §505(b)) The Dec. 31, 2010 date corresponds to the sunset of the 15% rate under Code Sec. 1445(e)(1), see ¶ 105. (Com Rept, see ¶ 5024)

To the extent the above exception for distributions by regularly-traded qualified entities to not more than 5% shareholders applies to a distribution to a RIC, the amount of the distribution that would otherwise be included in computing long-term capital gains for the shareholders of the RIC is not included in computing long-term capital gains for the shareholders. (Code Sec. 852(b)(3)(E)(i) as amended by Tax Increase Prevention Act §505(c)(1)) Instead, that portion is treated as a dividend from the RIC. (Code Sec. 852(b)(3)(E)(ii)) Similarly, the amount of the distribution is not treated as a short-term capital gains dividend to the RIC shareholders, (Code Sec. 871(k)(2)(E)(i) as amended by Tax Increase Prevention Act §505(c)(2)) but as a dividend from the RIC. (Code Sec. 871(k)(2)(E)(ii))

> ***illustration (1):*** R, a REIT, has realized a $1,000,000 capital gain. T, another REIT, holds a 10% interest in R. Both T and R shares are regularly traded on a U.S. securities market. R makes a $200,000 distribution to T. The distribution results in T recognizing a $100,000 gain that is treated as effectively connected with the conduct of a U.S. trade or business. T then makes a $100,000 distribution that is attributable to the $100,000 gain that is treated as effectively connected with the conduct of a U.S. trade or business. A, a U.S. citizen who is a 10% shareholder of T, receives a $10,000 distribution and treats the distribution as capital gain. B, a nonresident alien who is a 10% shareholder of T, receives a $10,000 distribution and treats the distribution as FIRPTA gain. C, a nonresident alien who is a 4% shareholder of T, receives a $4,000 distribution and treats the distribution as an ordinary dividend subject to Code Sec. 1441 withholding.

For rules regarding wash sales of interests in qualified investment entities, see ¶ 604.

Limitation of RIC look-through treatment to USRPHC RICs. The Tax Increase Prevention Act also amends the definition of a qualified investment entity to include only a RIC which is a USRPHC or which would be a USRPHC if the exceptions (i) for shareholders with interests of not more than 5% of the corporation's regularly traded class of stock and (ii) for shareholders of domestically controlled qualified investment entities didn't apply. (Code Sec. 897(h)(4)(A)(i)(II) as amended by Tax Increase Prevention Act §504(a))

This means that look-through treatment does not apply unless 50% or more of the RIC's value is represented by its USRPIs, including investments in USRPHCs. However, in determining whether a RIC is a USRPHC for this purpose, the RIC must include as USRPIs its holdings of RIC or REIT stock if the RIC or REIT is a USRPHC without regard to the "not more than 5% of regularly traded stock" exception and without regard to the exception for domestically controlled qualified investment entities. (Com Rept, see ¶ 5024)

> ***illustration (2):*** S, a RIC, invests entirely in regularly-traded USRPHCs, but never holds more than 5% of the stock of each

USRPHC. In addition, 60% of S's stock is held by U.S. persons. S is subject to the look-through rules.

observation: Since this provision narrows the application of the look-through rules to RICs retroactively, foreign persons who paid tax because of the application of the look-through rules to non-USRPHC RICs may be able to apply for refunds of taxes paid because of the look-through rules.

☐ **Effective:** Tax years of qualified investment entities beginning after Dec. 31, 2005, except that no Code Sec. 1441, Code Sec. 1442, or Code Sec. 1445 withholding is required before May 17, 2006 if withholding was not required under pre-Tax Increase Prevention Act law. (Tax Increase Prevention Act §505(d))

The amendment to the definition of qualified investment entities applies for distributions relating to tax years of RICs beginning after Dec. 31, 2004. (Tax Increase Prevention Act §504(b)) The Tax Increase Prevention Act §504(d) provides that the above provision is effective as if included in the 2004 Jobs Act §411 (Sec. 411, PL 108-357, 10/22/2004), which was effective after Dec. 31, 2004. 2004 Jobs Act §411(d)(3) (Sec. 411(d)(3), PL 108-357, 10/22/2004).

¶ 604. Certain wash sales of interests in domestically controlled qualified investment entities result in gain recognition under FIRPTA

Code Sec. 897(h)(5), as amended by Tax Increase Prevention Act § 506(a)
Code Sec. 1445(b)(8), as amended by Tax Increase Prevention Act § 506(b)
Generally effective: Tax years beginning after Dec. 31, 2005
Committee Reports, see ¶ 5024

Under the Code Sec. 897 FIRPTA rules, a nonresident alien or a foreign corporation is taxed on the gain or loss on the disposition of a U.S. real property interest (USRPI) as if it were effectively connected with the conduct of a U.S. trade or business. In addition to real property interests in the U.S. or the Virgin Islands, USRPIs include interests in a domestic corporation unless the taxpayer establishes that the corporation was not, during the 5-year period ending on the disposition date, a U.S. real property holding corporation (USRPHC), generally, a corporation in which the fair market value of its USRPIs is at least 50% of the fair market values of the sum of its USRPIs, non-U.S. real property inter-

FTC 2d References are to Federal Tax Coordinator 2d
FIN References are to RIA's Analysis of Federal Taxes: Income
USTR References are to United States Tax Reporter: Income, Estate & Gift, and Excise
PCA References are to Pension Analysis (print & electronic)
PE References are to the Pension Explanations (print & electronic)

ests, and other assets used or held for use in a trade or business. (FTC 2d/FIN ¶ O-10701, ¶ O-10735, ¶ O-10771; USTR ¶ 8974; TaxDesk ¶ 643,001, ¶ 643,016, ¶ 643,022)

An exception applies under which an interest in a domestically controlled (i.e., less than 50% of the stock is held by foreign persons) qualified investment entity (generally, either a RIC or a REIT, see ¶ 603) is not a USRPI. Under pre-Tax Increase Prevention Act law, distributions by a qualified investment entity to a nonresident alien or a foreign corporation were looked through so that the recipient was treated as recognizing gain on the recipient's portion of the distribution attributable to the gain on the sale or exchange of USRPIs. However, look-through treatment did not apply to distributions by REITs on a class of shares that was regularly traded on a U.S. established securities market to shareholders that held not more than 5% of the regularly-traded class of stock during the tax year of the distribution. (FTC 2d/FIN ¶ O-10734, ¶ O-10753; USTR ¶ 8974.02; TaxDesk ¶ 643,015, ¶ 643,016)

Under pre-Tax Increase Prevention Act law, foreign persons could avoid FIRPTA tax on a distribution from a RIC or a REIT by selling the RIC or REIT stock shortly before the distribution and buying back the stock shortly after the distribution. If the RIC or REIT was domestically controlled, and, thus, not a USRPI in the hands of the foreign seller, the seller would take the position that the gain on the sale of the stock was capital gain not subject to U.S. tax.

New Law. The Tax Increase Prevention Act adds a new rule under which a wash sale of an interest in a domestically controlled qualified investment entity can trigger gain recognition under FIRPTA. Under this rule, if an interest in a domestically controlled qualified investment entity is disposed of in an applicable wash sale transaction, the seller is treated as having gain from the sale or exchange of a USRPI in an amount equal to the portion of the distribution relating to the interest which, but for the disposition, would have been treated as gain from the sale or exchange of a USRPI as a result of the look-though rule described above. (Code Sec. 897(h)(5)(A) as amended by Tax Increase Prevention Act §506(a))

An applicable wash sale transaction is any transaction (or series of transactions) under which a nonresident alien individual, foreign corporation, or qualified investment entity:

- disposes of an interest in a domestically controlled qualified investment entity during the 30-day period before the ex-dividend date of a distribution relating to the interest where any portion of the distribution would, but for the disposition, have been treated by the seller as gain from the sale or exchange of a USRPI under the look-through rule, and
- acquires (or enters into a contract or option to acquire) an identical interest in the entity during the 61-day period beginning with the first day of the 30-

day period described above. For this purpose, a nonresident alien individual, foreign corporation, or qualified investment entity is treated as having acquired any interest that a person related (under the Code Sec. 267(b) or Code Sec. 707(b)(1) rules, see FTC 2d/FIN ¶ I-3504; USTR ¶ 2674.03; TaxDesk ¶ 227,904 and FTC 2d/FIN ¶ B-2016; USTR ¶ 7074.03; TaxDesk ¶ 584,514) to the individual, corporation, or entity acquired (or entered into a contract or option to acquire). (Code Sec. 897(h)(5)(B)(i))

For this purpose, a RIC is treated as a qualified investment entity even after Dec. 31, 2007. (Code Sec. 897(h)(4)(A)(ii) as amended by Tax Increase Prevention Act §505(a)(2))

> ***observation:*** This change means that the foreign person must include in income the amount that he would have to include in income under FIRPTA if he had held his stock.

> ***illustration:*** R, a REIT, has realized a $1,000,000 capital gain. A, a nonresident alien holds a 10% interest in R. A sells its 10% interest on May 1, Year 1. On May 15, Year 1, R makes a distribution to shareholders who hold shares on that date. If A had held its interest in R on May 15, Year 1, the distribution would result in A recognizing a $100,000 gain that would be treated as effectively connected with the conduct of a U.S. trade or business. On June 1, Year 1, A buys back the same number of shares it held before the sale of its R shares. A is treated as recognizing $100,000 of gain that is effectively connected with the conduct of a U.S. trade or business on the sale of its R shares.

The wash sale rule applies to any substitute dividend payment (within the meaning of Code Sec. 861) or any other similar payment specified in regs which IRS determines necessary to prevent avoidance of the purposes of the wash sale rule. The portion of the payment treated by the taxpayer as gain from the sale or exchange of a USRPI under the wash sale rule is determined by looking at the payment for which the substitute payment is in lieu of. To the extent that the underlying payment would have been treated as gain from the sale or exchange of a USRPI, the substitute payment will be treated as gain from the sale or exchange of a USRPI. (Code Sec. 897(h)(5)(B)(ii)) A substitute dividend payment, which under Code Sec. 861 is generally sourced and treated in the same manner as the underlying payment, is defined in Reg §1.861-3(a)(6) (see FTC 2d/FIN ¶ O-10930; USTR ¶ 8614.13) as a payment made to the transferor of a security, in a securities-lending transaction or a sale-repurchase transaction, of an amount equivalent to a dividend distribution which the owner of the transferred security is entitled to receive during the term of the transaction. (Com Rept, see ¶ 5024)

However, a transaction is not treated as an applicable wash sale transaction if the nonresident alien individual, foreign corporation, or qualified investment entity receives the distribution relating to either the interest that was disposed of, or acquired, in the transaction. (Code Sec. 897(h)(5)(B)(iii))

A transaction is also not treated as an applicable wash sale transaction if it involves the disposition of any class of shares that is regularly traded on a U.S.-established securities market by a nonresident alien, foreign corporation, or qualified investment entity that did not hold more than 5% of the regularly-traded class of stock during the one-year period ending on the date of the distribution. (Code Sec. 897(h)(5)(B)(iv)) Since the taxpayer would not have been subject to FIRPTA tax if it received the payment (see ¶ 603), it is not subject to the wash sale rule. (Com Rept, see ¶ 5024)

An applicable wash sale transaction does not require any person to deduct and withhold any amount that is treated as a disposition of a USRPI. (Code Sec. 1445(b)(8) as amended by Tax Increase Prevention Act §506(b))

For other changes to the rules regarding qualified investment entities for FIRPTA purposes, see ¶ 603.

☐ **Effective:** Tax years beginning after Dec. 31, 2005, except that the rules do not apply to distributions or substitute dividend payments before the date that is 30 days after May 17, 2006. (Tax Increase Prevention Act §506(c))

¶ 700. Exempt Organization Tax-Shelter Reforms

¶ 701. Excise tax is imposed on tax-exempt entities that are parties to prohibited tax shelter transactions, and on entity managers who knowingly approve prohibited tax shelter transactions

Code Sec. 4965, as added by Tax Increase Prevention Act § 516(a)
Generally effective: Tax years ending after May 17, 2006
Committee Reports, see ¶ 5034

Every taxpayer that has participated in a "reportable transaction" (including a "listed transaction"), and who is required to file a tax return, must attach a disclosure statement to its return. (FTC 2d/FIN ¶ S-4427.1; USTR ¶ 60,114.02)

Under Code Sec. 6707A, a penalty is imposed on any person who fails to include, on any return or statement, any required information with respect to a "reportable transaction." (FTC 2d/FIN ¶ V-2531; USTR ¶ 67,07A4; TaxDesk ¶ 866,501)

Code Sec. 6707A(c)(1) defines a "reportable transaction" as any transaction with respect to which information is required to be included with a return or statement because, as determined under regs issued under Code Sec. 6011 (relating to the filing of returns and statements), the transaction is of a type which IRS determines as having a potential for tax avoidance or evasion. (FTC 2d/FIN ¶ V-2533; USTR ¶ 67,07A4; TaxDesk ¶ 866,503) Under regs issued under Code Sec. 6011, a reportable transaction includes a "listed transaction" and four other categories of transactions: (1) confidential transactions, (2) transactions with contractual protection, (3) loss transactions, and (4) transactions involving a brief asset holding period. (FTC 2d/FIN ¶ S-4427.1; USTR ¶ 60,114.02; TaxDesk ¶ 817,007)

Code Sec. 6707A(c)(2) defines a "listed transaction" as a reportable transaction which is the same as, or substantially similar to, a transaction specifically identified by the IRS as a tax avoidance transaction for purposes of Code Sec. 6011. (FTC 2d/FIN ¶ V-2534; USTR ¶ 67,07A4; TaxDesk ¶ 866,504)

A taxpayer has participated in a listed transaction if the taxpayer's tax return reflects tax consequences or a tax strategy described in the published guidance that lists the transaction, or if the taxpayer knows or has reason to know that the

FTC 2d References are to Federal Tax Coordinator 2d
FIN References are to RIA's Analysis of Federal Taxes: Income
USTR References are to United States Tax Reporter: Income, Estate & Gift, and Excise
PCA References are to Pension Analysis (print & electronic)
PE References are to the Pension Explanations (print & electronic)

taxpayer's tax benefits are derived directly or indirectly from tax consequences or a tax strategy described in published guidance that lists a transaction. A taxpayer has participated in a confidential transaction if the taxpayer's tax return reflects a tax benefit from the transaction, and the taxpayer's disclosure of the tax treatment or tax structure of the transaction is limited under conditions of confidentiality. A taxpayer has participated in a transaction with contractual protection if the taxpayer's tax return reflects a tax benefit from the transaction, and the taxpayer has the right to the full or partial refund of fees, or if the fees are contingent, see FTC 2d/FIN ¶ S-4427.4 *et seq.*; USTR ¶ 60,114.002; TaxDesk ¶ 817,002.

Under pre-Tax Increase Prevention Act law, no excise tax was imposed on a tax-exempt entity for being a party to a reportable transaction, or on the entity manager of a tax-exempt entity for approving the entity as a party to a reportable transaction.

New Law. Under the Tax Increase Prevention Act—

(1) If a transaction is a "prohibited tax shelter transaction" (as defined below) at the time any tax-exempt entity described in items (a), (b), or (c) of the "tax-exempt entity" list, below, becomes a party (see below) to the transaction, the entity must pay a tax for the tax year in which the entity becomes a party to the transaction, and any later tax year, in an amount determined as described below. (Code Sec. 4965(a)(1)(A) as added by Tax Increase Prevention Act §516(a)(1))

(2) If any tax-exempt entity described in items (a), (b), (c) of the "tax-exempt entity" list, below, is a party to a "subsequently listed transaction" (as defined below) at any time during a tax year, the entity must pay a tax for the tax year in an amount determined as described below. (Code Sec. 4965(a)(1)(B))

(3) If any "entity manager" (as defined below) of a tax-exempt entity approves the entity as (or otherwise causes the entity to be) a party to a prohibited tax shelter transaction at any time during the tax year, and the entity manager knows, or has reason to know (see below), that the transaction is a prohibited tax shelter transaction, the entity manager must pay a tax for the tax year in an amount determined as described below. (Code Sec. 4965(a)(2))

The taxes imposed under (1) and (2), above, are referred to as "entity level taxes." (Com Rept, see ¶ 5034)

Amount of the entity level taxes. The amount of the tax imposed on a tax-exempt entity that is a party to a prohibited tax shelter transaction depends on whether the tax-exempt entity knew, or had reason to know, that the transaction is a prohibited tax shelter transaction.

Amount of tax where the tax-exempt entity does not know, or have reason to know, that the transaction is a prohibited tax shelter transaction. In general, the amount of the entity level tax imposed for any transaction for a tax year is an amount equal to the product of—

- the highest unrelated business taxable income rate ((Com Rept, see ¶ 5034)) under Code Sec. 11, and
- the greater of—

... the entity's net income (after taking into account any tax imposed on the transaction, other than the tax imposed by new Code Sec. 4965) for the tax year which (a) for a prohibited tax shelter transaction (other than a subsequently listed transaction) is attributable to the transaction, or (b) for a subsequently listed transaction, is attributable to the transaction and is properly allocable to the period beginning on the later of (i) the date on which the transaction is identified by IRS guidance as a listed transaction, or (ii) the first day of the tax year, or

... 75% of the proceeds received by the entity for the tax year which (a) for a prohibited tax shelter transaction (other than a subsequently listed transaction) are attributable to the transaction, or (b) for a subsequently listed transaction, are attributable to the transaction and are properly allocable to the period beginning on the later of (i) the date on which the transaction is identified by IRS guidance as a listed transaction, or (ii) the first day of the tax year. (Code Sec. 4965(b)(1)(A))

Amount of the entity level tax where the tax-exempt entity knows, or has reason to know, that the transaction is a prohibited tax shelter transaction. For a tax-exempt entity which knew, or had reason to know, that a transaction was a prohibited tax shelter transaction at the time the entity became a party to the transaction, the amount of the entity level tax imposed under (1), above, for any transaction for a tax year is the greater of—

... 100% of the entity's net income (after taking into account any tax imposed on the prohibited tax shelter transaction, other than the tax imposed by new Code Sec. 4965) for the tax year which is attributable to the prohibited tax shelter transaction, or

... 75% of the proceeds received by the entity which are attributable to the prohibited tax shelter transaction. (Code Sec. 4965(b)(1)(B))

The entity level tax rate that applies if the entity knows, or has reason to know, that a transaction is a prohibited tax shelter transaction does not apply to—

. . . any prohibited tax shelter transaction to which a tax-exempt entity became a party on or before May 17, 2006, (Code Sec. 4965(b)(1)(B)) or to

. . . subsequently listed transactions. (Com Rept, see ¶ 5034)

Amount of the tax on an entity manager. The amount of the tax imposed on an entity manager who approves the entity as a party to a prohibited tax shelter transaction is $20,000 for each approval (or other act causing participation). (Code Sec. 4965(b)(2))

When an entity or entity manager knows, or has reason to know, that a transaction is a prohibited tax shelter transaction. In general, in order for an entity or entity manager to have reason to know that a transaction is a prohibited tax shelter transaction, the entity or entity manager must have knowledge of sufficient facts that would lead a reasonable person to conclude that the transaction is a prohibited tax shelter transaction. If there is justifiable reliance on a reasoned written opinion of legal counsel (including in-house counsel), or of an independent accountant with expertise in tax matters, after making full disclosure of relevant facts about a transaction to the counsel or accountant, that a transaction is not a prohibited tax shelter transaction, then, absent knowledge of facts not considered in the reasoned written opinion that would lead a reasonable person to conclude that the transaction is a prohibited tax shelter transaction, the "reason to know" standard is not met.

Not obtaining a reasoned written opinion of legal counsel does not, by itself, indicate whether a person has reason to know. However, if a transaction (1) is extraordinary for the entity, (2) promises a return for the organization that is exceptional considering the amount invested by, the participation of, or the absence of risk to the organization, or (3) is of significant size, either in an absolute sense or relative to the receipts of the entity, then, in general, the presence of those factors may indicate that the entity or entity manager has a responsibility to inquire further about whether a transaction is a prohibited tax shelter transaction, or, in the absence of such an inquiry, that the "reason to know" standard is satisfied.

For example, if a tax-exempt entity's investment in a transaction is $1,000, and the entity is promised or expects to receive $10,000 in the near term, in general, the rate of return would be considered exceptional and the entity should make inquiries about the transaction. As another example, if a tax-exempt entity's expected income from a transaction is greater than 5% of the entity's annual receipts, or exceeds $1 million, and the entity fails to make appropriate inquiries with respect to its participation in the transaction, the failure is a factor tending to show that the "reason to know" standard is met. Appropriate inquiries do not have to involve obtaining a reasoned written opinion.

In general, if a transaction does not present the factors described above and the organization is a small (measured by receipts and assets) Code

Sec. 501(c)(3) organization, it is expected that the "reason to know" standard will not be met. (Com Rept, see ¶ 5034)

When a tax-exempt entity is a party to a prohibited tax shelter transaction. In determining whether a tax-exempt entity is a "party" to a prohibited tax shelter transaction, all the facts and circumstances should be taken into account. Absence of a written agreement is not determinative. Certain indirect involvement in a prohibited tax shelter transaction would not result in an entity being considered a party to the transaction. For example, investment by a tax-exempt entity in a mutual fund that in turn invests in, or participates in, a prohibited tax shelter transaction does not, in general, make the tax-exempt entity a party to the transaction, in the absence of facts or circumstances indicating that the purpose of the tax exempt entity's investment in the mutual fund was specifically to participate in the transaction.

However, whether a tax-exempt entity is a party to a transaction will be informed by whether the entity or entity manager knew, or had reason to know, that an investment of the entity would be used in a prohibited tax shelter transaction. Presence of such knowledge or reason to know may indicate that the purpose of the investment was to participate in the prohibited tax shelter transaction, and that the tax-exempt entity is a party to the transaction. (Com Rept, see ¶ 5034)

"Tax-exempt entity" defined. For purposes of the Code Sec. 4965 excise taxes, the term "tax-exempt entity" means an entity which is—

(a) described in Code Sec. 501(c) (exempt organizations) or Code Sec. 501(d) (religious and apostolic organizations),

(b) described in Code Sec. 170(c) (charitable organizations other than an agency or instrumentality of the U.S.) to which item (a), above, does not apply,

(c) an Indian tribal government, within the meaning of Code Sec. 7701(a)(40),

(d) described in Code Sec. 4979(e)(1), Code Sec. 4979(e)(2), or Code Sec. 4979(e)(3), (i.e., a Code Sec. 401(a) plan, a Code Sec. 403(a) annuity plan, or a Code Sec. 403(b) annuity contract),

(e) a qualified tuition program described in Code Sec. 529,

(f) an eligible deferred compensation plan described in Code Sec. 457(b) which is maintained by an employer described in Code Sec. 4457(e)(1)(A) (sic; presumably, the reference should be to Code Sec. 457(e)(1)(A)) (i.e., a deferred compensation plan of a state or local government, or of a tax-exempt organization), or

---

FTC 2d References are to Federal Tax Coordinator 2d
FIN References are to RIA's Analysis of Federal Taxes: Income
USTR References are to United States Tax Reporter: Income, Estate & Gift, and Excise
PCA References are to Pension Analysis (print & electronic)
PE References are to the Pension Explanations (print & electronic)

(g) an arrangement described in Code Sec. 4973(a) (i.e., a Code Sec. 408(a) individual retirement account, a Code Sec. 220(d) Archer MSA, a Code Sec. 408(b) individual retirement annuity, a custodial account treated as an annuity contract under Code Sec. 403(b)(7)(A) (relating to custodial accounts for regulated investment company stock), a Code Sec. 530 Coverdell education savings account, or a Code Sec. 223(d) health savings account). (Code Sec. 4965(c))

> ***observation:*** As noted above, the entity level taxes do not apply to a tax-exempt entity described in items (d), (e), (f), and (g) of the list immediately above. Thus, the entity level taxes do not apply to qualified pension plans, IRAs, and similar tax-favored savings arrangements, such as Coverdell education savings accounts, health savings accounts, and qualified tuition plans. However, the excise tax imposed on entity managers applies to entity managers of *all* tax-exempt entities described in the list immediately above. Thus, if the entity manager of a qualified pension plan, IRA, or similar tax-favored savings arrangement approves the entity as (or otherwise causes the entity to be) a party to a prohibited tax shelter transaction, the entity manager is subject to the $20,000-per-approval excise tax.

"Entity manager" defined. For a tax-exempt entity described in items (a), (b), or (c) of the "tax-exempt entity defined" list above, the term "entity manager" means—

. . . the person with authority or responsibility similar to that exercised by an officer, director, or trustee of an organization, and

. . . for any act, the person having authority or responsibility for that act. (Code Sec. 4965(d)(1))

For a tax-exempt entity described in items (d), (e), (f), or (g) of the "tax-exempt entity defined" list above, the term "entity manager" means the person who approves or otherwise causes the entity to be a party to the prohibited tax shelter transaction. (Code Sec. 4965(d)(2))

For a qualified pension plan, IRA, or similar tax-favored savings arrangement (such as a Coverdell education savings account, health savings account, or qualified tuition plan), in general, a person who decides that the assets of the plan, IRA, or other savings arrangement are to be invested in a prohibited tax shelter transaction is the entity manager. Except for a fully self-directed plan or other savings arrangement for which a participant or beneficiary decides to invest in the prohibited tax shelter transaction, a participant or beneficiary generally is not an entity manager. Thus, for example, a participant or beneficiary is not an entity manager merely by reason of choosing among pre-selected investment options (as is typically the case if a qualified retirement plan provides for participant-directed investments). (Depending on the circumstances, the person who is responsible for determining the pre-selected investment options may be an entity manager.) Similarly, if an individual has an IRA and may choose among various mutual funds offered by the IRA trustee, but has no control over the investments held in the mutual funds, the individual is not an entity manager. (Com Rept, see ¶ 5034)

"Prohibited tax shelter transaction" defined as "listed transaction" and "prohibited reportable transaction". For purposes of the Code Sec. 4965 excise taxes, the term "prohibited tax shelter transaction" means—

. . . any "listed transaction" (as defined below), and

. . . any "prohibited reportable transaction" (as defined below). (Code Sec. 4965(e)(1)(A))

For this purpose—

. . . the term "listed transaction" has the meaning given to it by Code Sec. 6707A(c)(2), (Code Sec. 4965(e)(1)(B)) and

. . . the term "prohibited reportable transaction" means any confidential transaction or any transaction with contractual protection (as defined under regs to be prescribed by IRS) which is a reportable transaction, as defined in Code Sec. 6707A(c)(1). (Code Sec. 4965(e)(1)(C))

"Subsequently listed transaction" defined. For purposes of the Code Sec. 4965 excise taxes, the term "subsequently listed transaction" means any transaction to which a tax-exempt entity is a party, and which is determined by IRS to be a listed transaction at any time after the entity has become a party to the transaction. The term does not include a transaction which is a "prohibited reportable transaction" (see immediately above) at the time the entity became a party to the transaction. (Code Sec. 4965(e)(2))

Regs may provide guidance on the allocation of net income attributable to a transaction to various periods. IRS is authorized to issue regs which provide guidance on the allocation of a tax-exempt entity's net income or proceeds attributable to a transaction to various periods, including before and after the listing of the transaction, or the date which is 90 days after May 17, 2006 (see the effective date provision, below). (Code Sec. 4965(f))

Coordination with other taxes and penalties. The excise taxes imposed by Code Sec. 4965 apply in addition to any other tax, any addition to tax, or any penalty imposed under the Internal Revenue Code. (Code Sec. 4965(g))

FTC 2d References are to Federal Tax Coordinator 2d
FIN References are to RIA's Analysis of Federal Taxes: Income
USTR References are to United States Tax Reporter: Income, Estate & Gift, and Excise
PCA References are to Pension Analysis (print & electronic)
PE References are to the Pension Explanations (print & electronic)

For rules requiring a tax-exempt entity to disclose its participation in any prohibited tax shelter transaction to IRS, see ¶ 702.

For rules requiring any taxable party to a prohibited tax shelter transaction to disclose that tax shelter status to any tax-exempt entity that is a party to the transaction, see ¶ 703.

For penalties that are imposed on tax-exempt entities that fail to make the required disclosures with respect to prohibited tax shelter transactions, see ¶ 704.

☐ **Effective:** Tax years ending after May 17, 2006 (with respect to transactions occurring before, on, and after May 17, 2006), except that no Code Sec. 4965 tax applies to income or proceeds that are properly allocable to any period on or before the date which is 90 days after May 17, 2006. (Tax Increase Prevention Act §516(d)(1))

¶ 702. Tax-exempt entities must disclose participation in prohibited tax shelter transactions to IRS

Code Sec. 6033(a)(2), as amended by Tax Increase Prevention Act § 516(b)(1)(A)
Generally effective: Disclosures the due date for which is after May 17, 2006
Committee Reports, see ¶ 5034

Under pre-Tax Increase Prevention Act law, a taxpayer that participates in a reportable transaction (including a listed transaction) and that is required to file a tax return must attach to its return a disclosure statement. For this purpose, "taxpayer" includes any person, including an individual, trust, estate, partnership, association, company, or corporation.

A reportable transaction includes a listed transaction and four other categories of transactions: (1) confidential transactions, (2) transactions with contractual protection, (3) loss transactions, and (4) transactions involving a brief asset holding period. The fact that a transaction is a reportable transaction does not affect the legal determination of whether the taxpayer's treatment of the transaction is proper. IRS is authorized to define reportable transaction on the basis of the transaction being of a type which IRS determines as having a potential for tax avoidance or evasion, see FTC 2d/FIN ¶ S-4427.1 *et seq.*; USTR ¶ 60,114.02; TaxDesk ¶ 817,002.

> ***observation:*** The reporting requirement also applies to tax-exempt entities with unrelated business taxable income (UBTI), see FTC 2d/FIN ¶ S-4427.1; USTR ¶ 60,114.02.

A taxpayer has participated in a listed transaction if the taxpayer's tax return reflects tax consequences or a tax strategy described in the published guidance that lists the transaction, or if the taxpayer knows or has reason to know that the taxpayer's tax benefits are derived directly or indirectly from tax consequences or a tax strategy described in published guidance that lists a transaction. A taxpayer has participated in a confidential transaction if the taxpayer's tax return reflects a tax benefit from the transaction and the taxpayer's disclosure of the tax treatment or tax structure of the transaction is limited under conditions of confidentiality. A taxpayer has participated in a transaction with contractual protection if the taxpayer's tax return reflects a tax benefit from the transaction, and the taxpayer has the right to the full or partial refund of fees or the fees are contingent, see FTC 2d/FIN ¶ S-4427.4 *et seq.*; USTR ¶ 60,114.02; TaxDesk ¶ 817,002.

Under pre-Tax Increase Prevention Act law, a penalty is imposed on any person who fails to include on any return or statement any required information with respect to a reportable transaction. The penalty applies without regard to whether the transaction ultimately results in an understatement of tax, and applies in addition to any other penalty that may be imposed, see FTC 2d/FIN ¶ V-2531; USTR ¶ 67,074; TaxDesk ¶ 866,501.

Under pre-Tax Increase Prevention Act law, every material advisor for a tax shelter reportable transaction is required to file an information return with IRS identifying and describing the transaction and the potential tax benefits that are expected to be derived from the transaction. For this purpose, a material advisor is any person:

. . . who provides any material aid, assistance, or advice with respect to organizing, managing, promoting, selling, implementing, insuring, or carrying out any reportable transaction; and

. . . who directly or indirectly derives gross income in excess of a threshold amount (or such other amount prescribed by IRS) for that assistance or advice.

The threshold amount is:

. . . $50,000 for a reportable transaction substantially all of the tax benefits from which are provided to natural persons, and

. . . $250,000 in any other case, see FTC 2d/FIN ¶ S-4401.2; USTR ¶ 61,114; TaxDesk ¶ 817,003.

observation: A tax-exempt entity that meets the above tests is subject to the material advisor disclosure requirement.

New Law. Under the Tax Increase Prevention Act, every tax-exempt entity described in Code Sec. 4965(c), see ¶ 701, must file a disclosure of: (Code Sec. 6033(a)(2) as amended by Tax Increase Prevention Act §516(b)(1)(A))

. . . the entity's being a party to any prohibited tax shelter transaction defined in Code Sec. 4965(e), see ¶ 701, and (Code Sec. 6033(a)(2)(A))

. . . the identity of any other party participating in the transaction whose identity is known by the tax-exempt entity. (Code Sec. 6033(a)(2)(B))

For the excise tax that is imposed under Code Sec. 4965 on certain tax-exempt entities entering into prohibited transactions, see ¶ 701.

> ***observation:*** The required disclosure by a tax-exempt entity is related to enforcement of the excise tax described at ¶ 701.

The disclosure is to be made in the form and manner, and at the time determined by IRS. (Code Sec. 6033(a)(2))

For the penalty that is imposed for failure to make the disclosure required under the above rules, see ¶ 704.

For disclosure by taxable parties to a prohibited tax shelter transaction to a tax-exempt entity that is a party to the transaction, see ¶ 703.

Redesignation. Pre-Tax Increase Prevention Act Code Sec. 6033(a)(2) (which provides exceptions to the annual information return filing requirements for certain tax-exempt organizations, see FTC 2d/FIN ¶s S-2813 *et seq.*, S-2823 *et seq.*; USTR ¶ 60,334; TaxDesk ¶ 688,005) is redesignated as Code Sec. 6033(a)(3). (Tax Increase Prevention Act §516(b)(1)(A))

☐ **Effective:** Disclosures the due date for which are after May 17, 2006. (Tax Increase Prevention Act §516(d)(2))

¶ 703. Taxable parties to a prohibited tax shelter transaction must disclose that tax shelter status to any tax-exempt entity that is a party to the transaction

Code Sec. 6011(g), as amended by Tax Increase Prevention Act § 516(b)(2)
Generally effective: Disclosures the due date for which is after May 17, 2006
Committee Reports, see ¶ 5034

Under pre-Tax Increase Prevention Act law, a taxpayer that participates in a reportable transaction (including a listed transaction) and who is required to file a tax return must attach to its return a disclosure statement. For this purpose, "taxpayer" includes any person, including an individual, trust, estate, partnership, association, company, or corporation.

A reportable transaction includes a listed transaction and four other categories of transactions: (1) confidential transactions, (2) transactions with contractual protection, (3) loss transactions, and (4) transactions involving a brief asset holding period. The fact that a transaction is a reportable transaction does not affect the legal determination of whether the taxpayer's treatment of the transaction is proper. IRS is authorized to define reportable transaction on the basis of the transaction being of a type which IRS determines as having a potential for tax avoidance or evasion, see FTC 2d/FIN ¶ S-4427.1 *et seq.*; USTR ¶ 60,114.02; TaxDesk ¶ 817,002.

> ***observation:*** The reporting requirement also applies to tax-exempt entities with unrelated business taxable income (UBTI), see FTC 2d/FIN ¶ S-4427.1; USTR ¶ 60,114.02.

A taxpayer has participated in a listed transaction if the taxpayer's tax return reflects tax consequences or a tax strategy described in the published guidance that lists the transaction, or if the taxpayer knows or has reason to know that the taxpayer's tax benefits are derived directly or indirectly from tax consequences or a tax strategy described in published guidance that lists a transaction. A taxpayer has participated in a confidential transaction if the taxpayer's tax return reflects a tax benefit from the transaction and the taxpayer's disclosure of the tax treatment or tax structure of the transaction is limited under conditions of confidentiality. A taxpayer has participated in a transaction with contractual protection if the taxpayer's tax return reflects a tax benefit from the transaction, and the taxpayer has the right to the full or partial refund of fees or the fees are contingent, see FTC 2d/FIN ¶ S-4427.4 *et seq.*; USTR ¶ 60,114.002; TaxDesk ¶ 817,002.

Under pre-Tax Increase Prevention Act law, a penalty is imposed on any person who fails to include on any return or statement any required information with respect to a reportable transaction. The penalty applies without regard to whether the transaction ultimately results in an understatement of tax, and applies in addition to any other penalty that may be imposed, see FTC 2d/FIN ¶ V-2531; USTR ¶ 67,074; TaxDesk ¶ 866,501.

Under pre-Tax Increase Prevention Act law, every material advisor for a tax shelter reportable transaction is required to file an information return with IRS identifying and describing the transaction and the potential tax benefits that are expected to be derived from the transaction. For this purpose, a material advisor is any person:

. . . who provides any material aid, assistance, or advice with respect to organizing, managing, promoting, selling, implementing, insuring, or carrying out any reportable transaction; and

. . . who directly or indirectly derives gross income in excess of a threshold amount (or such other amount prescribed by IRS) for that assistance or advice.

The threshold amount is:

. . . $50,000 for a reportable transaction substantially all of the tax benefits from which are provided to natural persons, and

. . . $250,000 in any other case, see FTC 2d/FIN ¶ S-4401.2; USTR ¶ 61,114; TaxDesk ¶ 817,003.

> ***observation:*** A tax-exempt entity that meets the above tests is subject to the material advisor disclosure requirement.

A tax-exempt entity is subject to tax on unrelated trade or business income, i.e., income derived from any trade or business that is regularly carried on, and not substantially related to the organization's exempt purpose or function. The tax is generally imposed at the corporate income tax rate, see FTC 2d/FIN ¶ D-6801; USTR ¶ 5114; TaxDesk ¶ 681,001.

New Law. Under the Tax Increase Prevention Act, any taxable party to a prohibited tax shelter transaction, as defined in Code Sec. 4965(e)(1), see ¶ 701, must provide a statement to any tax-exempt entity which is a party to the transaction disclosing that the transaction is a prohibited tax shelter transaction. (Code Sec. 6011(g) as amended by Tax Increase Prevention Act §516(b)(2))

> ***observation:*** The requirement to provide a statement is imposed only on any *taxable party* to a prohibited tax shelter transaction. Thus, a tax-exempt entity that is a party to the transaction, and which does not have a tax liability as a result of unrelated business taxable income (UBTI), does not have to provide a statement to any other tax-exempt entity that is a party to the transaction.

For the excise tax that is imposed on certain tax-exempt entities entering into prohibited transactions, see ¶ 701.

For penalties that are imposed for failure to make a required disclosure, see ¶ 704.

For the requirement that tax-exempt entities disclose their participation in prohibited tax shelter transactions to IRS, see ¶ 702.

Redesignation. Pre-Tax Increase Prevention Act Code Sec. 6011(g) (which requires returns of income, estate, or gift tax to be made whether or not there is tax liability) is redesignated as Code Sec. 6011(h). (Tax Increase Prevention Act §516(b)(2))

☐ **Effective:** Disclosures the due date for which are after May 17, 2006. (Tax Increase Prevention Act §516(d)(2))

¶ 704. $100 per day penalties imposed where exempt organizations fail to make required disclosures to IRS relating to prohibited tax shelter transactions

Code Sec. 6652(c), as amended by Tax Increase Prevention Act § 516(c)
Generally effective: Disclosures the due date for which is after May 17, 2006
Committee Reports, see ¶ 5034

The 2004 Jobs Act added a tax shelter penalty under Code Sec. 6707A for any person who fails to include on any return or statement any information regarding a reportable transaction which is required under Code Sec. 6011 to be included with the return or statement. The penalty applies regardless of whether the transaction results in a tax understatement. The penalty also applies in addition to any other penalty that may be imposed under the Code. (FTC 2d/FIN ¶ V-2531; USTR ¶ 67,07A4; TaxDesk ¶ 866,501)

A "reportable transaction" for Code Sec. 6707A purposes means any transaction for which information must be included with a return or statement because, as determined under regs, the transaction is of a type that IRS determines as having a potential for tax avoidance or evasion. Regs describe five categories of reportable transactions. One category of reportable transactions is a transaction that is the same as (or substantially similar to) a transaction IRS has specified as a tax avoidance transaction and identified by notice, reg or other form of published guidance as a "listed transaction." The other four categories of reportable transactions are:

(1) A transaction that is offered under conditions of confidentiality and for which the taxpayer has paid an advisor a minimum fee.

(2) Transactions with contractual protection, including transactions for which the taxpayer has contractual protection against the possibility that part or all of the intended tax consequences from the transaction won't be sustained and transactions for which fees are contingent on realization of tax benefits.

FTC 2d References are to Federal Tax Coordinator 2d
FIN References are to RIA's Analysis of Federal Taxes: Income
USTR References are to United States Tax Reporter: Income, Estate & Gift, and Excise
PCA References are to Pension Analysis (print & electronic)
PE References are to the Pension Explanations (print & electronic)

(3) A transaction resulting in a taxpayer claiming a loss under Code Sec. 165 of at least (a) $10 million in any single year or $20 million in any combination of years by a corporate taxpayer or by a partnership that has only corporations as partners; (b) $2 million in any single year or $4 million in any combination of years by an individual, an S corporation, a trust, or a partnership that has noncorporate partners; or (c) $50,000 in any single year for individuals or trusts if the loss arises from foreign currency transaction losses.

(4) Any transaction that results in a tax credit exceeding $250,000 (including a foreign tax credit) if the taxpayer holds the underlying asset for less than 46 days. (FTC 2d/FIN ¶ V-2533; USTR ¶ 67,07A4; TaxDesk ¶ 866,503)

Penalties for failure to meet information reporting requirements are imposed on exempt organizations and certain other entities by Code Sec. 6652(c). No penalty is imposed under Code Sec. 6652(c) with respect to any failure if it is shown that the failure is due to reasonable cause. (FTC 2d/FIN ¶ V-1907; USTR ¶ 66,524)

New Law. The Tax Increase Prevention Act requires every tax-exempt entity described in Code Sec. 4965(c), to file a disclosure of its being a party to any prohibited tax shelter transaction and of the identity of any other party to the transaction which is known by the entity, see ¶ 702. In the case of a failure to file the disclosure statement, the tax-exempt entity (or the entity manager in the case of certain tax-exempt entities) must pay $100 for each day during which the failure continues. The maximum penalty on failures for any one disclosure is $50,000. (Code Sec. 6652(c)(3)(A) as amended by Tax Increase Prevention Act §516(c)(1))

> ***observation:*** For this purpose, a "prohibited tax shelter transaction" is defined in Code Sec. 4965(e), which refers to the Code Sec. 6707A(c)(2) definition of listed transaction and to certain reportable transactions. Thus, a prohibited tax shelter transaction is defined as: (a) any listed transaction, or (b) any "prohibited reportable transaction." A prohibited reportable transaction is any confidential transaction or any transaction with contractual protection (as defined under regs to be prescribed by IRS) which is a reportable transaction, see ¶ 701.

The entity manager is required to pay the penalty in the case of exempt entities described in (4), (5), (6), or (7) of Code Sec. 4965(c), see ¶ 701. (Code Sec. 6652(c)(3)(A))

> ***observation:*** Thus, the entity manager must pay the penalty in the case of:
>
> - an employee benefit plan under Code Sec. 401(a) that includes an exempt trust,
> - an annuity plan under Code Sec. 403(a),

- an annuity contract under Code Sec. 403(b),
- a qualified tuition program described in Code Sec. 529,
- certain Code Sec. 457(b) eligible deferred compensation plans, and
- an arrangement described in Code Sec. 4973(a) (relating to individual retirement accounts and annuities, Archer MSAs, custodial accounts for RICs, Coverdell education savings accounts, and HSAs).

observation: The manager also pays any Code Sec. 4965 excise tax relating to the entities listed above, see ¶ 701.

IRS may make a written demand on any entity or manager subject to the above penalty specifying a reasonable future date by which the disclosure will be filed. (Code Sec. 6652(c)(3)(B)(i)) If any entity or manager fails to comply with any such demand on or before the date specified in the demand, that entity or manager must pay $100 for each day after the expiration of the time specified in that demand during which the failure continues. The maximum penalty imposed under this rule on all entities and managers for failures regarding any one disclosure is $10,000. (Code Sec. 6652(c)(3)(B)(ii))

As under Code Sec. 6652 before amended by the Tax Increase Prevention Act, no penalty is imposed on any failure if it is shown that the failure is due to reasonable cause. (Com Rept, see ¶ 5034)

Any term used in Code Sec. 6652, which is also used in Code Sec. 4965, has the same meaning as that term has under Code Sec. 4965. (Code Sec. 6652(c)(3)(C))

observation: Thus, for example, an entity manager would be defined as in Code Sec. 4965, see ¶ 701.

☐ **Effective:** Disclosures the due dates for which are after May 17, 2006. (Tax Increase Prevention Act §516(d)(2))

¶ 800. Tax Payment, Withholding & Reporting

¶ 801. Tax-exempt interest is subject to information reporting in the same manner as interest paid on taxable obligations

Code Sec. 6049(b)(2)(B), as amended by Tax Increase Prevention Act § 502(a)
Generally effective: Interest paid after Dec. 31, 2005
Committee Reports, see ¶ 5021

Every person who makes payments of interest aggregating $10 or more or receives payments of interest as a nominee aggregating $10 or more must file an information return setting forth the amount of interest payments for the calendar year and the name, address, and TIN of the person to whom interest is paid (see FTC 2d/FIN ¶ S-3001; USTR ¶ 60,494.01; TaxDesk ¶ 811,501). Regs prescribe the form and manner for filing interest payment information returns. Regs require the reporting of the account or serial number, or other identifying information with respect to obligations on which interest is paid (see FTC 2d/FIN ¶ S-3011; USTR ¶ 60,494.01; TaxDesk ¶ 811,501). The regs also require that every person acting as a middleman (e.g., a broker) file information returns for the calendar year (see FTC 2d/FIN ¶ S-3008; USTR ¶ 60,494.01; TaxDesk ¶ 811,501). Penalties are imposed for failure to file interest payment information returns or payee statements (see FTC 2d/FIN ¶ V-1803; USTR ¶ 66,524; TaxDesk ¶ 861,025). The regs also impose recordkeeping requirements on persons required to file information returns (see FTC 2d/FIN ¶ G-2012; USTR ¶ 60,014).

Payments of interest are reported on Form 1099-INT, and Form 1096, Annual Summary and Transmittal of U.S. Information Returns. A copy of the information return must be mailed by the payor to the payee indicating the amount of interest paid for the tax year and contact information for the payor. See FTC 2d/FIN ¶ S-3002; USTR ¶ 60,494.01; TaxDesk ¶ 811,506.

Under pre-Tax Increase Prevention Act law, interest paid on tax-exempt bonds was exempt from interest reporting requirements. Thus, for example, payors of tax-exempt interest did not have to file annual information returns (Form 1099-INT) as payors of taxable interest were required to do. (FTC 2d/FIN ¶ S-3040; USTR ¶ 60,494.03; TaxDesk ¶ 811,501)

FTC 2d References are to Federal Tax Coordinator 2d
FIN References are to RIA's Analysis of Federal Taxes: Income
USTR References are to United States Tax Reporter: Income, Estate & Gift, and Excise
PCA References are to Pension Analysis (print & electronic)
PE References are to the Pension Explanations (print & electronic)

New Law. The Tax Increase Prevention Act eliminates the exception from information reporting by payors of tax-exempt interest. (Code Sec. 6049(b)(2)(B) as amended by Tax Increase Prevention Act §502(a))

Thus, interest paid on tax-exempt bonds is subject to information reporting in the same manner as interest paid on taxable obligations. (Com Rept, see ¶ 5021)

> ***observation:*** Thus, payors of tax-exempt interest will presumably have to file annual information returns.

> ***observation:*** The statute and the Committee Reports do not indicate whether tax-exempt interest is to be reported on Form 1099-INT, the same form used for information reporting for payments of taxable interest. Presumably, IRS will either instruct payors to use Form 1099-INT, or issue a new information reporting form for payors of tax-exempt interest.

> ***observation:*** The above rule will allow IRS to track both who is paying and who is receiving tax-exempt interest. All taxpayers are required to report the tax-exempt interest received or accrued for the tax year on their returns for that tax year (see FTC 2d/FIN ¶ J-3001.1; USTR ¶ 60,124; TaxDesk ¶ 158,003). Although this interest is not subject to federal income tax, it is necessary for other calculations, such as the taxable portion of Social Security benefits (see FTC 2d/FIN ¶ J-1459; USTR ¶ 864.02; TaxDesk ¶ 146,001) or the AMT preference for tax-exempt interest from private activity bonds (see FTC 2d/FIN ¶ A-8201; USTR ¶ 574; TaxDesk ¶ 696,501). Adherence to this reporting rule allows IRS to match the amount of tax-exempt interest being reported as received by taxpayers with that reported as paid by payors.

☐ **Effective:** Interest paid after Dec. 31, 2005. (Tax Increase Prevention Act §502(c))

¶ 802. Government entities will have to report and withhold income tax on certain payments made after 2010

Code Sec. 3402(t), as amended by Tax Increase Prevention Act § 511(a)
Generally effective: For payments made after Dec. 31, 2010
Committee Reports, see ¶ 5029

Employers are required to withhold income tax on wages paid to employees, including wages and salaries of employees or elected officials of federal, state, and local governments. (FTC 2d/FIN ¶ H-4486 *et seq.*; USTR ¶ 34,024 *et seq.*; TaxDesk ¶ 538,001 *et seq.*) Certain non-wage payments are also subject to mandatory or voluntary withholding. (FTC 2d/FIN ¶ H-4475 *et seq.*; USTR ¶ 34,024.25; TaxDesk ¶ 538,049) But other payments, including certain payments made by government entities, aren't subject to withholding. (FTC 2d/FIN ¶ H-4258 *et seq.*; USTR ¶ 34,014.37 *et seq.*; TaxDesk ¶ 535,007 *et seq.*)

Employers required to deduct and withhold tax from employees' income are subject to information reporting requirements. (FTC 2d/FIN ¶ S-3151 *et seq.*; USTR ¶ 60,514; TaxDesk ¶ 812,001) In addition, any service recipient engaged in a trade or business and paying for services is required to report payments totalling $600 or more. (FTC 2d/FIN ¶ S-3656 *et seq.*; USTR ¶ 60,414; TaxDesk ¶ 814,001)

Government entities are specifically required to make an information return, reporting certain payments to corporations as well as individuals. (FTC 2d/FIN ¶ H-4226 *et seq.*; USTR ¶ 34,044 *et seq.*; TaxDesk ¶ 534,001 *et seq.*) And the head of every federal executive agency that enters into certain contracts must file an information return with information regarding the contractor and the contract. (FTC 2d/FIN ¶ S-3679 *et seq.*; USTR ¶ 60,50M4.01; TaxDesk ¶ 816,014)

New Law. Under the Tax Increase Prevention Act, beginning in 2011 (Tax Increase Prevention Act §511(b)), the federal government and the government of every state, political subdivision of a state, and instrumentality of a state or state subdivision (including multi-state agencies) making certain payments to a person providing any property or services will have to deduct and withhold tax from that payment in an amount equal to 3% of the payment. The withholding requirement will also apply to a payment made in connection with a government voucher or certificate program that functions as a payment for property or services. (Code Sec. 3402(t)(1) as amended by Tax Increase Prevention Act §511(a)) The withholding requirement will apply regardless of whether the government entity making the payment is the recipient of the property or services. For example, payments to a commodity producer under a government commodity support program will be subject to the withholding requirement. (Com Rept, see ¶ 5029)

> ***observation:*** Presumably, the new rules are intended, in part, to address the perceived problem of government contractors not paying taxes.

Payments not subject to withholding The new withholding rules won't apply to payments of wages or to any other payment with respect to which mandatory (e.g., U.S.-source income of foreign taxpayers, see (A), below) or voluntary (e.g., unemployment benefits) withholding applies. (Com Rept, see ¶ 5029)

The Tax Increase Prevention Act provides that withholding under the new rules won't apply to any payment:

(A) except as provided in (B), below, that is subject to withholding under any other Code provision of chapter 3 (dealing with withholding on nonresident aliens and foreign corporations, see FTC 2d/FIN ¶ O-11900 *et seq.*; USTR ¶ 14,414 *et seq.*; TaxDesk ¶ 634,000 *et seq.*), or Chapter 24 (dealing with collection of income tax at source on wages, see FTC 2d/FIN ¶ H-4486 *et seq.*; USTR ¶ 34,024 *et seq.*; TaxDesk ¶ 538,001 *et seq.*) (Code Sec. 3402(t)(2)(A))

(B) that is subject to backup withholding under Code Sec. 3406 and from which amounts are being withheld under that section. (Code Sec. 3402(t)(2)(B)) Thus, payments that are potentially subject to backup withholding under Code Sec. 3406 won't be excluded from withholding under the new rules unless the payments are actually being withheld under backup withholding. (Com Rept, see ¶ 5029)

(C) of interest (Code Sec. 3402(t)(2)(C))

(D) for real property (Code Sec. 3402(t)(2)(D))

(E) to any governmental entity subject to the new withholding rules, any tax-exempt entity, or any foreign government (Code Sec. 3402(t)(2)(E))

(F) made under a classified or confidential contract described in section Code Sec. 6050M(e)(3), see FTC 2d/FIN ¶ S-3683; USTR ¶ 60,41A4; TaxDesk ¶ 816,014 (Code Sec. 3402(t)(2)(F))

(G) made by a political subdivision of a state (or any state instrumentality) that makes less than $100 million of these payments annually (Code Sec. 3402(t)(2)(G))

(H) that is made in connection with a public assistance or public welfare program for which eligibility is determined by a needs or income test. (Code Sec. 3402(t)(2)(H)). For example, payments under government programs providing food vouchers or medical assistance to low-income individuals won't be subject to withholding under the new rules. However, payments under government programs to provide health care or other services that aren't based on the recipients' needs or income will be subject to withholding, including programs where eligibility is based on the beneficiary's age. (Com Rept, see ¶ 5029)

(I) to any government employee not otherwise excludable with respect to his services as an employee. (Code Sec. 3402(t)(2)(I))

Information reporting requirements and liability for withholding tax Payments to any person for property or services that are subject to withholding will be treated as if those payments were wages paid by an employer to an employee for purposes of:

. . . Code Sec. 3403, dealing with liability for withholding tax (FTC 2d/FIN ¶ H-4222 *et seq.*; USTR ¶ 34,034 *et seq.*; TaxDesk ¶ 531,002 *et seq.*);

. . . Code Sec. 3404, dealing with return and payment requirements for government employers (FTC 2d/FIN ¶ H-4226 *et seq.*; USTR ¶ 34,044 *et seq.*; TaxDesk ¶ 534,001 *et seq.*); and

. . . so much of subtitle F (dealing with procedure and administration, see FTC 2d/FIN ¶ J-9100 *et seq.*; USTR ¶ 60,414 *et seq.*; TaxDesk ¶ 814,001 *et seq.*) (except Code Sec. 7205, see FTC 2d/FIN ¶ V-4106; USTR ¶ 72,054; TaxDesk ¶ 554,012) as relates to chapter 24 of the Code. (Code Sec. 3402(t)(3))

Thus, payments subject to withholding under the new rules will also be subject to information reporting requirements. (Com Rept, see ¶ 5029)

☐ **Effective:** Payments made after Dec. 31, 2010. (Tax Increase Prevention Act §511(b))

¶ 803. Percentages and due dates of otherwise required estimated tax payments due from corporations are changed for some installment due dates in 2006, and 2010 to 2013

Code Sec. 6655, Tax Increase Prevention Act § 401
Generally effective: May 17, 2006
Committee Reports, see ¶ 5018

Under pre-Tax Increase Prevention Act law, corporations are generally required to make quarterly estimated tax payments of their income tax liability. Generally, each payment must be at least 25% of the required annual payment. The required annual payment is generally the lesser of 100% of the current year's tax or 100% of the tax for the preceding year.

A calendar year corporation's estimated tax installments are required to be paid in four installments no later than Apr. 15, June 15, Sept. 15 and Dec. 15. For corporations with tax years beginning on any date other than Jan. 1 (i.e., corporations with fiscal years), there is substituted, for the months set forth above, the months that correspond thereto; that is, the due dates for installment payments are on the 15th day of the fourth, sixth, ninth, and twelfth months, respectively, of the corporation's fiscal tax year. If any due date falls on a Saturday, Sunday, or legal holiday, the due date is extended to the next succeeding day which is not a Saturday, Sunday, or legal holiday.

> ***illustration (1):*** If a corporation uses a fiscal year beginning on Apr. 1, Year 1, the due dates for its installment payments are July 15, Sept.

FTC 2d References are to Federal Tax Coordinator 2d
FIN References are to RIA's Analysis of Federal Taxes: Income
USTR References are to United States Tax Reporter: Income, Estate & Gift, and Excise
PCA References are to Pension Analysis (print & electronic)
PE References are to the Pension Explanations (print & electronic)

15, and Dec. 15 of Year 1, and Mar. 15 of Year 2. A corporation with a fiscal year beginning on July 1, Year 1 must make the first two estimated tax payments by Oct. 15, Year 1 and Dec. 15, Year 1. The third and fourth payments are due Mar. 15 and June 15 of Year 2.

observation: July 15, 2006 falls on a Saturday. Thus, estimated tax payments otherwise due on that date are timely if made by the following Monday, July 17, 2006.

observation: Penalties may apply to estimated tax payments that are not paid in full by the due date.

Congress has on occasion accelerated or delayed the due date of all or part of an installment payment. It has also increased or decreased the percentage of the required annual payment for particular payments. Thus, for example, the installment payment that was otherwise due in Sept. 2001 was not due until Oct. 1, 2001. Similarly, for a corporate estimated tax installment that otherwise was due in Sept. 2004, 20% of the amount of that estimated tax installment was not due until Oct. 1, 2004. As a result, for the corporate estimated tax payments that were otherwise due on Sept. 15, 2004, only 80% had to be paid by Sept. 15, 2004. (FTC 2d/FIN ¶ S-5353; USTR ¶ 66,554; TaxDesk ¶ 609,201)

New Law. The Tax Increase Prevention Act changes the amount and timing of certain estimated tax payments for certain large corporations. The Tax Increase Prevention Act also changes the amount and timing of estimated tax payments of *all* corporations otherwise due in 2010 and 2011. (Tax Increase Prevention Act §401)

Estimated tax payments for large ($1 billion or more in assets) corporations. Under the Tax Increase Prevention Act, for a corporation with assets of $1 billion or more (determined as of the end of the preceding tax year) (Tax Increase Prevention Act §401(1)), the amount of any required installment of corporate estimated tax that is otherwise due in July, Aug., or Sept. of 2006 is 105% of that amount. (Tax Increase Prevention Act §401(1)(A)) The amount of the next required installment after an installment due in the months described above is appropriately reduced to reflect the amount of the increase to 105% in the earlier installment. (Tax Increase Prevention Act §401(1)(D))

observation: The net effect of these changes is to increase by 5% the amount of the estimated tax installment due in July, Aug., or Sept. of 2006, and reduce the next installment payment by the same dollar amount.

illustration (2): The required annual payment of Corp X, a calendar year taxpayer which has assets of more than $1 billion, is $500 million for 2006. X made estimated tax payments of $125 million each on Apr.

15 and June 15, 2006. X is required to make an estimated tax payment of $131.25 million (i.e., 105% of $125 million) by Sept. 15, 2006, and reduces its Dec. 15, 2006 payment appropriately, i.e., to $118.75 million ($125 million – $6.25 million).

observation: The required annual payment of Corp X in the above example remains unchanged, i.e., $500 million. The effect of the Tax Increase Protection Act is to shift 5% ($6.25 million) of the required installment that otherwise would have to be paid by Dec. 15, 2006 to the required installment due on Sept. 15, 2006.

observation: A corporation with a fiscal year beginning on Apr. 1, 2006 has to make required installment payments in July 2006 and in Sept. 2006. Thus, in the case of a large corporation, both of those payments would presumably have to be for 105% of the required amount. However, under Tax Increase Prevention Act §401(1)(D), the Sept. payment is presumably reduced by the amount of the increase in the July payment. Thus, apparently, the Sept. payment would be 100% of the required amount.

illustration (3): The required annual payment of Corp Y, a large corporation, for its fiscal year that began on Apr. 1, 2006, is $800 million. The first required installment, due July 17, 2006 (because July 15 is a Saturday), is $210 million ($200 million × 105%). The second required installment, due Sept. 15, is presumably $200 million ($200 million × 105% = $210 million, which is reduced by the $10 million increase in the July installment under Tax Increase Prevention Act §401(1)(A)). The third required installment, due Dec. 15, is presumably $190 million ($200 million reduced by the $10 million increase in the Sept. payment under Tax Increase Prevention Act §401(1)(A)).

observation: Large corporations with a fiscal year that begins July 1, 2006 are not affected by these rules because they do not have any estimated tax payments due in July, Aug., or Sept. of 2006.

illustration (4): Corp Z has a fiscal year beginning on July 1 and ending on June 30. The final installment of Z's estimated tax for the 2005/2006 fiscal year is due on June 15, 2006. The first installment of the 2006/2007 estimated tax isn't due until Oct. 15, 2006.

observation: A major consequence of this change is to increase government revenue for its fiscal year ending Sept. 30, 2006 with an equivalent reduction in fiscal 2007 revenue.

For corporations with assets of $1 billion or more (determined as of the end of the preceding tax year): (Tax Increase Prevention Act §401(1))

. . . the amount of any required installment of corporate estimated that is otherwise due in July, Aug., or Sept. of 2012 is 106.25% of that amount, (Tax Increase Prevention Act §401(1)(B))

. . . the amount of any required installment of corporate estimated that is otherwise due in July, Aug., or Sept. of 2013 is 100.75% of that amount, (Tax Increase Prevention Act §401(1)(C)) and

. . . the amount of the next required installment after the installment in Tax Increase Prevention Act §401(1)(B) or Tax Increase Prevention Act §401(1)(C), above, is appropriately reduced to reflect the amount of the increase in the earlier installment. (Tax Increase Prevention Act §401(1)(D))

Estimated tax changes affecting all corporations. For any required installment of corporate estimated tax that is otherwise due in Sept. 2010, 20.5% of the amount of that installment is not due until Oct. 1, 2010. (Tax Increase Prevention Act §401(2))

illustration (5): The required installment of ABC Corp's estimated tax that is due on Sept. 15, 2010 is $300,000. ABC must pay $238,500 (79.5% of $300,000) by Sept. 15, 2010. The remaining $61,500 (20.5% of $300,000) is due Oct. 1, 2010.

For any required installment of corporate estimated tax that is otherwise due in Sept. 2011, 27.5% of the amount of that installment is not due until Oct. 1, 2011. (Tax Increase Prevention Act §401(3))

illustration (6): The required installment of DEF Corp's estimated tax that is due on Sept. 15, 2011 is $200,000. DEF must pay $145,000 (72.5% of $200,000) by Sept. 15, 2011. The remaining $55,000 (27.5% of $200,000) is due Oct. 1, 2011.

observation: The changes in due dates for a portion of the installments due on Sept. 15, 2010 and Sept. 15, 2011 will affect corporations using:

. . . a calendar year (the third installment of estimated tax is due Sept. 15);

. . . a fiscal year ending Mar. 30 (the second installment of estimated tax is due Sept. 15);

. . . a fiscal year ending May 30 (the first installment of estimated tax is due Sept. 15); and

. . . a fiscal year ending Sept. 30 (the fourth installment of estimated tax is due Sept. 15).

The due dates for other estimated tax payments aren't changed by this Tax Increase Prevention Act provision.

☐ **Effective:** May 17, 2006. (Com Rept, see ¶ 5018)

¶ 804. Partial payments are required with submissions of offers in compromise; offers are deemed accepted if not rejected within a certain period

Code Sec. 7122(c), as amended by Tax Increase Prevention Act § 509(a)
Code Sec. 7122(c)(3), as amended and redesignated by Tax Increase Prevention Act § 509
Code Sec. 7122(f), as amended by Tax Increase Prevention Act § 509(b)(2)
Generally effective: Offers in compromise submitted on and after the date that is 60 days after May 17, 2006
Committee Reports, see ¶ 5027

IRS has the authority to settle a tax debt under an offer in compromise. (FTC 2d/FIN ¶ T-9601; USTR ¶ 71,224.01; TaxDesk ¶ 842,001) Under pre-Tax Increase Prevention Act law, offers proposing to compromise tax liabilities weren't required to include partial payment of the tax proposed to be compromised. (FTC 2d/FIN ¶ T-9612; USTR ¶ 71,224.03; TaxDesk ¶ 842,012) An offer wasn't deemed to be accepted merely because IRS hadn't rejected it. (FTC 2d/FIN ¶ T-9618, ¶ T-9620; USTR ¶ 71,224.03; TaxDesk ¶ 842,022) And a user fee was imposed on a taxpayer entering into an offer in compromise. (FTC 2d/FIN ¶ T-10024; USTR ¶ 71,224.03; TaxDesk ¶ 901,006)

New Law. The Tax Increase Prevention Act adds a requirement that any *lump-sum* offer in compromise must be accompanied by the payment of 20% of the amount of the offer. (Code Sec. 7122(c)(1)(A)(i) as amended by Tax Increase Prevention Act §509(a)) For this purpose, a lump-sum offer in compromise is any offer of payment made in five or fewer installments. (Code Sec. 7122(c)(1)(A)(ii))

Any *periodic payment* offer in compromise must be accompanied by the payment of the amount of the first proposed installment. (Code Sec.

FTC 2d References are to Federal Tax Coordinator 2d
FIN References are to RIA's Analysis of Federal Taxes: Income
USTR References are to United States Tax Reporter: Income, Estate & Gift, and Excise
PCA References are to Pension Analysis (print & electronic)
PE References are to the Pension Explanations (print & electronic)

7122(c)(1)(B)(i)) IRS will treat any failure to make an installment (other than the first installment) due under a periodic payment offer in compromise while the offer is being evaluated by IRS as a withdrawal of the offer. (Code Sec. 7122(c)(1)(B)(ii))

> ***observation:*** The requirement that a taxpayer continue to make installment payments under the offer doesn't appear to apply to lump-sum offers of five or fewer installments under Code Sec. 7122(c)(1)(A).

Any offer in compromise (whether lump-sum or periodic payment) that isn't accompanied by the required payment will be returned to the taxpayer as unprocessable. (Code Sec. 7122(d)(3)(C) as amended and redesignated by Tax Increase Prevention Act §509)

> ***observation:*** The partial payment requirement may make it difficult (and in some cases impossible) for a taxpayer to file an offer in compromise.

The taxpayer can specify the application of any payment made under the above rules to the assessed tax or to other amounts (i.e., penalties or interest) imposed with respect to that tax. (Code Sec. 7122(c)(2)(A))

> ***recommendation:*** The application of any partial payment won't matter if the offer is accepted, but it might if the offer is rejected. To prepare for that possibility, if the offer is being made with respect to more than one tax year, the taxpayer should consider applying any payments made under the offer to more recent years, rather than to those nearing the expiration of the limitation period for collection. This will avoid having the payments credited to a tax liability that might be rendered uncollectible by the running of the statute of limitations.

An offer in compromise is deemed to be accepted by IRS if IRS doesn't reject it within 24 months after the offer is submitted. For this purpose, any period during which any tax liability that's the subject of an offer in compromise is in dispute in any judicial proceeding isn't taken into account in determining the expiration of the 24-month period. (Code Sec. 7122(f) as amended by Tax Increase Prevention Act §509(b)(2))

Any assessed tax or other amounts (i.e., interest or penalties) imposed with respect to a tax that is the subject of an offer in compromise subject to the above rules will be reduced by any user fee imposed with respect to that offer in compromise. (Code Sec. 7122(c)(2)(B))

> ***observation:*** Under this rule, the user fee is applied *against* the underlying tax, interest, or penalties, and thus is not imposed *in addition* to those amounts.

IRS is authorized to issue regs waiving any payment required under Code Sec. 7122(c)(1), consistent with the practices established in accordance with the Code Sec. 7122(d)(3) requirements (Code Sec. 7122(c)(2)(C)), which deal with offers filed by low-income taxpayers or based only on doubt as to liability. (FTC 2d/FIN ¶ T-9627; USTR ¶ 71,224.05; TaxDesk ¶ 842,027)

☐ **Effective:** Offers in compromise submitted on and after the date that's 60 days after May 17, 2006. (Tax Increase Prevention Act §509(d))

FTC 2d References are to Federal Tax Coordinator 2d
FIN References are to RIA's Analysis of Federal Taxes: Income
USTR References are to United States Tax Reporter: Income, Estate & Gift, and Excise
PCA References are to Pension Analysis (print & electronic)
PE References are to the Pension Explanations (print & electronic)

¶ 900. Tax-Exempt Bonds

¶ 901. Allowance of additional $10 million capital expenditures (i.e., $20 million total maximum) for small issue bonds generally is accelerated to bonds issued after 2006 (instead of Sept. 30, 2009)

Code Sec. 144(a)(4)(G), as amended by Tax Increase Prevention Act § 208(a)
Code Sec. 144(a)(4)(F), as amended by Tax Increase Prevention Act § 208(b)
Generally effective: May 17, 2006 for bonds issued after Dec. 31, 2006
Committee Reports, see ¶ 5012

Interest on certain "small issue" bonds is exempt from federal income tax if at least 95% of the issue's net proceeds are used to finance the acquisition, construction, reconstruction, or improvement of depreciable property or land (other than to provide real property for family units) and certain financing limits are met. Generally, no more than $1 million of small issue bond financing may be outstanding at any time for property of a business (including related parties) located in the same municipality or county (see FTC 2d/FIN ¶ J-3227; USTR ¶ 1444.01). This limit may be increased to $10 million (at the issuer's election), but only if all other same-municipality-or-county capital expenditures (except specified capital expenditures) made over the six-year period that starts three years before the issue date of the bonds and ends three years after that date—and not financed by the issues taken into account—are counted toward that limit. Thus, where the $10 million small issue bond limit is elected, the amount of same-municipality-or-county capital expenditures made (from other financing) during the six-year measurement period can't exceed $10 million. (See FTC 2d/FIN ¶s J-3233, J-3236; USTR ¶ 1444.01.)

An additional $10 million of capital expenditures is allowed (because those expenditures aren't taken into account in applying the $10 million limit), in effect increasing the maximum allowable amount of total same-county-or-municipality capital expenditures to $20 million, but only for issues where 95% or more of the net proceeds are used to provide facilities with respect to which an urban development action grant (UDAG) has been made. The 2004 Jobs Act (Sec. 340, PL 108-357, 10/22/2004) expanded the allowance of the additional $10 million capital expenditures to all small issue bonds (i.e., not just UDAG financings). Under pre-Tax Increase Prevention Act law, the "general" allow-

FTC 2d References are to Federal Tax Coordinator 2d
FIN References are to RIA's Analysis of Federal Taxes: Income
USTR References are to United States Tax Reporter: Income, Estate & Gift, and Excise
PCA References are to Pension Analysis (print & electronic)
PE References are to the Pension Explanations (print & electronic)

ance of the additional $10 million capital expenditures (i.e., the $20 million total capital expenditures maximum) was to go into effect for bonds issued after Sept. 30, 2009. (FTC 2d/FIN ¶ J-3233.1, ¶ J-3233.2; USTR ¶ 1444.01)

New Law. The Tax Increase Prevention Act accelerates the application of the $20 million capital expenditures limitation for small issue bonds generally from bonds issued after Sept. 30, 2009, to bonds issued after Dec. 31, 2006. (Com Rept, see ¶ 5012) That is, with respect to bonds issued after Dec. 31, 2006 (instead of bonds issued after Sept. 30, 2009), in addition to the capital expenditures described in Code Sec. 144(a)(4)(C) (i.e., the "specified capital expenditures" that aren't counted in applying the $10 million limit, see below), capital expenditures of up to $10 million won't be taken into account in applying the $10 million small issue bond limit. (Code Sec. 144(a)(4)(G) as amended by Tax Increase Prevention Act §208(a))

> ***observation:*** The $20 million maximum allowable amount of capital expenditures consists of: (1) the $10 million counted in applying the $10 million small issue bond limit, plus (2) the $10 million that isn't taken into account in applying that limit.

> ***observation:*** In other words, the pre-Tax Increase Prevention Act law rule that permitted an additional $10 million of capital expenditures (because those expenditures aren't taken into account in applying the $10 million small issue bond limit) for issues used to provide UDAG-financed facilities will—for bonds issued after Dec. 31, 2006—apply to small issue bonds generally. However, the bond still must qualify as a small issue bond. That is, at least 95% or more of the issue's net proceeds must be used to finance the acquisition, construction, reconstruction, or improvement of land or depreciable property (see FTC 2d/FIN ¶ J-3227; USTR ¶ 1444.01).

> ***observation:*** Code Sec. 144(a)(4)(C) describes capital expenditures that are: (1) to replace property destroyed or damaged by casualty, (2) required by a post-issuance law change, (3) required by circumstances not reasonably foreseen on the issue date or arising out of a mistake of law or fact, and (4) certain in-house research expenses the taxpayer elects to deduct currently (see FTC 2d/FIN ¶ J-3236; J-3237; USTR ¶ 1444.01). The capital expenditures that aren't taken into account in applying the $10 million small issue bond limit are $10 million of capital expenditures that don't fall into those four categories. Because these $10 million "other" capital expenses don't enter into the determination as to whether a bond issue has exceeded the $10 million small issue bond limit, they won't preclude the bond issue from being a qualified small bond issue.

The Tax Increase Prevention Act also accelerates the termination of the rule that allows an additional $10 million of capital expenditures (because those expenditures aren't taken into account in applying the $10 million limit) specifically for issues where 95% or more of the net proceeds are used to finance UDAG facilities, so that it won't apply to bonds issued after Dec. 31, 2006 (instead of Sept. 30, 2009). (Code Sec. 144(a)(4)(F) as amended by Tax Increase Prevention Act §208(b))

> ***observation:*** The allowance of $10 million additional capital expenditures will apply to small issue bonds generally (which include bonds used 95% to finance UDAG facilities), for bonds issued after Dec. 31, 2006. The specific rule for issues used to finance urban action grant facilities won't be necessary.

The Tax Increase Prevention Act doesn't change the rule that no more than $10 million of bond financing may be outstanding at any time for property of an eligible business (including related parties) located in the same municipality or county. (Com Rept, see ¶ 5012)

The Tax Increase Prevention Act also doesn't change the rule limiting the outstanding aggregate borrowing to $40 million per borrower (including related parties) regardless of where the property is located (see FTC 2d/FIN ¶ J-3238; USTR ¶ 1444.01). (Com Rept, see ¶ 5012)

☐ **Effective:** May 17, 2006 for bonds issued after Dec. 31, 2006. (Com Rept, see ¶ 5012)

FTC 2d References are to Federal Tax Coordinator 2d
FIN References are to RIA's Analysis of Federal Taxes: Income
USTR References are to United States Tax Reporter: Income, Estate & Gift, and Excise
PCA References are to Pension Analysis (print & electronic)
PE References are to the Pension Explanations (print & electronic)

¶ 902. Pooled financing bonds must meet requirements relating to loan origination, written loan commitments, and redemptions, and are counted in applying small issuer exception to arbitrage rebate requirements

Code Sec. 149(f)(2)(A), as amended by Tax Increase Prevention Act § 508(a)
Code Sec. 149(f)(4), as amended by Tax Increase Prevention Act § 508(b)
Code Sec. 149(f)(5), as amended by Tax Increase Prevention Act § 508(b)
Code Sec. 148(f)(4)(D)(ii), as amended by Tax Increase Prevention Act § 508(c)
Code Sec. 149(f)(1), as amended by Tax Increase Prevention Act § 508(d)(1)
Generally effective: Bonds issued after May 17, 2006
Committee Reports, see ¶ 5026

Interest on bonds issued by state and local governments isn't exempt from federal income tax unless the bond meets the requirements for tax-exempt bonds generally (including the arbitrage restrictions, see below), and the applicable requirements for the specific type of bond issue, e.g., the specific requirements for pooled financing bonds. (See FTC 2d/FIN ¶ J-3001 *et seq.*; TG ¶ 158,001 *et seq.*; USTR ¶ 1034)

Pooled financing bonds are issues of more than $5 million where the proceeds are used to provide financing for the benefit of a third party (a "conduit party" or "ultimate borrower"), unless the conduit loans are to be used to finance a single project. Under pre-Tax Increase Prevention Act law, pooled financing bonds had to meet only these two specific requirements to be tax-exempt (FTC 2d/FIN ¶ J-3664; USTR ¶ 1494.05):

(1) the "reasonable expectations" requirement—i.e., the issuer must reasonably expect that at least 95% of the net proceeds will be lent to ultimate borrowers by the end of the third year after the date of issue (see FTC 2d/FIN ¶ J-3665; USTR ¶ 1494.05); and

(2) the "cost of issuance" requirement—i.e., all legal and underwriting costs associated with the issuance of the bonds may not be contingent, and must be substantially paid within 180 days of the date of issuance (see FTC 2d/FIN ¶ J-3666; USTR ¶ 1494.05).

An arbitrage bond is any bond that is part of an issue if any proceeds of the issue are reasonably expected to be (or intentionally are) used to acquire higher yielding investments. However, if the arbitrage profits—the amounts earned from investing the bond proceeds in investments that have a materially higher yield than the bonds and are unrelated to the governmental purpose of the financing—are rebated to the U.S., the bond will be tax-exempt. (See FTC 2d/FIN ¶ J-3431; USTR ¶ 1484.04; TaxDesk ¶ 158,013.)

Under a "small issuer exception," the above-described arbitrage rebate requirement is treated as satisfied for an issue issued by a governmental unit with general taxing powers, if the aggregate face amount of all tax-exempt bonds (other than "private activity bonds" issued to finance certain activities of private persons) issued by the unit during the calendar year of the issue is not reasonably expected, as of the issue date, to exceed $5 million, and certain other requirements are met. Pre-Tax Increase Prevention Act law provided that, in the case of a pooled financing bond where the ultimate borrowers were governmental units with general taxing powers not subordinate to the issuer of the pooled bond, the pooled bond didn't count against the issuer's $5 million limitation, as long as the issuer wasn't a borrower from the pooled bond. However, the issuer remained subject to the arbitrage rebate requirement for unloaned proceeds. (Com Rept, see ¶ 5026) (FTC 2d/FIN ¶ J-3462; USTR ¶ 1484.04)

New Law. The Tax Increase Prevention Act imposes new requirements on pooled financing bonds as a condition of tax exemption, with respect to loan origination expectations, loan commitments, redemption requirement, and the small issuer exception to the arbitrage rebate requirement. (Com Rept, see ¶ 5026)

Loan origination expectations. The Tax Increase Prevention Act imposes new reasonable expectations requirement for loan originations. (Com Rept, see ¶ 5026)

For the reasonable expectation requirements to be met with respect to an issue, the issuer must reasonably expect that (Code Sec. 149(f)(2)(A) as amended by Tax Increase Prevention Act §508(a)), as of the close of the one-year period beginning on the date of issuance of the issue, at least 30% of the net proceeds of the issue (as of the close of the period) will have been used directly or indirectly to make or finance loans to ultimate borrowers. (Code Sec. 149(f)(2)(A)(i))

This means that the issuer must reasonably expect that at least 30% of the net proceeds of the pooled financing bond will be lent to ultimate borrowers one year after the date of issue. This is in addition to the three-year reasonable expectations requirement that at least 95% of the net proceeds will be lent to ultimate borrowers by the end of the third year after the date of issue. (Com Rept, see ¶ 5026)

FTC 2d References are to Federal Tax Coordinator 2d
FIN References are to RIA's Analysis of Federal Taxes: Income
USTR References are to United States Tax Reporter: Income, Estate & Gift, and Excise
PCA References are to Pension Analysis (print & electronic)
PE References are to the Pension Explanations (print & electronic)

> ***observation:*** Thus, the issuer must meet two separate "reasonable expectations" tests as to the use, at different times, of specific percentages of the issue proceeds:
>
> (1) The one-year/30% test. This first test relates to the issuer's reasonable expectations for how at least 30% of the issue proceeds will be used by the end of the first year after the issuance, i.e., by the end of the one-year loan origination period.
>
> (2) The three-year/95% test. This second test relates to the issuer's reasonable expectations for how at least 95% of the issue proceeds will be used by the end of the third year after the issuance, i.e., by the end of the three-year loan origination period.

An issuer's past experience regarding loan origination is a criterion upon which the reasonableness of its expectations can be based. (Com Rept, see ¶ 5026)

For the requirement to use bond proceeds that aren't loaned within the one- and three-year loan origination periods to redeem outstanding bonds, see "Redemption Requirement," below.

Written loan commitment requirements—borrower identification. The Tax Increase Prevention Act imposes a written loan commitment requirement to restrict the issuance of pooled bonds where potential borrowers have not been identified ("blind pools"). (Com Rept, see ¶ 5026)

The written loan commitment requirement is met with respect to an issue if the issuer receives written loan commitments identifying the ultimate potential borrowers of at least 30% of the net proceeds of the issue, before the issuance. (Code Sec. 149(f)(4)(A) as amended by Tax Increase Prevention Act §508(b)) Thus, interest on an otherwise qualifying pooled financing bond is tax-exempt only if the issuer gets written commitments with ultimate borrowers for loans equal to at least 30% of the net proceeds of the pooled bond before the issuance. (Com Rept, see ¶ 5026) For an exception, see below.

> ***observation:*** In JCX-77-05, which is related to a predecessor Senate bill (S. 2020) to the Tax Increase Prevention Act, the Joint Committee on Taxation indicates that a loan commitment exists for this purpose only if: (a) the issuer is committed to lend bond proceeds to the borrower identified in the commitment, and (b) the borrower has applied for, and agreed to execute, a loan in an amount certain to finance a specifically identified project and, as part of that application, has paid a nonrefundable commitment fee in an amount that is commensurate with fees customarily paid for similar loan commitments. (Com Rept, see ¶ 5026)

The written loan commitment requirement doesn't apply with respect to these issuers (Code Sec. 149(f)(4)(B)):

(a) any issuer that is a state (or an integral part of a state) issuing pooled financing bonds to make or finance loans to subordinate governmental units of that state. (Code Sec. 149(f)(4)(B)(i)) That is, the written loan commitment requirement doesn't apply to bonds issued by states (or an integral part of a state) to provide loans to subordinate governmental units (Com Rept, see ¶ 5026); or

(b) any issuer that is a state-created entity providing financing for water-infrastructure projects through the federally-sponsored state revolving fund (SRF) program. (Code Sec. 149(f)(4)(B)(ii)) That is, the written loan commitment requirement doesn't apply to bonds issued by state entities created to provide financing for water-infrastructure projects through the federally-sponsored SRF Program. (Com Rept, see ¶ 5026)

> ***observation:*** The Senate Finance Committee Summary of the Tax Increase Prevention Act indicates that the federally-sponsored SRF Programs referred to in (b), above, are those sponsored by the Environmental Protection Agency (EPA). That is, the written loan commitment requirement doesn't apply to bonds issued by state entities created to provide financing for water-infrastructure projects through EPA-sponsored SRF Programs such as the Clean Water SRF Program and the Safe Drinking Water SRF Program.

Redemption requirement. The Tax Increase Prevention Act requires the redemption of outstanding bonds with proceeds that are not loaned to borrowers as required under the one- and three-year rules for the reasonable expectations requirement. (Com Rept, see ¶ 5026)

The redemption requirement is met if, to the extent that less than the percentage of the proceeds of an issue required to be used under Code Sec. 149(f)(2)(A)(i) (i.e., 30%, see above) or Code Sec. 149(f)(2)(A)(ii) (i.e., 95%, see above) is used by the close of the one- or three-year period, respectively, beginning on the date of the issuance, the issuer uses a specified amount of the proceeds to redeem outstanding bonds within 90 days after the end of the period. The specified amount is equal to the excess of (Code Sec. 149(f)(5)):

(A) the amount required to be used under Code Sec. 149(f)(2)(A)(i) (30%, for the one-year period) or Code Sec. 149(f)(2)(A)(ii) (95%, for the three-year period) (Code Sec. 149(f)(5)), over

(B) the amount actually used by the close of the period. (Code Sec. 149(f)(5))

> ***observation:*** Under Code Sec. 149(f)(2)(A)(i) and Code Sec. 149(f)(2)(A)(ii), the issuer must reasonably expect that 30% and 95%, respectively, of the bond proceeds will be used directly or indirectly to make or finance loans to ultimate borrowers within the one- and three-year loan origination periods, respectively (see "Loan origination requirements," above). The redemption requirement comes into play if either of those two "reasonable expectations" is not met. That is, the redemption requirement is triggered if 30% or 95% of the bond proceeds is not loaned to the ultimate borrower, or to an entity that provides financing to the ultimate borrower, within the applicable one- or three-year period.

Thus, if bond proceeds are not loaned to borrowers within prescribed periods, outstanding bonds equal to the amount of proceeds that were not loaned within the required period must be redeemed within 90 days. (Com Rept, see ¶ 5026)

> ***observation:*** In other words, the amount of the net proceeds that wasn't used to make or finance loans to ultimate borrowers within the applicable one- or three-year periods won't be available for use by the ultimate borrower.

> ***Illustration (1):*** An amount equal to 25% of the net proceeds of an issue is used to make loans to ultimate borrowers as of one year after the bonds are issued. An amount equal to 5% of the net proceeds of the issue (30% required to be used – 25% actually used) must be used to redeem bonds within the following 90-day period. That 5% amount is no longer available for lending. (Com Rept, see ¶ 5026)

> ***Illustration (2):*** An amount equal to 85% of the net proceeds of an issue is used to make qualifying loans (or to redeem bonds) as of three years after the bonds are issued. Of the remaining net proceeds, 10% (95% – 85%) is no longer available for lending, and must be used to redeem bonds within the following 90-day period. (Com Rept, see ¶ 5026)

Small issuer exception. The Tax Increase Prevention Act eliminates the rule disregarding pooled financing bonds from the issuer's $5 million annual limitation for purposes of the small issuer exception to the arbitrage rebate requirement. (Code Sec. 148(f)(4)(D)(ii) as amended by Tax Increase Prevention Act §508(c)) That is, the rule allowing an issuer of pooled financing bonds to disregard the pooled financing bonds for purposes of determining whether the issuer qualifies for the small issuer exception is eliminated. (Com Rept, see ¶ 5026)

Conforming amendment. The written loan commitment requirement and the redemption requirement are added to the specific "section 149 requirements" (i.e., the "reasonable expectations" and "cost of issuance" requirements, see FTC 2d/FIN ¶ J-3664) that a pooled financing bond must meet to qualify for as a tax-exempt state or local bond. (Code Sec. 149(f)(1) as amended by Tax Increase Prevention Act §508(d)(1))

☐ **Effective:** Bonds issued after May 17, 2006. (Tax Increase Prevention Act §508(e))

¶ 903. New $25 million volume limits on qualified veterans' mortgage bonds issued by Alaska, Oregon, and Wisconsin will be phased in from 2006 to 2009; issuance will terminate after 2010

Code Sec. 143(l)(3)(B), as amended by Tax Increase Prevention Act § 203(b)(1)
Generally effective: Allocations of state volume limit after Apr. 5, 2006
Committee Reports, see ¶ 5007

Qualified veterans' mortgage bonds are private activity bonds whose proceeds are used to make mortgage loans to certain veterans. Only states that had issued veterans' mortgage bonds before June 22, 1984 are eligible to issue them. (FTC 2d/FIN ¶ J-3182; USTR ¶ 1434.019) Those states are Alaska, California, Oregon, Texas, and Wisconsin. (Com Rept, see ¶ 5007)

Under pre-Tax Increase Prevention Act law, each state's issuance of qualified veterans' mortgage bonds was subject to an annual limit based on the volume of those bonds issued by that state between Jan. 1, 1979 and June 22, 1984. (FTC 2d/FIN ¶ J-3182; USTR ¶ 1434.019)

New Law. The Tax Increase Prevention Act provides new annual state volume limits of $25 million each for Alaska, Oregon, and Wisconsin. The limits are phased in during calendar years 2006–2009, and are reduced to zero for 2011 and thereafter. (Com Rept, see ¶ 5007)

The volume limits for California and Texas are unchanged. (Com Rept, see ¶ 5007) They continue to be based on the volume of bonds issued by those states between Jan. 1, 1979 and June 22, 1984. (Code Sec. 143(l)(3)(B)(i) as amended by Tax Increase Prevention Act §203(b)(1)(B))

FTC 2d References are to Federal Tax Coordinator 2d
FIN References are to RIA's Analysis of Federal Taxes: Income
USTR References are to United States Tax Reporter: Income, Estate & Gift, and Excise
PCA References are to Pension Analysis (print & electronic)
PE References are to the Pension Explanations (print & electronic)

observation: Thus, for California and Texas there is no phase-in from 2006 to 2009 and no sunset after 2010.

$25 million limits for Alaska, Oregon, and Wisconsin. For calendar year 2010, the limit on the total volume of qualified veterans' mortgage bonds will be (Code Sec. 143(l)(3)(B)(ii) as amended by Tax Increase Prevention Act §203(b)(1)(C)):

. . . $25 million for Alaska (Code Sec. 143(l)(3)(B)(ii)(I));

. . . $25 million for Oregon (Code Sec. 143(l)(3)(B)(ii)(II)); and

. . . $25 million for Wisconsin. (Code Sec. 143(l)(3)(B)(ii)(III))

Phase-in of limits during 2006–2009. The above volume limits for Alaska, Oregon, and Wisconsin will be phased-in over calendar years 2006–2009 by allowing the applicable percentage of the 2010 volume limits in accordance with the following table (Code Sec. 143(l)(3)(B)(iii)):

Calendar year:	Applicable percentage is:
2006	20 percent
2007	40 percent
2008	60 percent
2009	80 percent

observation: Thus, each of the three states can issue:

. . . $5 million (20% of $25 million) of qualified veterans' mortgage bonds in 2006;

. . . $10 million (40% of $25 million) of qualified veterans' mortgage bonds in 2007;

. . . $15 million (60% of $25 million) of qualified veterans' mortgage bonds in 2008; and

. . . $20 million (80% of $25 million) of qualified veterans' mortgage bonds in 2009.

In 2010, each of the three states can issue the full $25 million of qualified veterans' mortgage bonds.

Termination after 2010. The volume limits for Alaska, Oregon, and Wisconsin will be zero for 2011 and any later year. (Code Sec. 143(l)(3)(B)(iv))

No carryforwards allowed. Any unused allocation of volume limit can't be carried forward to later years. (Com Rept, see ¶ 5007)

For changes to the eligibility requirements for veterans to apply for a loan under this program, see ¶ 904.

☐ **Effective:** Allocations of state volume limit after Apr. 5, 2006. (Tax Increase Prevention Act §203(b)(2))

¶ 904. Loans financed with veterans' mortgage bonds issued by Alaska, Oregon, and Wisconsin made available to post-1976 veterans for 25 years after leaving active service

Code Sec. 143(l)(4), as amended by Tax Increase Prevention Act § 203(a)(1)
Generally effective: Bonds issued on or after May 17, 2006
Committee Reports, see ¶ 5007

Qualified veterans' mortgage bonds are private activity bonds whose proceeds are used to make mortgage loans to certain veterans. (FTC 2d/FIN ¶ J-3182; USTR ¶ 1434.019) These bonds can be issued by Alaska, California, Oregon, Texas, and Wisconsin. (Com Rept, see ¶ 5007)

Under pre-Tax Increase Prevention Act law, veterans' mortgage bond loans could be made only to veterans who served on active duty at some time before Jan. 1, 1977, and who applied for the loan before the date 30 years after the last date on which the veteran left active service. (FTC 2d/FIN ¶ J-3182; USTR ¶ 1434.019)

New Law. The Tax Increase Prevention Act changes the eligibility requirements for loans financed with qualified veterans' mortgage bonds issued by Alaska, Oregon, and Wisconsin, by:

- making loans available to any veteran who served on active duty (Code Sec. 143(l)(4)(A)(i) as amended by Tax Increase Prevention Act §203(a)(1)), thus repealing the requirement that veterans had to have served before Jan. 1, 1977, and making loans available to more recent veterans, including potentially those on active duty today (Com Rept, see ¶ 5007), and
- reducing to 25 years (from 30 years) the period after leaving active service in which veterans can apply for a loan. (Code Sec. 143(l)(4)(A)(ii))

> ***observation:*** This change will help veterans who began their active duty after 1976 and who apply for a loan within 25 years after leaving active service. For some veterans, this 25-year period has already ended.

FTC 2d References are to Federal Tax Coordinator 2d
FIN References are to RIA's Analysis of Federal Taxes: Income
USTR References are to United States Tax Reporter: Income, Estate & Gift, and Excise
PCA References are to Pension Analysis (print & electronic)
PE References are to the Pension Explanations (print & electronic)

illustration (1): Veteran A served on active duty from 1977 to 1980. Veteran A isn't eligible for a loan, because his 25-year period ended in 2005.

illustration (2): Veteran B served on active duty from 1979 to 1982. Veteran B is eligible for a loan if she applies before the end of her 25-year period, which will end in 2007.

recommendation: Veterans who are nearing the end of the 25-year period should be sure to make a loan application before the deadline.

The eligibility requirements for loans financed with qualified veterans' bonds issued by California and Texas are unchanged. (Com Rept, see ¶ 5007) In those states, veterans must have served on active duty at some time before Jan. 1, 1977 (Code Sec. 143(l)(4)(B)(i)), and must apply for the loan within 30 years after leaving active service. (Code Sec. 143(l)(4)(B)(ii))

For changes to the volume caps on issuance of qualified veterans' mortgage bonds, see ¶ 903.

☐ **Effective:** Bonds issued on or after May 17, 2006. (Tax Increase Prevention Act §203(a)(2))

¶ 1000. Client Letters

¶ 1001. Extension of relief from the AMT in the Tax Increase Prevention and Reconciliation Act

To the practitioner: You can use the following client letter to inform clients of these important provisions in the Tax Increase Prevention and Reconciliation Act. For analysis of the AMT relief provisions, see ¶ 201 and ¶ 202.

Dear Client,

I am writing to provide details regarding two key provisions in the recently enacted Tax Increase Prevention and Reconciliation Act which extend partial relief to individual taxpayers from the alternative minimum tax, or AMT. Earlier temporary measures to deal with the AMT expired at the end of last year, meaning that an estimated 15 million additional taxpayers would have faced paying the tax on their 2006 returns without the new relief.

Brief overview of the AMT.

The AMT is a parallel tax system which does not permit several of the deductions permissible under the regular tax system, such as state, local and property taxes. Taxpayers who may be subject to the AMT must calculate their tax liability under the regular federal tax system and under the AMT system. If their liability is found to be greater under the AMT system, that's what they owe the federal government. Originally enacted to make sure that wealthy Americans did not escape paying taxes, the AMT has started to apply to more middle-income taxpayers, due in part to the fact that the AMT parameters are not indexed for inflation.

In recent years, Congress has provided a measure of relief from the AMT by raising the AMT "exemption amounts"—allowances that reduce the amount of alternative minimum taxable income (AMTI), reducing or eliminating AMT liability. (However, these exemption amounts are phased out for taxpayers whose AMTI exceeds specified amounts.) For 2005, the AMT exemption amounts were $58,000 for married couples filing jointly and surviving spouses; $40,250 for single taxpayers; and $29,000 for marrieds filing separately. However, for 2006, those amounts were scheduled to fall back to the amounts that applied in 2000: $45,000, $33,750, and $22,500, respectively. This would have brought millions of additional mid-

FTC 2d References are to Federal Tax Coordinator 2d
FIN References are to RIA's Analysis of Federal Taxes: Income
USTR References are to United States Tax Reporter: Income, Estate & Gift, and Excise
PCA References are to Pension Analysis (print & electronic)
PE References are to the Pension Explanations (print & electronic)

dle-income Americans under the AMT system, resulting in higher federal tax bills for many of them, along with higher compliance costs associated with filling out and filing the complicated AMT tax form.

New law provides one-year stopgap fix.

To prevent the unintended result of having millions of middle-income taxpayers fall prey to the AMT, Congress has once again relied on a temporary "patch" to the problem, this time a one-year extension of the 2005 AMT exemption amounts, increased slightly. Under the new law, for tax years beginning in 2006, the AMT exemption amounts are increased to: (1) $62,550 in the case of married individuals filing a joint return and surviving spouses; (2) $42,500 in the case of unmarried individuals other than surviving spouses; and (3) $31,275 in the case of married individuals filing a separate return.

Personal credits may be used to offset AMT through 2006.

Another provision in the new law provides AMT relief for personal tax credits. The tax liability limitation rules generally provide that certain nonrefundable personal credits (including dependent care, elderly and disabled, and Hope Scholarship and Lifetime Learning) are allowed only to the extent that a taxpayer has regular income tax liability in excess of the tentative minimum tax, which has the effect of disallowing these credits against AMT. Temporary provisions had been enacted which permitted these credits to offset the entire regular and AMT liability through the end of 2005. The new law extends this temporary provision to tax years beginning in 2006.

I hope this information is helpful. If you would like more details about these changes, or any other aspects of the new law, please do not hesitate to call.

Very truly yours,

¶ 1002. Beginning in 2010, income limitations on Roth IRA conversions are eliminated under the Tax Increase Prevention and Reconciliation Act

To the practitioner: You can use the following client letter to inform clients of this important provision in the Tax Increase Prevention and Reconciliation Act. For analysis of the provision eliminating income limitations on Roth IRA conversions beginning in 2010, see ¶ 203.

Dear Client,

Taxpayers with six-figure incomes who like to plan far ahead should be aware of a potentially lucrative provision contained in the recently enacted Tax Increase Prevention and Reconciliation Act. The new law provides that, beginning in 2010, the rules that currently prevent a taxpayer with more than $100,000 in modified adjusted gross income from converting a regular individual retirement account (IRA) into a Roth IRA will be eliminated.

A taxpayer who makes deductible contributions to a regular individual retirement account (IRA) gets a tax break now for the dollars he puts in and his earnings grow tax free, but he pays ordinary income tax on every dollar he takes out, and withdrawals are subject to significant restrictions. In a Roth IRA, the taxpayer gets no tax deduction for contributions, but his money grows tax free and there's no tax, and few restrictions, on qualifying withdrawals.

Under pre-Tax Increase Prevention and Reconciliation Act law, only taxpayers with $100,000 or less in modified adjusted gross income can convert a regular IRA into a Roth IRA. A taxpayer making the conversion generally must pay tax on money he takes out of his regular IRA, but once it's in his Roth IRA, he won't pay tax on that money or the money it earns. Generally speaking, Roth conversions appeal to taxpayers who either think their tax rate will go up in retirement, or believe that the value of their account will rise significantly, and thus are willing to make an upfront tax payment when they convert in order to reap large tax savings in later years.

Under the new law, beginning in 2010, taxpayers with more than $100,000 of modified adjusted gross income also will be able to convert a regular IRA into a Roth IRA. To make such conversions more attractive in 2010, the new law permits taxpayers who convert in 2010 to spread the income and resulting tax payments on the converted funds over two years—2011 and 2012.

I hope this information is helpful. If you would like more details about this provision of the new law, or if you would like to discuss any aspect of your retirement planning, please do not hesitate to call.

Very truly yours,

¶ 1003. Kiddie tax age limit raised from under 14 to under 18 in the Tax Increase Prevention and Reconciliation Act

To the practitioner: You can use the following client letter to inform clients of these important changes in the Tax Increase Prevention and Reconciliation Act. For analysis of the provision increasing the age to which the kiddie tax rules apply from under age 14 to under age 18, see ¶ 204. For analysis of the provision excepting distributions from certain qualified disability trusts from the kiddie tax, see ¶ 205.

Dear Client,

For parents thinking about trying to save taxes by transferring assets into their children's names, Congress has just thrown up another roadblock. In the recently enacted Tax Increase Prevention and Reconciliation Act, Congress raised the age at which the unearned income of minor children is taxed at the parents' tax rate from under age 14 to under age 18. Here are the details.

At one time, wealthy parents could significantly lower their family's tax bill by transferring investment assets to minor children. This tax technique, called income shifting, worked by taking income out of the parents' higher tax bracket and placing it in the lower tax brackets of their children. To curtail the use of this tax technique, Congress enacted the "kiddie tax" rules, which said that children under 14 who had more than a small amount of unearned (investment) income had to pay tax at their parents' marginal tax rate (the rate of tax on the last dollar earned). The threshold amount at which the kiddie tax kicks in is two times the amount allowed as a standard deduction for a dependent who has only investment income. For 2006, that amount is $850, so the kiddie tax begins to apply when the child has more than $1,700 in unearned income.

Under the new law, the age limit below which a child's income from investments is taxed at the parents' rate is raised from 14 to 18. The new law specifies, however, that the kiddie tax does not apply to a child who is married and files a joint return for the tax year. It also adds an exception to the kiddie tax for distributions from certain qualified disability trusts. The new provisions apply to tax years beginning after Dec. 31, 2005.

I hope this information is helpful. If you would like more details about this or any other aspect of the new law, please do not hesitate to call.

Very truly yours,

FTC 2d References are to Federal Tax Coordinator 2d
FIN References are to RIA's Analysis of Federal Taxes: Income
USTR References are to United States Tax Reporter: Income, Estate & Gift, and Excise
PCA References are to Pension Analysis (print & electronic)
PE References are to the Pension Explanations (print & electronic)

¶ 1004. Tax provisions affecting individuals in the Tax Increase Prevention and Reconciliation Act

To the practitioner: You can use the following client letter to provide clients with an overview of the tax provisions affecting individuals in the Tax Increase Prevention and Reconciliation Act. For analysis of AMT relief, see ¶ 201 and ¶ 202. For analysis of investor tax breaks, see ¶ 101, ¶ 102, ¶ 103, ¶ 104, ¶ 105, ¶ 106, ¶ 107, ¶ 108, ¶ 109, ¶ 110, ¶ 111, ¶ 112, and ¶ 113. For analysis of the elimination, beginning in 2010, of the income limitations on Roth IRA conversions, see ¶ 203. For analysis of the provision raising the kiddie tax age limit from under 14 to under 18, see ¶ 204. For analysis of the capital gain treatment for self-created musical works, see ¶ 208. For analysis of the changes to the foreign earned income exclusion and housing allowance for U.S. citizens working abroad, see ¶ 206.

Dear Client,

The recently enacted Tax Increase Prevention and Reconciliation Act contains investor tax breaks, alternative minimum tax (AMT) relief, and several other provisions with immediate and long-term impact on individuals. Although the new legislation also contains several provisions affecting primarily businesses and corporations, I am writing this to provide you with a quick overview of the provisions in the new law that directly affect individual taxpayers.

AMT relief.

Originally enacted to make sure that wealthy Americans did not escape paying taxes, the AMT, which is a parallel tax system which does not permit several of the deductions permissible under the regular tax system, such as state, local and property taxes, has started to affect more middle-income taxpayers. This is in part due to the fact that the AMT parameters are not indexed for inflation. In recent years, Congress has provided a measure of relief from the AMT by raising the AMT "exemption amounts"—allowances that reduce the amount of alternative minimum taxable income (AMTI), reducing or eliminating AMT liability. (However, these exemption amounts are phased out for taxpayers whose AMTI exceeds specified amounts.) For 2005, the AMT exemption amounts were $58,000 for married couples filing jointly and surviving spouses; $40,250 for single taxpayers; and $29,000 for marrieds filing separately. However, for 2006, those amounts were scheduled to fall back to the amounts that applied in 2000: $45,000, $33,750, and $22,500, respectively. This would have brought millions of additional middle-income Americans under the AMT system, resulting in higher federal tax bills for many of them, along with higher compliance costs associated with filling out and filing the complicated AMT tax form.

To prevent the unintended result of having millions of middle-income taxpayers pay tax under the AMT rules, Congress has once again relied on a temporary fix to the problem, this time a one-year extension of the 2005 AMT exemption amounts, increased slightly. Under the new law, for tax years beginning in 2006, the AMT exemption amounts are increased to: (1) $62,550 in the case of married individuals filing a joint return and surviving spouses; (2) $42,500 in the case of unmarried individuals other than surviving spouses; and (3) $31,275 in the case of married individuals filing a separate return.

Another provision in the new law provides AMT relief for those who have personal tax credits. The tax liability limitation rules generally provide that certain nonrefundable personal credits (including dependent care, elderly and disabled, and Hope Scholarship and Lifetime Learning) are allowed only to the extent that a taxpayer has regular income tax liability in excess of the tentative minimum tax, which has the effect of disallowing these credits against AMT. Temporary provisions had been enacted which permitted these credits to offset the entire regular and AMT liability through the end of 2005. The new law extends this temporary provision to tax years beginning in 2006.

Investor tax breaks extended.

In 2003, Congress passed a measure to lower the tax rate on most dividends to 15 percent from as high as 38.6 percent, and to lower the rate on most capital gains from 20 percent to 15 percent. That measure was due to expire at the end of 2008, but the new law extends the favorable tax rates through 2010.

Income limitations on Roth IRA conversions eliminated, beginning in 2010.

A taxpayer who makes deductible contributions to a regular individual retirement account (IRA) gets a tax break now for the dollars he puts in and his earnings grow tax free, but he pays ordinary income tax on every dollar he takes out, and withdrawals are subject to significant restrictions. In a Roth IRA, the taxpayer gets no tax deduction for contributions, but his money grows tax free and there's no tax, and few restrictions, on qualifying withdrawals.

Under pre-Act law, only taxpayers with $100,000 or less in modified adjusted gross income can convert a regular IRA into a Roth IRA. A taxpayer making the conversion generally must pay tax on money he takes out of his regular IRA, but once it's in his Roth IRA, he won't pay tax on that money or the money it earns. Generally speaking, Roth conversions appeal to taxpayers who either think their tax rate will go up in retirement, or believe that the value of their account will rise significantly, and thus are willing to make an upfront tax payment when they convert in order to reap large tax savings in later years.

Under the new law, beginning in 2010, taxpayers with more than $100,000 of modified adjusted gross income also will be able to convert a regular IRA into a Roth IRA. To make such conversions more attractive in 2010, the new law permits taxpayers who convert in 2010 to spread the income and resulting tax payments on the converted funds over two years—2011 and 2012.

Kiddie tax age limit raised from under 14 to under 18.

At one time, wealthy parents could significantly lower their family's tax bill by transferring investment assets to minor children. This tax technique, called income shifting, worked by taking income out of the parents' higher tax bracket and placing it in the lower tax brackets of their children. To curtail the use of this tax technique, Congress enacted the "kiddie tax" rules, which said that children under 14 who had more than a small amount of unearned (investment) income had to pay tax at their parents' marginal tax rate (the rate of tax on the last dollar earned). The threshold amount at which the kiddie tax kicks in is two times the amount allowed as a standard deduction for a dependent who has only investment income. For 2006, that amount is $850, so the kiddie tax begins to apply when the child has more than $1,700 in unearned income.

Under the new law, the age limit below which a child's income from investments is taxed at the parents' rates is raised from 14 to 18. The new law specifies, however, that the kiddie tax does not apply to a child who is married and files a joint return for the tax year. It also adds an exception to the kiddie tax for distributions from certain qualified disability trusts. The new provisions apply to tax years beginning after Dec. 31, 2005.

Capital gain treatment for self-created musical works.

Under pre-Act law, capital assets do not include copyrights, literary, musical, or artistic compositions, letters or memoranda, or similar property held by a taxpayer whose personal efforts created the property. As a result, when a taxpayer sells copyrights he owns in, for example, books, songs, or paintings that he created, gain from the sale is treated as ordinary income, not capital gain, which is generally taxed at a lower rate.

Under the new law, at the election of a taxpayer, the sale or exchange before Jan. 1, 2011 of musical compositions or copyrights in musical works created by the taxpayer's personal efforts is treated as the sale or exchange of a capital asset. The change applies for sales or exchanges in tax years beginning after May 17, 2006.

Changes to the foreign earned income exclusion and housing allowance for U.S. citizens working abroad.

The new law makes three changes to the foreign earned income exclusion and housing allowance. First, the income exclusion is indexed for inflation starting in 2006 (rather than 2008 under pre-Act law). Second, the base housing amount used in calculating the foreign housing cost exclusion in a taxable year is 16 percent of the amount of the foreign earned income exclusion limitation (instead of the pre-Act law 16 percent of the U.S. government employee grade GS-14, step 1 amount). Reasonable foreign housing expenses in excess of the base housing amount remain excluded from gross income, but the amount of the exclusion is limited to 30 percent of the taxpayer's foreign earned income exclusion. Third, income excluded as either foreign earned income or as a housing allowance is included for purposes of determining the marginal tax rates applicable to non-excluded income.

Please keep in mind that I've described only the highlights of the new law. If you would like more details on any aspect of this legislation, please call me at your earliest convenience.

Very truly yours,

¶ 1005. Business and corporate changes in the Tax Increase Prevention and Reconciliation Act

To the practitioner: You can use the following client letter to provide clients with an overview of the business and corporate tax provisions in the Tax Increase Prevention and Reconciliation Act. For analysis of the extension of increased expensing for small business, see ¶ 401, ¶ 402, and ¶ 403. For analysis of the modifications to the wage limitation on the Code Sec. 199 production deduction, see ¶ 301 and ¶ 302. For analysis of the changes regarding controlled foreign corporations, see ¶ 601 and ¶ 602. For analysis of the modified rules for distributions of controlled corporations, see ¶ 501. For analysis of the elective five-year amortization of expenses paid for musical works and copyrights, see ¶ 405. For analysis of changes to corporate estimated tax, see ¶ 803. For analysis of the requirement that partial payments have to be made with offer in compromise submissions, see ¶ 804. For analysis of changes to the earnings-stripping rules that apply to certain corporate partners, see ¶ 503. For analysis of the denial of Code Sec. 355 treatment for disqualified investment companies, see ¶ 502. For analysis of the requirement that certain major integrated oil companies have to amortize geological and geophysical costs over five years, see ¶ 404.

Dear Client,

As you probably know, Congress recently passed the Tax Increase Prevention and Reconciliation Act, the core provisions of which are a two-year extension of investor tax breaks and a one-year extension of alternative minimum tax (AMT) relief for individuals. However, the new legislation also contains an assortment of business and corporate tax breaks, as well as some revenue raisers affecting business taxpayers. I am writing to provide you with a quick overview of the provisions in the new law that directly impact business.

Extension of increased expensing for small business.

A taxpayer, other than an estate, trust, and certain noncorporate lessors, may elect under Code Sec. 179 to deduct as an expense, rather than to depreciate, up to a specified amount of the cost of new or used tangible personal property placed in service during the tax year in his trade or business. The maximum dollar amount that may be deducted annually is $100,000 ($108,000 for 2006, as adjusted for inflation). Under pre-Act law, this amount was to drop to $25,000 for property placed in service in tax years beginning after 2007.

The taxpayer's maximum annual Code Sec. 179 expensing amount is reduced dollar-for-dollar by the amount of qualified expensing-eligible property that he places in service during the tax year in excess of a phaseout amount. This amount is $400,000 ($430,000 for 2006, as adjusted for infla-

FTC 2d References are to Federal Tax Coordinator 2d
FIN References are to RIA's Analysis of Federal Taxes: Income
USTR References are to United States Tax Reporter: Income, Estate & Gift, and Excise
PCA References are to Pension Analysis (print & electronic)
PE References are to the Pension Explanations (print & electronic)

tion). Under pre-Act law, this amount was to drop to $200,000 for property placed in service in tax years beginning after 2007.

Off-the-shelf computer software qualifies as "section 179 property" eligible for the Code Sec. 179 expense election, but under pre-Act law, could not qualify in tax years beginning in 2008 and later.

A Code Sec. 179 election or a revocation may be made, without IRS's consent, on an amended federal tax return for the tax year to which the election or revocation applies, but under pre-Act law, could not be so made in tax years beginning after 2007.

The new law extends the $100,000 expense election limit and the $400,000 phaseout ceiling (as inflation adjusted), the inclusion of off-the-shelf computer software in eligible "section 179 property," and the right to amend or revoke an expense election without IRS's consent for two years, to tax years beginning before 2010.

50% W-2 wage limit on the Code Sec. 199 domestic production deduction modified.

The domestic production deduction is limited to 50% of the W-2 wages paid by the taxpayer. Under the new law, the W-2 wages taken into account for purposes of this limitation must be properly allocable to domestic production gross receipts—that is, the gross receipts from the activities that give rise to the deduction. In addition, the new law repeals the special limitation on the amount of W-2 wages that may be taken into account by partners and S corporation shareholders. The changes are effective for tax years beginning after May 17, 2006.

Controlled foreign corporations (CFCs).

The new law makes two changes regarding controlled foreign corporations. First, it provides a two-year extension of the "active financing exemption," due to expire at the end of this year and important to the financial-services industry. The exemption, which dates back to 1997, says that U.S. companies shouldn't be taxed on the active business income earned abroad by their foreign subsidiaries until the income is returned to the American parent. Second, regarding look-through treatment of payments between related CFCs under the foreign personal holding company income rules, the Act adds a new temporary exception from subpart F for dividends, interest, rents and royalties received by one CFC from a related CFC to the extent attributable to non-subpart F income of the payor. This provision is effective for tax years beginning after Dec. 31, 2005 and before Jan. 1, 2009.

Modified rules for distributions of controlled corporations.

The new law simplifies the active business test for tax-free corporate spin-offs by looking at all corporations in the distributing corporation's and the spun-off subsidiary's respective affiliated group to determine if the active business test is satisfied. This change applies for distributions after May 17, 2006 and before 2011.

Amortization of expenses paid for musical works and copyrights.

The new law allows taxpayers to elect to amortize over five years expenses paid or incurred in creating or acquiring certain musical works and copyrights. This five-year amortization method is an alternative to the income forecast method of accounting for these expenses.

Revenue offsets.

The new law pays for the extended and new tax breaks highlighted above with a number of revenue-raising provisions, including the following:

. . . Corporations with assets of at least $1 billion face a modified schedule of estimated tax payments. Those payments due in July, Aug., or Sept. of 2006 will be increased to 105% of the payment otherwise due, and the next required payment will be reduced accordingly. Payments due in July, Aug., or Sept. of 2012, will be increased to 106.25% of the payment otherwise due, and the next required payment will be reduced accordingly. Finally, payments due in July, Aug., or Sept. of 2013, will be increased to 100.75% of the payment otherwise due, and the next required payment will be reduced accordingly.

. . . In another estimated tax change, with respect to corporate estimated tax payments due on Sept. 15, 2010, 20.5% won't be due until Oct. 1, 2010, and for Sept. 15, 2011, 27.5% won't be due until Oct. 1, 2011.

. . . Information reporting will be required for tax-exempt interest paid on tax-exempt bonds after Dec. 31, 2005.

. . . Taxpayers will be required to make partial payments to the IRS with any offer in compromise. For lump-sum offers (which include single payments, as well as payments made in 5 or fewer installments), taxpayers will have to make a down payment of 20% of the amount of the offer with any application. Any periodic payment offer in compromise will have to be accompanied by the payment of the amount of the first proposed installment. User fees will be applied against tax, interest or penalties due under the offer in compromise.

. . . The new law codifies proposed regs that provide that, for purposes of applying the earnings-stripping rules to a corporation that owns, directly or indirectly, an interest in a partnership, the corporation's share of partnership liabilities, interest income, and interest expense will be treated as those of the corporation. This provision is effective for tax years beginning on or after May 17, 2006.

. . . The new law denies tax-free treatment to certain spin-offs where either the distributing corporation or the controlled corporation is a "disqualified investment corporation."

. . . The new law requires amortization of geological and geophysical (G&G) costs over five years (instead of the more favorable 24 months) for certain major integrated oil companies, effective for amounts paid or incurred after May 17, 2006. The five year amortization rule for G&G costs will apply only to integrated oil companies that have an average daily worldwide production of crude oil of at least 500,000 barrels for the tax year, gross receipts in excess of $1 billion in the last tax year ending during calendar year 2005, and an ownership interest in a crude oil refiner of 15% or more.

Please keep in mind that I've described only the highlights of the most important changes in the new law. Give me a call at your earliest convenience for more details on how you may be affected by this important tax legislation.

Very truly yours,

[¶3000] Code As Amended

This section reproduces Code as Amended by HR4297, the Tax Increase Prevention and Reconciliation Act of 2005. Code sections appear in order, as amended, added or repealed. New matter is shown in *italics*. All changes and effective dates are shown in the endnotes.

[¶3001] Code Sec. 1. Tax imposed.

* * * * * * * * * * * *

(g) Certain unearned income of minor children taxed as if parent's income.

* * * * * * * * * * * *

(2) Child to whom subsection applies. This subsection shall apply to any child for any taxable year if—

(A) such child has not attained [1]*age 18* before the close of the taxable year,[2]

(B) either parent of such child is alive at the close of the taxable year[3], *and*

[4]*(C) such child does not file a joint return for the taxable year.*

* * * * * * * * * * * *

(4) Net unearned income. For purposes of this subsection—

(A) In general. The term "net unearned income" means the excess of—

(i) the portion of the adjusted gross income for the taxable year which is not attributable to earned income (as defined in section 911(d)(2)), over

(ii) the sum of—

(I) the amount in effect for the taxable year under section 63(c)(5)(A) (relating to limitation on standard deduction in the case of certain dependents), plus

(II) the greater of the amount described in subclause (I) or, if the child itemizes his deductions for the taxable year, the amount of the itemized deductions allowed by this chapter for the taxable year which are directly connected with the production of the portion of adjusted gross income referred to in clause (i).

(B) Limitation based on taxable income. The amount of the net unearned income for any taxable year shall not exceed the individual's taxable income for such taxable year.

[5]*(C) Treatment of distributions from qualified disability trusts. For purposes of this subsection, in the case of any child who is a beneficiary of a qualified disability trust (as defined in section 642(b)(2)(C)(ii)), any amount included in the income of such child under sections 652 and 662 during a taxable year shall be considered earned income of such child for such taxable year.*

* * * * * * * * * * * *

[For Analysis, see ¶101, ¶102, ¶107, ¶108, ¶204, ¶205. For Committee Reports, see ¶5002, ¶5028.]

[Endnote Code Sec. 1]

Matter in *italics* in Code Sec. 1(g)(2)(A), Code Sec. 1(g)(2)(B), Code Sec. 1(g)(2)(C), and Code Sec. 1(g)(4)(C) was added by Sec. 510(a)-(c) of the Tax Increase Prevention and Reconciliation Act of 2005, HR4297, 5/17/2006, which struck out:

1. "age 14"
2. "and"
3. ","
4. added subpara. (g)(2)(C)
5. added subpara. (g)(4)(C)

Effective Date (Sec. 510(d), HR4297, 5/17/2006) effective for tax. yrs. begin. after 12/31/2005.

Sec. 102, HR4297, 5/17/2006, amended Sec. 303, P.L. 108-27, relating to the sunset of the amendments made by Secs. 301 and 302 of P.L. 108-27, by substituting "December 31, 2010" for "December 31, 2008". Sec. 303 as amended by Sec. 102, HR4297, 5/17/2006, reads as follows:

"SEC. 303. SUNSET OF TITLE. All provisions of, and amendments made by, this title [Secs. 301 and 302] shall not apply to taxable years beginning after December 31, 2010, and the Internal Revenue Code of 1986 shall be applied and administered to such years as if such provisions and amendments had never been enacted."

[¶3002] Code Sec. 26. Limitation based on tax liability; definition of tax liability.

(a) Limitation based on amount of tax.

* * * * * * * * * * * * *

(2) Special rule for taxable years 2000 through [1]*2006*. For purposes of any taxable year beginning during 2000, 2001, 2002, 2003, 2004, [2]*2005, or 2006*, the aggregate amount of credits allowed by this subpart for the taxable year shall not exceed the sum of—

(A) the taxpayer's regular tax liability for the taxable year reduced by the foreign tax credit allowable under section 27(a), and

(B) the tax imposed by section 55(a) for the taxable year.

* * * * * * * * * * * * *

[For Analysis, see ¶202. For Committee Reports, see ¶5016.]

[Endnote Code Sec. 26]

Matter in *italics* in Code Sec. 26(a)(2) was added by Sec. 302(a)(1) and (2) of the Tax Increase Prevention and Reconciliation Act of 2005, HR4297, 5/17/2006, which struck out:

1. "2005"
2. "or 2005"

Effective Date (Sec. 302(b), HR4297, 5/17/2006) effective for tax. yrs. begin. after 12/31/2005.

[¶3003] Code Sec. 54. Credit to holders of clean renewable energy bonds.

* * * * * * * * * * * * *

(l) Other definitions and special rules. For purposes of this section—

* * * * * * * * * * * * *

(2) Pooled financing bond. The term "pooled financing bond" shall have the meaning given such term by [1]*section 149(f)(6)(A)*.

* * * * * * * * * * * * *

[Endnote Code Sec. 54]

Matter in *italics* in Code Sec. 54(l)(2) was added by Sec. 508(d)(3) of the Tax Increase Prevention and Reconciliation Act of 2005, HR4297, 5/17/2006, which struck out:

1. "section 149(f)(4)(A)"

Effective Date (Sec. 508(e), HR4297, 5/17/2006) effective for bonds issued after 5/17/2006.

[¶3004] Code Sec. 55. Alternative minimum tax imposed.

* * * * * * * * * * * * *

(d) Exemption amount. For purposes of this section—

(1) Exemption amount for taxpayers other than corporations. In the case of a taxpayer other than a corporation, the term "exemption amount" means—

(A) $45,000 ([1]*$62,550 in the case of taxable years beginning in 2006*) in the case of—

(i) a joint return, or

(ii) a surviving spouse,

(B) $33,750 ([2]*$42,500 in the case of taxable years beginning in 2006*) in the case of an individual who—

(i) is not a married individual, and

(ii) is not a surviving spouse,

(C) 50 percent of the dollar amount applicable under paragraph (1)(A) in the case of a married individual who files a separate return, and

(D) $22,500 in the case of an estate or trust.

For purposes of this paragraph, the term "surviving spouse" has the meaning given to such term by section 2(a), and marital status shall be determined under section 7703.

* * * * * * * * * * * * *

[For Analysis, see ¶ 103, ¶ 201. For Committee Reports, see ¶ 5002, ¶ 5015.]

[Endnote Code Sec. 55]

Matter in *italics* in Code Sec. 55(d)(1)(A) and Code Sec. 55(d)(1)(B) was added by Sec. 301(a)(1) and (2) of the Tax Increase Prevention and Reconciliation Act of 2005, HR4297, 5/17/2006, which struck out:

1. "$58,000 in the case of taxable years beginning in 2003, 2004, and 2005"
2. "$40,250 in the case of taxable years beginning in 2003, 2004, and 2005"

Effective Date (Sec. 301(b), HR4297, 5/17/2006) effective for tax. yrs. begin. after 12/31/2005.

Sec. 102, HR4297, 5/17/2006, amended Sec. 303, P.L. 108-27, relating to the sunset of the amendments made by Secs. 301 and 302 of P.L. 108-27, by substituting "December 31, 2010" for "December 31, 2008". Sec. 303 as amended by Sec. 102, HR4297, 5/17/2006, reads as follows:

"SEC. 303. SUNSET OF TITLE. All provisions of, and amendments made by, this title [Secs. 301 and 302] shall not apply to taxable years beginning after December 31, 2010, and the Internal Revenue Code of 1986 shall be applied and administered to such years as if such provisions and amendments had never been enacted."

[¶ 3005] Code Sec. 142. Exempt facility bond.

* * * * * * * * * * * * *

(d) Qualified residential rental project. For purposes of this section—

* * * * * * * * * * * * *

(2) Definitions and special rules. For purposes of this subsection—

(A) Qualified project period. The term "qualified project period" means the period beginning on the 1st day on which 10 percent of the residential units in the project are occupied and ending on the latest of—

(i) the date which is 15 years after the date on which 50 percent of the residential units in the project are occupied,

(ii) the 1st day on which no tax-exempt private activity bond issued with respect to the project is outstanding, or

(iii) the date on which any assistance provided with respect to the project under section 8 of the United States Housing Act of 1937 terminates.

(B) Income of individuals; area median gross income. The income of individuals and area median gross income shall be determined by the Secretary in a manner consistent with determinations of lower income families and area median gross income under section 8 of the United States Housing Act of 1937 (or, if such program is terminated, under such program as in effect immediately before such termination). Determinations under the preceding sentence shall include adjustments for family size. [1]*Subsections (g) and (h) of section 7872* shall not apply in determining the income of individuals under this subparagraph.

* * * * * * * * * * * * *

[Endnote Code Sec. 142]

Matter in *italics* in Code Sec. 142(d)(2)(B) was added by Sec. 209(b)(2) of the Tax Increase Prevention and Reconciliation Act of 2005, HR4297, 5/17/2006, which struck out:

1. "Section 7872(g)"

Effective Date (Sec. 209(c), HR4297, 5/17/2006) effective for calendar yrs. begin. after 12/31/2005, for loans made before, on, or after 12/31/2005.

[¶3006] Code Sec. 143. Mortgage revenue bonds: qualified mortgage bond and qualified veterans' mortgage bond.

* * * * * * * * * * * *

(l) Additional requirements for qualified veterans' mortgage bonds. An issue meets the requirements of this subsection only if it meets the requirements of paragraphs (1), (2), and (3).

(1) Veterans to whom financing may be provided. An issue meets the requirements of this paragraph only if each mortgagor to whom financing is provided under the issue is a qualified veteran.

(2) Requirement that state program be in effect before June 22, 1984. An issue meets the requirements of this paragraph only if it is a general obligation of a State which issued qualified veterans' mortgage bonds before June 22, 1984.

(3) Volume limitation.

(A) In general. An issue meets the requirements of this paragraph only if the aggregate amount of bonds issued pursuant thereto (when added to the aggregate amount of qualified veterans' mortgage bonds previously issued by the State during the calendar year) does not exceed the State veterans limit for such calendar year.

[1]*(B) State veterans limit.*

(i) In general. In the case of any State to which clause (ii) does not apply, the State veterans limit for any calendar year is the amount equal to—

[2]*(I)* the aggregate amount of qualified veterans bonds issued by such State during the period beginning on January 1, 1979, and ending on June 22, 1984 (not including the amount of any qualified veterans bond issued by such State during the calendar year (or portion thereof) in such period for which the amount of such bonds so issued was the lowest), divided by

[3]*(II)* the number (not to exceed 5) of calendar years after 1979 and before 1985 during which the State issued qualified veterans bonds (determined by only taking into account bonds issued on or before June 22, 1984).

[4]*(ii) Alaska, Oregon, and Wisconsin. In the case of the following States, the State veterans limit for any calendar year is the amount equal to—*

(I) $25,000,000 for the State of Alaska,

(II) $25,000,000 for the State of Oregon, and

(III) $25,000,000 for the State of Wisconsin.

(iii) Phasein. In the case of calendar years beginning before 2010, clause (ii) shall be applied by substituting for each of the dollar amounts therein an amount equal to the applicable percentage of such dollar amount. For purposes of the preceding sentence, the applicable percentage shall be determined in accordance with the following table:

For Calendar Year:	*Applicable percentage is:*
2006	*20 percent*
2007	*40 percent*
2008	*60 percent*
2009	*80 percent.*

(iv) Termination. The State veterans limit for the States specified in clause (ii) for any calendar year after 2010 is zero.

(C) Treatment of refunding issues.

(i) In general. For purposes of subparagraph (A), the term "qualified veterans' mortgage bond" shall not include any bond issued to refund another bond but only if the maturity date of the refunding bond is not later than the later of—

(I) the maturity date of the bond to be refunded, or

(II) the date 32 years after the date on which the refunded bond was issued (or in the case of a series of refundings, the date on which the original bond was issued).

The preceding sentence shall apply only to the extent that the amount of the refunding bond does not exceed the outstanding amount of the refunded bond.

(ii) Exception for advance refunding. Clause (i) shall not apply to any bond issued to advance refund another bond.

[5]***(4) Qualified veteran.*** *For purposes of this subsection, the term "qualified veteran" means—*

(A) in the case of the States of Alaska, Oregon, and Wisconsin, any veteran—

(i) who served on active duty, and

(ii) who applied for the financing before the date 25 years after the last date on which such veteran left active service, and

(B) in the case of any other State, any veteran—

(i) who served on active duty at some time before January 1, 1977, and

(ii) who applied for the financing before the later of—

(I) the date 30 years after the last date on which such veteran left active service, or

(II) January 31, 1985.

* * * * * * * * * * * *

[For Analysis, see ¶ 903, ¶ 904. For Committee Reports, see ¶ 5007.]

[Endnote Code Sec. 143]

Matter in *italics* in Code Sec. 143(l)(3)(B), Code Sec. 143(l)(3)(B)(i), Code Sec. 143(l)(3)(B)(i)(I), Code Sec. 143(l)(3)(B)(i)(II), Code Sec. 143(l)(3)(B)(ii), Code Sec. 143(l)(3)(B)(iii), and Code Sec. 143(l)(3)(B)(iv) was added by Sec. 203(b)(1)(A)-(C) of the Tax Increase Prevention and Reconciliation Act of 2005, HR4297, 5/17/2006, which struck out:

1. "(B) State veterans limit. A State veterans limit for any calendar year is the amount equal to—"
2. "(i)"
3. "(ii)"
4. added clauses (l)(3)(B)(ii)-(iv)

Effective Date (Sec. 203(b)(2), HR4297, 5/17/2006) effective for allocations of State volume limit after 4/5/2006.

Code Sec. 143(l)(4), in *italics*, was added by Sec. 203(a)(1), HR4297, 5/17/2006, which struck out:

5. "(4) Qualified veteran. For purposes of this subsection, the term 'qualified veteran' means any veteran—

"(A) who served on active duty at some time before January 1, 1977, and

"(B) who applied for the financing before the later of—

"(i) the date 30 years after the last date on which such veteran left active service, or

"(ii) January 31, 1985."

Effective Date (Sec. 203(a)(2), HR4297, 5/17/2006) effective for bonds issued on or after 5/17/2006.

[¶ 3007] Code Sec. 144. Qualified small issue bond; qualified student loan bond; qualified redevelopment bond.

(a) Qualified small issue bond.

* * * * * * * * * * * *

(4) $10,000,000 limit in certain cases.

(A) In general. At the election of the issuer with respect to any issue, this subsection shall be applied—

(i) by substituting "$10,000,000" for "$1,000,000" in paragraph (1), and

(ii) in determining the aggregate face amount of such issue, by taking into account not only the amount described in paragraph (2), but also the aggregate amount of capital expenditures with respect to facilities described in subparagraph (B) paid or incurred during the 6-year period beginning 3 years before the date of such issue and ending 3 years after such date (and financed otherwise than out of the proceeds of outstanding tax-exempt issues to which paragraph (1) (or the corresponding provision of prior law) applied), as if the aggregate amount of such capital expenditures constituted the face amount of a prior outstanding issue described in paragraph (2).

(B) Facilities taken into account. For purposes of subparagraph (A)(ii), the facilities described in this subparagraph are facilities—

(i) located in the same incorporated municipality or located in the same county (but not in any incorporated municipality), and

(ii) the principal user of which is or will be the same person or 2 or more related persons.

For purposes of clause (i), the determination of whether or not facilities are located in the same governmental unit shall be made as of the date of issue of the issue in question.

(C) Certain capital expenditures not taken into account. For purposes of subparagraph (A)(ii), any capital expenditure—

(i) to replace property destroyed or damaged by fire, storm, or other casualty, to the extent of the fair market value of the property replaced,

(ii) required by a change made after the date of issue of the issue in question in a Federal or State law or local ordinance of general application or required by a change made after such date in rules and regulations of general application issued under such a law or ordinance,

(iii) required by circumstances which could not be reasonably foreseen on such date of issue or arising out of a mistake of law or fact (but the aggregate amount of expenditures not taken into account under this clause with respect to any issue shall not exceed $1,000,000), or

(iv) described in clause (i) or (ii) of section 41(b)(2)(A) for which a deduction was allowed under section 174(a), shall not be taken into account.

(D) Limitation on loss of tax exemption. In applying subparagraph (A)(ii) with respect to capital expenditures made after the date of any issue, no bond issued as a part of such issue shall cease to be treated as a qualified small issue bond by reason of any such expenditure for any period before the date on which such expenditure is paid or incurred.

(E) Certain refinancing issues. In the case of any issue described in paragraph (1)(B), an election may be made under subparagraph (A) of this paragraph only if all of the prior issues being redeemed are issues to which paragraph (1) (or the corresponding provision of prior law) applied. In applying subparagraph (A)(ii) with respect to such a refinancing issue, capital expenditures shall be taken into account only for purposes of determining whether the prior issues being redeemed qualified (and would have continued to qualify) under paragraph (1) (or the corresponding provision of prior law).

(F) Aggregate amount of capital expenditures where there is urban development action grant. In the case of any issue 95 percent or more of the net proceeds of which are to be used to provide facilities with respect to which an urban development action grant has been made under section 119 of the Housing and Community Development Act of 1974, capital expenditures of not to exceed $10,000,000 shall not be taken into account for purposes of applying subparagraph (A)(ii). This subparagraph shall not apply to bonds issued after [1]*December 31, 2006.*

(G) Additional capital expenditures not taken into account. With respect to bonds issued after [2]*December 31, 2006,* in addition to any capital expenditure described in subparagraph (C), capital expenditures of not to exceed $10,000,000 shall not be taken into account for purposes of applying subparagraph (A)(ii).

* * * * * * * * * * * *

[For Analysis, see ¶ 901. For Committee Reports, see ¶ 5012.]

[Endnote Code Sec. 144]

Matter in *italics* in Code Sec. 144(a)(4)(F) and Code Sec. 144(a)(4)(G) was added by Sec. 208(a) and (b) of the Tax Increase Prevention and Reconciliation Act of 2005, HR4297, 5/17/2006, which struck out:

1. "September 30, 2009"
2. "September 30, 2009"
Effective Date Enacted 5/17/2006.

[¶ 3008] Code Sec. 148. Arbitrage.

* * * * * * * * * * * *

(f) Required rebate to the United States.

* * * * * * * * * * * *

(4) Special rules for applying paragraph (2).

* * * * * * * * * * * *

(D) Exception for governmental units issuing $5,000,000 or less of bonds.—

(i) In general. An issue shall, for purposes of this subsection, be treated as meeting the requirements of paragraphs (2) and (3) if—

(I) the issue is issued by a governmental unit with general taxing powers,

(II) no bond which is part of such issue is a private activity bond,

(III) 95 percent or more of the net proceeds of such issue are to be used for local governmental activities of the issuer (or of a governmental unit the jurisdiction of which is entirely within the jurisdiction of the issuer), and

(IV) the aggregate face amount of all tax-exempt bonds (other than private activity bonds) issued by such unit during the calendar year in which such issue is issued is not reasonably expected to exceed $5,000,000.

(ii) Aggregation of issuers. For purpose of subclause (IV) of clause (i)—

(I) an issuer and all entities which issue bonds on behalf of such issuer shall be treated as 1 issuer,

[1]*(II)* all bonds issued by a subordinate entity shall, for purposes of applying such subclause to each other entity to which such entity is subordinate, be treated as issued by such other entity, and

[2]*(III)* an entity formed (or, to the extent provided by the Secretary, availed of) to avoid the purposes of such subclause (IV) and all other entities benefiting thereby shall be treated as 1 issuer.

(iii) Certain refunding bonds not taken into account in determining small issuer status. There shall not be taken into account under subclause (IV) of clause (i) any bond issued to refund (other than to advance refund) any bond to the extent the amount of the refunding bond does not exceed the outstanding amount of the refunded bond.

(iv) Certain issues issued by subordinate governmental units, etc., exempt from rebate requirement. An issue issued by a subordinate entity of a governmental unit with general taxing powers shall be treated as described in clause (i)(I) if the aggregate face amount of such issue does not exceed the lesser of—

(I) $5,000,000, or

(II) the amount which, when added to the aggregate face amount of other issues issued by such entity, does not exceed the portion of the $5,000,000 limitation under clause (i)(IV) which such governmental unit allocates to such entity.

For purposes of the preceding sentence, an entity which issues bonds on behalf of a governmental unit with general taxing powers shall be treated as a subordinate entity of such unit. An allocation shall be taken into account under subclause (II) only if it is irrevocable and made before the issuance date of such issue and only to the extent that the limitation so allocated bears a reasonable relationship to the benefits received by such governmental unit from issues issued by such entity.

(v) Determination of whether refunding bonds eligible for exception from rebate requirement. If any portion of an issue is issued to refund other bonds, such portion shall be treated as a separate issue which does not meet the requirements of paragraphs (2) and (3) by reason of this subparagraph unless—

(I) the aggregate face amount of such issue does not exceed $5,000,000,

(II) each refunded bond was issued as part of an issue which was treated as meeting the requirements of paragraphs (2) and (3) by reason of this subparagraph,

(III) the average maturity date of the refunding bonds issued as part of such issue is not later than the average maturity date of the bonds to be refunded by such issue, and

(IV) no refunding bond has a maturity date which is later than the date which is 30 years after the date the original bond was issued.

Subclause (III) shall not apply if the average maturity of the issue of which the original bond was a part (and of the issue of which the bonds to be refunded are a part) is 3 years or less. For purposes of this clause, average maturity shall be determined in accordance with section 147(b)(2)(A).

(vi) Refundings of bonds issued under law prior to Tax Reform Act of 1986. If section 141(a) did not apply to any refunded bond, the issue of which such refunded bond was a part shall be treated as meeting the requirements of subclause (II) of clause (v) if—

(I) such issue was issued by a governmental unit with general taxing powers,

(II) no bond issued as part of such issue was an industrial development bond (as defined in section 103(b)(2), but without regard to subparagraph (B) of section 103(b)(3)) or a private loan bond (as defined in section 103(o)(2)(A), but without regard to any exception from such definition other than section 103(o)(2)(C)), and

(III) the aggregate face amount of all tax-exempt bonds (other than bonds described in subclause (II)) issued by such unit during the calendar year in which such issue was issued did not exceed $5,000,000.

References in subclause (II) to section 103 shall be to such section as in effect on the day before the date of the enactment [10/22/86] of the Tax Reform Act of 1986. Rules similar to the rules of clauses (ii) and (iii) shall apply for purposes of subclause (III). For purposes of subclause (II) of clause (i), bonds described in subclause (II) of this clause to which section 141(a) does not apply shall not be treated as private activity bonds.

(vii) Increase in exception for bonds financing public school capital expenditures. Each of the $5,000,000 amounts in the preceding provisions of this subparagraph shall be increased by the lesser of $10,000,000 or so much of the aggregate face amount of the bonds as are attributable to financing the construction (within the meaning of subparagraph (C)(iv)) of public school facilities.

* * * * * * * * * * * * *

[For Analysis, see ¶ 902. For Committee Reports, see ¶ 5026.]

[Endnote Code Sec. 148]

Matter in *italics* in Code Sec. 148(f)(4)(D)(ii)(II) and Code Sec. 148(f)(4)(D)(ii)(III) was added by Sec. 508(c) of the Tax Increase Prevention and Reconciliation Act of 2005, HR4297, 5/17/2006, which struck out:

1. "(II) all bonds issued by a governmental unit to make loans to other governmental units with general taxing powers not subordinate to such unit shall, for purposes of applying such subclause to such unit, be treated as not issued by such unit,"

"(III)"

2. "(IV)"

Effective Date (Sec. 508(e), HR4297, 5/17/2006) effective for bonds issued after 5/17/2006.

[¶ 3009] Code Sec. 149. Bonds must be registered to be tax exempt; other requirements.

* * * * * * * * * * * *

(f) Treatment of certain pooled financing bonds.

(1) In general. Section 103(a) shall not apply to any pooled financing bond unless, with respect to the issue of which such bond is a part, the requirements of [1]*paragraphs (2), (3), (4), and (5)* are met.

(2) Reasonable expectation requirement.

[2]*(A) In general. The requirements of this paragraph are met with respect to an issue if the issuer reasonably expects that—*

(i) as of the close of the 1-year period beginning on the date of issuance of the issue, at least 30 percent of the net proceeds of the issue (as of the close of such period) will have been used directly or indirectly to make or finance loans to ultimate borrowers, and

(ii) as of the close of the 3-year period beginning on such date of issuance, at least 95 percent of the net proceeds of the issue (as of the close of such period) will have been so used.

(B) Certain factors may not be taken into account in determining expectations. Expectations as to changes in interest rates or in the provisions of this title (or in the regulations or rulings thereunder) may not be taken into account in determining whether expectations are reasonable for purposes of this paragraph.

(C) Net proceeds. For purposes of subparagraph (A), the term "net proceeds" has the meaning given such term by section 150 but shall not include proceeds used to finance issuance costs and shall not include proceeds necessary to pay interest (during such period) on the bonds which are part of the issue.

(D) Refunding bonds. For purposes of subparagraph (A), in the case of a refunding bond, the date of issuance taken into account is the date of issuance of the original bond.

(3) Cost of issuance payment requirements. The requirements of this paragraph are met with respect to an issue if—

(A) the payment of legal and underwriting costs associated with the issuance of the issue is not contingent, and

(B) at least 95 percent of the reasonably expected legal and underwriting costs associated with the issuance of the issue are paid not later than the 180th day after the date of the issuance of the issue.

[3]***(4) Written loan commitment requirement.***

(A) In general. The requirement of this paragraph is met with respect to an issue if the issuer receives prior to issuance written loan commitments identifying the ultimate potential borrowers of at least 30 percent of the net proceeds of such issue.

(B) Exception. Subparagraph (A) shall not apply with respect to any issuer which—

(i) is a State (or an integral part of a State) issuing pooled financing bonds to make or finance loans to subordinate governmental units of such State, or

(ii) is a State-created entity providing financing for water-infrastructure projects through the federally-sponsored State revolving fund program.

[4]***(5) Redemption requirement.*** *The requirement of this paragraph is met if to the extent that less than the percentage of the proceeds of an issue required to be used under clause (i) or (ii) of paragraph (2)(A) is used by the close of the period identified in such clause, the issuer uses an amount of proceeds equal to the excess of—*

(A) the amount required to be used under such clause, over

(B) the amount actually used by the close of such period,

to redeem outstanding bonds within 90 days after the end of such period.

[5]***(6)*** **Pooled financing bond.** For purposes of this subsection—

(A) In general. The term "pooled financing bond" means any bond issued as part of an issue more than $5,000,000 of the proceeds of which are reasonably expected (at the time of the issuance of the bonds) to be used (or are intentionally used) directly or indirectly to make or finance loans to 2 or more ultimate borrowers.

(B) Exceptions. Such term shall not include any bond if—

(i) section 146 applies to the issue of which such bond is a part (other than by reason of section 141(b)(5)) or would apply but for section 146(i), or

(ii) section 143(l)(3) applies to such issue.

[6]*(7)* **Definition of loan; treatment of mixed use issues.**

(A) Loan. For purposes of this subsection, the term "loan" does not include—

(i) any loan which is a nonpurpose investment (within the meaning of section 148(f)(6)(A), determined without regard to section 148(b)(3)), and

(ii) any use of proceeds by an agency of the issuer unless such agency is a political subdivision or instrumentality of the issuer.

(B) Portion of issue to be used for loans treated as separate issue. If only a portion of the proceeds of an issue is reasonably expected (at the time of issuance of the bond) to be used (or is intentionally used) as described in [7]*paragraph (6)(A)*, such portion and the other portion of such issue shall be treated as separate issues for purposes of determining whether such portion meets the requirements of this subsection.

[For Analysis, see ¶ 902. For Committee Reports, see ¶ 5026.]

[Endnote Code Sec. 149]

Matter in *italics* in Code Sec. 149(f)(1), Code Sec. 149(f)(2)(A), Code Sec. 149(f)(4), Code Sec. 149(f)(5), Code Sec. 149(f)(6), and Code Sec. 149(f)(7) was added by Sec. 508(a), (b), (d)(1) and (2) of the Tax Increase Prevention and Reconciliation Act of 2005, HR4297, 5/17/2006, which struck out:

1. "paragraphs (2) and (3)"
2. "(A) In general. The requirements of this paragraph are met with respect to an issue if the issuer reasonably expects that as of the close of the 3-year period beginning on the date of issuance of the issue, at least 95 percent of the net proceeds of the issue (as of the close of such period) will have been used directly or indirectly to make or finance loans to ultimate borrowers."
3. added para. (f)(4)
4. added para. (f)(5)
5. "(4)"
6. "(5)"
7. "paragraph (4)(A)"

Effective Date (Sec. 508(e), HR4297, 5/17/2006) effective for bonds issued after 5/17/2006.

[¶ 3010] Code Sec. 163. Interest.

* * * * * * * * * * * * *

(j) Limitation of deduction for interest on certain indebtedness.

* * * * * * * * * * * * *

[1]***(8) Treatment of corporate partners.*** *Except to the extent provided by regulations, in applying this subsection to a corporation which owns (directly or indirectly) an interest in a partnership—*

(A) such corporation's distributive share of interest income paid or accrued to such partnership shall be treated as interest income paid or accrued to such corporation,

(B) such corporation's distributive share of interest paid or accrued by such partnership shall be treated as interest paid or accrued by such corporation, and

(C) such corporation's share of the liabilities of such partnership shall be treated as liabilities of such corporation.

[2]*(9)* **Regulations.** The Secretary shall prescribe such regulations as may be appropriate to carry out the purposes of this subsection, including—

(A) such regulations as may be appropriate to prevent the avoidance of the purposes of this subsection,

(B) regulations providing such adjustments in the case of corporations which are members of an affiliated group as may be appropriate to carry out the purposes of this subsection, [3]

(C) regulations for the coordination of this subsection with section 884[4], *and*

[5]*(D) regulations providing for the reallocation of shares of partnership indebtedness, or distributive shares of the partnership's interest income or interest expense.*

* * * * * * * * * * * *

[For Analysis, see ¶ 109, ¶ 503. For Committee Reports, see ¶ 5002, ¶ 5020.]

[Endnote Code Sec. 163]

Matter in *italics* in Code Sec. 163(j)(8) and Code Sec. 163(j)(9) was added by Sec. 501(a) and (b) of the Tax Increase Prevention and Reconciliation Act of 2005, HR4297, 5/17/2006, which struck out:

1. added para. (j)(8)
2. "(8)"
3. "and"
4. "."
5. added subpara. (j)(9)(D)

Effective Date (Sec. 501(c), HR4297, 5/17/2006) effective for tax. yrs. begin. on or after 5/17/2006.

Sec. 102, HR4297, 5/17/2006, amended Sec. 303, P.L. 108-27, relating to the sunset of the amendments made by Secs. 301 and 302 of P.L. 108-27, by substituting "December 31, 2010" for "December 31, 2008". Sec. 303 as amended by Sec. 102, HR4297, 5/17/2006, reads as follows:

"SEC. 303. SUNSET OF TITLE. All provisions of, and amendments made by, this title [Secs. 301 and 302] shall not apply to taxable years beginning after December 31, 2010, and the Internal Revenue Code of 1986 shall be applied and administered to such years as if such provisions and amendments had never been enacted."

[¶ 3011] Code Sec. 167. Depreciation.

* * * * * * * * * * * *

(g) Depreciation under income forecast method.

* * * * * * * * * * * *

[1]***(8) Special rules for certain musical works and copyrights.***

(A) In general. If an election is in effect under this paragraph for any taxable year, then, notwithstanding paragraph (1), any expense which—

(i) is paid or incurred by the taxpayer in creating or acquiring any applicable musical property placed in service during the taxable year, and

(ii) is otherwise properly chargeable to capital account,

shall be amortized ratably over the 5-year period beginning with the month in which the property was placed in service. The preceding sentence shall not apply to any expense which, without regard to this paragraph, would not be allowable as a deduction.

(B) Exclusive method. Except as provided in this paragraph, no depreciation or amortization deduction shall be allowed with respect to any expense to which subparagraph (A) applies.

(C) Applicable musical property. For purposes of this paragraph—

(i) In general. The term "applicable musical property" means any musical composition (including any accompanying words), or any copyright with respect to a musical composition, which is property to which this subsection applies without regard to this paragraph.

(ii) Exceptions. Such term shall not include any property—

(I) with respect to which expenses are treated as qualified creative expenses to which section 263A(h) applies,

(II) to which a simplied procedure established under section 263A(j)(2) applies, or

(III) which is an amortizable section 197 intangible (as defined in section 197(c)).

(D) Election. An election under this paragraph shall be made at such time and in such form as the Secretary may prescribe and shall apply to all applicable musical property placed in service during the taxable year for which the election applies.

(E) Termination. An election may not be made under this paragraph for any taxable year beginning after December 31, 2010.

(h) Amortization of geological and geophysical expenditures.

* * * * * * * * * * * * *

[2]***(5) Special rule for major integrated oil companies.***

(A) In general. In the case of a major integrated oil company, paragraphs (1) and (4) shall be applied by substituting "5-year" for "24 month".

(B) Major integrated oil company. For purposes of this paragraph, the term "major integrated oil company" means, with respect to any taxable year, a producer of crude oil—

(i) which has an average daily worldwide production of crude oil of at least 500,000 barrels for the taxable year,

(ii) which had gross receipts in excess of $1,000,000,000 for its last taxable year ending during calendar year 2005, and

(iii) to which subsection (c) of section 613A does not apply by reason of paragraph (4) of section 613A(d), determined—

(I) by substituting "15 percent" for "5 percent" each place it occurs in paragraph (3) of section 613A(d), and

(II) without regard to whether subsection (c) of section 613A does not apply by reason of paragraph (2) of section 613A(d).

For purposes of clauses (i) and (ii), all persons treated as a single employer under subsections (a) and (b) of section 52 shall be treated as 1 person and, in case of a short taxable year, the rule under section 448(c)(3)(B) shall apply.

* * * * * * * * * * * * *

[For Analysis, see ¶ 404, ¶ 405. For Committee Reports, see ¶ 5011, ¶ 5022.]

[Endnote Code Sec. 167]

Code Sec. 167(g)(8), in *italics*, was added by Sec. 207(a) of the Tax Increase Prevention and Reconciliation Act of 2005, HR4297, 5/17/2006.

1. added para. (g)(8)

Effective Date (Sec. 207(b), HR4297, 5/17/2006) effective for expenses paid or incurred with respect to property placed in service in tax. yrs. begin. after 12/31/2005.

Code Sec. 167(h)(5), in *italics*, was added by Sec. 503(a), HR4297, 5/17/2006.

2. added para. (h)(5)

Effective Date (Sec. 503(b), HR4297, 5/17/2006) effective for amounts paid or incurred after 5/17/2006.

[¶ 3012] Code Sec. 170. Charitable, etc., contributions and gifts.

* * * * * * * * * * * * *

(e) Certain contributions of ordinary income and capital gain property.

(1) General rule. The amount of any charitable contribution of property otherwise taken into account under this section shall be reduced by the sum of—

(A) the amount of gain which would not have been long-term capital gain [1]*(determined without regard to section 1221(b)(3))* if the property contributed had been sold by the taxpayer at its fair market value (determined at the time of such contribution), and

(B) in the case of a charitable contribution—

(i) of tangible personal property, if the use by the donee is unrelated to the purpose or function constituting the basis for its exemption under section 501 (or, in the case of a governmental unit, to any purpose or function described in subsection (c)),

(ii) to or for the use of a private foundation (as defined in section 509(a)), other than a private foundation described in subsection (b)(1)(E), or

(iii) of any patent, copyright (other than a copyright described in section 1221(a)(3) or 1231(b)(1)(C)), trademark, trade name, trade secret, know-how, software (other than software described in section 197(e)(3)(A)(i)), or similar property, or applications or registrations of such property,

the amount of gain which would have been long-term capital gain if the property contributed had been sold by the taxpayer at its fair market value (determined at the time of such contribution).

For purposes of applying this paragraph (other than in the case of gain to which section 617(d)(1), 1245(a), 1250(a), 1252(a), or 1254(a) applies), property which is property used in the trade or business (as defined in section 1231(b)) shall be treated as a capital asset. For purposes of applying this paragraph in the case of a charitable contribution of stock in an S corporation, rules similar to the rules of section 751 shall apply in determining whether gain on such stock would have been long-term capital gain if such stock were sold by the taxpayer.

* * * * * * * * * * * * *

[For Analysis, see ¶ 208. For Committee Reports, see ¶ 5008.]

[Endnote Code Sec. 170]

Matter in *italics* in Code Sec. 170(e)(1)(A) was added by Sec. 204(b) of the Tax Increase Prevention and Reconciliation Act of 2005, HR4297, 5/17/2006.

1. added matter in subpara. (e)(1)(A)

Effective Date (Sec. 204(c), HR4297, 5/17/2006) effective for sales and exchanges in tax. yrs. begin. after 5/17/2006.

[¶ 3013] Code Sec. 179. Election to expense certain depreciable business assets.

* * * * * * * * * * * * *

(b) Limitations.

(1) Dollar limitation. The aggregate cost which may be taken into account under subsection (a) for any taxable year shall not exceed $25,000 ($100,000 in the case of taxable years beginning after 2002 and before [1]*2010*).

(2) Reduction in limitation. The limitation under paragraph (1) for any taxable year shall be reduced (but not below zero) by the amount by which the cost of section 179 property placed in service during such taxable year exceeds $200,000 ($400,000 in the case of taxable years beginning after 2002 and before [2]*2010*).

(3) Limitation based on income from trade or business.

(A) In general. The amount allowed as a deduction under subsection (a) for any taxable year (determined after the application of paragraphs (1) and (2)) shall not exceed the aggregate amount of taxable income of the taxpayer for such taxable year which is derived from the active conduct by the taxpayer of any trade or business during such taxable year.

(B) Carryover of disallowed deduction. The amount allowable as a deduction under subsection (a) for any taxable year shall be increased by the lesser of

(i) the aggregate amount disallowed under subparagraph (A) for all prior taxable years (to the extent not previously allowed as a deduction by reason of this subparagraph), or

(ii) the excess (if any) of—

(I) the limitation of paragraphs (1) and (2) (or if lesser, the aggregate amount of taxable income referred to in subparagraph (A)), over

(II) the amount allowable as a deduction under subsection (a) for such taxable year without regard to this subparagraph.

(C) Computation of taxable income. For purposes of this paragraph, taxable income derived from the conduct of a trade or business shall be computed without regard to the deduction allowable under this section.

(4) Married individuals filing separately. In the case of a husband and wife filing separate returns for the taxable year—

(A) such individuals shall be treated as 1 taxpayer for purposes of paragraphs (1) and (2), and

(B) unless such individuals elect otherwise, 50 percent of the cost which may be taken into account under subsection (a) for such taxable year (before application of paragraph (3)) shall be allocated to each such individual.

(5) Inflation adjustments.

(A) In general. In the case of any taxable year beginning in a calendar year after 2003 and before [3]*2010*, the $100,000 and $400,000 amounts in paragraphs (1) and (2) shall each be increased by an amount equal to—

(i) such dollar amount, multiplied by

(ii) the cost-of-living adjustment determined under section 1(f)(3) for the calendar year in which the taxable year begins, by substituting "calendar year 2002" for "calendar year 1992" in subparagraph (B) thereof.

(B) Rounding.

(i) Dollar limitation. If the amount in paragraph (1) as increased under subparagraph (A) is not a multiple of $1,000, such amount shall be rounded to the nearest multiple of $1,000.

(ii) Phaseout amount. If the amount in paragraph (2) as increased under subparagraph (A) is not a multiple of $10,000, such amount shall be rounded to the nearest multiple of $10,000.

(6) Limitation on cost taken into account for certain passenger vehicles.

(A) In general. The cost of any sport utility vehicle for any taxable year which may be taken into account under this section shall not exceed $25,000.

(B) Sport utility vehicle. For purposes of subparagraph (A)—

(i) In general. The term "sport utility vehicle" means any 4-wheeled vehicle—

(I) which is primarily designed or which can be used to carry passengers over public streets, roads, or highways (except any vehicle operated exclusively on a rail or rails),

(II) which is not subject to section 280F, and

(III) which is rated at not more than 14,000 pounds gross vehicle weight.

(ii) Certain vehicles excluded. Such term does not include any vehicle which—

(I) is designed to have a seating capacity of more than 9 persons behind the driver's seat,

(II) is equipped with a cargo area of at least 6 feet in interior length which is an open area or is designed for use as an open area but is enclosed by a cap and is not readily accessible directly from the passenger compartment, or

(III) has an integral enclosure, fully enclosing the driver compartment and load carrying device, does not have seating rearward of the driver's seat, and has no body section protruding more than 30 inches ahead of the leading edge of the windshield.

(c) Election.

* * * * * * * * * * * * *

(2) Election irrevocable. Any election made under this section, and any specification contained in any such election, may not be revoked except with the consent of the Secretary. Any such election or specification with respect to any taxable year beginning after 2002 and before [4]*2010* may be revoked by the taxpayer with respect to any property, and such revocation, once made, shall be irrevocable.

(d) Definitions and special rules.

(1) Section 179 property. For purposes of this section, the term "section 179 property" means property—

(A) which is—

(i) tangible property (to which section 168 applies), or

(ii) computer software (as defined in section 197(e)(3)(B)) which is described in section 197(e)(3)(A)(i), to which section 167 applies, and which is placed in service in a taxable year beginning after 2002 and before [5]*2010,*

(B) which is section 1245 property (as defined in section 1245(a)(3)), and

(C) which is acquired by purchase for use in the active conduct of a trade or business.

Such term shall not include any property described in section 50(b) and shall not include air conditioning or heating units.

* * * * * * * * * * * *

[For Analysis, see ¶ 401, ¶ 402, ¶ 403. For Committee Reports, see ¶ 5001.]

[Endnote Code Sec. 179]

Matter in *italics* in Code Sec. 179(b)(1), Code Sec. 179(b)(2), Code Sec. 179(b)(5), Code Sec. 179(c)(2), and Code Sec. 179(d)(1)(A)(ii) was added by Sec. 101 of the Tax Increase Prevention and Reconciliation Act of 2005, HR4297, 5/17/2006, which struck out:

1. "2008"
2. "2008"
3. "2008"
4. "2008"
5. "2008"

Effective Date Enacted 5/17/2006.

[¶ 3014] Code Sec. 199. Income attributable to domestic production activities.

(a) Allowance of deduction.

* * * * * * * * * * * *

(2) Phasein. In the case of any taxable year beginning after 2004 and before 2010, paragraph (1) [1]shall be applied by substituting for the percentage contained therein the transition percentage determined under the following table:

For taxable years beginning in:	The transition percentage is:
2005 or 2006	3
2007, 2008, or 2009	6

(b) Deduction limited to wages paid.

* * * * * * * * * * * *

[2]*(2)* ***W-2 wages.*** *For purposes of this section—*

(A) In general. The term "W-2 wages" means, with respect to any person for any taxable year of such person, the sum of the amounts described in paragraphs (3) and (8) of section 6051(a) paid by such person with respect to employment of employees by such person during the calendar year ending during such taxable year.

(B) Limitation to wages attributable to domestic production. Such term shall not include any amount which is not properly allocable to domestic production gross receipts for purposes of subsection (c)(1).

(C) Return requirement. Such term shall not include any amount which is not properly included in a return filed with the Social Security Administration on or before the 60th day after the due date (including extensions) for such return.

* * * * * * * * * * * *

(d) Definitions and special rules.

(1) Application of section to pass-thru entities.

(A) Partnerships and S corporations. In the case of a partnership or S corporation—

(i) this section shall be applied at the partner or shareholder level,

(ii) each partner or shareholder shall take into account such person's allocable share of each item described in subparagraph (A) or (B) of subsection (c)(1) (determined without regard to whether the items described in such subparagraph (A) exceed the items described in such subparagraph (B)), and

[3]*(iii) each partner or shareholder shall be treated for purposes of subsection (b) as having W-2 wages for the taxable year in an amount equal to such person's allocable share of the W-2 wages of the partnership or S corporation for the taxable year (as determined under regulations prescribed by the Secretary).*

(B) Trusts and estates. In the case of a trust or estate—

(i) the items referred to in subparagraph (A)(ii) (as determined therein) and the W-2 wages of the trust or estate for the taxable year, shall be apportioned between the beneficiaries and the fiduciary (and among the beneficiaries) under regulations prescribed by the Secretary, and

(ii) for purposes of paragraph (2), adjusted gross income of the trust or estate shall be determined as provided in section 67(e) with the adjustments described in such paragraph.

(C) Regulations. The Secretary may prescribe rules requiring or restricting the allocation of items and wages under this paragraph and may prescribe such reporting requirements as the Secretary determines appropriate.

* * * * * * * * * * * *

[For Analysis, see ¶301, ¶302. For Committee Reports, see ¶5032.]

[Endnote Code Sec. 199]

Matter in *italics* in Code Sec. 199(a)(2), Code Sec. 199(b)(2), and Code Sec. 199(d)(1)(A)(iii) was added by Sec. 514(a), (b)(1) and (2) of the Tax Increase Prevention and Reconciliation Act of 2005, HR4297, 5/17/2006, which struck out:

1. "and subsection (d)(1)"

2. "(2) W-2 wages.

"For purposes of this section, the term 'W-2 wages' means, with respect to any person for any taxable year of such person, the sum of the amounts described in paragraphs (3) and (8) of section 6051(a) paid by such person with respect to employment of employees by such person during the calendar year ending during such taxable year. Such term shall not include any amount which is not properly included in a return filed with the Social Security Administration on or before the 60th day after the due date (including extensions) for such return."

3. "(iii) each partner or shareholder shall be treated for purposes of subsection (b) as having W-2 wages for the taxable year in an amount equal to the lesser of—

"(I) such person's allocable share of the W-2 wages of the partnership or S corporation for the taxable year (as determined under regulations prescribed by the Secretary), or

"(II) 2 times 9 percent of so much of such person's qualified production activities income as is attributable to items allocated under clause (ii) for the taxable year."

Effective Date (Sec. 514(c), HR4297, 5/17/2006) effective for tax. yrs. begin. after 5/17/2006.

[¶3015] Code Sec. 355. Distribution of stock and securities of a controlled corporation.

* * * * * * * * * * * *

(b) Requirements as to active business.

* * * * * * * * * * * *

[1]***(3) Special rule relating to active business requirement.***

(A) In general. In the case of any distribution made after the date of the enactment of this paragraph and on or before December 31, 2010, a corporation shall be treated as

meeting the requirement of paragraph (2)(A) if and only if such corporation is engaged in the active conduct of a trade or business.

(B) Affiliated group rule. For purposes of subparagraph (A), all members of such corporation's separate affiliated group shall be treated as one corporation. For purposes of the preceding sentence, a corporation's separate affiliated group is the affiliated group which would be determined under section 1504(a) if such corporation were the common parent and section 1504(b) did not apply.

(C) Transition rule. Subparagraph (A) shall not apply to any distribution pursuant to a transaction which is—

(i) made pursuant to an agreement which was binding on the date of the enactment of this paragraph and at all times thereafter,

(ii) described in a ruling request submitted to the Internal Revenue Service on or before such date, or

(iii) described on or before such date in a public announcement or in a filing with the Securities and Exchange Commission.

The preceding sentence shall not apply if the distributing corporation elects not to have such sentence apply to distributions of such corporation. Any such election, once made, shall be irrevocable.

(D) Special rule for certain pre-enactment distributions. For purposes of determining the continued qualification under paragraph (2)(A) of distributions made on or before the date of the enactment of this paragraph as a result of an acquisition, disposition, or other restructuring after such date and on or before December 31, 2010, such distribution shall be treated as made on the date of such acquisition, disposition, or restructuring for purposes of applying subparagraphs (A) through (C) of this paragraph.

* * * * * * * * * * * *

[2]***(g) Section not to apply to distributions involving disqualified investment corporations.***

(1) In general. *This section (and so much of section 356 as relates to this section) shall not apply to any distribution which is part of a transaction if—*

(A) either the distributing corporation or controlled corporation is, immediately after the transaction, a disqualified investment corporation, and

(B) any person holds, immediately after the transaction, a 50-percent or greater interest in any disqualified investment corporation, but only if such person did not hold such an interest in such corporation immediately before the transaction.

(2) Disqualified investment corporation. *For purposes of this subsection—*

(A) In general. The term "disqualified investment corporation" means any distributing or controlled corporation if the fair market value of the investment assets of the corporation is—

(i) in the case of distributions after the end of the 1-year period beginning on the date of the enactment of this subsection, ⅔ or more of the fair market value of all assets of the corporation, and

(ii) in the case of distributions during such 1-year period, ¾ or more of the fair market value of all assets of the corporation.

(B) Investment assets.

(i) In general. Except as otherwise provided in this subparagraph, the term "investment assets" means—

(I) cash,

(II) any stock or securities in a corporation,

(III) any interest in a partnership,

(IV) any debt instrument or other evidence of indebtedness,

(V) any option, forward or futures contract, notional principal contract, or derivative,

(VI) foreign currency, or

(VII) any similar asset.

(ii) Exception for assets used in active conduct of certain financial trades or businesses. Such term shall not include any asset which is held for use in the active and regular conduct of—

(I) a lending or finance business (within the meaning of section 954(h)(4)),

(II) a banking business through a bank (as defined in section 581), a domestic building and loan association (within the meaning of section 7701(a)(19)), or any similar institution specified by the Secretary, or

(III) an insurance business if the conduct of the business is licensed, authorized, or regulated by an applicable insurance regulatory body.

This clause shall only apply with respect to any business if substantially all of the income of the business is derived from persons who are not related (within the meaning of section 267(b) or 707(b)(1)) to the person conducting the business.

(iii) Exception for securities marked to market. Such term shall not include any security (as defined in section 475(c)(2)) which is held by a dealer in securities and to which section 475(a) applies.

(iv) Stock or securities in a 20-percent controlled entity.

(I) In general. Such term shall not include any stock and securities in, or any asset described in subclause (IV) or (V) of clause (i) issued by, a corporation which is a 20-percent controlled entity with respect to the distributing or controlled corporation.

(II) Look-thru rule. The distributing or controlled corporation shall, for purposes of applying this subsection, be treated as owning its ratable share of the assets of any 20-percent controlled entity.

(III) 20-percent controlled entity. For purposes of this clause, the term "20-percent controlled entity" means, with respect to any distributing or controlled corporation, any corporation with respect to which the distributing or controlled corporation owns directly or indirectly stock meeting the requirements of section 1504(a)(2), except that such section shall be applied by substituting "20-percent" for "80-percent" and without regard to stock described in section 1504(a)(4).

(v) Interests in certain partnerships.

(I) In general. Such term shall not include any interest in a partnership, or any debt instrument or other evidence of indebtedness, issued by the partnership, if 1 or more of the trades or businesses of the partnership are (or, without regard to the 5-year requirement under subsection (b)(2)(B), would be) taken into account by the distributing or controlled corporation, as the case may be, in determining whether the requirements of subsection (b) are met with respect to the distribution.

(II) Look-thru rule. The distributing or controlled corporation shall, for purposes of applying this subsection, be treated as owning its ratable share of the assets of any partnership described in subclause (I).

***(3) 50-percent or greater interest.** For purposes of this subsection—*

(A) In general. The term "50-percent or greater interest" has the meaning given such term by subsection (d)(4).

(B) Attribution rules. The rules of section 318 shall apply for purposes of determining ownership of stock for purposes of this paragraph.

***(4) Transaction.** For purposes of this subsection, the term "transaction" includes a series of transactions.*

***(5) Regulations.** The Secretary shall prescribe such regulations as may be necessary to carry out, or prevent the avoidance of, the purposes of this subsection, including regulations—*

(A) to carry out, or prevent the avoidance of, the purposes of this subsection in cases involving—

(i) the use of related persons, intermediaries, pass-thru entities, options, or other arrangements, and

(ii) the treatment of assets unrelated to the trade or business of a corporation as investment assets if, prior to the distribution, investment assets were used to acquire such unrelated assets,

(B) which in appropriate cases exclude from the application of this subsection a distribution which does not have the character of a redemption which would be treated as a sale or exchange under section 302, and

(C) which modify the application of the attribution rules applied for purposes of this subsection.

[For Analysis, see ¶ 501, ¶ 502. For Committee Reports, see ¶ 5006, ¶ 5025.]

[Endnote Code Sec. 355]

Code Sec. 355(b)(3), in *italics*, was added by Sec. 202 of the Tax Increase Prevention and Reconciliation Act of 2005, HR4297, 5/17/2006.

1. added para. (b)(3)

Effective Date Enacted 5/17/2006.

Code Sec. 355(g), in *italics*, was added by Sec. 507(a), HR4297, 5/17/2006.

2. added subsec. (g)

Effective Date (Sec. 507(b), HR4297, 5/17/2006) effective for distributions after 5/17/2006. Sec. 507(b)(2) of this Act, provides:

"(2) Transition rule. The amendments made by this section shall not apply to any distribution pursuant to a transaction which is—

"(A) made pursuant to an agreement which was binding on such date of enactment and at all times thereafter,

"(B) described in a ruling request submitted to the Internal Revenue Service on or before such date, or

"(C) described on or before such date in a public announcement or in a filing with the Securities and Exchange Commission."

[¶ 3016] Code Sec. 408A. Roth IRAs.

* * * * * * * * * * * *

(c) Treatment of contributions.

* * * * * * * * * * * *

(3) Limits based on modified adjusted gross income.

(A) Dollar limit. The amount determined under paragraph (2) for any taxable year shall not exceed an amount equal to the amount determined under paragraph (2)(A) for such taxable year, reduced (but not below zero) by the amount which bears the same ratio to such amount as—

(i) the excess of—

(I) the taxpayer's adjusted gross income for such taxable year, over

(II) the applicable dollar amount, bears to

(ii) $15,000 ($10,000 in the case of a joint return or a married individual filing a separate return).

The rules of subparagraphs (B) and (C) of section 219(g)(2) shall apply to any reduction under this subparagraph.

[1]*(B)* Definitions. For purposes of this paragraph—

(i) adjusted gross income shall be determined in the same manner as under section 219(g)(3), [2]*except that any amount included in gross income under subsection (d)(3) shall not be taken into account, and*

(ii) the applicable dollar amount is—

(I) in the case of a taxpayer filing a joint return, $150,000,

(II) in the case of any other taxpayer (other than a married individual filing a separate return), $95,000, and

(III) in the case of a married individual filing a separate return, zero.

[3]*(C)* Marital status. Section 219(g)(4) shall apply for purposes of this paragraph.

* * * * * * * * * * * *

(d) **Distribution rules.** For purposes of this title—

* * * * * * * * * * * *

(3) **Rollovers from an IRA other than a Roth IRA.**

(A) In general. Notwithstanding section 408(d)(3), in the case of any distribution to which this paragraph applies—

(i) there shall be included in gross income any amount which would be includible were it not part of a qualified rollover contribution,

(ii) section 72(t) shall not apply, and

[4]*(iii) unless the taxpayer elects not to have this clause apply, any amount required to be included in gross income for any taxable year beginning in 2010 by reason of this paragraph shall be so included ratably over the 2-taxable-year period beginning with the first taxable year beginning in 2011.*

Any election under clause (iii) for any distributions during a taxable year may not be changed after the due date for such taxable year.

(B) Distributions to which paragraph applies. This paragraph shall apply to a distribution from an individual retirement plan (other than a Roth IRA) maintained for the benefit of an individual which is contributed to a Roth IRA maintained for the benefit of such individual in a qualified rollover contribution.

(C) Conversions. The conversion of an individual retirement plan (other than a Roth IRA) to a Roth IRA shall be treated for purposes of this paragraph as a distribution to which this paragraph applies.

(D) Additional reporting requirements. Trustees of Roth IRAs, trustees of individual retirement plans, or both, whichever is appropriate, shall include such additional information in reports required under section 408(i) as the Secretary may require to ensure that amounts required to be included in gross income under subparagraph (A) are so included.

(E) Special rules for contributions to which [5]*2-year* averaging applies. In the case of a qualified rollover contribution to a Roth IRA of a distribution to which subparagraph (A)(iii) applied, the following rules shall apply:

[6]*(i) Acceleration of inclusion.*

(I) In general. The amount otherwise required to be included in gross income for any taxable year beginning in 2010 or the first taxable year in the 2-year period under subparagraph (A)(iii) shall be increased by the aggregate distributions from Roth IRAs for such taxable year which are allocable under paragraph (4) to the portion of such qualified rollover contribution required to be included in gross income under subparagraph (A)(i).

(II) Limitation on aggregate amount included. The amount required to be included in gross income for any taxable year under subparagraph (A)(iii) shall not exceed the aggregate amount required to be included in gross income under subparagraph (A)(iii) for all taxable years in the 2-year period (without regard to subclause (I)) reduced by amounts included for all preceding taxable years.

(ii) Death of distributee.

(I) In general. If the individual required to include amounts in gross income under such subparagraph dies before all of such amounts are included, all remaining amounts shall be included in gross income for the taxable year which includes the date of death.

(II) Special rule for surviving spouse. If the spouse of the individual described in subclause (I) acquires the individual's entire interest in any Roth IRA to which such qualified rollover contribution is properly allocable, the spouse may elect to treat the remaining amounts described in subclause (I) as includible in the spouse's gross income in the taxable years of the spouse ending with or within the taxable years of such individual in which such amounts would otherwise have been includible. Any such election may not be made or changed after the due date for the spouse's taxable year which includes the date of death.

(F) Special rule for applying section 72.

(i) In general. If—

(I) any portion of a distribution from a Roth IRA is properly allocable to a qualified rollover contribution described in this paragraph; and

(II) such distribution is made within the 5-taxable year period beginning with the taxable year in which such contribution was made,

then section 72(t) shall be applied as if such portion were includible in gross income.

(ii) Limitation. Clause (i) shall apply only to the extent of the amount of the qualified rollover contribution includible in gross income under subparagraph (A)(i).

* * * * * * * * * * * *

[For Analysis, see ¶ 203. For Committee Reports, see ¶ 5030.]

[Endnote Code Sec. 408A]

Matter in *italics* in Code Sec. 408A(c)(3)(B), Code Sec. 408A(c)(3)(B)(i), Code Sec. 408A(c)(3)(C), Code Sec. 408A(d)(3)(A)(iii), Code Sec. 408A(d)(3)(E), and Code Sec. 408A(d)(3)(E)(i) was added by Sec. 512(a)(1) and (2) and (b)(1) and (2) of the Tax Increase Prevention and Reconciliation Act of 2005, HR4297, 5/17/2006, which struck out:

1. "(B) Rollover from IRA. A taxpayer shall not be allowed to make a qualified rollover contribution to a Roth IRA from an individual retirement plan other than a Roth IRA during any taxable year if, for the taxable year of the distribution to which such contribution relates—

"(i) the taxpayer's adjusted gross income exceeds $100,000, or

"(ii) the taxpayer is a married individual filing a separate return."

"(C)"

2. "except that—

"(I) any amount included in gross income under subsection (d)(3) shall not be taken into account; and

"(II) any amount included in gross income by reason of a required distribution under a provision described in paragraph (5) shall not be taken into account for purposes of subparagraph (B)(i), and"

3. "(D)"

4. "(iii) unless the taxpayer elects not to have this clause apply for any taxable year, any amount required to be included in gross income for such taxable year by reason of this paragraph for any distribution before January 1, 1999, shall be so included ratably over the 4-taxable year period beginning with such taxable year."

5. "4-year"

6. "(i) Acceleration of inclusion.

"(I) In general. The amount required to be included in gross income for each of the first 3 taxable years in the 4-year period under subparagraph (A)(iii) shall be increased by the aggregate distributions from Roth IRAs for such taxable year which are allocable under paragraph (4) to the portion of such qualified rollover contribution required to be included in gross income under subparagraph (A)(i).

"(II) Limitation on aggregate amount included. The amount required to be included in gross income for any taxable year under subparagraph (A)(iii) shall not exceed the aggregate amount required to be included in gross income under subparagraph (A)(iii) for all taxable years in the 4-year period (without regard to subclause (I)) reduced by amounts included for all preceding taxable years."

Effective Date (Sec. 512(c), HR4297, 5/17/2006) effective for tax. yrs. begin. after 12/31/2009.

[¶ 3017] Code Sec. 468B. Special rules for designated settlement funds.

* * * * * * * * * * * *

[1]***(g) Clarification of taxation of certain funds.***

(1) In general. *Except as provided in paragraph (2), nothing in any provision of law shall be construed as providing that an escrow account, settlement fund, or similar fund is not subject to current income tax. The Secretary shall prescribe regulations providing for the taxation of any such account or fund whether as a grantor trust or otherwise.*

(2) Exemption from tax for certain settlement funds. *An escrow account, settlement fund, or similar fund shall be treated as beneficially owned by the United States and shall be exempt from taxation under this subtitle if—*

(A) it is established pursuant to a consent decree entered by a judge of a United States District Court,

(B) it is created for the receipt of settlement payments as directed by a government entity for the sole purpose of resolving or satisfying one or more claims asserting liabil-

ity under the Comprehensive Environmental Response, Compensation, and Liability Act of 1980,

(C) the authority and control over the expenditure of funds therein (including the expenditure of contributions thereto and any net earnings thereon) is with such government entity, and

(D) upon termination, any remaining funds will be disbursed to such government entity for use in accordance with applicable law.

For purposes of this paragraph, the term "government entity" means the United States, any State or political subdivision thereof, the District of Columbia, any possession of the United States, and any agency or instrumentality of any of the foregoing.

***(3) Termination.** Paragraph (2) shall not apply to accounts and funds established after December 31, 2010.*

[For Analysis, see ¶ 303. For Committee Reports, see ¶ 5005.]

[Endnote Code Sec. 468B]

Code Sec. 468B(g), in *italics*, was added by Sec. 201(a) of the Tax Increase Prevention and Reconciliation Act of 2005, HR4297, 5/17/2006, which struck out:

1. "(g) Clarification of taxation of certain funds. Nothing in any provision of law shall be construed as providing that an escrow account, settlement fund, or similar fund is not subject to current income tax. The Secretary shall prescribe regulations providing for the taxation of any such account or fund whether as a grantor trust or otherwise."

Effective Date (Sec. 201(b), HR4297, 5/17/2006) effective for accounts and funds established after 5/17/2006.

[¶ 3018] Code Sec. 852. Taxation of regulated investment companies and their shareholders.

* * * * * * * * * * * *

(b) Method of taxation of companies and shareholders.

* * * * * * * * * * * *

(3) Capital gains.

(A) Imposition of tax. There is hereby imposed for each taxable year in the case of every regulated investment company a tax, determined as provided in section 1201(a), on the excess, if any, of the net capital gain over the deduction for dividends paid (as defined in section 561) determined with reference to capital gain dividends only.

(B) Treatment of capital gain dividends by shareholders. A capital gain dividend shall be treated by the shareholders as a gain from the sale or exchange of a capital asset held for more than 1 year.

(C) Definition of capital gain dividend. For purposes of this part, a capital gain dividend is any dividend, or part thereof, which is designated by the company as a capital gain dividend in a written notice mailed to its shareholders not later than 60 days after the close of its taxable year; except that, if there is an increase in the excess described in subparagraph (A) of this paragraph for such year which results from a determination (as defined in section 860(e)), such designation may be made with respect to such increase at any time before the expiration of 120 days after the date of such determination. If the aggregate amount so designated with respect to a taxable year of the company (including capital gains dividends paid after the close of the taxable year described in section 855) is greater than the net capital gain of the taxable year, the portion of each distribution which shall be a capital gain dividend shall be only that proportion of the amount so designated which such net capital gain bears to the aggregate amount so designated. For purposes of this subparagraph, the amount of the net capital gain for a taxable year (to which an election under section 4982(e)(4) does not apply) shall be determined without regard to any net capital loss or net long-term capital loss attributable to transactions after October 31 of such year, and any such net capital loss or net long-term capital loss shall be treated as arising on the 1st day of the next taxable year. To the extent provided in regulations, the preceding sentence shall apply also for purposes of computing the taxable income of the regulated investment company.

(D) Treatment by shareholders of undistributed capital gains.

(i) Every shareholder of a regulated investment company at the close of the company's taxable year shall include, in computing his long-term capital gains in his return for his taxable year in which the last day of the company's taxable year falls, such amount as the company shall designate in respect of such shares in a written notice mailed to its shareholders at any time prior to the expiration of 60 days after close of its taxable year, but the amount so includible by any shareholder shall not exceed that part of the amount subjected to tax in subparagraph (A) which he would have received if all of such amount had been distributed as capital gain dividends by the company to the holders of such shares at the close of its taxable year.

(ii) For purposes of this title, every such shareholder shall be deemed to have paid, for his taxable year under clause (i), the tax imposed by subparagraph (A) on the amounts required by this subparagraph to be included in respect of such shares in computing his long-term capital gains for that year; and such shareholder shall be allowed credit or refund, as the case may be, for the tax so deemed to have been paid by him.

(iii) The adjusted basis of such shares in the hands of the shareholder shall be increased, with respect to the amounts required by this subparagraph to be included in computing his long-term capital gains, by the difference between the amount of such includible gains and the tax deemed paid by such shareholder in respect of such shares under clause (ii).

(iv) In the event of such designation the tax imposed by subparagraph (A) shall be paid by the regulated investment company within 30 days after close of its taxable year.

(v) The earnings and profits of such regulated investment company, and the earnings and profits of any such shareholder which is a corporation, shall be appropriately adjusted in accordance with regulations prescribed by the Secretary.

[1]*(E) Certain distributions. In the case of a distribution to which section 897 does not apply by reason of the second sentence of section 897(h)(1), the amount of such distribution which would be included in computing long-term capital gains for the shareholder under subparagraph (B) or (D) (without regard to this subparagraph)—*

(i) shall not be included in computing such shareholder's long-term capital gains, and

(ii) shall be included in such shareholder's gross income as a dividend from the regulated investment company.

* * * * * * * * * * * *

[For Analysis, see ¶603. For Committee Reports, see ¶5023, ¶5024.]

[Endnote Code Sec. 852]

Code Sec. 852(b)(3)(E), in *italics*, was added by Sec. 505(c)(1) of the Tax Increase Prevention and Reconciliation Act of 2005, HR4297, 5/17/2006.

1. added subpara. (b)(3)(E)

Effective Date (Sec. 505(d), HR4297, 5/17/2006) effective for tax. yrs. of qualified investment entities begin. after 12/31/2005, except that no amount shall be required to be withheld under Code Secs. 1441, 1442, or 1445 with respect to any distribution before 5/17/2006 if such amount was not otherwise required to be withheld under any such section as in effect before such amendments.

[¶3019] Code Sec. 871. Tax on nonresident alien individuals.

* * * * * * * * * * * *

(k) Exemption for certain dividends of regulated investment companies.

* * * * * * * * * * * *

(2) Short-term capital gain dividends.

(A) In general. Except as provided in subparagraph (B), no tax shall be imposed under paragraph (1)(A) of subsection (a) on any short-term capital gain dividend received from a regulated investment company.

(B) Exception for aliens taxable under subsection (a)(2). Subparagraph (A) shall not apply in the case of any nonresident alien individual subject to tax under subsection (a)(2).

(C) Short-term capital gain dividend. For purposes of this paragraph, the term "short-term capital gain dividend" means any dividend (or part thereof) which is designated by the regulated investment company as a short-term capital gain dividend in a written notice mailed to its shareholders not later than 60 days after the close of its taxable year. If the aggregate amount so designated with respect to a taxable year of the company (including amounts so designated with respect to dividends paid after the close of the taxable year described in section 855) is greater than the qualified short-term gain of the company for such taxable year, the portion of each distribution which shall be a short-term capital gain dividend shall be only that portion of the amounts so designated which such qualified short-term gain bears to the aggregate amount so designated. Such term shall not include any dividend with respect to any taxable year of the company beginning after December 31, 2007.

(D) Qualified short-term gain. For purposes of subparagraph (C), the term "qualified short-term gain" means the excess of the net short-term capital gain of the regulated investment company for the taxable year over the net long-term capital loss (if any) of such company for such taxable year. For purposes of this subparagraph—

(i) the net short-term capital gain of the regulated investment company shall be computed by treating any short-term capital gain dividend includible in gross income with respect to stock of another regulated investment company as a short-term capital gain, and

(ii) the excess of the net short-term capital gain for a taxable year over the net long-term capital loss for a taxable year (to which an election under section 4982(e)(4) does not apply) shall be determined without regard to any net capital loss or net short-term capital loss attributable to transactions after October 31 of such year, and any such net capital loss or net short-term capital loss shall be treated as arising on the 1st day of the next taxable year.

To the extent provided in regulations, clause (ii) shall apply also for purposes of computing the taxable income of the regulated investment company.

[1]*(E) Certain distributions. In the case of a distribution to which section 897 does not apply by reason of the second sentence of section 897(h)(1), the amount which would be treated as a short-term capital gain dividend to the shareholder (without regard to this subparagraph)—*

(i) shall not be treated as a short-term capital gain dividend, and

(ii) shall be included in such shareholder's gross income as a dividend from the regulated investment company.

* * * * * * * * * * * *

[For Analysis, see ¶ 603. For Committee Reports, see ¶ 5023, ¶ 5024.]

[Endnote Code Sec. 871]

Code Sec. 871(k)(2)(E), in *italics*, was added by Sec. 505(c)(2) of the Tax Increase Prevention and Reconciliation Act of 2005, HR4297, 5/17/2006.

1. added subpara. (k)(2)(E)

Effective Date (Sec. 505(d), HR4297, 5/17/2006) effective for tax. yrs. of qualified investment entities begin. after 12/31/2005, except that no amount shall be required to be withheld under Code Secs. 1441, 1442, or 1445 with respect to any distribution before 5/17/2006 if such amount was not otherwise required to be withheld under any such section as in effect before such amendments.

[¶ 3020] Code Sec. 897. Disposition of investment in United States real property.

* * * * * * * * * * * * *

(h) Special rules for certain investment entities. For purposes of this section—

(1) Look-through of distributions. Any distribution by a qualified investment entity to [1]*a nonresident alien individual, a foreign corporation, or other qualified investment entity* shall, to the extent attributable to gain from sales or exchanges by the qualified investment entity of United States real property interests, be treated as gain recognized by [2]*such nonresident alien individual, foreign corporation, or other qualified investment entity* from the sale or exchange of a United States real property interest. [3]*Notwithstanding the preceding sentence, any distribution by a qualified investment entity to a nonresident alien individual or a foreign corporation with respect to any class of stock which is regularly traded on an established securities market located in the United States shall not be treated as gain recognized from the sale or exchange of a United States real property interest if such individual or corporation did not own more than 5 percent of such class of stock at any time during the 1-year period ending on the date of such distribution.*

(2) Sale of stock in domestically controlled entity not taxed. The term "United States real property interest" does not include any interest in a domestically controlled qualified investment entity.

(3) Distributions by domestically controlled qualified investment entities. In the case of a domestically controlled qualified investment entity, rules similar to the rules of subsection (d) shall apply to the foreign ownership percentage of any gain.

(4) Definitions.

(A) Qualified investment entity.

(i) In general. The term "qualified investment entity" means—

(I) any real estate investment trust, and

(II) any regulated investment company [4]*which is a United States real property holding corporation or which would be a United States real property holding corporation if the exceptions provided in subsections (c)(3) and (h)(2) did not apply to interests in any real estate investment trust or regulated investment company* .

(ii) Termination. Clause (i)(II) shall not apply after December 31, 2007. [5]*Notwithstanding the preceding sentence, an entity described in clause (i)(II) shall be treated as a qualified investment entity for purposes of applying paragraphs (1) and (5) and section 1445 with respect to any distribution by the entity to a nonresident alien individual or a foreign corporation which is attributable directly or indirectly to a distribution to the entity from a real estate investment trust.*

(B) Domestically controlled. The term "domestically controlled qualified investment entity" means any qualified investment entity in which at all times during the testing period less than 50 percent in value of the stock was held directly or indirectly by foreign persons.

(C) Foreign ownership percentage. The term "foreign ownership percentage" means that percentage of the stock of the qualified investment entity which was held (directly or indirectly) by foreign persons at the time during the testing period during which the direct and indirect ownership of stock by foreign persons was greatest.

(D) Testing period. The term "testing period" means whichever of the following periods is the shortest:

(i) the period beginning on June 19, 1980, and ending on the date of the disposition or of the distribution, as the case may be,

(ii) the 5-year period ending on the date of the disposition or of the distribution, as the case may be, or

(iii) the period during which the qualified investment entity was in existence.

[6]***(5) Treatment of certain wash sale transactions.***

(A) In general. If an interest in a domestically controlled qualified investment entity is disposed of in an applicable wash sale transaction, the taxpayer shall, for purposes of this section, be treated as having gain from the sale or exchange of a United States real

property interest in an amount equal to the portion of the distribution described in subparagraph (B) with respect to such interest which, but for the disposition, would have been treated by the taxpayer as gain from the sale or exchange of a United States real property interest under paragraph (1).

(B) Applicable wash sales transaction. For purposes of this paragraph—

(i) In general. The term "applicable wash sales transaction" means any transaction (or series of transactions) under which a nonresident alien individual, foreign corporation, or qualified investment entity—

(I) disposes of an interest in a domestically controlled qualified investment entity during the 30-day period preceding the ex-dividend date of a distribution which is to be made with respect to the interest and any portion of which, but for the disposition, would have been treated by the taxpayer as gain from the sale or exchange of a United States real property interest under paragraph (1), and

(II) acquires, or enters into a contract or option to acquire, a substantially identical interest in such entity during the 61-day period beginning with the 1st day of the 30-day period described in subclause (I).

For purposes of subclause (II), a nonresident alien individual, foreign corporation, or qualified investment entity shall be treated as having acquired any interest acquired by a person related (within the meaning of section 267(b) or 707(b)(1)) to the individual, corporation, or entity, and any interest which such person has entered into any contract or option to acquire.

(ii) Application to substitute dividend and similar payments. Subparagraph (A) shall apply to—

(I) any substitute dividend payment (within the meaning of section 861), or

(II) any other similar payment specified in regulations which the Secretary determines necessary to prevent avoidance of the purposes of this paragraph.

The portion of any such payment treated by the taxpayer as gain from the sale or exchange of a United States real property interest under subparagraph (A) by reason of this clause shall be equal to the portion of the distribution such payment is in lieu of which would have been so treated but for the transaction giving rise to such payment.

(iii) Exception where distribution actually received. A transaction shall not be treated as an applicable wash sales transaction if the nonresident alien individual, foreign corporation, or qualified investment entity receives the distribution described in clause (i)(I) with respect to either the interest which was disposed of, or acquired, in the transaction.

(iv) Exception for certain publicly traded stock. A transaction shall not be treated as an applicable wash sales transaction if it involves the disposition of any class of stock in a qualified investment entity which is regularly traded on an established securities market within the United States but only if the nonresident alien individual, foreign corporation, or qualified investment entity did not own more than 5 percent of such class of stock at any time during the 1-year period ending on the date of the distribution described in clause (i)(I).

* * * * * * * * * * * * *

[For Analysis, see ¶ 603, ¶ 604. For Committee Reports, see ¶ 5023, ¶ 5024.]

[Endnote Code Sec. 897]

Matter in *italics* in Code Sec. 897(h)(1) was added by Sec. 505(a)(1)(A)-(C) of the Tax Increase Prevention and Reconciliation Act of 2005, HR4297, 5/17/2006, which struck out:

1. "a nonresident alien individual or a foreign corporation"
2. "such nonresident alien individual or foreign corporation."
3. "Notwithstanding the preceding sentence, any distribution by a real estate investment trust with respect to any class of stock which is regularly traded on an established securities market located in the United States shall not be treated as gain recognized from the sale or exchange of a United States real property interest if the shareholder did not own more than 5 percent of such class of stock at any time during the 1-year period ending on the date of the distribution."

Effective Date (Sec. 505(d), HR4297, 5/17/2006) effective for tax. yrs. of qualified investment entities begin. after 12/31/2005, except that no amount shall be required to be withheld under Code Secs. 1441, 1442, or 1445 with respect to any distribution before the 5/17/2006 if such amount was not otherwise required to be withheld under any such section as in effect before such amendments.

Matter in *italics* in Code Sec. 897(h)(4)(A)(i)(II) was added by Sec. 504(a), HR4297, 5/17/2006.
4. added matter in subclause (h)(4)(A)(i)(II)
Effective Date (Sec. 504(b), HR4297, 5/17/2006) effective after 12/31/2004, as if included with the amendments made by Sec. 411 of the American Jobs Creation Act of 2004 [P.L. 108-357].

Matter in *italics* in Code Sec. 897(h)(4)(A)(ii) was added by Sec. 505(a)(2), HR4297, 5/17/2006.
5. added matter in clause (h)(4)(A)(ii)
Effective Date (Sec. 505(d), HR4297, 5/17/2006) effective for tax. yrs. of qualified investment entities begin. after 12/31/2005, except that no amount shall be required to be withheld under Code Secs. 1441, 1442, or 1445 with respect to any distribution before the 5/17/2006 if such amount was not otherwise required to be withheld under any such section as in effect before such amendments.

Code Sec. 897(h)(5), in *italics*, was added by Sec. 506(a), HR4297, 5/17/2006.
6. added para. (h)(5)
Effective Date (Sec. 506(c), HR4297, 5/17/2006) effective for tax. yrs. begin. after 12/31/2005, except that such amendments shall not apply to any distribution, or substitute dividend payment, occurring before the date that is 30 days after 5/17/2006.

[¶ 3021] Code Sec. 911. Citizens or residents of the United States living abroad.

* * * * * * * * * * * * *

(b) Foreign earned income.

* * * * * * * * * * * * *

(2) Limitation on foreign earned income.

(A) In general. The foreign earned income of an individual which may be excluded under subsection (a)(1) for any taxable year shall not exceed the amount of foreign earned income computed on a daily basis at an annual rate equal to the exclusion amount for the calendar year in which such taxable year begins.

(B) Attribution to year in which services are performed. For purposes of applying subparagraph (A), amounts received shall be considered received in the taxable year in which the services to which the amounts are attributable are performed.

(C) Treatment of community income. In applying subparagraph (A) with respect to amounts received from services performed by a husband or wife which are community income under community property laws applicable to such income, the aggregate amount which may be excludable from the gross income of such husband and wife under subsection (a)(1) for any taxable year shall equal the amount which would be so excludable if such amounts did not constitute community income.

(D) Exclusion amount.

(i) In general. The exclusion amount for any calendar year is the exclusion amount determined in accordance with the following table (as adjusted by clause (ii)):

For calendar year—	The exclusion amount is—
1998	$72,000
1999	74,000
2000	76,000
2001	78,000
2002 and thereafter	80,000

(ii) Inflation adjustment. In the case of any taxable year beginning in a calendar year after [1]*2005*, the $80,000 amount in clause (i) shall be increased by an amount equal to the product of—

(I) such dollar amount, and

(II) the cost-of-living adjustment determined under section 1(f)(3) for the calendar year in which the taxable year begins, determined by substituting "[2]*2004*" for "1992" in subparagraph (B) thereof.

If any increase determined under the preceding sentence is not a multiple of $100, such increase shall be rounded to the next lowest multiple of $100.

(c) Housing cost amount. For purposes of this section—

(1) In general. The term "housing cost amount" means an amount equal to the excess of—

(A) the housing expenses of an individual for the taxable year [3]*to the extent such expenses do not exceed the amount determined under paragraph (2)*, over

(B) an amount equal to the product of—

[4]*(i) 16 percent of the amount (computed on a daily basis) in effect under subsection (b)(2)(D) for the calendar year in which such taxable year begins, multiplied by*

(ii) the number of days of such taxable year within the applicable period described in subparagraph (A) or (B) of subsection (d)(1).

[5]***(2) Limitation.***

(A) In general. The amount determined under this paragraph is an amount equal to the product of—

(i) 30 percent (adjusted as may be provided under subparagraph (B)) of the amount (computed on a daily basis) in effect under subsection (b)(2)(D) for the calendar year in which the taxable year of the individual begins, multiplied by

(ii) the number of days of such taxable year within the applicable period described in subparagraph (A) or (B) of subsection (d)(1).

(B) Regulations. The Secretary may issue regulations or other guidance providing for the adjustment of the percentage under subparagraph (A)(i) on the basis of geographic differences in housing costs relative to housing costs in the United States.

[6]***(3)* Housing expenses.**

(A) In general. The term "housing expenses" means the reasonable expenses paid or incurred during the taxable year by or on behalf of an individual for housing for the individual (and, if they reside with him, for his spouse and dependents) in a foreign country. The term—

(i) includes expenses attributable to the housing (such as utilities and insurance), but

(ii) does not include interest and taxes of the kind deductible under section 163 or 164 or any amount allowable as a deduction under section 216(a).

Housing expenses shall not be treated as reasonable to the extent such expenses are lavish or extravagant under the circumstances.

(B) Second foreign household.

(i) In general. Except as provided in clause (ii), only housing expenses incurred with respect to that abode which bears the closest relationship to the tax home of the individual shall be taken into account under paragraph (1).

(ii) Separate household for spouse and dependents. If an individual maintains a separate abode outside the United States for his spouse and dependents and they do not reside with him because of living conditions which are dangerous, unhealthful, or otherwise adverse, then—

(I) the words "if they reside with him" in subparagraph (A) shall be disregarded, and

(II) the housing expenses incurred with respect to such abode shall be taken into account under paragraph (1).

[7]***(4)* Special rules where housing expenses not provided by employer.**

(A) In general. To the extent the housing cost amount of any individual for any taxable year is not attributable to employer provided amounts, such amount shall be treated as a deduction allowable in computing adjusted gross income to the extent of the limitation of subparagraph (B).

(B) Limitation. For purposes of subparagraph (A), the limitation of this subparagraph is the excess of—

(i) the foreign earned income of the individual for the taxable year, over

(ii) the amount of such income excluded from gross income under subsection (a) for the taxable year.

(C) 1-year carryover of housing amounts not allowed by reason of subparagraph (B).

(i) In general. The amount not allowable as a deduction for any taxable year under subparagraph (A) by reason of the limitation of subparagraph (B) shall be treated as a deduction allowable in computing adjusted gross income for the succeeding taxable year (and only for the succeeding taxable year) to the extent of the limitation of clause (ii) for such succeeding taxable year.

(ii) Limitation. For purposes of clause (i), the limitation of this clause for any taxable year is the excess of—

(I) the limitation of subparagraph (B) for such taxable year, over

(II) amounts treated as a deduction under subparagraph (A) for such taxable year.

(D) Employer provided amounts. For purposes of this paragraph, the term "employer provided amounts" means any amount paid or incurred on behalf of the individual by the individual's employer which is foreign earned income included in the individual's gross income for the taxable year (without regard to this section).

(E) Foreign earned income. For purposes of this paragraph, an individual's foreign earned income for any taxable year shall be determined without regard to the limitation of subparagraph (A) of subsection (b)(2).

(d) Definitions and special rules. For purposes of this section—

* * * * * * * * * * * *

(4) Waiver of period of stay in foreign country. Notwithstanding paragraph (1), an individual who—

(A) is a bona fide resident of, or is present in, a foreign country for any period,

(B) leaves such foreign country after August 31, 1978—

(i) during any period during which the Secretary determines, after consultation with the Secretary of State or his delegate, that individuals were required to leave such foreign country because of war, civil unrest, or similar adverse conditions in such foreign country which precluded the normal conduct of business by such individuals, and

(ii) before meeting the requirements of such paragraph (1), and

(C) establishes to the satisfaction of the Secretary that such individual could reasonably have been expected to have met such requirements but for the conditions referred to in clause (i) of subparagraph (B),

shall be treated as a qualified individual with respect to the period described in subparagraph (A) during which he was a bona fide resident of, or was present in, the foreign country, and in applying subsections (b)(2)(A)[8], *(c)(1)(B)(ii), and (c)(2)(A)(ii)* with respect to such individual, only the days within such period shall be taken into account.

* * * * * * * * * * * *

(7) Aggregate benefit cannot exceed foreign earned income. The sum of the amount excluded under subsection (a) and the amount deducted under [9]*subsection (c)(4)*(A) for the taxable year shall not exceed the individual's foreign earned income for such year.

* * * * * * * * * * * *

[10]***(f) Determination of tax liability on nonexcluded amounts.*** *For purposes of this chapter, if any amount is excluded from the gross income of a taxpayer under subsection (a) for any taxable year, then, notwithstanding section 1 or 55—*

(1) *the tax imposed by section 1 on the taxpayer for such taxable year shall be equal to the excess (if any) of—*

(A) the tax which would be imposed by section 1 for the taxable year if the taxpayer's taxable income were increased by the amount excluded under subsection (a) for the taxable year, over

(B) the tax which would be imposed by section 1 for the taxable year if the taxpayer's taxable income were equal to the amount excluded under subsection (a) for the taxable year, and

(2) *the tentative minimum tax under section 55 for such taxable year shall be equal to the excess (if any) of—*

(A) the amount which would be such tentative minimum tax for the taxable year if the taxpayer's taxable excess were increased by the amount excluded under subsection (a) for the taxable year, over

(B) the amount which would be such tentative minimum tax for the taxable year if the taxpayer's taxable excess were equal to the amount excluded under subsection (a) for the taxable year.

For purposes of this subsection, the amount excluded under subsection (a) shall be reduced by the aggregate amount of any deductions or exclusions disallowed under subsection (d)(6) with respect to such excluded amount.

[11]***(g)*** **Cross references.** For administrative and penal provisions relating to the exclusions provided for in this section, see sections 6001, 6011, 6012(c), and the other provisions of subtitle F.

[For Analysis, see ¶ 206. For Committee Reports, see ¶ 5033.]

[Endnote Code Sec. 911]

Matter in *italics* in Code Sec. 911(b)(2)(D)(ii), Code Sec. 911(b)(2)(D)(ii)(II), Code Sec. 911(c)(1)(A), Code Sec. 911(c)(1)(B)(i), Code Sec. 911(c)(2), Code Sec. 911(c)(3), Code Sec. 911(c)(4), Code Sec. 911(d)(4), Code Sec. 911(d)(7), Code Sec. 911(f), and Code Sec. 911(g) was added by Sec. 515(a)-(c) of the Tax Increase Prevention and Reconciliation Act of 2005, HR4297, 5/17/2006, which struck out:

1. "2007"
2. "2006"
3. added matter in subpara. (c)(1)(A)
4. "(i) 16 percent of the salary (computed on a daily basis) of an employee of the United States who is compensated at a rate equal to the annual rate paid for step 1 of grade GS-14, multiplied by"
5. added para. (c)(2)
6. "(2)"
7. "(3)"
8. "and (c)(1)(B)(ii)"
9. "subsection (c)(3)"
10. added subsec. (f)
11. "(f)"

Effective Date (Sec. 515(d), HR4297, 5/17/2006) effective for tax. yrs. begin. after 12/31/2005.

[¶ 3022] Code Sec. 953. Insurance income.

* * * * * * * * * * * *

(e) Exempt insurance income. For purposes of this section—

* * * * * * * * * * * *

(10) Application. This subsection and section 954(i) shall apply only to taxable years of a foreign corporation beginning after December 31, 1998, and before [1]*January 1, 2009,* and to taxable years of United States shareholders with or within which any such taxable year of such foreign corporation ends. If this subsection does not apply to a taxable year of a foreign corporation beginning after [2]*December 31, 2008* (and taxable years of United States shareholders ending with or within such taxable year), then, notwithstanding the preceding sentence, subsection (a) shall be applied to such taxable years in the same manner as it would if the taxable year of the foreign corporation began in 1998.

* * * * * * * * * * * *

[For Analysis, see ¶601. For Committee Reports, see ¶5003.]

[Endnote Code Sec. 953]

Matter in *italics* in Code Sec. 953(e)(10) was added by Sec. 103(a)(1)(A) and (B) of the Tax Increase Prevention and Reconciliation Act of 2005, HR4297, 5/17/2006, which struck out:

1. "January 1, 2007"
2. "December 31, 2006"

Effective Date Enacted 5/17/2006.

[¶3023] Code Sec. 954. Foreign base company income.

* * * * * * * * * * * *

(c) Foreign personal holding company income.

* * * * * * * * * * * *

[1]***(6) Look-thru rule for related controlled foreign corporations.***

(A) In general. For purposes of this subsection, dividends, interest, rents, and royalties received or accrued from a controlled foreign corporation which is a related person shall not be treated as foreign personal holding company income to the extent attributable or properly allocable (determined under rules similar to the rules of subparagraphs (C) and (D) of section 904(d)(3)) to income of the related person which is not subpart F income. For purposes of this subparagraph, interest shall include factoring income which is treated as income equivalent to interest for purposes of paragraph (1)(E). The Secretary shall prescribe such regulations as may be appropriate to prevent the abuse of the purposes of this paragraph.

(B) Application. Subparagraph (A) shall apply to taxable years of foreign corporations beginning after December 31, 2005, and before January 1, 2009, and to taxable years of United States shareholders with or within which such taxable years of foreign corporations end.

* * * * * * * * * * * *

(h) Special rule for income derived in the active conduct of banking, financing, or similar businesses.

* * * * * * * * * * * *

(9) Application. This subsection, subsection (c)(2)(C)(ii), and the last sentence of subsection (e)(2) shall apply only to taxable years of a foreign corporation beginning after December 31, 1998, and before [2]*January 1, 2009*, and to taxable years of United States shareholders with or within which any such taxable year of such foreign corporation ends.

* * * * * * * * * * * *

[For Analysis, see ¶601, ¶602. For Committee Reports, see ¶5003, ¶5004.]

[Endnote Code Sec. 954]

Code Sec. 954(c)(6), in *italics*, was added by Sec. 103(b)(1) of the Tax Increase Prevention and Reconciliation Act of 2005, HR4297, 5/17/2006.

1. added para. (c)(6)

Effective Date (Sec. 103(b)(2), HR4297, 5/17/2006) effective for tax. yrs. of foreign corporations begin. after 12/31/2005, and for tax. yrs. of United States shareholders with or within which such tax. yrs. of foreign corporations end.

Matter in *italics* in Code Sec. 954(h)(9) was added by Sec. 103(a)(2), HR4297, 5/17/2006, which struck out:

2. "January 1, 2007"

Effective Date Enacted 5/17/2006.

[¶ 3024] Code Sec. 1221. Capital asset defined.

* * * * * * * * * * * *

(b) Definitions and special rules.

* * * * * * * * * * * *

[1]***(3) Sale or exchange of self-created musical works.*** *At the election of the taxpayer, paragraphs (1) and (3) of subsection (a) shall not apply to musical compositions or copyrights in musical works sold or exchanged before January 1, 2011, by a taxpayer described in subsection (a)(3).*

[2]***(4)*** **Regulations.** The Secretary shall prescribe such regulations as are appropriate to carry out the purposes of paragraph (6) and (7) of subsection (a) in the case of transactions involving related parties.

[For Analysis, see ¶ 208. For Committee Reports, see ¶ 5008.]

[Endnote Code Sec. 1221]

Matter in *italics* in Code Sec. 1221(b)(3) and Code Sec. 1221(b)(4) was added by Sec. 204(a) of the Tax Increase Prevention and Reconciliation Act of 2005, HR4297, 5/17/2006, which struck out:

1. added para. (b)(3)
2. "(3)"

Effective Date (Sec. 204(c), HR4297, 5/17/2006) effective for sales and exchanges in tax. yrs. begin. after 5/17/2006.

[¶ 3025] Code Sec. 1355. Definitions and special rules.

(a) Definitions. For purposes of this subchapter—

* * * * * * * * * * * *

(4) Qualifying vessel. The term "qualifying vessel" means a self-propelled (or a combination self-propelled and non-self-propelled) United States flag vessel of not less than 10,000 [1]*(6,000, in the case of taxable years beginning after December 31, 2005, and ending before January 1, 2011)* deadweight tons used exclusively in the United States foreign trade during the period that the election under this subchapter is in effect.

* * * * * * * * * * * *

[For Analysis, see ¶ 305. For Committee Reports, see ¶ 5009.]

[Endnote Code Sec. 1355]

Matter in *italics* in Code Sec. 1355(a)(4) was added by Sec. 205(a) of the Tax Increase Prevention and Reconciliation Act of 2005, HR4297, 5/17/2006.

1. added matter in para. (a)(4)

Effective Date (Sec. 205(b), HR4297, 5/17/2006) effective for tax. yrs. begin. after 12/31/2005.

[¶ 3026] Code Sec. 1445. Withholding of tax on dispositions of United States real property interests.

* * * * * * * * * * * *

(b) Exemptions.

* * * * * * * * * * * *

[1]***(8) Applicable wash sales transactions.*** *No person shall be required to deduct and withhold any amount under subsection (a) with respect to a disposition which is treated as a disposition of a United States real property interest solely by reason of section 897(h)(5).*

* * * * * * * * * * * *

(e) Special rules relating to distributions, etc., by corporations, partnerships, trusts, or estates.

* * * * * * * * * * * * *

[2]*(6)* ***Distributions by regulated investment companies and real estate investment trusts.*** *If any portion of a distribution from a qualified investment entity (as defined in section 897(h)(4)) to a nonresident alien individual or a foreign corporation is treated under section 897(h)(1) as gain realized by such individual or corporation from the sale or exchange of a United States real property interest, the qualified investment entity shall deduct and withhold under subsection (a) a tax equal to 35 percent (or, to the extent provided in regulations, 15 percent (20 percent in the case of taxable years beginning after December 31, 2010)) of the amount so treated.*

[3]*(7)* **Regulations.** The Secretary shall prescribe such regulations as may be necessary to carry out the purposes of this subsection, including regulations providing for exceptions from provisions of this subsection and regulations for the application of this subsection in the case of payments through 1 or more entities.

* * * * * * * * * * * * *

[For Analysis, see ¶ 105, ¶ 603, ¶ 604. For Committee Reports, see ¶ 5002, ¶ 5023, ¶ 5024.]

[Endnote Code Sec. 1445]

Code Sec. 1445(b)(8), in *italics*, was added by Sec. 506(b) of the Tax Increase Prevention and Reconciliation Act of 2005, HR4297, 5/17/2006.

1. added para. (b)(8)

Effective Date (Sec. 506(c), HR4297, 5/17/2006) effective for tax. yrs. begin. after 12/31/2005, except that such amendment shall not apply to any distribution, or substitute dividend payment, occurring before the date that is 30 days after 5/17/2006.

Matter in *italics* in Code Sec. 1445(e)(6) and Code Sec. 1445(e)(7) was added by Sec. 505(b), HR4297, 5/17/2006, which struck out:

2. added para. (e)(6)

3. "(6)"

Effective Date (Sec. 505(d), HR4297, 5/17/2006) effective for tax. yrs. of qualified investment entities begin. after 12/31/2005, except that no amount shall be required to be withheld under Code Sec. 1441, 1442, or 1445 with respect to any distribution before 5/17/2006 if such amount was not otherwise required to be withheld under any such section as in effect before such amendments.

Sec. 102, HR4297, 5/17/2006, amended Sec. 303, P.L. 108-27, relating to the sunset of the amendments made by Secs. 301 and 302 of P.L. 108-27, by substituting "December 31, 2010" for "December 31, 2008". Sec. 303 as amended by Sec. 102, HR4297, 5/17/2006, reads as follows:

"SEC. 303. SUNSET OF TITLE. All provisions of, and amendments made by, this title [Secs. 301 and 302] shall not apply to taxable years beginning after December 31, 2010, and the Internal Revenue Code of 1986 shall be applied and administered to such years as if such provisions and amendments had never been enacted."

[¶ 3027] Code Sec. 3402. Income tax collected at source.

* * * * * * * * * * * * *

[1]***(t) Extension of withholding to certain payments made by government entities.***

(1) General rule. *The Government of the United States, every State, every political subdivision thereof, and every instrumentality of the foregoing (including multi-State agencies) making any payment to any person providing any property or services (including any payment made in connection with a government voucher or certificate program which functions as a payment for property or services) shall deduct and withhold from such payment a tax in an amount equal to 3 percent of such payment.*

(2) Property and services subject to withholding. *Paragraph (1) shall not apply to any payment—*

(A) except as provided in subparagraph (B), which is subject to withholding under any other provision of this chapter or chapter 3,

(B) which is subject to withholding under section 3406 and from which amounts are being withheld under such section,

(C) of interest,

(D) for real property,

(E) to any governmental entity subject to the requirements of paragraph (1), any tax-exempt entity, or any foreign government,

(F) made pursuant to a classified or confidential contract described in section 6050M(e)(3),

(G) made by a political subdivision of a State (or any instrumentality thereof) which makes less than $100,000,000 of such payments annually,

(H) which is in connection with a public assistance or public welfare program for which eligibility is determined by a needs or income test, and

(I) to any government employee not otherwise excludable with respect to their services as an employee.

(3) Coordination with other sections. *For purposes of sections 3403 and 3404 and for purposes of so much of subtitle F (except section 7205) as relates to this chapter, payments to any person for property or services which are subject to withholding shall be treated as if such payments were wages paid by an employer to an employee.*

[For Analysis, see ¶ 802. For Committee Reports, see ¶ 5029.]

[Endnote Code Sec. 3402]

Code Sec. 3402(t), in *italics*, was added by Sec. 511(a) of the Tax Increase Prevention and Reconciliation Act of 2005, HR4297, 5/17/2006.

1. added subsec. (t)

Effective Date (Sec. 511(b), HR4297, 5/17/2006) effective for payments made after 12/31/2010.

[¶ 3028] Code Sec.[1] 4965. ***Excise tax on certain tax-exempt entities entering into prohibited tax shelter transactions.***

(a) Being a party to and approval of prohibited transactions.

(1) Tax-exempt entity.

(A) In general. If a transaction is a prohibited tax shelter transaction at the time any tax-exempt entity described in paragraph (1), (2), or (3) of subsection (c) becomes a party to the transaction, such entity shall pay a tax for the taxable year in which the entity becomes such a party and any subsequent taxable year in the amount determined under subsection (b)(1).

(B) Post-transaction determination. If any tax-exempt entity described in paragraph (1), (2), or (3) of subsection (c) is a party to a subsequently listed transaction at any time during a taxable year, such entity shall pay a tax for such taxable year in the amount determined under subsection (b)(1).

(2) Entity manager. *If any entity manager of a tax-exempt entity approves such entity as (or otherwise causes such entity to be) a party to a prohibited tax shelter transaction at any time during the taxable year and knows or has reason to know that the transaction is a prohibited tax shelter transaction, such manager shall pay a tax for such taxable year in the amount determined under subsection (b)(2).*

(b) Amount of tax.

(1) Entity. *In the case of a tax-exempt entity—*

(A) In general. Except as provided in subparagraph (B), the amount of the tax imposed under subsection (a)(1) with respect to any transaction for a taxable year shall be an amount equal to the product of the highest rate of tax under section 11, and the greater of—

(i) the entity's net income (after taking into account any tax imposed by this subtitle (other than by this section) with respect to such transaction) for such taxable year which—

(I) in the case of a prohibited tax shelter transaction (other than a subsequently listed transaction), is attributable to such transaction, or

(II) in the case of a subsequently listed transaction, is attributable to such transaction and which is properly allocable to the period beginning on the later of the date such transaction is identified by guidance as a listed transaction by the Secretary or the first day of the taxable year, or

(ii) 75 percent of the proceeds received by the entity for the taxable year which—

(I) in the case of a prohibited tax shelter transaction (other than a subsequently listed transaction), are attributable to such transaction, or

(II) in the case of a subsequently listed transaction, are attributable to such transaction and which are properly allocable to the period beginning on the later of the date such transaction is identified by guidance as a listed transaction by the Secretary or the first day of the taxable year.

(B) Increase in tax for certain knowing transactions. In the case of a tax-exempt entity which knew, or had reason to know, a transaction was a prohibited tax shelter transaction at the time the entity became a party to the transaction, the amount of the tax imposed under subsection (a)(1)(A) with respect to any transaction for a taxable year shall be the greater of—

(i) 100 percent of the entity's net income (after taking into account any tax imposed by this subtitle (other than by this section) with respect to the prohibited tax shelter transaction) for such taxable year which is attributable to the prohibited tax shelter transaction, or

(ii) 75 percent of the proceeds received by the entity for the taxable year which are attributable to the prohibited tax shelter transaction.

This subparagraph shall not apply to any prohibited tax shelter transaction to which a tax exempt entity became a party on or before the date of the enactment of this section.

(2) Entity manager. *In the case of each entity manager, the amount of the tax imposed under subsection (a)(2) shall be $20,000 for each approval (or other act causing participation) described in subsection (a)(2).*

(c) Tax-exempt entity. *For purposes of this section, the term "tax-exempt entity" means an entity which is—*

(1) *described in section 501(c) or 501(d),*

(2) *described in section 170(c) (other than the United States),*

(3) *an Indian tribal government (within the meaning of section 7701(a)(40)),*

(4) *described in paragraph (1), (2), or (3) of section 4979(e),*

(5) *a program described in section 529,*

(6) *an eligible deferred compensation plan described in section 457(b) which is maintained by an employer described in section 4457(e)(1)(A) [sic 457(e)(1)(A)], or*

(7) *an arrangement described in section 4973(a).*

(d) Entity manager. *For purposes of this section, the term "entity manager" means—*

(1) *in the case of an entity described in paragraph (1), (2), or (3) of subsection (c)—*

(A) the person with authority or responsibility similar to that exercised by an officer, director, or trustee of an organization, and

(B) with respect to any act, the person having authority or responsibility with respect to such act, and

(2) *in the case of an entity described in paragraph (4), (5), (6), or (7) of subsection (c), the person who approves or otherwise causes the entity to be a party to the prohibited tax shelter transaction.*

(e) Prohibited tax shelter transaction; subsequently listed transaction. *For purposes of this section—*

(1) Prohibited tax shelter transaction.

(A) In general. The term "prohibited tax shelter transaction" means—

(i) any listed transaction, and

(ii) any prohibited reportable transaction.

(B) Listed transaction. The term "listed transaction" has the meaning given such term by section 6707A(c)(2).

(C) Prohibited reportable transaction. The term "prohibited reportable transaction" means any confidential transaction or any transaction with contractual protection (as defined under regulations prescribed by the Secretary) which is a reportable transaction (as defined in section 6707A(c)(1)).

(2) Subsequently listed transaction. *The term "subsequently listed transaction" means any transaction to which a tax-exempt entity is a party and which is determined by the Secretary to be a listed transaction at any time after the entity has become a party to the transaction. Such term shall not include a transaction which is a prohibited reportable transaction at the time the entity became a party to the transaction.*

(f) Regulatory authority. *The Secretary is authorized to promulgate regulations which provide guidance regarding the determination of the allocation of net income or proceeds of a tax-exempt entity attributable to a transaction to various periods, including before and after the listing of the transaction or the date which is 90 days after the date of the enactment of this section.*

(g) Coordination with other taxes and penalties. *The tax imposed by this section is in addition to any other tax, addition to tax, or penalty imposed under this title.*

[For Analysis, see ¶ 701. For Committee Reports, see ¶ 5034.]

[Endnote Code Sec. 4965]

Code Sec. 4965, in *italics*, was added by Sec. 516(a)(1) of the Tax Increase Prevention and Reconciliation Act of 2005, HR4297, 5/17/2006.

1. added Code Sec. 4965

Effective Date (Sec. 516(d)(1), HR4297, 5/17/2006) effective for tax. yrs. end. after 5/17/2006, for transactions before, on, or after 5/17/2006, except that no tax under Code Sec. 4965(a) (as added by Sec. 516(a)(1) of HR4297) shall apply with respect to income or proceeds that are properly allocable to any period end. on or before the date which is 90 days after 5/17/2006.

[¶ 3029] Code Sec. 6011. General requirement of return, statement, or list.

* * * * * * * * * * * *

[1]***(g) Disclosure of reportable transaction to tax-exempt entity.*** *Any taxable party to a prohibited tax shelter transaction (as defined in section 4965(e)(1)) shall by statement disclose to any tax-exempt entity (as defined in section 4965(c)) which is a party to such transaction that such transaction is such a prohibited tax shelter transaction.*

[2]***(h)*** **Income, estate, and gift taxes.** For requirement that returns of income, estate, and gift taxes be made whether or not there is tax liability, see subparts B and C.

[For Analysis, see ¶ 703. For Committee Reports, see ¶ 5034.]

[Endnote Code Sec. 6011]

Matter in *italics* in Code Sec. 6011(g) and Code Sec. 6011(h) was added by Sec. 516(b)(2) of the Tax Increase Prevention and Reconciliation Act of 2005, HR4297, 5/17/2006, which struck out:

1. added subsec. (g)
2. "(g)"

Effective Date (Sec. 516(d)(2), HR4297, 5/17/2006) effective for disclosures the due dates for which are after 5/17/2006.

[¶ 3030] Code Sec. 6033. Returns by exempt organizations.

(a) Organizations required to file.

(1) In general. Except as provided in [1]*paragraph (3)*, every organization exempt from taxation under section 501(a) shall file an annual return, stating specifically the items of gross income, receipts, and disbursements, and such other information for the purpose of carrying out the internal revenue laws as the Secretary may by forms or regulations prescribe, and shall keep such records, render under oath such statements, make such other returns, and comply with such rules and regulations as the Secretary may from time to time prescribe; except that, in the discretion of the Secretary, any organization described in section 401(a) may be relieved from stating in its return any information which is reported in returns filed by the employer which established such organization.

[2]***(2) Being a party to certain reportable transactions.*** *Every tax-exempt entity described in section 4965(c) shall file (in such form and manner and at such time as determined by the Secretary) a disclosure of—*

(A) such entity's being a party to any prohibited tax shelter transaction (as defined in section 4965(e)), and

(B) the identity of any other party to such transaction which is known by such tax-exempt entity.

[3]***(3)*** **Exceptions from filing.**

(A) Mandatory exceptions. Paragraph (1) shall not apply to—

(i) churches, their integrated auxiliaries, and conventions or associations of churches,

(ii) any organization (other than a private foundation, as defined in section 509(a)) described in subparagraph (C), the gross receipts of which in each taxable year are normally not more than $5,000, or

(iii) the exclusively religious activities of any religious order.

(B) Discretionary exceptions. The Secretary may relieve any organization required under paragraph (1) to file an information return from filing such a return where he determines that such filing is not necessary to the efficient administration of the internal revenue laws.

(C) Certain organizations. The organizations referred to in subparagraph (A)(ii) are—

(i) a religious organization described in section 501(c)(3);

(ii) an educational organization described in section 170(b)(1)(A)(ii);

(iii) a charitable organization, or an organization for the prevention of cruelty to children or animals, described in section 501(c)(3), if such organization is supported, in whole or in part, by funds contributed by the United States or any State or political subdivision thereof, or is primarily supported by contributions of the general public;

(iv) an organization described in section 501(c)(3), if such organization is operated, supervised, or controlled by or in connection with a religious organization described in clause (i);

(v) an organization described in section 501(c)(8); and

(vi) an organization described in section 501(c)(1), if such organization is a corporation wholly owned by the United States or any agency or instrumentality thereof, or a wholly-owned subsidiary of such a corporation.

* * * * * * * * * * * * *

[For Analysis, see ¶ 702. For Committee Reports, see ¶ 5034.]

[Endnote Code Sec. 6033]

Matter in *italics* in Code Sec. 6033(a)(1), Code Sec. 6033(a)(2), and Code Sec. 6033(a)(3) was added by Sec. 516(b)(1)(A) and (B) of the Tax Increase Prevention and Reconciliation Act of 2005, HR4297, 5/17/2006, which struck out:

1. "paragraph (2)"
2. added para. (a)(2)
3. "(2)"

Effective Date (Sec. 516(d)(2), HR4297, 5/17/2006) effective for disclosures the due dates for which are after 5/17/2006.

[¶ 3031] Code Sec. 6049. Returns regarding payments of interest.

* * * * * * * * * * * *

(b) Interest defined.

* * * * * * * * * * * *

(2) Exceptions. For purposes of subsection (a), the term "interest" does not include—

(A) interest on any obligation issued by a natural person,

[1]*(B)* except to the extent otherwise provided in regulations—

(i) any amount paid to any person described in paragraph (4), or

(ii) any amount described in paragraph (5), and

[2]*(C)* except to the extent otherwise provided in regulations, any amount not described in [3]*subparagraph (B)* of this paragraph which is income from sources outside the United States or which is paid by—

(i) a foreign government or international organization or any agency or instrumentality thereof,

(ii) a foreign central bank of issue,

(iii) a foreign corporation not engaged in a trade or business in the United States,

(iv) a foreign corporation, the interest payments of which would be exempt from withholding under subchapter A of chapter 3 if paid to a person who is not a United States person, or

(v) a partnership not engaged in a trade or business in the United States and composed in whole of nonresident alien individuals and persons described in clause (i), (ii), or (iii).

* * * * * * * * * * * *

[For Analysis, see ¶ 801. For Committee Reports, see ¶ 5021.]

[Endnote Code Sec. 6049]

Matter in *italics* in Code Sec. 6049(b)(2)(B) and Code Sec. 6049(b)(2)(C) was added by Sec. 502(a) and (b) of the Tax Increase Prevention and Reconciliation Act of 2005, HR4297, 5/17/2006, which struck out:

1. "(B) interest on any obligation if such interest is exempt from tax under section 103(a) or if such interest is exempt from tax (without regard to the identity of the holder) under any other provision of this title,"

"(C)"

2. "(D)"

3. "subparagraph (C)"

Effective Date (Sec. 502(c), HR4297, 5/17/2006) effective for interest paid after 12/31/2005.

[¶ 3032] Code Sec. 6159. Agreements for payment of tax liability in installments.

* * * * * * * * * * * *

(f) Cross reference. For rights to administrative review and appeal, see [1]*section 7122(e).*

[Endnote Code Sec. 6159]

Matter in *italics* in Code Sec. 6159(f) was added by Sec. 509(c) of the Tax Increase Prevention and Reconciliation Act of 2005, HR4297, 5/17/2006, which struck out:

1. "section 7122(d)"

Effective Date (Sec. 509(d), HR4297, 5/17/2006) effective for offers-in-compromise submitted on and after the date which is 60 days after 5/17/2006.

[¶ 3033] Code Sec. 6652. Failure to file certain information returns, registration statements, etc.

* * * * * * * * * * * *

(c) Returns by exempt organizations and by certain trusts.

(1) Annual returns under section [1]*6033(a)(1)* or 6012(a)(6).

(A) Penalty on organization. In the case of—

(i) a failure to file a return required under [2]*6033(a)(1)* (relating to returns by exempt organizations) or section 6012(a)(6) (relating to returns by political organizations) on the date and in the manner prescribed therefor (determined with regard to any extension of time for filing), or

(ii) a failure to include any of the information required to be shown on a return filed under [3]*6033(a)(1)* or section 6012(a)(6) or to show the correct information,

there shall be paid by the exempt organization $20 for each day during which such failure continues. The maximum penalty under this subparagraph on failures with respect to any 1 return shall not exceed the lesser of $10,000 or 5 percent of the gross receipts of the organization for the year. In the case of an organization having gross receipts exceeding $1,000,000 for any year, with respect to the return required under [4]*6033(a)(1)* or section 6012(a)(6) for such year, the first sentence of this subparagraph shall be applied by substituting "100" for "20" and, in lieu of applying the second sentence of this subparagraph, the maximum penalty under this subparagraph shall not exceed $50,000.

(B) Managers.

(i) In general. The Secretary may make a written demand on any organization subject to penalty under subparagraph (A) specifying therein a reasonable future date by which the return shall be filed (or the information furnished) for purposes of this subparagraph.

(ii) Failure to comply with demand. If any person fails to comply with any demand under clause (i) on or before the date specified in such demand, there shall be paid by the person failing to so comply $10 for each day after the expiration of the time specified in such demand during which such failure continues. The maximum penalty imposed under this subparagraph on all persons for failures with respect to any 1 return shall not exceed $5,000.

(C) Public inspection of annual returns and reports. In the case of a failure to comply with the requirements of section 6104(d) with respect to any annual return on the date and in the manner prescribed therefor (determined with regard to any extension of time for filing) or report required under section 527(j), there shall be paid by the person failing to meet such requirements $20 for each day during which such failure continues. The maximum penalty imposed under this subparagraph on all persons for failures with respect to any 1 return or report shall not exceed $10,000.

(D) Public inspection of applications for exemption and notice of status. In the case of a failure to comply with the requirements of section 6104(d) with respect to any exempt status application materials (as defined in such section) or notice materials (as defined in such section) on the date and in the manner prescribed therefor, there shall be paid by the person failing to meet such requirements $20 for each day during which such failure continues.

(2) Returns under section 6034 or 6043(b).

(A) Penalty on organization or trust. In the case of a failure to file a return required under section 6034 (relating to returns by certain trusts) or section 6043(b) (relating to terminations, etc., of exempt organizations), on the date and in the manner prescribed therefor (determined with regard to any extension of time for filing), there shall be paid by the exempt organization or trust failing so to file $10 for each day during which such failure continues, but the total amount imposed under this subparagraph on any organization or trust for failure to file any 1 return shall not exceed $5,000.

(B) Managers. The Secretary may make written demand on an organization or trust failing to file under subparagraph (A) specifying therein a reasonable future date by which such filing shall be made for purposes of this subparagraph. If such filing is not made on or before such date, there shall be paid by the person failing so to file $10 for each day after the expiration of the time specified in the written demand during which such failure continues, but the total amount imposed under this subparagraph on all persons for failure to file any 1 return shall not exceed $5,000.

[5]*(3)* ***Disclosure under section 6033(a)(2).***

(A) Penalty on entities. In the case of a failure to file a disclosure required under section 6033(a)(2), there shall be paid by the tax-exempt entity (the entity manager in the case of a tax-exempt entity described in paragraph (4), (5), (6), or (7) of section 4965(c)) $100 for each day during which such failure continues. The maximum penalty under this subparagraph on failures with respect to any 1 disclosure shall not exceed $50,000.

(B) Written demand.

(i) In general. The Secretary may make a written demand on any entity or manager subject to penalty under subparagraph (A) specifying therein a reasonable future date by which the disclosure shall be filed for purposes of this subparagraph.

(ii) Failure to comply with demand. If any entity or manager fails to comply with any demand under clause (i) on or before the date specified in such demand, there shall be paid by such entity or manager failing to so comply $100 for each day after the expiration of the time specified in such demand during which such failure continues. The maximum penalty imposed under this subparagraph on all entities and managers for failures with respect to any 1 disclosure shall not exceed $10,000.

(C) Definitions. Any term used in this section which is also used in section 4965 shall have the meaning given such term under section 4965.

[6]*(4)* **Reasonable cause exception.** No penalty shall be imposed under this subsection with respect to any failure if it is shown that such failure is due to reasonable cause.

[7]*(5)* **Other special rules.**

(A) Treatment as tax. Any penalty imposed under this subsection shall be paid on notice and demand of the Secretary and in the same manner as tax.

(B) Joint and several liability. If more than 1 person is liable under this subsection for any penalty with respect to any failure, all such persons shall be jointly and severally liable with respect to such failure.

(C) Person. For purposes of this subsection, the term "person" means any officer, director, trustee, employee, or other individual who is under a duty to perform the act in respect of which the violation occurs.

* * * * * * * * * * * * * *

[For Analysis, see ¶ 704. For Committee Reports, see ¶ 5034.]

[Endnote Code Sec. 6652]

Matter in *italics* in Code Sec. 6652(c)(1), Code Sec. 6652(c)(3), Code Sec. 6652(c)(4), and Code Sec. 6652(c)(5) was added by Sec. 516(c)(1) and (2) of the Tax Increase Prevention and Reconciliation Act of 2005, HR4297, 5/17/2006, which struck out:

1. "6033"
2. "6033"
3. "6033"
4. "6033"
5. added para. (c)(3)
6. "(3)"
7. "(4)"

Effective Date (Sec. 516(d)(2), HR4297, 5/17/2006) effective for disclosures the due dates for which are after 5/17/2006.

[¶ 3034] **Code Sec. 7122. Compromises.**

* * * * * * * * * * * *

[1]***(c) Rules for submission of offers-in-compromise.***

(1) Partial payment required with submission.

(A) Lump-sum offers.

(i) In general. The submission of any lump-sum offer-in-compromise shall be accompanied by the payment of 20 percent of the amount of such offer.

(ii) Lump-sum offer-in-compromise. For purposes of this section, the term "lump-sum offer-in-compromise" means any offer of payments made in 5 or fewer installments.

(B) Periodic payment offers.

(i) In general. The submission of any periodic payment offer-in-compromise shall be accompanied by the payment of the amount of the first proposed installment.

(ii) Failure to make installment during pendency of offer. Any failure to make an installment (other than the first installment) due under such offer-in-compromise during the period such offer is being evaluated by the Secretary may be treated by the Secretary as a withdrawal of such offer-in-compromise.

(2) Rules of application.

(A) Use of payment. The application of any payment made under this subsection to the assessed tax or other amounts imposed under this title with respect to such tax may be specified by the taxpayer.

(B) Application of user fee. In the case of any assessed tax or other amounts imposed under this title with respect to such tax which is the subject of an offer-in-compromise to which this subsection applies, such tax or other amounts shall be reduced by any user fee imposed under this title with respect to such offer-in-compromise.

(C) Waiver authority. The Secretary may issue regulations waiving any payment required under paragraph (1) in a manner consistent with the practices established in accordance with the requirements under subsection (d)(3).

[2]***(d)*** **Standards for evaluation of offers.**

(1) In general. The Secretary shall prescribe guidelines for officers and employees of the Internal Revenue Service to determine whether an offer-in-compromise is adequate and should be accepted to resolve a dispute.

(2) Allowances for basic living expenses.

(A) In general. In prescribing guidelines under paragraph (1), the Secretary shall develop and publish schedules of national and local allowances designed to provide that taxpayers entering into a compromise have an adequate means to provide for basic living expenses.

(B) Use of schedules. The guidelines shall provide that officers and employees of the Internal Revenue Service shall determine, on the basis of the facts and circumstances of each taxpayer, whether the use of the schedules published under subparagraph (A) is appropriate and shall not use the schedules to the extent such use would result in the taxpayer not having adequate means to provide for basic living expenses.

(3) Special rules relating to treatment of offers. The guidelines under paragraph (1) shall provide that—

(A) an officer or employee of the Internal Revenue Service shall not reject an offer-in-compromise from a low-income taxpayer solely on the basis of the amount of the offer[3],

(B) in the case of an offer-in-compromise which relates only to issues of liability of the taxpayer—

(i) such offer shall not be rejected solely because the Secretary is unable to locate the taxpayer's return or return information for verification of such liability; and

(ii) the taxpayer shall not be required to provide a financial statement[4], *and*

[5]*(C) any offer-in-compromise which does not meet the requirements of subparagraph (A)(i) or (B)(i), as the case may be, of subsection (c)(1) may be returned to the taxpayer as unprocessable.*

[6]***(e)*** **Administrative review.** The Secretary shall establish procedures—

(1) for an independent administrative review of any rejection of a proposed offer-in-compromise or installment agreement made by a taxpayer under this section or section 6159 before such rejection is communicated to the taxpayer; and

(2) which allow a taxpayer to appeal any rejection of such offer or agreement to the Internal Revenue Service Office of Appeals.

[7]***(f) Deemed acceptance of offer not rejected within certain period.*** *Any offer-in-compromise submitted under this section shall be deemed to be accepted by the Secretary if such offer is not rejected by the Secretary before the date which is 24 months after the date of the submission of such offer. For purposes of the preceding sentence, any period during which any tax liability which is the subject of such offer-in-compromise is in dispute in any judicial proceeding shall not be taken into account in determining the expiration of the 24-month period.*

[For Analysis, see ¶ 804. For Committee Reports, see ¶ 5027.]

[Endnote Code Sec. 7122]

Matter in *italics* in Code Sec. 7122(c), Code Sec. 7122(d), Code Sec. 7122(e), and Code Sec. 7122(f) was added by Sec. 509(a) and (b)(1) and (2) of the Tax Increase Prevention and Reconciliation Act of 2005, HR4297, 5/17/2006, which struck out:

1. added subsec. (c)
2. "(c)"
3. "; and"
4. "."
5. added subpara. (d)(3)(C)
6. "(d)"
7. added subsec. (f)

Effective Date (Sec. 509(d), HR4297, 5/17/2006) effective for offers-in-compromise submitted on and after the date which is 60 days after 5/17/2006.

[¶ 3035] Code Sec. 7872. Treatment of loans with below-market interest rates.

* * * * * * * * * * * *

(g) Exception for certain loans to qualified continuing care facilities.

* * * * * * * * * * * *

[1]***(6) Suspension of application.*** *Paragraph (1) shall not apply for any calendar year to which subsection (h) applies.*

[2]***(h) Exception for loans to qualified continuing care facilities.***

(1) In general. *This section shall not apply for any calendar year to any below-market loan owed by a facility which on the last day of such year is a qualified continuing care facility, if such loan was made pursuant to a continuing care contract and if the lender (or the lender's spouse) attains age 62 before the close of such year.*

(2) Continuing care contract. *For purposes of this section, the term "continuing care contract" means a written contract between an individual and a qualified continuing care facility under which—*

(A) the individual or individual's spouse may use a qualified continuing care facility for their life or lives,

(B) the individual or individual's spouse will be provided with housing, as appropriate for the health of such individual or individual's spouse—

(i) in an independent living unit (which has additional available facilities outside such unit for the provision of meals and other personal care), and

(ii) in an assisted living facility or a nursing facility, as is available in the continuing care facility, and

(C) the individual or individual's spouse will be provided assisted living or nursing care as the health of such individual or individual's spouse requires, and as is available in the continuing care facility.

The Secretary shall issue guidance which limits such term to contracts which provide only facilities, care, and services described in this paragraph.

(3) Qualified continuing care facility.

(A) In general. For purposes of this section, the term "qualified continuing care facility" means 1 or more facilities—

(i) which are designed to provide services under continuing care contracts,

(ii) which include an independent living unit, plus an assisted living or nursing facility, or both, and

(iii) substantially all of the independent living unit residents of which are covered by continuing care contracts.

(B) Nursing homes excluded. The term "qualified continuing care facility" shall not include any facility which is of a type which is traditionally considered a nursing home.

(4) Termination. *This subsection shall not apply to any calendar year after 2010.*

[3]***(i)*** **Regulations.**

(1) In general. The Secretary shall prescribe such regulations as may be necessary or appropriate to carry out the purposes of this section, including—

(A) regulations providing that where, by reason of varying rates of interest, conditional interest payments, waivers of interest, disposition of the lender's or borrower's interest in the loan, or other circumstances, the provisions of this section do not carry out the purposes of this section, adjustments to the provisions of this section will be made to the extent necessary to carry out the purposes of this section,

(B) regulations for the purpose of assuring that the positions of the borrower and lender are consistent as to the application (or nonapplication) of this section, and

(C) regulations exempting from the application of this section any class of transactions the interest arrangements of which have no significant effect on any Federal tax liability of the lender or the borrower.

(2) Estate tax coordination. Under regulations prescribed by the Secretary, any loan which is made with donative intent and which is a term loan shall be taken into account for purposes of chapter 11 in a manner consistent with the provisions of subsection (b).

[For Analysis, see ¶ 207. For Committee Reports, see ¶ 5013.]

[Endnote Code Sec. 7872]

Matter in *italics* in Code Sec. 7872(g)(6), Code Sec. 7872(h), and Code Sec. 7872(i) was added by Sec. 209(a) and (b)(1) of the Tax Increase Prevention and Reconciliation Act of 2005, HR4297, 5/17/2006, which struck out:

1. added para. (g)(6)
2. added susbec. (h)
3. "(h)"

Effective Date (Sec. 209(c), HR4297, 5/17/2006) effective for calendar yrs. begin. after 12/31/2005, for loans made before, on, or after 12/31/2005.

Tax Increase Prevention and Reconciliation Act of 2005

One Hundred Ninth Congress

2nd Session

HR4297

[¶ 4000] Act sections of the Tax Increase Prevention and Reconciliation Act of 2005, HR4297, or portions thereof, that do not amend specific Internal Revenue Code sections follow. Sections of the Internal Revenue Code as amended are reproduced at *Code as Amended.* Section 102 of HR4297 extends the sunset of amendments made by Secs. 301 and 302 of the Jobs and Growth Tax Relief Reconciliation Act of 2003, P.L. 108-27, from 12/31/2008 until 12/31/2010. This includes amendments to the following Code sections: 1, 55, 57, 163, 301, 306, 338, 341 (repealed), 467, 531, 541, 584, 691, 702, 854, 857, 1255, 1257, 1445, and 7518.

[¶ 4001] Sec. 1. SHORT TITLE, ETC.

(a) SHORT TITLE. This Act may be cited as the "Tax Increase Prevention and Reconciliation Act of 2005".

(b) AMENDMENT OF 1986 CODE. Except as otherwise expressly provided, whenever in this Act an amendment or repeal is expressed in terms of an amendment to, or repeal of, a section or other provision, the reference shall be considered to be made to a section or other provision of the Internal Revenue Code of 1986.

(c) TABLE OF CONTENTS. The table of contents for this Act is as follows:

Sec. 503. 5-year amortization of geological and geophysical expenditures for certain major integrated oil companies.

Sec. 504. Application of FIRPTA to regulated investment companies.

Sec. 505. Treatment of distributions attributable to FIRPTA gains.

Sec. 506. Prevention of avoidance of tax on investments of foreign persons in United States real property through wash sale transactions.

Sec. 507. Section 355 not to apply to distributions involving disqualified investment companies.

Sec. 508. Loan and redemption requirements on pooled financing requirements.

Sec. 509. Partial payments required with submission of offers-in-compromise.

Sec. 510. Increase in age of minor children whose unearned income is taxed as if parent's income.

Sec. 511. Imposition of withholding on certain payments made by government entities.

Sec. 512. Conversions to Roth IRAs.

Sec. 513. Repeal of FSC/ETI binding contract relief.

Sec. 514. Only wages attributable to domestic production taken into account in determining deduction for domestic production.

Sec. 515. Modification of exclusion for citizens living abroad.

Sec. 516. Tax involvement of accommodation parties in tax shelter transactions.

TITLE I— EXTENSION AND MODIFICATION OF CERTAIN PROVISIONS

[¶ 4002] Sec. 101. INCREASED EXPENSING FOR SMALL BUSINESS.

* * * * * * * * * * * * *

[¶ 4003] Sec. 102. CAPITAL GAINS AND DIVIDENDS RATES. Section 303 of the Jobs and Growth Tax Relief Reconciliation Act of 2003 is amended by striking "December 31, 2008" and inserting "December 31, 2010".

[¶ 4004] Sec. 103. CONTROLLED FOREIGN CORPORATIONS.

* * * * * * * * * * * * *

(b) LOOK-THROUGH TREATMENT OF PAYMENTS BETWEEN RELATED CONTROLLED FOREIGN CORPORATIONS UNDER THE FOREIGN PERSONAL HOLDING COMPANY RULES.

* * * * * * * * * * * * *

(2) EFFECTIVE DATE. The amendment made by this subsection shall apply to taxable years of foreign corporations beginning after December 31, 2005, and to taxable years of United States shareholders with or within which such taxable years of foreign corporations end.

TITLE II— OTHER PROVISIONS

[¶ 4005] Sec. 201. CLARIFICATION OF TAXATION OF CERTAIN SETTLEMENT FUNDS.

* * * * * * * * * * * * *

(b) EFFECTIVE DATE. The amendment made by subsection (a) shall apply to accounts and funds established after the date of the enactment of this Act.

[¶ 4006] Sec. 202. MODIFICATION OF ACTIVE BUSINESS DEFINITION UNDER SECTION 355.

* * * * * * * * * * * * *

[¶4007] Sec. 203. VETERANS' MORTGAGE BONDS.

(a) EXPANSION OF DEFINITION OF VETERANS ELIGIBLE FOR STATE HOME LOAN PROGRAMS FUNDED BY QUALIFIED VETERANS' MORTGAGE BONDS.

* * * * * * * * * * * * *

(2) EFFECTIVE DATE. The amendments made by this subsection shall apply to bonds issued on or after the date of the enactment of this Act.

(b) REVISION OF STATE VETERANS LIMIT.

* * * * * * * * * * * * *

(2) EFFECTIVE DATE. The amendments made by this subsection shall apply to allocations of State volume limit after April 5, 2006.

[¶4008] Sec. 204. CAPITAL GAINS TREATMENT FOR CERTAIN SELF-CREATED MUSICAL WORKS.

* * * * * * * * * * * * *

(c) EFFECTIVE DATE. The amendments made by this section shall apply to sales and exchanges in taxable years beginning after the date of the enactment of this Act.

[¶4009] Sec. 205. VESSEL TONNAGE LIMIT.

* * * * * * * * * * * * *

(b) EFFECTIVE DATE. The amendment made by subsection (a) shall apply to taxable years beginning after December 31, 2005.

[¶4010] Sec. 206. MODIFICATION OF SPECIAL ARBITRAGE RULE FOR CERTAIN FUNDS. In the case of bonds issued after the date of the enactment of this Act and before August 31, 2009—

(1) the requirement of paragraph (1) of section 648 of the Deficit Reduction Act of 1984 [P.L. 98-369] (98 Stat. 941) shall be treated as met with respect to the securities or obligations referred to in such section if such securities or obligations are held in a fund the annual distributions from which cannot exceed 7 percent of the average fair market value of the assets held in such fund except to the extent distributions are necessary to pay debt service on the bond issue, and

(2) paragraph (3) of such section shall be applied by substituting "distributions from" for "the investment earnings of" both places it appears.

[¶4011] Sec. 207. AMORTIZATION OF EXPENSES INCURRED IN CREATING OR ACQUIRING MUSIC OR MUSIC COPYRIGHTS.

* * * * * * * * * * * * *

(b) EFFECTIVE DATE. The amendments made by this section shall apply to expenses paid or incurred with respect to property placed in service in taxable years beginning after December 31, 2005.

[¶4012] Sec. 208. MODIFICATION OF EFFECTIVE DATE OF DISREGARD OF CERTAIN CAPITAL EXPENDITURES FOR PURPOSES OF QUALIFIED SMALL ISSUE BONDS.

* * * * * * * * * * * * *

[¶4013] Sec. 209. MODIFICATION OF TREATMENT OF LOANS TO QUALIFIED CONTINUING CARE FACILITIES.

* * * * * * * * * * * * *

(c) EFFECTIVE DATE. The amendment made by this section shall apply to calendar years beginning after December 31, 2005, with respect to loans made before, on, or after such date.

TITLE III— ALTERNATIVE MINIMUM TAX RELIEF

[¶ 4014] Sec. 301. INCREASE IN ALTERNATIVE MINIMUM TAX EXEMPTION AMOUNT FOR 2006.

* * * * * * * * * * * *

(b) EFFECTIVE DATE. The amendments made by this section shall apply to taxable years beginning after December 31, 2005.

[¶ 4015] Sec. 302. ALLOWANCE OF NONREFUNDABLE PERSONAL CREDITS AGAINST REGULAR AND ALTERNATIVE MINIMUM TAX LIABILITY.

* * * * * * * * * * * *

(b) EFFECTIVE DATE. The amendments made by this section shall apply to taxable years beginning after December 31, 2005.

TITLE IV— CORPORATE ESTIMATED TAX PROVISIONS

[¶ 4016] Sec. 401. TIME FOR PAYMENT OF CORPORATE ESTIMATED TAXES. Notwithstanding section 6655 of the Internal Revenue Code of 1986—

(1) in the case of a corporation with assets of not less than $1,000,000,000 (determined as of the end of the preceding taxable year)—

(A) the amount of any required installment of corporate estimated tax which is otherwise due in July, August, or September of 2006 shall be 105 percent of such amount,

(B) the amount of any required installment of corporate estimated tax which is otherwise due in July, August, or September of 2012 shall be 106.25 percent of such amount,

(C) the amount of any required installment of corporate estimated tax which is otherwise due in July, August, or September of 2013 shall be 100.75 percent of such amount, and

(D) the amount of the next required installment after an installment referred to in subparagraph (A), (B), or (C) shall be appropriately reduced to reflect the amount of the increase by reason of such subparagraph,

(2) 20.5 percent of the amount of any required installment of corporate estimated tax which is otherwise due in September 2010 shall not be due until October 1, 2010, and

(3) 27.5 percent of the amount of any required installment of corporate estimated tax which is otherwise due in September 2011 shall not be due until October 1, 2011.

TITLE V— REVENUE OFFSET PROVISIONS

[¶ 4017] Sec. 501. APPLICATION OF EARNINGS STRIPPING RULES TO PARTNERS WHICH ARE CORPORATIONS.

* * * * * * * * * * * *

(c) EFFECTIVE DATE. The amendments made by this section shall apply to taxable years beginning on or after the date of the enactment of this Act.

[¶ 4018] Sec. 502. REPORTING OF INTEREST ON TAX-EXEMPT BONDS.

* * * * * * * * * * * *

(c) EFFECTIVE DATE. The amendments made by this section shall apply to interest paid after December 31, 2005.

[¶ 4019] Sec. 503. 5-YEAR AMORTIZATION OF GEOLOGICAL AND GEOPHYSICAL EXPENDITURES FOR CERTAIN MAJOR INTEGRATED OIL COMPANIES.

* * * * * * * * * * * *

(b) EFFECTIVE DATE. The amendment made by this section shall apply to amounts paid or incurred after the date of the enactment of this Act.

[¶ 4020] Sec. 504. APPLICATION OF FIRPTA TO REGULATED INVESTMENT COMPANIES.

* * * * * * * * * * * *

(b) EFFECTIVE DATE. The amendment made by this section shall take effect as if included in the provisions of section 411 of the American Jobs Creation Act of 2004 [P.L. 108-357] to which it relates.

[¶ 4021] Sec. 505. TREATMENT OF DISTRIBUTIONS ATTRIBUTABLE TO FIRPTA GAINS.

* * * * * * * * * * * *

(d) EFFECTIVE DATES. The amendments made by this section shall apply to taxable years of qualified investment entities beginning after December 31, 2005, except that no amount shall be required to be withheld under section 1441, 1442, or 1445 of the Internal Revenue Code of 1986 with respect to any distribution before the date of the enactment of this Act if such amount was not otherwise required to be withheld under any such section as in effect before such amendments.

[¶ 4022] Sec. 506. PREVENTION OF AVOIDANCE OF TAX ON INVESTMENTS OF FOREIGN PERSONS IN UNITED STATES REAL PROPERTY THROUGH WASH SALE TRANSACTIONS.

* * * * * * * * * * * *

(c) EFFECTIVE DATE. The amendments made by this section shall apply to taxable years beginning after December 31, 2005, except that such amendments shall not apply to any distribution, or substitute dividend payment, occurring before the date that is 30 days after the date of the enactment of this Act.

[¶ 4023] Sec. 507. SECTION 355 NOT TO APPLY TO DISTRIBUTIONS INVOLVING DISQUALIFIED INVESTMENT COMPANIES.

* * * * * * * * * * * *

(b) EFFECTIVE DATES.

(1) IN GENERAL. The amendments made by this section shall apply to distributions after the date of the enactment of this Act.

(2) TRANSITION RULE. The amendments made by this section shall not apply to any distribution pursuant to a transaction which is—

(A) made pursuant to an agreement which was binding on such date of enactment and at all times thereafter,

(B) described in a ruling request submitted to the Internal Revenue Service on or before such date, or

(C) described on or before such date in a public announcement or in a filing with the Securities and Exchange Commission.

[¶ 4024] Sec. 508. LOAN AND REDEMPTION REQUIREMENTS ON POOLED FINANCING REQUIREMENTS.

* * * * * * * * * * * *

(e) EFFECTIVE DATE. The amendments made by this section shall apply to bonds issued after the date of the enactment of this Act.

[¶ 4025] Sec. 509. PARTIAL PAYMENTS REQUIRED WITH SUBMISSION OF OFFERS-IN-COMPROMISE.

* * * * * * * * * * * *

(d) EFFECTIVE DATE. The amendments made by this section shall apply to offers-in-compromise submitted on and after the date which is 60 days after the date of the enactment of this Act.

[¶ 4026] Sec. 510. INCREASE IN AGE OF MINOR CHILDREN WHOSE UNEARNED INCOME IS TAXED AS IF PARENT'S INCOME.

* * * * * * * * * * * *

(d) EFFECTIVE DATE. The amendments made by this section shall apply to taxable years beginning after December 31, 2005.

[¶ 4027] Sec. 511. IMPOSITION OF WITHHOLDING ON CERTAIN PAYMENTS MADE BY GOVERNMENT ENTITIES.

* * * * * * * * * * * *

(b) EFFECTIVE DATE. The amendment made by this section shall apply to payments made after December 31, 2010.

[¶ 4028] Sec. 512. CONVERSIONS TO ROTH IRAS.

* * * * * * * * * * * *

(c) EFFECTIVE DATE. The amendments made by this section shall apply to taxable years beginning after December 31, 2009.

[¶ 4029] Sec. 513. REPEAL OF FSC/ETI BINDING CONTRACT RELIEF.

(a) FSC PROVISIONS. Paragraph (1) of section 5(c) of the FSC Repeal and Extraterritorial Income Exclusion Act of 2000 is amended by striking "which occurs—" and all that follows and inserting "which occurs before January 1, 2002.".

(b) ETI PROVISIONS. Section 101 of the American Jobs Creation Act of 2004 is amended by striking subsection (f).

(c) EFFECTIVE DATE. The amendments made by this section shall apply to taxable years beginning after the date of the enactment of this Act.

[¶ 4030] Sec. 514. ONLY WAGES ATTRIBUTABLE TO DOMESTIC PRODUCTION TAKEN INTO ACCOUNT IN DETERMINING DEDUCTION FOR DOMESTIC PRODUCTION.

* * * * * * * * * * * *

(c) EFFECTIVE DATE. The amendments made by this section shall apply to taxable years beginning after the date of the enactment of this Act.

[¶ 4031] Sec. 515. MODIFICATION OF EXCLUSION FOR CITIZENS LIVING ABROAD.

* * * * * * * * * * * *

(d) EFFECTIVE DATE. The amendments made by this section shall apply to taxable years beginning after December 31, 2005.

[¶ 4032] Sec. 516. TAX INVOLVEMENT OF ACCOMMODATION PARTIES IN TAX SHELTER TRANSACTIONS.

* * * * * * * * * * * *

(d) EFFECTIVE DATES.

(1) IN GENERAL. Except as provided in paragraph (2), the amendments made by this section shall apply to taxable years ending after the date of the enactment of this Act, with respect to transactions before, on, or after such date, except that no tax under section 4965(a) of the Internal Revenue Code of 1986 (as added by this section) shall apply with respect to income or proceeds that are properly allocable to any period ending on or before the date which is 90 days after such date of enactment.

(2) DISCLOSURE. The amendments made by subsections (b) and (c) shall apply to disclosures the due date for which are after the date of the enactment of this Act.

[¶5000] Congressional Committee Reports Accompanying the Tax Increase Prevention and Reconciliation Act

This section, in ¶5001 through ¶5034, reproduces all relevant parts of the Conference Report (Conf Rept 109-455, 5/9/2006) relating to H.R. 4297, the Tax Increase Prevention and Reconciliation Act, which was signed into law on May 17, 2006 (P.L. 109-xxx, 5/17/2006). Also reproduced are all relevant parts of the House Report relating to H.R. 4297, the Tax Relief Extension Reconciliation Act of 2005 (H Rept 109-304, 11/17/2005), and the Joint Committee on Taxation Report relating to S. 2020, a predecessor to H.R. 4297, the Description of the Chairman's Modification to the Provisions of the "Tax Relief Act of 2005" (JCX-77-05, 11/14/2005).

[¶5001] Section 101. Increased expensing for small business.

(Code Sec. 179)

[House Report]

Present Law

In lieu of depreciation, a taxpayer with a sufficiently small amount of annual investment may elect to deduct (or "expense") such costs. Present law provides that the maximum amount a taxpayer may expense, for taxable years beginning in 2003 through 2007, is $100,000 of the cost of qualifying property placed in service for the taxable year.[29] In general, qualifying property is defined as depreciable tangible personal property that is purchased for use in the active conduct of a trade or business. Off-the-shelf computer software placed in service in taxable years beginning before 2008 is treated as qualifying property. The $100,000 amount is reduced (but not below zero) by the amount by which the cost of qualifying property placed in service during the taxable year exceeds $400,000. The $100,000 and $400,000 amounts are indexed for inflation for taxable years beginning after 2003 and before 2008.

The amount eligible to be expensed for a taxable year may not exceed the taxable income for a taxable year that is derived from the active conduct of a trade or business (determined without regard to this provision). Any amount that is not allowed as a deduction because of the taxable income limitation may be carried forward to succeeding taxable years (subject to similar limitations). No general business credit under section 38 is allowed with respect to any amount for which a deduction is allowed under section 179. An expensing election is made under rules prescribed by the Secretary.[30]

For taxable years beginning in 2008 and thereafter (or before 2003), the following rules apply. A taxpayer with a sufficiently small amount of annual investment may elect to deduct up to $25,000 of the cost of qualifying property placed in service for the taxable year. The $25,000 amount is reduced (but not below zero) by the amount by which the cost of qualifying property placed in service during the taxable year exceeds $200,000. The $25,000 and $200,000 amounts are not indexed. In general, qualifying property is defined as depreciable tangible personal property that is purchased for use in the active conduct of a trade or business (not including off the-shelf computer software). An expensing election may be revoked only with consent of the Commissioner.[31]

29. Additional section 179 incentives are provided with respect to a qualified property used by a business in the New York Liberty Zone (sec. 1400L(f)), an empowerment zone (sec. 1397A), or a renewal community (sec. 1400J).
30. Sec. 179(c)(1). Under Treas. Reg. sec. 179-5, applicable to property placed in service in taxable years beginning after 2002 and before 2008, a taxpayer is permitted to make or revoke an election under section 179 without the consent of the Commissioner on an amended Federal tax return for that taxable year. This amended return must be filed within the time prescribed by law for filing an amended return for the taxable year. T.D. 9209, July 12, 2005.
31. Sec. 179(c)(2).

Reasons for Change

The Committee believes that section 179 expensing provides two important benefits for small businesses. First, it lowers the cost of capital for property used in a trade or business. With a lower cost of capital, the Committee believes small businesses will invest in more equipment and employ more workers. Second, it eliminates depreciation recordkeeping requirements with respect to expensed property. In 2004, Congress acted to increase the value of these benefits and to increase the number of taxpayers eligible for taxable years through 2007. The Committee believes that the changes to section 179 expensing will continue to provide important benefits if extended, and the bill therefore extends these changes for an additional two years.

Explanation of Provision

The provision extends for two years the increased amount that a taxpayer may deduct and the other section 179 rules applicable in taxable years beginning before 2008. Thus, under the provision, these present-law rules continue in effect for taxable years beginning after 2007 and before 2010.

[Conference Report]

Senate Amendment

The Senate amendment provision is the same as the House bill.

Conference Agreement

The conference agreement includes the provision in the House bill and the Senate amendment.

Effective Date

The provision is effective for taxable years beginning after 2007 and before 2010.

[¶5002] Section 102. Capital gains and dividends rates.

(Code Sec. 1)

[House Report]

Present Law

Capital gains

In general

In general, gain or loss reflected in the value of an asset is not recognized for income tax purposes until a taxpayer disposes of the asset. On the sale or exchange of a capital asset, any gain generally is included in income. Any net capital gain of an individual is taxed at maximum rates lower than the rates applicable to ordinary income. Net capital gain is the excess of the net long-term capital gain for the taxable year over the net short-term capital loss for the year. Gain or loss is treated as long-term if the asset is held for more than one year.

Capital losses generally are deductible in full against capital gains. In addition, individual taxpayers may deduct capital losses against up to $3,000 of ordinary income in each year. Any remaining unused capital losses may be carried forward indefinitely to another taxable year.

A capital asset generally means any property except (1) inventory, stock in trade, or property held primarily for sale to customers in the ordinary course of the taxpayer's trade or business, (2) depreciable or real property used in the taxpayer's trade or business, (3) specified literary or artistic property, (4) business accounts or notes receivable,

(5) certain U.S. publications, (6) certain commodity derivative financial instruments, (7) hedging transactions, and (8) business supplies. In addition, the net gain from the disposition of certain property used in the taxpayer's trade or business is treated as long-term capital gain. Gain from the disposition of depreciable personal property is not treated as capital gain to the extent of all previous depreciation allowances. Gain from the disposition of depreciable real property is generally not treated as capital gain to the extent of the depreciation allowances in excess of the allowances that would have been available under the straight-line method of depreciation.

Tax rates before 2009

Under present law, for taxable years beginning before January 1, 2009, the maximum rate of tax on the adjusted net capital gain of an individual is 15 percent. Any adjusted net capital gain which otherwise would be taxed at a 10- or 15-percent rate is taxed at a five-percent rate (zero for taxable years beginning after 2007). These rates apply for purposes of both the regular tax and the alternative minimum tax.

Under present law, the "adjusted net capital gain" of an individual is the net capital gain reduced (but not below zero) by the sum of the 28-percent rate gain and the unrecaptured section 1250 gain. The net capital gain is reduced by the amount of gain that the individual treats as investment income for purposes of determining the investment interest limitation under section 163(d).

The term "28-percent rate gain" means the amount of net gain attributable to long-term capital gains and losses from the sale or exchange of collectibles (as defined in section 408(m) without regard to paragraph (3) thereof), an amount of gain equal to the amount of gain excluded from gross income under section 1202 (relating to certain small business stock), the net short-term capital loss for the taxable year, and any long-term capital loss carryover to the taxable year.

"Unrecaptured section 1250 gain" means any long-term capital gain from the sale or exchange of section 1250 property (i.e., depreciable real estate) held more than one year to the extent of the gain that would have been treated as ordinary income if section 1250 applied to all depreciation, reduced by the net loss (if any) attributable to the items taken into account in computing 28-percent rate gain. The amount of unrecaptured section 1250 gain (before the reduction for the net loss) attributable to the disposition of property to which section 1231 (relating to certain property used in a trade or business) applies may not exceed the net section 1231 gain for the year.

An individual's unrecaptured section 1250 gain is taxed at a maximum rate of 25 percent, and the 28-percent rate gain is taxed at a maximum rate of 28 percent. Any amount of unrecaptured section 1250 gain or 28-percent rate gain otherwise taxed at a 10- or 15-percent rate is taxed at the otherwise applicable rate.

Tax rates after 2008

For taxable years beginning after December 31, 2008, the maximum rate of tax on the adjusted net capital gain of an individual is 20 percent. Any adjusted net capital gain which otherwise would be taxed at a 10- or 15-percent rate is taxed at a 10-percent rate.

In addition, any gain from the sale or exchange of property held more than five years that would otherwise have been taxed at the 10-percent rate is taxed at an eight-percent rate. Any gain from the sale or exchange of property held more than five years and the holding period for which began after December 31, 2000, that would otherwise have been taxed at a 20-percent rate is taxed at an 18-percent rate.

The tax rates on 28-percent gain and unrecaptured section 1250 gain are the same as for taxable years beginning before 2009.

Dividends

In general

A dividend is the distribution of property made by a corporation to its shareholders out of its after-tax earnings and profits.

Tax rates before 2009

Under present law, dividends received by an individual from domestic corporations and qualified foreign corporations are taxed at the same rates that apply to capital gains. This treatment applies for purposes of both the regular tax and the alternative minimum tax. Thus, for taxable years beginning before 2009, dividends received by an individual are taxed at rates of five (zero for taxable years beginning after 2007) and 15 percent.

If a shareholder does not hold a share of stock for more than 60 days during the 121-day period beginning 60 days before the exdividend date (as measured under section 246(c)), dividends received on the stock are not eligible for the reduced rates. Also, the reduced rates are not available for dividends to the extent that the taxpayer is obligated to make related payments with respect to positions in substantially similar or related property.

Qualified dividend income includes otherwise qualified dividends received from qualified foreign corporations. The term "qualified foreign corporation" includes a foreign corporation that is eligible for the benefits of a comprehensive income tax treaty with the United States which the Treasury Department determines to be satisfactory and which includes an exchange of information program. In addition, a foreign corporation is treated as a qualified foreign corporation with respect to any dividend paid by the corporation with respect to stock that is readily tradable on an established securities market in the United States.

Dividends received from a corporation that is a passive foreign investment company (as defined in section 1297) in either the taxable year of the distribution, or the preceding taxable year, are not qualified dividends.

Special rules apply in determining a taxpayer's foreign tax credit limitation under section 904 in the case of qualified dividend income. For these purposes, rules similar to the rules of section 904(b)(2)(B) concerning adjustments to the foreign tax credit limitation to reflect any capital gain rate differential will apply to any qualified dividend income.

If a taxpayer receives an extraordinary dividend (within the meaning of section 1059(c)) eligible for the reduced rates with respect to any share of stock, any loss on the sale of the stock is treated as a long-term capital loss to the extent of the dividend.

A dividend is treated as investment income for purposes of determining the amount of deductible investment interest only if the taxpayer elects to treat the dividend as not eligible for the reduced rates.

The amount of dividends qualifying for reduced rates that may be paid by a regulated investment company ("RIC") for any taxable year in which the qualified dividend income received by the company is less than 95 percent of its gross income (as specially computed) may not exceed the sum of (i) the qualified dividend income of the RIC for the taxable year and (ii) the amount of earnings and profits accumulated in a non-RIC taxable year that were distributed by the RIC during the taxable year.

The amount of dividends qualifying for reduced rates that may be paid by a real estate investment trust ("REIT") for any taxable year may not exceed the sum of (i) the qualified dividend income of the REIT for the taxable year, (ii) an amount equal to the excess of the income subject to the taxes imposed by 857(b)(1) and the regulations prescribed under section 337(d) for the preceding taxable year over the amount of these taxes for the preceding taxable year, and (iii) the amount of earnings and profits accumulated in a non-REIT taxable year that were distributed by the REIT during the taxable year.

The reduced rates do not apply to dividends received from an organization that was exempt from tax under section 501 or was a tax-exempt farmers' cooperative in either the taxable year of the distribution or the preceding taxable year; dividends received from a mutual savings bank that received a deduction under section 591; or deductible dividends paid on employer securities.[27]

Tax rates after 2008

For taxable years beginning after 2008, dividends received by an individual are taxed as ordinary income at rates of up to 35 percent.

Reasons for Change

The Committee believes that the lower capital gain and dividend rates have had a positive effect on the economy and should be extended to continue to promote economic growth by increasing the after-tax return to saving and investment. The Committee further believes that the extension will encourage the payment of dividends by corporations.

Explanation of Provision

The bill extends for two years the present-law provisions relating to lower capital gain and dividend tax rates (through taxable years beginning on or before December 31, 2010).

[Conference Report]

Senate Amendment

No provision.

Conference Agreement

The conference agreement includes the House bill provision.

Effective Date

The provision applies to taxable years beginning after December 31, 2008.

[¶5003] Section 103(a). Controlled foreign corporations; subpart F exception for active financing.

(Code Sec. 953, 954)

[House Report]

Present law

Under the subpart F rules, 10-percent U.S. shareholders of a controlled foreign corporation ("CFC") are subject to U.S. tax currently on certain income earned by the CFC, whether or not such income is distributed to the shareholders. The income subject to current inclusion under the subpart F rules includes, among other things, insurance income and foreign base company income. Foreign base company income includes, among other things, foreign personal holding company income and foreign base company ser-

27. In addition, for taxable years beginning before 2009, amounts treated as ordinary income on the disposition of certain preferred stock (sec. 306) are treated as dividends for purposes of applying the reduced rates; the tax rate for the accumulated earnings tax (sec. 531) and the personal holding company tax (sec. 541) is reduced to 15 percent; and the collapsible corporation rules (sec. 341) are repealed.

vices income (i.e., income derived from services performed for or on behalf of a related person outside the country in which the CFC is organized).

Foreign personal holding company income generally consists of the following: (1) dividends, interest, royalties, rents, and annuities; (2) net gains from the sale or exchange of (a) property that gives rise to the preceding types of income, (b) property that does not give rise to income, and (c) interests in trusts, partnerships, and REMICs; (3) net gains from commodities transactions; (4) net gains from certain foreign currency transactions; (5) income that is equivalent to interest; (6) income from notional principal contracts; (7) payments in lieu of dividends; and (8) amounts received under personal service contracts.

Insurance income subject to current inclusion under the subpart F rules includes any income of a CFC attributable to the issuing or reinsuring of any insurance or annuity contract in connection with risks located in a country other than the CFC's country of organization. Subpart F insurance income also includes income attributable to an insurance contract in connection with risks located within the CFC's country of organization, as the result of an arrangement under which another corporation receives a substantially equal amount of consideration for insurance of other country risks. Investment income of a CFC that is allocable to any insurance or annuity contract related to risks located outside the CFC's country of organization is taxable as subpart F insurance income.[22]

Temporary exceptions from foreign personal holding company income, foreign base company services income, and insurance income apply for subpart F purposes for certain income that is derived in the active conduct of a banking, financing, or similar business, or in the conduct of an insurance business (so-called "active financing income").[23]

With respect to income derived in the active conduct of a banking, financing, or similar business, a CFC is required to be predominantly engaged in such business and to conduct substantial activity with respect to such business in order to qualify for the exceptions. In addition, certain nexus requirements apply, which provide that income derived by a CFC or a qualified business unit ("QBU") of a CFC from transactions with customers is eligible for the exceptions if, among other things, substantially all of the activities in connection with such transactions are conducted directly by the CFC or QBU in its home country, and such income is treated as earned by the CFC or QBU in its home country for purposes of such country's tax laws. Moreover, the exceptions apply to income derived from certain cross border transactions, provided that certain requirements are met. Additional exceptions from foreign personal holding company income apply for certain income derived by a securities dealer within the meaning of section 475 and for gain from the sale of active financing assets.

In the case of insurance, in addition to a temporary exception from foreign personal holding company income for certain income of a qualifying insurance company with respect to risks located within the CFC's country of creation or organization, certain temporary exceptions from insurance income and from foreign personal holding company income apply for certain income of a qualifying branch of a qualifying insurance company with respect to risks located within the home country of the branch, provided certain requirements are met under each of the exceptions. Further, additional temporary exceptions from insurance income and from foreign personal holding company income apply for certain income of certain CFCs or branches with respect to risks located in a country other than the United States, provided that the requirements for these exceptions are met.

22. Prop. Treas. Reg. sec. 1.953-1(a).
23. Temporary exceptions from the subpart F provisions for certain active financing income applied only for taxable years beginning in 1998. Those exceptions were modified and extended for one year, applicable only for taxable years beginning in 1999. The Tax Relief Extension Act of 1999 (Pub. L. No. 106-170) clarified and extended the temporary exceptions for two years, applicable only for taxable years beginning after 1999 and before 2002. The Job Creation and Worker Assistance Act of 2002 (Pub. L. No. 107-147) modified and extended the temporary exceptions for five years, for taxable years beginning after 2001 and before 2007.

In the case of a life insurance or annuity contract, reserves for such contracts are determined as follows for purposes of these provisions. The reserves equal the greater of: (1) the net surrender value of the contract (as defined in section 807(e)(1)(A)), including in the case of pension plan contracts; or (2) the amount determined by applying the tax reserve method that would apply if the qualifying life insurance company were subject to tax under Subchapter L of the Code, with the following modifications. First, there is substituted for the applicable Federal interest rate an interest rate determined for the functional currency of the qualifying insurance company's home country, calculated (except as provided by the Treasury Secretary in order to address insufficient data and similar problems) in the same manner as the mid-term applicable Federal interest rate (within the meaning of section 1274(d)). Second, there is substituted for the prevailing State assumed rate the highest assumed interest rate permitted to be used for purposes of determining statement reserves in the foreign country for the contract. Third, in lieu of U.S. mortality and morbidity tables, mortality and morbidity tables are applied that reasonably reflect the current mortality and morbidity risks in the foreign country. Fourth, the Treasury Secretary may provide that the interest rate and mortality and morbidity tables of a qualifying insurance company may be used for one or more of its branches when appropriate. In no event may the reserve for any contract at any time exceed the foreign statement reserve for the contract, reduced by any catastrophe, equalization, or deficiency reserve or any similar reserve.

Present law permits a taxpayer in certain circumstances, subject to approval by the IRS through the ruling process or in published guidance, to establish that the reserve of a life insurance company for life insurance and annuity contracts is the amount taken into account in determining the foreign statement reserve for the contract (reduced by catastrophe, equalization, or deficiency reserve or any similar reserve). IRS approval is to be based on whether the method, the interest rate, the mortality and morbidity assumptions, and any other factors taken into account in determining foreign statement reserves (taken together or separately) provide an appropriate means of measuring income for Federal income tax purposes. In seeking a ruling, the taxpayer is required to provide the IRS with necessary and appropriate information as to the method, interest rate, mortality and morbidity assumptions and other assumptions under the foreign reserve rules so that a comparison can be made to the reserve amount determined by applying the tax reserve method that would apply if the qualifying insurance company were subject to tax under Subchapter L of the Code (with the modifications provided under present law for purposes of these exceptions). The IRS also may issue published guidance indicating its approval. Present law continues to apply with respect to reserves for any life insurance or annuity contract for which the IRS has not approved the use of the foreign statement reserve. An IRS ruling request under this provision is subject to the present-law provisions relating to IRS user fees.

Reason of Change

In the Taxpayer Relief Act of 1997, one-year temporary exceptions from foreign personal holding company income were enacted for income from the active conduct of an insurance, banking, financing, or similar business.[24] In 1998, 1999, and 2002, the provisions were extended, and in some cases, modified.[25] The Committee believes that it is

24. The President canceled this provision in 1997 pursuant to the Line Item Veto Act. On June 25, 1998, the Supreme Court held that the cancellation procedures set forth in the Line Item Veto Act are unconstitutional. Clinton v. City of New York, 524 U.S. 417 (1998).

25. The Tax and Trade Relief Extension Act of 1998, Division J, Making Omnibus Consolidated and Emergency Supplemental Appropriations for Fiscal Year 1999, Pub. L. No. 105-277 sec. 1005, (1998), provided a one-year extension, with modifications. The Tax Relief Extension Act of 1999, Pub.L. No. 106-170, sec. 503 (1999), provided an additional two-year extension, with a clarification. The Job Creation and Worker Assistance Act of 2002 (Pub. L. No. 107-147, sec. 614) provided an additional five-year extension and provided that in certain circumstances an insurance company may establish reserves taking into account foreign statement reserves. The House bill, H.R. 3090, the "Economic Security and Recovery Act of 2001," had provided for a permanent extension (H. R. Rep. No. 107-251 at 50 (2001)), while the Senate bill, the "Economic Recovery and Assistance for American Workers Act of 2001," had provided for a one-year extension. See S. Prt. No. 107-49 at 58-60 (2001).

appropriate to extend the temporary provisions, as modified by the previous legislation, for an additional two years.

Explanation of Provision

The provision extends for two years (for taxable years beginning before 2009) the present-law temporary exceptions from subpart F foreign personal holding company income, foreign base company services income, and insurance income for certain income that is derived in the active conduct of a banking, financing, or similar business, or in the conduct of an insurance business.

[Conference Report]

Senate Amendment

No provision.

Conference Agreement

The conference agreement includes the House bill provision.

Effective Date

The provision is effective for taxable years of foreign corporations beginning after December 31, 2006, and before January 1, 2009, and for taxable years of U.S. shareholders with or within which such taxable years of such foreign corporations end.

[¶ 5004] Section 103(b). Controlled foreign corporations; look-through treatment of payments between related controlled foreign corporations under foreign personal holding company rules.

(Code Sec. 954)

[House Report]

Present Law

In general, the rules of subpart F (secs. 951-964) require U.S. shareholders with a 10-percent or greater interest in a controlled foreign corporation ("CFC") to include certain income of the CFC (referred to as "subpart F income") on a current basis for U.S. tax purposes, regardless of whether the income is distributed to the shareholders.

Subpart F income includes foreign base company income. One category of foreign base company income is foreign personal holding company income. For subpart F purposes, foreign personal holding company income generally includes dividends, interest, rents, and royalties, among other types of income. However, foreign personal holding company income does not include dividends and interest received by a CFC from a related corporation organized and operating in the same foreign country in which the CFC is organized, or rents and royalties received by a CFC from a related corporation for the use of property within the country in which the CFC is organized. Interest, rent, and royalty payments do not qualify for this exclusion to the extent that such payments reduce the subpart F income of the payor.

Reasons for Change

Most countries allow their companies to redeploy active foreign earnings with no additional tax burden. The Committee believes that this provision will make U.S. companies and U.S. workers more competitive with respect to such countries. By allowing U.S. companies to reinvest their active foreign earnings where they are most needed without incurring the immediate additional tax that companies based in many other countries never incur, the Committee believes that the provision will enable U.S. companies to make more sales overseas, and thus produce more goods in the United States.

Explanation of Provision

Under the provision, for taxable years beginning after 2005 and before 2009, dividends, interest,[26] rents, and royalties received by one CFC from a related CFC are not treated as foreign personal holding company income to the extent attributable or properly allocable to non-subpart-F income of the payor. For this purpose, a related CFC is a CFC that controls or is controlled by the other CFC, or a CFC that is controlled by the same person or persons that control the other CFC. Ownership of more than 50 percent of the CFC's stock (by vote or value) constitutes control for these purposes.

[Conference Report]

Senate Amendment

No provision.

Conference Agreement

The conference agreement includes the House bill provision.

Effective date

The provision in the House bill is effective for taxable years of foreign corporations beginning after December 31, 2005 but before January 1, 2009, and for taxable years of U.S. shareholders with or within which such taxable years of such foreign corporations end.

[¶ 5005] Section 201. Clarification of taxation of certain settlement funds.

(Code Sec. 468B)

[House Report]

Present Law

Present law provides that if a taxpayer makes a payment to a designated settlement fund pursuant to a court order, the deduction timing rules that require economic performance generally are deemed to be met as the payments are made by the taxpayer to the fund. A designated settlement fund means a fund which: is established pursuant to a court order; extinguishes completely the taxpayer's tort liability arising out of personal injury, death or property damage; is administered by persons a majority of whom are independent of the taxpayer; and under the terms of the fund the taxpayer (or any related person) may not hold any beneficial interest in the income or corpus of the fund.

Generally, a designated or qualified settlement fund is taxed as a separate entity at the maximum trust rate on its modified income. Modified income is generally gross income less deductions for administrative costs and other incidental expenses incurred in connection with the operation of the settlement fund.

The cleanup of hazardous waste sites is sometimes funded by environmental "settlement funds" or escrow accounts. These escrow accounts are established in consent decrees between the Environmental Protection Agency ("EPA") and the settling parties under the jurisdiction of a Federal district court. The EPA uses these accounts to resolve claims against private parties under Comprehensive Environmental Response, Compensation and Liability Act of 1980 ("CERCLA").

Present law provides that nothing in any provision of law is to be construed as providing that an escrow account, settlement fund, or similar fund is not subject to current income tax.

26. Interest for this purpose includes factoring income which is treated as equivalent to interest under sec. 954(c)(1)(E).

Reasons for Change

The Committee believes that environmental escrow accounts established under court consent decrees are essential for the EPA to resolve or satisfy claims under the CERCLA. The tax treatment of these settlement funds may prevent taxpayers from entering into prompt settlements with the EPA for the cleanup of Superfund hazardous waste sites and reduce the ultimate amount of funds available for the sites' cleanup. Because these settlement funds are controlled by the government and, upon termination, any remaining funds belong to the government, the Committee believes it is appropriate to establish that these funds are to be treated as beneficially owned by the United States.

Explanation of Provision

The provision provides that certain settlement funds established in consent decrees for the sole purpose of resolving claims under CERCLA are to be treated as beneficially owned by the United States government and therefore, not subject to Federal income tax.

To qualify the settlement fund must be: (1) established pursuant to a consent decree entered by a judge of a United States District Court; (2) created for the receipt of settlement payments for the sole purpose of resolving claims under CERCLA; (3) controlled (in terms of expenditures of contributions and earnings thereon) by the government or an agency or instrumentality thereof; and (4) upon termination, any remaining funds will be disbursed to such government entity and used in accordance with applicable law. For purposes of the provision, a government entity means the United States, any State of political subdivision thereof, the District of Columbia, any possession of the United States, and any agency or instrumentality of the foregoing.

The provision does not apply to accounts or funds established after December 31, 2010.

[Conference Report]

Senate Amendment

No provision.

Conference Agreement

The conference agreement includes the House bill provision.

Effective Date

The provision is effective for accounts and funds established after the date of enactment.

[¶ 5006] Section 202. Modification of active business definition under Section 355.

(Code Sec. 355)

[House Report]

Present Law

A corporation generally is required to recognize gain on the distribution of property (including stock of a subsidiary) to its shareholders as if such property had been sold for its fair market value. An exception to this rule applies if the distribution of the stock of a controlled corporation satisfies the requirements of section 355 of the Code. To qualify for tax-free treatment under section 355, both the distributing corporation and the controlled corporation must be engaged immediately after the distribution in the active conduct of a trade or business that has been conducted for at least five years and was not acquired in a taxable transaction during that period.[32] For this purpose, a corporation is engaged in the active conduct of a trade or business only if (1) the corporation is directly engaged in the active conduct of a trade or business, or (2) the corporation is not directly engaged in an active business, but substantially all of its assets consist of stock and securities of a corporation it controls that is engaged in the active conduct of a trade or business.[33]

In determining whether a corporation is directly engaged in an active trade or business that satisfies the requirement, old IRS guidelines for advance ruling purposes required that the value of the gross assets of the trade or business being relied on must ordinarily constitute at least five percent of the total fair market value of the gross assets of the corporation directly conducting the trade or business.[34] More recently, the IRS has suspended this specific rule in connection with its general administrative practice of moving IRS resources away from advance rulings on factual aspects of section 355 transactions in general.[35]

If the distributing or controlled corporation is not directly engaged in an active trade or business, then the IRS takes the position that the "substantially all" test requires that at least 90 percent of the fair market value of the corporation's gross assets consist of stock and securities of a controlled corporation that is engaged in the active conduct of a trade or business.[36]

Reasons for Change

Prior to a spin-off under section 355 of the Code, corporate groups that have conducted business in separate corporate entities often must undergo elaborate restructurings to place active businesses in the proper entities to satisfy the five-year active business requirement. If the top-tier corporation of a chain that is being spun off or retained is a holding company, then the requirements regarding the activities of its subsidiaries are more stringent than if the top-tier corporation itself engaged in some active business. The Committee believes that it is appropriate to simplify planning for corporate groups that use a holding company structure to engage in distributions that qualify for tax-free treatment under section 355.

Explanation of Provision

Under the bill, the active business test is determined by reference to the relevant affiliated group. For the distributing corporation, the relevant affiliated group consists of the distributing corporation as the common parent and all corporations affiliated with the distributing corporation through stock ownership described in section 1504(a)(1)(B (regardless of whether the corporations are includible corporations under section 1504(b)), immediately after the distribution. The relevant affiliated group for a controlled corporation is determined in a similar manner (with the controlled corporation as the common parent).

Effective Date

The bill applies to distributions after the date of enactment and before December 31, 2010, with three exceptions. The bill does not apply to distributions (1) made pursuant to an agreement which is binding on the date of enactment and at all times thereafter, (2) described in a ruling request submitted to the IRS on or before the date of enactment, or (3) described on or before the date of enactment in a public announcement or in a filing with the Securities and Exchange Commission. The distributing corporation may irrevocably elect not to have the exceptions described above apply.

---

32. Section 355(b).
33. Section 355(b)(2)(A).
34. Rev. Proc. 2003-3, sec. 4.01(30), 2003-1 I.R.B. 113.
35. Rev. Proc. 2003-48, 2003-29 I.R.B. 86.
36. Rev. Proc. 96-30, sec. 4.03(5), 1996-1 C.B. 696; Rev. Proc. 77-37, sec. 3.04, 1977-2 C.B. 568.

In the case of any distribution prior to the date of enactment, solely for the purpose of determining whether, after the date of enactment, the taxpayer continues to satisfy the requirements of section 355(b)(2)(A) as a result of an acquisition, disposition, or other restructuring after such date and before December 31, 2010, the provisions of the bill apply as if the distribution had occurred after the date of enactment.[37]

[Conference Report]

Present Law

A corporation generally is required to recognize gain on the distribution of property (including stock of a subsidiary) to its shareholders as if the corporation had sold such property for its fair market value. In addition, the shareholders receiving the distributed property are ordinarily treated as receiving a dividend of the value of the distribution (to the extent of the distributing corporation's earnings and profits), or capital gain in the case of a stock buyback that significantly reduces the shareholder's interest in the parent corporation.

An exception to these rules applies if the distribution of the stock of a controlled corporation satisfies the requirements of section 355 of the Code. If all the requirements are satisfied, there is no tax to the distributing corporation or to the shareholders on the distribution.

In determining whether assets are part of a five-year qualifying active business, assets acquired more recently than five years prior to the distribution, in a taxable transaction, are permitted to qualify as five-year "active business" assets if they are considered to have been acquired as part of an expansion of an existing business that does so qualify.[45]

Senate Amendment

The Senate amendment provision is the same as the House bill with respect to the House bill provision described above, except for the date on which that provision sunsets.[49]

Effective Date

The effective date of the first provision of the Senate amendment generally is the same as the effective date of the identical provision of the House bill, except that the Senate amendment provision sunsets for distributions (and for acquisitions, dispositions, or other restructurings as relating to continuing qualification of pre-effective date distributions) after December 31, 2009, rather than for distributions (and for acquisitions, dispositions, or other restructurings as relating to continuing qualification of pre-effective date distributions) on or after December 31, 2010.

Conference Agreement

The conference agreement includes the House bill and the Senate amendment with modifications.

With respect to the provision that applies the active business test by reference to the relevant affiliated group, the conference agreement provision is the same as the House

37. For example, a holding company taxpayer that had distributed a controlled corporation in a spin-off prior to the date of enactment, in which spin-off the taxpayer satisfied the "substantially all" active business stock test of present law section 355(b)(2)(A) immediately after the distribution, would not be deemed to have failed to satisfy any requirement that it continue that same qualified structure for any period of time after the distribution, solely because of a restructuring that occurs after the date of enactment and that would satisfy the requirements of new section 355(b)(2)(A).

45. Treas. Reg. sec. 1.355-3(b)(ii).

49. See "Effective date" for the Senate Amendment, infra.

bill and the Senate amendment except for the date on which the conference agreement provision sunsets.[50]

Effective Date

The starting effective date of the provision that applies the active business test by reference to the relevant affiliated group is the same as that of the House bill and the Senate amendment provisions. The conference agreement changes the date on which the provision sunsets so that the provision does not apply for distributions (or for acquisitions, dispositions, or other restructurings as relating to continuing qualification of pre-effective date distributions) occurring after December 31, 2010.

[¶ 5007] Section 203. Veterans' mortgage bonds.

(Code Sec. 143)

[House Report]

Present Law

Qualified veterans' mortgage bonds are private activity bonds the proceeds of which are used to make mortgage loans to certain veterans. Authority to issue qualified veterans' mortgage bonds is limited to States that had issued such bonds before June 22, 1984. Qualified veterans' mortgage bonds are not subject to the State volume limitations generally applicable to private activity bonds. Instead, annual issuance in each State is subject to a State volume limitation based on the volume of such bonds issued by the State before June 22, 1984. The five States eligible to issue these bonds are Alaska, California, Oregon, Texas, and Wisconsin. Loans financed with qualified veterans' mortgage bonds can be made only with respect to principal residences and can not be made to acquire or replace existing mortgages. Mortgage loans made with the proceeds of these bonds can be made only to veterans who served on active duty before 1977 and who applied for the financing before the date 30 years after the last date on which such veteran left active service (the "eligibility period").

Reasons for Change

The Committee believes that the qualified veterans' mortgage bond program should be expanded to more recent veterans including potentially the men and women serving on active duty today. The Committee also believes that such an expansion requires modified volume limits for these bonds.

Explanation of Provision

The bill repeals the requirement that veterans receiving loans financed with veterans' bonds must have served before 1977. It also reduces the eligibility period to 25 years (rather than 30 years) following release from the military service. The bill provides new State volume limits for these bonds for the five eligible States. In 2010, the new annual limit on the total volume of veterans' bonds is $25 million for Alaska, $66.25 million for California, $25 million for Oregon, $53.75 million for Texas, and $25 million for Wisconsin. These volume limits are phased-in over the four-year period immediately preceding 2010 by allowing the applicable percentage of the 2010 volume limits. The following table provides those percentages.

50. See "Effective date" of the conference agreement provision, infra.

Calendar year:	Applicable percentage is:
2006	20 percent
2007	40 percent
2008	60 percent
2009	80 percent

The volume limits are zero for 2011 and each year thereafter. Unused allocation cannot be carried forward to subsequent years.

[Conference Report]

Present Law

Private activity bonds are bonds that nominally are issued by States or local governments, but the proceeds of which are used (directly or indirectly) by a private person and payment of which is derived from funds of such private person. The exclusion from income for State and local bonds does not apply to private activity bonds, unless the bonds are issued for certain permitted purposes ("qualified private activity bonds"). The definition of a qualified private activity bond includes both qualified mortgage bonds and qualified veterans' mortgage bonds.

Qualified mortgage bonds are issued to make mortgage loans to qualified mortgagors for owner-occupied residences. The Code imposes several limitations on qualified mortgage bonds, including income limitations for homebuyers and purchase price limitations for the home financed with bond proceeds. In addition, qualified mortgage bonds generally cannot be used to finance a mortgage for a homebuyer who had an ownership interest in a principal residence in the three years preceding the execution of the mortgage (the "first-time homebuyer" requirement).

Senate Amendment

No provision.

Conference Agreement

The conference agreement includes the House bill with the following modifications. The conference agreement does not amend present law as it relates to qualified veterans' mortgage bonds issued by the States of California and Texas. In the case of qualified veterans' mortgage bonds issued by the States of Alaska, Oregon, and Wisconsin, (1) the requirement that veterans must have served before 1977 is repealed and (2) the eligibility period for applying for a loan following release from the military service is reduced from 30 years to 25 years.

In addition, the annual issuance of qualified veterans' mortgage bonds in the States of Alaska, Oregon and Wisconsin is subject to new State volume limitations which are phased in between the years 2006 and 2010. The State volume limit in these States for any calendar year after 2010 is zero.

Effective Date

The provision expanding the definition of eligible veterans applies to bonds issued on or after date of enactment. The provision amending State volume limitations applies to allocations of volume limitation made after April 5, 2006.

[¶5008] Section 204. Capital gains treatment for certain self-created musical works.

(Code Sec. 1221)

[House Report]

Present Law

Capital gains

The maximum tax rate on the net capital gain income of an individual is 15 percent for taxable years beginning in 2005. By contrast, the maximum tax rate on an individual's ordinary income is 35 percent. The reduced 15-percent rate generally is available for gain from the sale or exchange of a capital asset for which the taxpayer has satisfied a holding-period requirement. Capital assets generally include all property held by a taxpayer with certain specified exclusions.

An exclusion from the definition of a capital asset applies to inventory property or property held by a taxpayer primarily for sale to customers in the ordinary course of the taxpayer's trade or business. Another exclusion from capital asset status applies to copyrights, literary, musical, or artistic compositions, letters or memoranda, or similar property held by a taxpayer whose personal efforts created the property (or held by a taxpayer whose basis in the property is determined by reference to the basis of the taxpayer whose personal efforts created the property). Consequently, when a taxpayer that owns copyrights in, for example, books, songs, or paintings that the taxpayer created (or when a taxpayer to which the copyrights have been transferred by the works' creator in a substituted basis transaction) sells the copyrights, gain from the sale is treated as ordinary income, not capital gain.

Charitable contributions

A taxpayer generally is allowed a deduction for the fair market value of property contributed to a charity. If a taxpayer makes a contribution of property that would have generated ordinary income (or short-term capital gain), the taxpayer's charitable contribution deduction generally is limited to the property's adjusted basis.

Reasons for Change

The Committee believes it is appropriate to allow taxpayers to treat as capital gain the income from a sale or exchange of musical compositions or copyrights in musical works the taxpayer created.

Explanation of Provision

The provision provides that at the election of a taxpayer, the sale or exchange before January 1, 2011 of musical compositions or copyrights in musical works created by the taxpayer's personal efforts (or having a basis determined by reference to the basis in the hands of the taxpayer whose personal efforts created the compositions or copyrights) is treated as the sale or exchange of a capital asset. The provision does not change the present law limitation on a taxpayer's charitable deduction for the contribution of such compositions or copyrights.

[Conference Report]

Senate Amendment

No provision.

Conference Agreement

The conference agreement includes the House bill provision.

Effective Date

The provision is effective for sales or exchanges in taxable years beginning after the date of enactment.

[¶ 5009] Section 205. Vessel tonnage limit.

(Code Sec. 1355)

[House Report]

Present Law

The United States employs a "worldwide" tax system, under which domestic corporations generally are taxed on all income, including income from shipping operations, whether derived in the United States or abroad. In order to mitigate double taxation, a foreign tax credit for income taxes paid to foreign countries is provided to reduce or eliminate the U.S. tax owed on such income, subject to certain limitations.

Generally, the United States taxes foreign corporations only on income that has a sufficient nexus to the United States. Thus, a foreign corporation is generally subject to U.S. tax only on income, including income from shipping operations, which is "effectively connected" with the conduct of a trade or business in the United States (sec. 882). Such "effectively connected income" generally is taxed in the same manner and at the same rates as the income of a U.S. corporation.

The United States imposes a four percent tax on the amount of a foreign corporation's U.S. source gross transportation income (sec. 887). Transportation income includes income from the use (or hiring or leasing for use) of a vessel and income from services directly related to the use of a vessel. Fifty percent of the transportation income attributable to transportation that either begins or ends (but not both) in the United States is treated as U.S. source gross transportation income. The tax does not apply, however, to U.S. source gross transportation income that is treated as income effectively connected with the conduct of a U.S. trade or business. U.S. source gross transportation income is not treated as effectively connected income unless (1) the taxpayer has a fixed place of business in the United States involved in earning the income, and (2) substantially all the income is attributable to regularly scheduled transportation.

The tax imposed by section 882 or 887 on income from shipping operations may be limited by an applicable U.S. income tax treaty or by an exemption of a foreign corporation's international shipping operations income in instances where a foreign country grants an equivalent exemption (sec. 883).

Notwithstanding the general rules described above, the American Jobs Creation Act of 2004 ("AJCA")[38] generally allows corporations that are qualifying vessel operators[39] to elect a "tonnage tax" in lieu of the corporate income tax on taxable income from certain shipping activities. Accordingly, an electing corporation's gross income does not include its income from qualifying shipping activities (and items of loss, deduction, or credit are disallowed with respect to such excluded income), and electing corporations are only subject to tax on these activities at the maximum corporate income tax rate on their notional shipping income, which is based on the net tonnage of the corporation's qualify-

38. Pub. L. No. 108-357, sec. 248. The tonnage tax regime is effective for taxable years beginning after the date of enactment of AJCA (October 22, 2004).

39. Generally, a qualifying vessel operator is a corporation that (1) operates one or more qualifying vessels and (2) meets certain requirements with respect to its shipping activities.

ing vessels.[40] No deductions are allowed against the notional shipping income of an electing corporation, and no credit is allowed against the notional tax imposed under the tonnage tax regime. In addition, special deferral rules apply to the gain on the sale of a qualifying vessel, if such vessel is replaced during a limited replacement period.

Generally, a "qualifying vessel" is defined as a self-propelled (or a combination of self-propelled and non-self-propelled) U.S.-flag vessel of not less than 10,000 deadweight tons[41] that is used exclusively in the U.S. foreign trade.

Reasons for Change

The Committee believes that the tonnage tax regime provides operators of qualifying U.S.-flag vessels in the U.S. foreign trade the opportunity to be competitive with their tax-advantaged foreign competitors. However, there are a number of U.S.-flag vessels that are operated in the U.S. foreign trade but which do not qualify for tonnage tax treatment because their carrying capacity is less than 10,000 deadweight tons. The Committee believes that the expansion of the tonnage tax regime to smaller vessels will permit the operators of such vessels to be competitive with their foreign competitors as well as with their larger U.S.-flag competitors.

Explanation of Provision

The provision expands the definition of "qualifying vessel" to include self-propelled (or a combination of self-propelled and non-self-propelled) U.S. flag vessels of not less than 6,000 deadweight tons used exclusively in the United States foreign trade. The modified definition applies for taxable years beginning after December 31, 2005 and ending before January 1, 2011.

[Conference Report]

Senate Amendment

No provision.

Conference Agreement

The conference agreement includes the provision in the House bill.

Effective Date

The provision applies to taxable years beginning after December 31, 2005 and ending before January 1, 2011.

40. An electing corporation's notional shipping income for the taxable year is the product of the following amounts for each of the qualifying vessels it operates: (1) the daily notional shipping income from the operation of the qualifying vessel, and (2) the number of days during the taxable year that the electing corporation operated such vessel as a qualifying vessel in the United States foreign trade. The daily notional shipping income from the operation of a qualifying vessel is (1) 40 cents for each 100 tons of so much of the net tonnage of the vessel as does not exceed 25,000 net tons, and (2) 20 cents for each 100 tons of so much of the net tonnage of the vessel as exceeds 25,000 net tons. "United States foreign trade" means the transportation of goods or passengers between a place in the United States and a foreign place or between foreign places. The temporary use in the United States domestic trade (i.e., the transportation of goods or passengers between places in the United States) of any qualifying vessel or the temporary ceasing to use a qualifying vessel may be disregarded, under special rules.

41. Deadweight measures the lifting capacity of a ship expressed in long tons (2,240 lbs.), including cargo, crew, and consumables such as fuel, lube oil, drinking water, and stores. It is the difference between the number of tons of water a vessel displaces without such items on board and the number of tons it displaces when fully loaded.

[¶5011] Section 207. Amortization of expenses incurred in creating or acquiring music or music copyrights.

(Code Sec. 167)

[Conference Report]

Present Law

A taxpayer is allowed to recover, through annual depreciation deductions, the cost of certain property used in a trade or business or for the production of income. Section 167(g) provides that the cost of motion picture films, sound recordings, copyrights, books, patents, and other property specified in regulations is eligible to be recovered using the income forecast method of depreciation.

Under the income forecast method, the depreciation deduction with respect to eligible property for a taxable year is determined by multiplying the adjusted basis of the property by a fraction, the numerator of which is the income generated by the property during the year, and the denominator of which is the total forecasted or estimated income expected to be generated prior to the close of the tenth taxable year after the year the property was placed in service. Any costs that are not recovered by the end of the tenth taxable year after the property was placed in service may be taken into account as depreciation in such year.

The adjusted basis of property that may be taken into account under the income forecast method includes only amounts that satisfy the economic performance standard of section 461(h) (except in the case of certain participations and residuals). In addition, taxpayers that claim depreciation deductions under the income forecast method are required to pay (or receive) interest based on a recalculation of depreciation under a "look-back" method.

The "look-back" method is applied in any "recomputation year" by (1) comparing depreciation deductions that had been claimed in prior periods to depreciation deductions that would have been claimed had the taxpayer used actual, rather than estimated, total income from the property; (2) determining the hypothetical overpayment or underpayment of tax based on this recalculated depreciation; and (3) applying the overpayment rate of section 6621 of the Code. Except as provided in Treasury regulations, a "recomputation year" is the third and tenth taxable year after the taxable year the property was placed in service, unless the actual income from the property for each taxable year ending with or before the close of such years was within 10 percent of the estimated income from the property for such years.

A special rule is provided under Treasury guidance in the case of certain authors and other taxpayers, with respect to their capitalization of costs under section 263A and with respect to the recovery or amortization of such costs. Specifically, IRS Notice 88-62 (1988-1 C.B. 548) provides an elective safe harbor under which eligible taxpayers capitalize qualified created costs incurred during the taxable year and amortize 50 percent of the costs in the taxable year incurred, and 25 percent in each of the two successive taxable years. Under the Notice, qualified creative costs generally are those incurred by a self-employed individual in the production of creative properties (such as films, sound recordings, musical and dance compositions including accompanying words, and other similar properties), provided the personal efforts of the individual predominantly create the properties. An eligible taxpayer is an individual, and also a corporation or partnership, substantially all of which is owned by one qualified employee owner (an individual and family members).

House Bill

No provision.

Senate Amendment

The Senate amendment provides that if any expense is paid or incurred by the taxpayer in creating or acquiring any musical composition (including accompanying words) or any copyright with respect to a musical composition that is required to be capitalized, then the income forecast method does not apply to such expenses, but rather, the expenses are amortized over a five-year period. The five-year period is the period beginning with the month in which the composition or copyright was acquired (or if created, the five-taxable-year period beginning with the taxable year in which the expenses were paid or incurred).

The provision does not apply to certain expenses. The expenses to which it does not apply are expenses: (1) that are qualified creative expenses under section 263A(h); (2) to which a simplified procedure established under section 263A(j)(2) applies; (3) that are an amortizable section 197 intangible; or (4) that, without regard to this provision, would not be allowable as a deduction.

Conference Agreement

The conference agreement includes the Senate amendment provision with the following modifications. Under the conference agreement, the five-year amortization period is elective for the taxable year. Thus, a taxpayer that places in service any musical composition or copyright with respect to a musical composition in a taxable year may elect to apply the provision with respect to all musical compositions and musical composition copyrights placed in service in that taxable year. An eligible taxpayer that does not make the election may recover the costs under any method allowable under present law, including the income forecast method.

Under the conference agreement, the election may be made for any taxable year which begins before January 1, 2011.

In addition, the conference agreement provides that the five-year amortization period begins in the month the property is placed in service.

Effective Date

The conference agreement is effective for expenses paid or incurred with respect to property placed in service in taxable years beginning after December 31, 2005 and before January 1, 2011.

[¶5012] Section 208. Modification of effective date of disregard of certain capital expenditures for purposes of qualified small issue bonds.

(Code Sec. 144)

[Conference Report]

Present Law

Qualified small-issue bonds are tax-exempt State and local government bonds used to finance private business manufacturing facilities (including certain directly related and ancillary facilities) or the acquisition of land and equipment by certain farmers. In both instances, these bonds are subject to limits on the amount of financing that may be provided, both for a single borrowing and in the aggregate. In general, no more than $1 million of small-issue bond financing may be outstanding at any time for property of a business (including related parties) located in the same municipality or county. Generally, this $1 million limit may be increased to $10 million if all other capital expenditures of the business in the same municipality or county are counted toward the limit over a six-year period that begins three years before the issue date of the bonds and ends three years after such date. Outstanding aggregate borrowing is limited to $40 million per borrower (including related parties) regardless of where the property is located.

For bonds issued after September 30, 2009, the Code permits up to $10 million of capital expenditures to be disregarded, in effect increasing from $10 million to $20 million the maximum allowable amount of total capital expenditures by an eligible business in the same municipality or county.[339] However, no more than $10 million of bond financing may be outstanding at any time for property of an eligible business (including related parties) located in the same municipality or county. Other limits (e.g., the $40 million per borrower limit) also continue to apply.

House Bill

No provision.

Senate Amendment

The provision accelerates the application of the $20 million capital expenditure limitation from bonds issued after September 30, 2009, to bonds issued after December 31, 2006.

Conference Agreement

The conference agreement includes the Senate amendment provision.

Effective Date

The provision is effective on the date of enactment for bonds issued after December 31, 2006.

[¶5013] Section 209. Modification of treatment of loans to qualified continuing care facilities.

(Code Sec. 7872)

[Conference Report]

Present Law

Present law provides generally that certain loans that bear interest at a below-market rate are treated as loans bearing interest at the market rate, accompanied by imputed payments characterized in accordance with the substance of the transaction (for example, as a gift, compensation, a dividend, or interest).[342]

An exception to this imputation rule is provided for any calendar year for a below-market loan made by a lender to a qualified continuing care facility pursuant to a continuing care contract, if the lender or the lender's spouse attains age 65 before the close of the calendar year.[343]

The exception applies only to the extent the aggregate outstanding loans by the lender (and spouse) to any qualified continuing care facility do not exceed $163,300 (for 2006).[344]

For this purpose, a continuing care contract means a written contract between an individual and a qualified continuing care facility under which: (1) the individual or the individual's spouse may use a qualified continuing care facility for their life or lives; (2) the individual or the individual's spouse will first reside in a separate, independent living unit with additional facilities outside such unit for the providing of meals and other personal care and will not require long-term nursing care, and then will be provided long-term and skilled nursing care as the health of the individual or the individual's

339. Sec. 144(a)(4)(G) as added by sec. 340(a) of the American Jobs Creation Act of 2004, Pub. L. No. 108-357 (2004).
342. Sec. 7872.
343. Sec. 7872(g).
344. Rev. Rul. 2005-75, 2005-49 I.R.B. 1073.

spouse requires; and (3) no additional substantial payment is required if the individual or the individual's spouse requires increased personal care services or long-term and skilled nursing care.

For this purpose, a qualified continuing care facility means one or more facilities that are designed to provide services under continuing care contracts, and substantially all of the residents of which are covered by continuing care contracts. A facility is not treated as a qualified continuing care facility unless substantially all facilities that are used to provide services required to be provided under a continuing care contract are owned or operated by the borrower. For these purposes, a nursing home is not a qualified continuing care facility.

House Bill

No provision.

Senate Amendment

The Senate amendment provision modifies the present-law exception under section 7872(g) relating to loans to continuing care facilities by eliminating the dollar cap on aggregate outstanding loans and making other modifications.

The Senate amendment provision provides an exception to the imputation rule of section 7872 for any calendar year for any below-market loan owed by a facility which on the last day of the year is a qualified continuing care facility, if the loan was made pursuant to a continuing care contract and if the lender or the lender's spouse attains age 62 before the close of the year.

For this purpose, a continuing care contract means a written contract between an individual and a qualified continuing care facility under which: (1) the individual or the individual's spouse may use a qualified continuing care facility for their life or lives; (2) the individual or the individual's spouse will be provided with housing in an independent living unit (which has additional available facilities outside such unit for the provision of meals and other personal care), an assisted living facility or nursing facility, as is available in the continuing care facility, as appropriate for the health of the individual or the individual's spouse; and (3) the individual or the individual's spouse will be provided assisted living or nursing care as the health of the individual or the individual's spouse requires, and as is available in the continuing care facility.

For this purpose, a qualified continuing care facility means one or more facilities: (1) that are designed to provide services under continuing care contracts; (2) that include an independent living unit, plus an assisted living or nursing facility, or both; and (3) substantially all of the independent living unit residents of which are covered by continuing care contracts. For these purposes, a nursing home is not a qualified continuing care facility.

Conference Agreement

The conference agreement includes the Senate amendment provision, with modifications. The conference agreement provision provides that a continuing care contract is a written contract between an individual and a qualified continuing care facility under which: (1) the individual or the individual's spouse may use a qualified continuing care facility for their life or lives; (2) the individual or the individual's spouse will be provided with housing, as appropriate for the health of such individual or individual's spouse, (i) in an independent living unit (which has additional available facilities outside such unit for the provision of meals and other personal care), and (ii) in an assisted living facility or a nursing facility, as is available in the continuing care facility; and (3) the individual or the individual's spouse will be provided assisted living or nursing care as the health of the individual or the individual's spouse requires, and as is available in the continuing care facility. The Secretary is required to issue guidance that limits the term "continuing care contract" to contracts that provide only facilities, care, and services described in the preceding sentence.

For purposes of defining the terms "continuing care contract" and "qualified continuing care facility" under the conference agreement provision, the term "assisted living facility" is intended to mean a facility at which assistance is provided (1) with activities of daily living (such as eating, toileting, transferring, bathing, dressing, and continence) or (2) in cases of cognitive impairment, to protect the health or safety of an individual. The term "nursing facility" is intended to mean a facility that offers care requiring the utilization of licensed nursing staff.

Effective Date

The conference agreement provision is generally effective for calendar years beginning after December 31, 2005, with respect to loans made before, on, or after such date. The conference agreement provision does not apply to any calendar year after 2010. Thus, the conference agreement provision does not apply with respect to interest imputed after December 31, 2010. After such date, the law as in effect prior to enactment applies.

[¶5015] Section 301. Increase in alternative minimum tax exemption amount for 2006.

(Code Sec. 55)

[Conference Report]

Present Law

Present law imposes an alternative minimum tax. The alternative minimum tax is the amount by which the tentative minimum tax exceeds the regular income tax. An individual's tentative minimum tax is the sum of (1) 26 percent of so much of the taxable excess as does not exceed $175,000 ($87,500 in the case of a married individual filing a separate return) and (2) 28 percent of the remaining taxable excess. The taxable excess is so much of the alternative minimum taxable income ("AMTI") as exceeds the exemption amount. The maximum tax rates on net capital gain and dividends used in computing the regular tax are used in computing the tentative minimum tax. AMTI is the individual's taxable income adjusted to take account of specified preferences and adjustments.

The exemption amount is: (1) $45,000 ($58,000 for taxable years beginning before 2006) in the case of married individuals filing a joint return and surviving spouses; (2) $33,750 ($40,250 for taxable years beginning before 2006) in the case of unmarried individuals other than surviving spouses; (3) $22,500 ($29,000 for taxable years beginning before 2006) in the case of married individuals filing a separate return; and (4) $22,500 in the case of estates and trusts. The exemption amount is phased out by an amount equal to 25 percent of the amount by which the individual's AMTI exceeds (1) $150,000 in the case of married individuals filing a joint return and surviving spouses, (2) $112,500 in the case of unmarried individuals other than surviving spouses, and (3) $75,000 in the case of married individuals filing separate returns, estates, and trusts. These amounts are not indexed for inflation.

House Bill

No provision.

Senate Amendment

Under the Senate amendment, for taxable years beginning in 2006, the exemption amounts are increased to: (1) $62,550 in the case of married individuals filing a joint return and surviving spouses; (2) $42,500 in the case of unmarried individuals other than surviving spouses; and (3) $31,275 in the case of married individuals filing a separate return.

Conference Agreement

The conference agreement includes the provision in the Senate amendment.

Effective Date

The provision applies to taxable years beginning after December 31, 2005.

[¶ 5016] Section 302. Allowance of nonrefundable personal credits against regular and alternative minimum tax liability.

(Code Sec. 26)

[House Report]

Present Law

Present law provides for certain nonrefundable personal tax credits (i.e., the dependent care credit, the credit for the elderly and disabled, the adoption credit, the child tax credit, the credit for interest on certain home mortgages, the HOPE Scholarship and Lifetime Learning credits, the credit for savers, the credit for certain nonbusiness energy property, the credit for residential energy efficient property, and the D.C. first-time homebuyer credit).

For taxable years beginning in 2005, the nonrefundable personal credits are allowed to the extent of the full amount of the individual's regular tax and alternative minimum tax.

For taxable years beginning after 2005, the nonrefundable personal credits (other than the adoption credit, child credit and saver's credit) are allowed only to the extent that the individual's regular income tax liability exceeds the individual's tentative minimum tax, determined without regard to the minimum tax foreign tax credit. The adoption credit, child credit, and saver's credit are allowed to the full extent of the individual's regular tax and alternative minimum tax.

The alternative minimum tax is the amount by which the tentative minimum tax exceeds the regular income tax. An individual's tentative minimum tax is the sum of (1) 26 percent of so much of the taxable excess as does not exceed $175,000 ($87,500 in the case of a married individual filing a separate return) and (2) 28 percent of the remaining taxable excess. The taxable excess is so much of the alternative minimum taxable income ("AMTI") as exceeds the exemption amount. The maximum tax rates on net capital gain and dividends used in computing the regular tax are used in computing the tentative minimum tax. AMTI is the individual's taxable income adjusted to take account of specified preferences and adjustments.

The exemption amount is: (1) $45,000 ($58,000 for taxable years beginning before 2006) in the case of married individuals filing a joint return and surviving spouses; (2) $33,750 ($40,250 for taxable years beginning before 2006) in the case of other unmarried individuals; (3) $22,500 ($29,000 for taxable years beginning before 2006) in the case of married individuals filing a separate return; and (4) $22,500 in the case of an estate or trust. The exemption amount is phased out by an amount equal to 25 percent of the amount by which the individual's AMTI exceeds (1) $150,000 in the case of married individuals filing a joint return and surviving spouses, (2) $112,500 in the case of other unmarried individuals, and (3) $75,000 in the case of married individuals filing separate returns, an estate, or a trust. These amounts are not indexed for inflation.

Reasons for Change

The Committee believes that the nonrefundable personal credits should be useable without limitation by reason of the alternative minimum tax.

Explanation of Provision

The provision extends for one year the present-law provision allowing nonrefundable personal credits to the full extent of the individual's regular tax and alternative minimum tax (through taxable years beginning on or before December 31, 2006).

[Conference Report]

Present Law

The Energy Tax Incentives Act of 2005 enacted, effective for 2006, nonrefundable tax credits for alternative motor vehicles, and alternative motor vehicle refueling property.[1]

Conference Agreement

The conference agreement includes the House bill provision.

Effective Date

The provision applies to taxable years beginning after December 31, 2005.

[¶5018] Section 401. Time for payment of corporate estimated taxes.

(Code Sec. None)

[Conference Report]

Present Law

In general, corporations are required to make quarterly estimated tax payments of their income tax liability. For a corporation whose taxable year is a calendar year, these estimated tax payments must be made by April 15, June 15, September 15, and December 15.

House Bill

No provision.

Senate Amendment

No provision.

Conference Agreement

In case of a corporation with assets of at least $1 billion, payments due in July, August, and September, 2006, shall be increased to 105 percent of the payment otherwise due and the next required payment shall be reduced accordingly.

In case of a corporation with assets of at least $1 billion, the payments due in July, August, and September, 2012, shall be increased to 106.25 percent of the payment otherwise due and the next required payment shall be reduced accordingly.

In case of a corporation with assets of at least $1 billion, the payments due in July, August, and September, 2013, shall be increased to 100.75 percent of the payment otherwise due and the next required payment shall be reduced accordingly.

With respect to corporate estimated tax payments due on September 15, 2010, 20.5 percent shall not be due until October 1, 2010.

With respect to corporate estimated tax payments due on September 15, 2011, 27.5 percent shall not be due until October 1, 2011.

Effective Date

The provision is effective on the date of enactment.

1. The portion of these credits relating to personal use property is subject to the same tax liability limitation as the nonrefundable personal tax credits (other than the adoption credit, child credit, and saver's credit).

[¶5020] Section 501. Application of earnings stripping rules to partners which are corporations.

(Code Sec. 163)

[Conference Report]

Present Law

Present law provides rules to limit the ability of U.S. corporations to reduce the U.S. tax on their U.S.-source income through earnings stripping transactions. Section 163(j) specifically addresses earnings stripping involving interest payments, by limiting the deductibility of interest paid to certain related parties ("disqualified interest"),[442] if the payor's debt-equity ratio exceeds 1.5 to 1 and the payor's net interest expense exceeds 50 percent of its "adjusted taxable income" (generally taxable income computed without regard to deductions for net interest expense, net operating losses, and depreciation, amortization, and depletion). Disallowed interest amounts can be carried forward indefinitely. In addition, excess limitation (i.e., any excess of the 50-percent limit over a company's net interest expense for a given year) can be carried forward three years.

Proposed Treasury regulations provide that a partner's proportionate share of partnership liabilities is treated as liabilities incurred directly by the partner, for purposes of applying the earnings stripping limitation to interest payments by a corporate partner of a partnership.[443] The proposed Treasury regulations provide that interest paid or accrued to a partnership is treated as paid or accrued to the partners of the partnership in proportion to each partner's distributive share of the partnership's interest income for the taxable year.[444] In addition, the proposed Treasury regulations provide that interest expense paid or accrued by a partnership is treated as paid or accrued by the partners of the partnership in proportion to each partner's distributive share of the partnership's interest expense.[445]

House Bill

No provision.

Senate Amendment

The Senate amendment provision codifies the approach of the proposed Treasury regulations by providing that, except to the extent provided by regulations, in the case of a corporation that owns, directly or indirectly, an interest in a partnership, the corporation's share of partnership liabilities is treated as liabilities of the corporation for purposes of applying the earnings stripping rules to the corporation. The provision provides that the corporation's distributive share of interest income of the partnership, and of interest expense of the partnership, is treated as interest income or interest expense of the corporation.

The provision provides Treasury regulatory authority to reallocate shares of partnership debt, or distributive shares of the partnership's interest income or interest expense, as may be appropriate to carry out the purposes of the provision. For example, it is not intended that the application of the earnings stripping rules to corporations with direct or indirect interests in partnerships be circumvented through the use of allocations of partnership interest income or expense (or partnership liabilities) to or away from partners.

Conference Agreement

The conference agreement includes the Senate amendment provision.

442. This interest also may include interest paid to unrelated parties in certain cases in which a related party guarantees the debt.
443. Prop. Treas. Reg. sec. 1.163(j)-3(b)(3).
444. Prop. Treas. Reg. sec. 1.163(j)-2(e)(4).
445. Prop. Treas. reg. sec. 1.163(j)-2(e)(5).

Effective Date

The provision is effective for taxable years beginning on or after the date of enactment.

[¶5021] Section 502. Reporting of interest on tax-exempt bonds.

(Code Sec. 6049)

[Conference Report]

Present Law

Tax-exempt bonds

Generally, gross income does not include interest on State or local bonds.[476] State and local bonds are classified generally as either governmental bonds or private activity bonds. Governmental bonds are bonds the proceeds of which are primarily used to finance governmental facilities or the debt is repaid with governmental funds. Private activity bonds are bonds in which the State or local government serves as a conduit providing financing to nongovernmental persons (e.g., private businesses or individuals). The exclusion from income for State and local bonds does not apply to private activity bonds, unless the bonds are issued for certain purposes ("qualified private activity bonds") permitted by the Code.[477]

Tax-exempt interest reporting by taxpayers

The Code provides that every person required to file a return must report the amount of tax-exempt interest received or accrued during any taxable year.[478] There are a number of reasons why the amount of tax-exempt interest received is relevant to determining tax liability despite the general exclusion from income. For example, the interest income from qualified private activity bonds (other than qualified 501(c)(3) bonds) issued after August 7, 1986, is a preference item for purposes of calculating the alternative minimum tax ("AMT").[479] Tax-exempt interest also is relevant for determining eligibility for the earned income credit (the"EIC")[480] and the amount of Social Security benefits includable in gross income.[481] Moreover, determining includable Social Security benefits is necessary for calculating either adjusted or modified adjusted gross income under several Code sections.[482]

Information reporting by payors

The Code generally requires every person who makes payments of interest aggregating $10 or more or receives payments of interest as a nominee and who makes payments aggregating $10 or more to file an information return setting forth the amount of interest payments for the calendar year and the name, address, and TIN[483] of the person to whom interest is paid.[484] Treasury regulations prescribe the form and manner for filing interest payment information returns. Penalties are imposed for failures to file interest payment information returns or payee statements.[485] Treasury Regulations also impose

476. Sec. 103.
477. Secs. 103(b)(1) and 141.
478. Sec. 6012(d).
479. Sec. 57(a)(5). Special rules apply to exclude refundings of bonds issued before August 8, 1986, and certain bonds issued before September 1, 1986.
480. Sec. 32(i).
481. Sec. 86.
482. See Secs. 135, 219, and 221.
483. The taxpayer's identification number, generally, for individuals is the taxpayer's social security number. Sec. 7701(a)(41).
484. Sec. 6049.
485. Secs. 6721 and 6722.

recordkeeping requirements on any person required to file information returns.[486] The Code excludes interest paid on tax-exempt bonds from interest reporting requirements.[487]

House Bill

No provision.

Senate Amendment

The provision eliminates the exception from information reporting requirements for interest paid on tax-exempt bonds.

Conference Agreement

The conference agreement includes the Senate amendment provision.

Effective Date

The provision is effective for interest paid on tax-exempt bonds after December 31, 2005.

[¶5022] Section 503. 5-year amortization of geological and geophysical expenditures for certain major integrated oil companies.

(Code Sec. 167)

[Conference Report]

Present Law

Geological and geophysical expenditures ("G&G costs") are costs incurred by a taxpayer the purpose of obtaining and accumulating data that will serve as the basis for the acquisition retention of mineral properties by taxpayers exploring for minerals. G&G costs incurred in connection with oil and gas exploration in the United States may be amortized over two years.[493] the case of abandoned property, remaining basis may not be recovered in the year of abandonment of a property as all basis is recovered over the two-year amortization period.

House Bill

No provision.

Senate Amendment.

The provision repeals the two-year amortization period with respect to G&G costs paid or incurred by certain large integrated oil companies, defined to include integrated oil companies (as defined in section 291(b)(4) of the Code) that have an average daily worldwide production of crude oil of at least 500,000 barrels. Thus, affected oil companies are required to capitalize their G&G costs associated with successful exploration projects that result in the acquisition of property. Such companies can recover any G&G costs associated with abandoned property in the year of abandonment.

Conference Agreement

The conference agreement extends the two-year amortization period for G&G costs to five years for certain major integrated oil companies. Under the conference agreement, the five-year amortization rule for G&G costs applies only to integrated oil companies that have an average daily worldwide production of crude oil of at least 500,000 barrels for the taxable year, gross receipts in excess of $1 billion in the last taxable year ending

486. Treas. Reg. sec. 1.6001-1(a).
487. Sec. 6049.
493. Sec. 167(h).

during calendar year 2005, and an ownership interest in a crude oil refiner of 15 percent or more.

Effective Date

The provision applies to amounts paid or incurred after the date of enactment.

[¶5023] Section 504. Application of FIRPTA to regulated investment companies.

(Code Sec. 897)

[Conference Report]

In general

A nonresident alien individual or foreign corporation is taxable on its taxable income which is effectively connected with the conduct of a trade or business within the United States, at the income tax rates applicable to U. S. persons. A nonresident alien individual is taxed (at a 30-percent rate) on gains, derived from sources within the United States, from the sale or exchange of capital assets if the individual is present in the United States for 183 days or more during the taxable year.

In addition, the Foreign Investment in Real Property Tax Act (FIRPTA)[497] generally treats a nonresident alien individual or foreign corporation's gain or loss from the disposition of a U.S. real property interest (USRPI) as income that is effectively connected with a U.S. trade or business, and thus taxable at the income tax rates applicable to U.S. persons, including the rates for net capital gain. A foreign investor subject to tax on this income is required to file a U.S. income tax return under the normal rules relating to receipt of income effectively connected with a U.S. trade or business.

The payor of FIRPTA effectively connected income to a foreign person is generally required to withhold U.S. tax from the payment. Withholding is generally 10 percent of the sales price in the case of a direct sale by the foreign person of a USRPI, and 35 percent of the amount of a distribution to a foreign person of proceeds attributable to such sales from an entity such as a partnership.[498] The foreign person can request a refund with its U.S. tax return, if appropriate based on that person's total U.S. effectively connected income and deductions (if any) for the taxable year.

USRPIs include interests in real property located in the United States or the U.S. Virgin Islands, and stock of a domestic U.S. real property holding company (USRPHC), generally defined as any corporation, unless the taxpayer established that the fair market value of its U.S. real property interests is less than 50 percent of the combined fair market value of all its real property interests (U.S. and worldwide) and of all its assets used or held for use in a trade or business.[499] However, any class of stock that is regularly traded on an established securities market located in the U.S. is treated as a U.S. real property interest only if the seller held more than 5 percent of the stock at any time during the 5-year period ending on the date of disposition of the stock.[500]

---

497. FIRPTA is codified in section 897 of the Code.

498. Sec. 1445 and Treasury regulations thereunder. The Treasury department is authorized to issue regulations that would reduce the 35 percent withholding on distributions to 15 percent during the time that the maximum income tax rate on dividends and capital gains of U.S. persons is 15 percent.

Section 1445 statutorily requires the 10 percent withholding by the purchaser of a USRPI and the 35 percent withholding (or less if directed by Treasury) on certain distributions by partnerships, trusts, and estates, among other situations. Treasury regulations prescribe the 35 percent withholding requirement for distributions by REITs to foreign shareholders. Treas. Reg. sec. 1.1445-8. No regulations have been issued relating specifically to RIC distributions, which first became subject to FIRPTA in 2005.

499. Sec. 897(c)(2).

500. Sec. 897(c)(3).

Special rules for certain investment entities

Real estate investment trusts and regulated investment companies are generally passive investment entities. They are organized as U.S. domestic entities and are taxed as U.S. domestic corporations. However, because of their special status, they are entitled to deduct amounts distributed to shareholders and, in some cases, to allow the shareholders to characterize these amounts based on the type of income the REIT or RIC received. Among numerous other requirements for qualification as a REIT or RIC, the entity is required to distribute to shareholders at least 90 percent its income (excluding net capital gain) annually.[501] A REIT or RIC may designate a capital gain dividend to its shareholders, who then treat the amount designated as capital gain.[502] A REIT or RIC is taxed at regular corporate rates on undistributed income; but the combination of the requirement to distribute income other than net capital gain, plus the ability to declare a capital gain dividend and avoid corporate level tax on such income, can result in little, if any, corporate level tax paid by a REIT or RIC. Instead, the shareholder level tax on distributions is the principal tax paid with respect to income of these entities. The requirements for REIT eligibility include primary investment in real estate assets (which assets can include mortgages). The requirements for RIC eligibility include primary investment in stocks and securities (which can include stock of REITs or of other RICs).

FIRPTA contains special rules for real estate investment trusts (REITs) and regulated investment companies (RICs).[503]

Stock of a "domestically controlled" REIT is not a USRPI. The term "domestically controlled" is defined to mean that less than 50 percent in value of the REIT has been owned by non-U.S. shareholders during the 5-year period ending on the date of disposition.[504] For 2005, 2006, and 2007, a similar exception applies to RIC stock. Thus, stock of a domestically controlled REIT or RIC can be sold without FIRPTA consequences. This exception applies regardless of whether the sale of stock is made directly by a foreign person, or by a REIT or RIC whose distributions to foreign persons of gain attributable to the sale of USRPI's would be subject to FIRPTA as described below.

A distribution by a REIT to a foreign shareholder, to the extent attributable to gain from the REIT's sale or exchange of USRPIs, is generally treated as FIRPTA gain to the shareholder. An exception enacted in 2004 applies if the distribution is made on a class of REIT stock that is regularly traded on an established securities market located in the United States and the foreign shareholder has not held more than 5 percent of the class of stock at any time during the one-year period ending on the date of the distribution.[505] Where the exception applies, the distribution to the foreign shareholder is treated as the distribution of an ordinary dividend (rather than as a capital gain dividend), subject to 30-percent (or lower treaty rate) withholding.[506]

Prior to 2005, distributions by RICs to foreign shareholders, to the extent attributable to the RIC's sale or exchange of USRPIs, were not treated as FIRPTA gain. If distributions were attributable to long-term capital gains, the RIC could designate the distributions as long-term capital gain dividends that would not be subject to any tax to the foreign shareholder, rather than as a regular dividends subject to 30-percent (or lower treaty rate) withholding.[507] For 2005, 2006, and 2007, RICs are subject to the rule that had applied to REITs prior to 2005, i.e., any distribution to a foreign shareholder attributable to

501. Secs. 852(a)(1) and 852(b)(2)(A); 857(a)(1).
502. Secs. 852(b)(3); 857(b)(3).
503. Sec. 897(h).
504. Sec. 897(h)(2) and (h)(4)(B).
505. This exception, effective beginning in 2005, was added by section 418 of the American Jobs Creation Act of 2004 ("AJCA"), Pub. L. No. 108-357, and modified by section 403(p) of the Tax Technical Corrections Act of 2005.
506. Sec. 857(b)(3)(F).
507. Sec. 852(b)(3)(C); Treas. Reg. sec. 1.1441-3(c)(2)(D).

gain from the RIC's sale of a USRPI is characterized as FIRPTA gain, without any exceptions.[508]

House Bill

No provision.

Senate Amendment

The Senate amendment provision provides that distributions by a RIC to foreign shareholders of amounts attributable to the sale of USRPIs are not treated as FIRPTA income unless the RIC itself is a U.S. real property holding corporation (i.e. 50 percent or more of its value is represented by its U.S. real property interests, including investments in U.S. real property holding corporations). In determining whether a RIC is a real property holding company for this purpose, a special rule applies that requires the RIC to include as U.S. real property interests its holdings of RIC or REIT stock if such RIC or REIT is a U.S. real property holding corporation, even if such stock is regularly traded on an established securities market and even if the RIC owns less than 5 percent of such stock. Another special rule requires the RIC to include as U.S. real property interests its interests in any domestically controlled RIC or REIT that is a U.S. real property holding corporation.

Conference Agreement

The conference agreement includes the Senate amendment provision with a clarification to the effective date. Under the clarification, the provision takes effect as if included in the provisions of section 411 of the American Jobs Creation Act of 2004 to which it relates.

Effective Date

The provision applies to distributions with respect to taxable years beginning after December 31, 2004.

[¶5024] Section 505, 506. Treatment of distributions attributable to FIRPTA gains and Prevention of avoidance of tax on investments of foreign persons in United States real property through wash sale transactions.

(Code Sec. 852, 897, 1445)

[Conference Report]

Present Law

General treatment of U.S.-source income of foreign investors

Fixed and determinable annual and periodical income

The United States generally imposes a flat 30-percent tax, collected by withholding, on the gross amount of U.S.-source investment income payments, such as interest, dividends, rents, royalties and similar types of fixed and determinable annual and periodical income, to nonresident alien individuals and foreign corporations ("foreign persons").[509] Under treaties, the United States may reduce or eliminate such taxes.

508. This requirement for RICs was added by section 411 of the American Jobs Creation Act of 2004 ("AJCA"), in connection with the enactment of other rules that allow RICs to identify certain types of distributions to foreign shareholders, attributable to the RIC's receipt of short-term capital gains or interest income, as distributions to such shareholders of such short-term gains or interest income and thus not taxed to the foreign shareholders, rather than as regular dividends that would be subject to withholding. See Secs. 871(k), 881(e), 1441(c)(12) and 1442(a). All these rules are scheduled to expire at the end of 2007, as is the rule subjecting to FIRPTA all distributions of RIC gain attributable to sales of U.S. real property interests and the rule excepting from FIRPTA a foreign person's sale of stock of a "domestically controlled" RIC.

509. Secs. 871(a), 881, 1441, and 1442.

Dividends

Even taking into account U.S. treaties, the tax on a dividend generally is not entirely eliminated. Instead, U.S.-source portfolio investment dividends received by foreign persons generally are subject to U.S. withholding tax at a rate of at least 15 percent.

Interest

Although payments of U.S.-source interest that is not effectively connected with a U.S. trade or business generally are subject to the 30-percent withholding tax, there are exceptions to that rule. For example, interest from certain deposits with banks and other financial institutions is exempt from tax.[510] Original issue discount on obligations maturing in 183 days or less from the date of original issue (without regard to the period held by the taxpayer) is also exempt from tax.[511] An additional exception is provided for certain interest paid on portfolio obligations.[512] Such "portfolio interest" generally is defined as any U.S.-source interest (including original issue discount), not effectively connected with the conduct of a U.S. trade or business, (i) on an obligation that satisfies certain registration requirements or specified exceptions thereto (i.e., the obligation is "foreign targeted"), and (ii) that is not received by a 10-percent shareholder.[513] With respect to a registered obligation, a statement that the beneficial owner is not a U.S. person is required.[514] This exception is not available for any interest received either by a bank on a loan extended in the ordinary course of its business (except in the case of interest paid on an obligation of the United States), or by a controlled foreign corporation from a related person.[515] Moreover, this exception is not available for certain contingent interest payments.[516] For 2005, 2006 and 2007, a regulated investment company ("RIC") may designate certain distributions to foreign shareholders that are attributable to the RIC's qualified interest income as non-taxable interest distributions to such foreign persons.[517]

Capital gains

A foreign person generally is not subject to U.S. tax on capital gain, including gain realized on the disposition of stock or securities issued by a U.S. person, unless the gain is effectively connected with the conduct of a trade or business in the United States or such person is an individual present in the United States for a period or periods aggregating 183 days or more during the taxable year.[518] A regulated investment company (RIC) can generally designate dividends to foreign persons that are attributable to the RIC's long term capital gain as a long-term gain dividends that are not subject to withholding.[519] For 2005, 2006 and 2007, RICs may also designate short-term capital gain dividends.[520]

For the years 2005, 2006 and 2007, RIC capital gain dividends that are attributable to the sale of U.S. real property interests (which can include stock of companies that are U.S. real property holding companies) are subject to special rules described below.

Real estate investment trusts (REITs) can also designate long-term capital gain dividends to shareholders; but when made to a foreign person such distributions attributable to the sale of U.S. real property interests are also subject to the special rules described below.

510. Secs. 871(i)(2)(A) and 881(d).
511. Sec. 871(g).
512. Secs. 871(h) and 881(c).
513. Secs. 871(h)(3) and 881(c)(3).
514. Secs. 871(h)(2), (5) and 881(c)(2).
515. Sec. 881(c)(3).
516. Secs. 871(h)(4) and 881(c)(4).
517. This interest distribution rule was added by section 411 of the American Jobs Creation Act of 2004 ("AJCA"), Pub. L. No. 108-357.
518. Secs. 871(a)(2) and 881.
519. Treas. Reg. sec. 1.1441-3(c)(2)(D).
520. This short-term gain distribution rule was added by section 411 of AJCA.

Foreign Investment in Real Property Tax Act ("FIRPTA")

Unlike most other U.S. source capital gains, which are generally not taxed to a foreign investor, the Foreign Investment in Real Property Tax Act of 1980 (FIRPTA) subjects gain or loss of a foreign person from the disposition of a U.S. real property interest (USRPI) to tax as if the taxpayer were engaged in a trade or business within the United States and the gain or loss were effectively connected with such trade or business.[521] In addition to an interest in real property located in the United States or the Virgin Islands, USRPIs include (among other things) any interest in a domestic corporation unless the taxpayer establishes that the corporation was not, during a five-year period ending on the date of the disposition of the interest, a U.S. real property holding corporation (which is defined generally to mean any corporation the fair market value of whose U.S. real property interests equals or exceeds 50 percent of the sum of the fair market values of its real property interests and any other of its assets used or held for use in a trade or business).

Distributions by a REIT to its foreign shareholders attributable to the sale of USRPI's are generally treated as income from the sale of USRPIs.[522] Treasury regulations require the REIT to withhold at 35 percent on such a distribution.[523] However, there is an exception for distributions by a REIT with respect to stock of the REIT that is regularly traded on an established securities market located in the U.S., to a foreign shareholder that has not held more than 5 percent of the stock of the REIT for the one year period ending with the date of the distribution.[524] In such cases, the REIT and the shareholder treat the distribution to a foreign shareholder as the distribution of an ordinary dividend,[525] subject to the 30-percent (or lower treaty rate) withholding applicable to dividends.

For 2005, 2006, and 2007, any RIC distribution to a foreign shareholder attributable to the sale of USRPIs is treated as FIRPTA income, without any exceptions.[526] However, no Treasury regulations have been issued addressing withholding obligations with respect to such distributions.

A more complete description of the provisions of FIRPTA and the special rules under FIRPTA that apply to RICs and REITs is contained under "Present Law" for the provision "Application of Foreign Investors in Real Property Tax Act (FIRPTA) to Regulated Investment Companies (RICS).

Although the law thus provides rules for taxing foreign persons under FIRPTA on distributions of gain from the sale of USRPIs by RICs or REITs, some taxpayers may be taking the position that if a foreign person invests in a RIC or REIT that, in turn, invests in a lower-tier RIC or REIT that is the entity that disposes of USRPIs and distributes the proceeds, then the proceeds from such disposition by the lower-tier RIC or REIT cease to be FIRPTA income when distributed to the upper-tier RIC or REIT (which is not itself a foreign person), and can thereafter be distributed by that latter entity to its foreign shareholders as non-FIRPTA income of such RIC or REIT, rather than continuing to be categorized as FIRPTA income. Furthermore, RICs may take the position that in the absence of regulations or a specific statutory rule addressing the withholding rules for FIRPTA capital gain that is treated as effectively connected with a U.S. trade or business, such gain should be considered capital gain for which no withholding is required.

In addition, some foreign persons may be attempting to avoid FIRPTA tax on a distribution from a RIC or a REIT, by selling the RIC or REIT stock shortly before the distribution and buying back the stock shortly after the distribution. If the stock is not a U.S.

521. Sec. 897.
522. Sec. 897(h)(1).
523. Treas. Reg. sec. 1.1445-8.
524. Sec. 897(h)(1)(second sentence).
525. Sec. Sec. 857(b)(3)(F).
526. Sec. Sec. 897(h)(1)

real property interest in the hands of the foreign seller, that person would take the position that the gain on the sale of the stock is capital gain not subject to U.S. tax. Stock of a RIC or REIT that is "domestically controlled" is not a U.S. real property interest.[527]

If the stock is a USRPI in the hands of the foreign person, the transferee generally is required to withhold 10 percent of the gross sales price under general FIRPTA withholding rules.[528]

House Bill

No provision.

Senate Amendment

The first part of the Senate amendment provision requires any distribution that is made by a RIC or a REIT that would otherwise be subject to FIRPTA because the distribution is attributable to the disposition of a U.S. real property interest (USRPI) to retain its character as FIRPTA income when distributed to any other RIC or REIT, and to be treated as if it were from the disposition of a USRPI by that other RIC or REIT. Under the provision, a RIC continues to be subject to FIRPTA, even after December 31, 2007, in any case in which a REIT makes a distribution to the RIC that is attributable to gain from the sale of U.S. real property interests.

The second part of the Senate amendment provision provides that a distribution by a RIC to a foreign shareholder, or to a RIC or REIT shareholder, attributable to sales of USRPIs is not treated as gain from the sale of a USRPI by that shareholder if the distribution is made with respect to a class of RIC stock that is regularly traded on an established securities market[529] located in the U.S. and if such shareholder did not hold more than 5 percent of such stock of within the one year period ending on the date of the distribution. Such distributions instead are treated as dividend distributions.[530]

The third part of the Senate amendment provision requires a foreign person that disposes of stock of a RIC or REIT during the 30-day period preceding a distribution on that stock that would have been treated as a distribution from the disposition of a USRPI, that acquires an identical stock interest during the 60 day period beginning the

527. Sec. 897(g)(3). A RIC or REIT is "domestically controlled" if less than 50 percent in value of the entity's stock is held by foreign persons. RIC stock ceases to be eligible for this exception as of the end of 2007. Distributions by a domestically controlled RIC or REIT, if attributable to the sale of U.S. real property interests, are not exempt from FIRPTA by reason of such domestic control. A foreign person that would be subject to FIRPTA on receipt of a distribution from such an entity might sell its stock before the distribution and repurchase stock after the distribution in an attempt to avoid FIRPTA consequences.

Under a different exception from FIRPTA, applicable to stock of all entities, neither RIC nor REIT stock is a U.S. real property interest if the RIC or REIT stock is regularly traded on an established securities market located in the United States and if the stock sale is made by a foreign shareholder that has not owned more than five percent of the stock during the five years ending with the date of the sale. Sec. 897(c)(3). Distributions by a REIT to a foreign person, attributable to the sale of U.S. real property interests, are also not subject to FIRPTA if made with respect to stock that is regularly traded on an established securities market located in the United States and made to a foreign person that has not held more than five percent of the REIT stock for the one-year period ending on the date of distribution. (Sec. 897(h)(1), second sentence.) Thus, any foreign shareholder of such a regularly traded REIT that would be exempt from FIRPTA on a sale of the REIT stock immediately before a distribution would also generally be exempt from FIRPTA on a distribution from the REIT if such shareholder held the stock through the date of the distribution, due to the holding period requirements. Distributions that are not subject to FIRPTA under this five percent exception are recharacterized as ordinary dividends and thus would normally be subject to ordinary dividend withholding rules. Secs. 857(b)(3)(F) and 1441.

528. Secs. 1445(a) and 1445(e).

529. It is intended that the rules generally applicable for this purpose under section 897 also apply under the provision in determining whether a class of interests is regularly traded on an established securities market located in the United Sates. For example, at the present time the rules currently in force for this purpose include Temp. Reg. sec. 1.897-9T(d)(2).

530. The provision treats such distributions as ordinary dividend distributions rather than as distributions of long term capital gain. This rule is the same as the present law rule for publicly traded REITs making a distribution to a foreign shareholder. In addition, under the immediately preceding provision (sec. 464) of the Senate amendment, for the years 2005, 2006 and 2007 that RICs are subject to FIRPTA, a RIC can make distributions from sales of USRPIs to shareholders who do not meet this rule, and such distributions will be treated not as dividends but as non-taxable long- or short-term capital gain, if so designated by the RIC, as long as the RIC itself is not a USRPHC after applying the special rules for counting the RIC's ownership of REIT or other RIC stock.

first day of such 30-day period preceding the distribution, and that does not in fact receive the distribution in a manner that subjects the person to tax under FIRPTA, to pay FIRPTA tax on an amount equal to the amount of the distribution that was not taxed under FIRPTA as a result of the disposition. A foreign person is treated as having acquired any interest acquired by any person treated as related to that foreign first person under section 465(b)(3)(C).[531]

This third part of the Senate amendment provision applies only in the case of a shareholder that would have been treated as receiving FIRPTA income on the distribution if that shareholder had in fact received the distribution, but that would not have been treated as receiving FIRPTA income if the form of the disposition transaction were respected. This category of persons consists of persons that are shareholders in a domestically controlled RIC or REIT (since sales of shares of such an entity are not subject to FIRPTA tax), but does not include a person who sells stock that is regularly traded on an established securities market located in the U.S. and who did not own more than five percent of such stock during the one year period ending on the date of the distribution (since such a person would not have been subject to FIRPTA tax under present law for REITs and under the second part of the Senate amendment provision for RICs, *supra.*, if that person had received the dividend instead of disposing of the stock).

Notwithstanding the recharacterization of the disposition as involving a FIRPTA distribution to the foreign person, no withholding on disposition proceeds to the foreign person on the disposition of such stock would be required. No inference is intended as to what situations under present law would or would not be respected as dispositions.

Conference Agreement

The conference agreement includes the Senate amendment provision with modifications and clarifications.

The conference agreement provides that the second part of the Senate amendment provision, treating certain distributions attributable to sales of U.S. real property interests as dividends subject to dividend withholding, applies when the distribution is made to a foreign shareholder of a RIC or REIT, but does not apply when the distribution is made to another RIC or a REIT. In such cases, the character of the distribution as FIRPTA gain is retained and must be tracked by the recipient RIC or REIT, but the distribution itself does not become dividend income in the hands of such RIC or REIT. Therefore, such recipient RIC or REIT can in turn distribute amounts attributable to that distribution (attributable to the sale of USRPIs) to its U.S shareholders as capital gain. However, if any recipient RIC or REIT in turn distributes to a foreign shareholder amounts that are attributable to a sale by a lower tier RIC or REIT of USRPIs, such amounts distributed to a foreign shareholder shall be treated as FIRPTA gain or as dividend income, according to whether or not such distribution to such foreign shareholder qualifies for dividend treatment.

The conference agreement amends section 1445 so that it explicitly requires withholding on RIC and REIT distributions to foreign persons, attributable to the sale of USRPIs, at 35 percent, or, to the extent provided by regulations, at 15 percent.[532]

531. These relationships generally include persons that are engaged in trades or businesses under common control (generally, a more than 50 percent relationship) and also include persons that have a more than 10 percent relationship, such as (for example) a corporation and an individual owning more than 10 percent of the corporation; or a corporation and a partnership if the same persons own more than 10 percent of the interests in each.

532. This provision is similar to present law section 1445(c)(1). The regulatory authority to reduce the withholding to 15 percent sunsets in accordance with the same sunset that applies to section 1445(c)(1), at the time that the present law maximum 15 percent rate on dividends is scheduled to sunset.

Treasury regulations under section 1445 already impose FIRPTA withholding on REITs under present law. Treasury has not yet written regulations applicable to RICs. No inference is intended regarding the existing Treasury regulations in force under section 1445 with respect to REITs

The conference agreement clarifies that the treatment of a RIC as a qualified investment entity continues after December 2007 with respect to a RIC that receives a distribution from a REIT, not only for purposes of the distribution rules, including withholding on distributions to foreign shareholders, but also for purposes of the new "wash sale" rules of the provision.

The conference agreement modifies the new "wash sale" rule. The period within which the basic "wash-sale" rule applies is changed from 60 days to 61 days.[533] The definition of "applicable wash sales transaction" is expanded to cover not only situations in which the taxpayer acquires a substantially identical interest, but also situations in which the taxpayer enters into a contract or option to acquire such an interest. The related party rule is also modified to apply the 50-percent relationship test under section 267(b) and 707(b)(1) rather than a 10-percent test.

In addition, treatment of a foreign shareholder of a RIC or REIT as if it had received a FIRPTA distribution that is treated as U.S. effectively connected income is extended to transactions that meet the definition of "substitute dividend payments" provided for purposes of section 861 and that would be properly treated by the foreign taxpayer as receipt of a distribution of FIRPTA gain if the distribution from the RIC or REIT had itself been received by the taxpayer, but that, by virtue of the substitute dividend payment, is not so treated but for the provision,[534] as well as to other similar arrangements to which Treasury may extend the rules.

Effective Date

The first part of the conference agreement provision, relating to distributions generally, applies to distributions with respect to taxable years of RICs and REITs beginning after December 31, 2005, except that no withholding is required under sections 1441, 1442, or 1445 with respect to any distribution before the date of enactment if such amount was not otherwise required to be withheld under any such section as in affect before the amendments made by the conference agreement.

The second part of the conference agreement, relating to the "wash sale" and substitute dividend payment transactions, is applicable to distributions and substitute dividend payments occurring on or after the 30th day following the date of enactment.

No inference is intended regarding the treatment under present law of any transactions addressed by the conference agreement.

533. Thus the period includes the 30 days before and the 30 days after the ex-dividend date, in addition to the ex-dividend date itself.

534. The conference agreement adopts the definition of "substitute dividend payment" used for purposes of section 861, which definition applies to determine substitute dividend payments under the conference agreement provision, even though the recipient may not be an individual and even though the underlying payment would not have been treated as a dividend to the recipient but as a distribution of FIRPTA gain. Treasury regulations section 1.861-3(a)(6) defines a "substitute dividend payment" as a payment, made to the transferor of a security in a securities lending transaction or a sale-repurchase transaction, of an amount equivalent to a dividend distribution which the owner of the transferred security is entitled to receive during the term of the transaction. The regulation applies to amounts received or accrued by the taxpayer. The regulation defines a securities lending transaction as a transfer of one or more securities that is described in section 1058(a) or a substantially similar transaction. The regulation defines a sale-repurchase transaction as an agreement under which a person transfers a security in exchange for cash and simultaneously agrees to receive substantially identical securities from the transferee in the future in exchange for cash. Under the regulation, a "substitute dividend payment" is generally sourced and in many instances characterized in the same manner as the underlying distribution with respect to the transferred security.

[¶ 5025] Section 507. Section 355 not to apply to distributions involving disqualified investment companies.

(Code Sec. 355)

[Conference Report]

Present Law

A corporation generally is required to recognize gain on the distribution of property (including stock of a subsidiary) to its shareholders as if the corporation had sold such property for its fair market value. In addition, the shareholders receiving the distributed property are ordinarily treated as receiving a dividend of the value of the distribution (to the extent of the distributing corporation's earnings and profits), or capital gain in the case of a stock buyback that significantly reduces the shareholder's interest in the parent corporation.

An exception to these rules applies if the distribution of the stock of a controlled corporation satisfies the requirements of section 355 of the Code. If all the requirements are satisfied, there is no tax to the distributing corporation or to the shareholders on the distribution.

One requirement to qualify for tax-free treatment under section 355 is that both the distributing corporation and the controlled corporation must be engaged immediately after the distribution in the active conduct of a trade or business that has been conducted for at least five years and was not acquired in a taxable transaction during that period (the "active business test").[40]

In determining whether assets are part of a five-year qualifying active business, assets acquired more recently than five years prior to the distribution, in a taxable transaction, are permitted to qualify as five-year "active business" assets if they are considered to have been acquired as part of an expansion of an existing business that does so qualify.[45]

When a corporation holds an interest in a partnership, IRS revenue rulings have allowed an active business of the partnership to count as an active business of a corporate partner in certain circumstances. One such case involved a situation in which the corporation owned at least 20 percent of the partnership, was actively engaged in management of the partnership, and the partnership itself had an active business.[46]

In addition to its active business requirements, section 355 does not apply to any transaction that is a "device" for the distribution of earnings and profits to a shareholder without the payment of tax on a dividend. A transaction is ordinarily not considered a "device" to avoid dividend tax if the distribution would have been treated by the shareholder as a redemption that was a sale or exchange of its stock, rather than as a dividend, if section 355 had not applied.[47]

Senate Amendment

* * *

In addition, the Senate amendment contains another provision that denies section 355 treatment if either the distributing or distributed corporation is a disqualified investment corporation immediately after the transaction (including any series of related transactions) and any person that did not hold 50 percent or more of the voting power or value of stock of such distributing or controlled corporation immediately before the transaction

40. Section 355(b).
45. Treas. Reg. sec. 1.355-3(b)(ii).
46. Rev. Rul. 92-17, 1002-1 C.B. 142; see also, Rev. Rul. 2002-49, 2002-2 C.B. 50.
47. Treas, Reg, sec, 1.355-2(d)(5)(iv).

does hold a such a 50 percent or greater interest immediately after such transaction. The attribution rules of section 318 apply for purposes of this determination.

A disqualified investment corporation is any distributing or controlled corporation if the fair market value of the investment assets of the corporation is 75 percent or more of the fair market value of all assets of the corporation. Except as otherwise provided, the term "investment assets" for this purpose means (i) cash, (ii) any stock or securities in a corporation, (iii) any interest in a partnership, (iv) any debt instrument or other evidence of indebtedness; (v) any option, forward or futures contract, notional principal contract, or derivative; (vi) foreign currency, or (vii) any similar asset.

The term "investment assets" does not include any asset which is held for use in the active and regular conduct of (i) a lending or finance business (as defined in section 954(h)(4)); (ii) a banking business through a bank (as defined in section 581), a domestic building and loan association (within the meaning of section 7701(a)(19), or any similar institution specified by the Secretary; or (iii) an insurance business if the conduct of the business is licensed, authorized, or regulated by an applicable insurance regulatory body. These exceptions only apply with respect to any business if substantially all the income of the business is derived from persons who are not related (within the meaning of section 267(b) or 707(b)(1) to the person conducting the business.

The term "investment assets" also does not include any security (as defined in section 475(c)(2)) which is held by a dealer in securities and to which section 475(a) applies.

The term "investment assets" also does not include any stock or securities in, or any debt instrument, evidence of indebtedness, option, forward or futures contract, notional principal contract, or derivative issued by, a corporation which is a 25-percent controlled entity with respect to the distributing or controlled corporation. Instead, the distributing or controlled corporation is treated as owning its ratable share of the assets of any 25-percent controlled entity.

The term 25-percent controlled entity means any corporation with respect to which the corporation in question (distributing or controlled) owns directly or indirectly stock possessing at least 25 percent of voting power and value, excluding stock that is not entitled to vote, is limited and preferred as to dividends and does not participate in corporate growth to any significant extent, has redemption and liquidation rights which do not exceed the issue price of such stock (except for a reasonable redemption or liquidation premium), and is not convertible into another class of stock.

The term "investment assets" also does not include any interest in a partnership, or any debt instrument or other evidence of indebtedness issued by the partnership, if one or more trades or businesses of the partnership are, (or without regard to the 5-year requirement of section 355(b)(2)(B), would be) taken into account by the distributing or controlled corporation, as the case may be, in determining whether the active business test of section 355 is met by such corporation.

The Treasury department shall provide regulations as may be necessary to carry out, or prevent the avoidance of, the purposes of the provision, including regulations in cases involving related persons, intermediaries, pass-through entities, or other arrangements; and the treatment of assets unrelated to the trade or business of a corporation as investment assets if, prior to the distribution, investment assets were used to acquire such assets. Regulations may also in appropriate cases exclude from the application of the provision a distribution which does not have the character of a redemption and which would be treated as a sale or exchange under section 302, and may modify the application of the attribution rules.

Effective Date

The second provision of the Senate amendment is effective for distributions after the date of enactment, except in transactions which are (i) made pursuant to an agreement which was binding on such date of enactment and at all times thereafter; (ii) described in a ruling request submitted to the Intetnal [*sic,* Internal] Revenue Service on or before such date, or (iii) described on or before such date in a public announcement or in a filing with the Securities and Exchange Commission.

Conference Agreement

The conference agreement includes the House bill and the Senate amendment with modifications.

With respect to the provision that affects transactions involving disqualified investment corporations, the conference agreement reduces the percentage of investment assets of a corporation that will cause such corporation to be a disqualified investment corporation, from 75 percent (three-quarters) to two-thirds of the fair market value of the corporation's assets, for distributions occurring after one year after the date of enactment.

The conference agreement also reduces from 25 percent to 20 percent the percentage stock ownership in a corporation that will cause such ownership to be disregarded as an investment asset itself, instead requiring "look-through" to the ratable share of the underlying assets of such corporation attributable to such stock ownership.

The conferees wish to clarify that the disqualified investment corporation provision applies when a person directly or indirectly holds 50 percent of either the vote or the value of a company immediately following a distribution, and such person did not hold such 50 percent interest directly or indirectly prior to the distribution. As one example, the provision applies if a person that held 50 percent or more of the vote, but not of the value, of a distributing corporation immediately prior to a transaction in which a controlled corporation that was 100 percent owned by that distributing corporation is distributed, directly or indirectly holds 50 percent of the value of either the distributing or controlled corporation immediately following such transaction.

The conferees further wish to clarify that the enumeration in subsection 355(g)(5)(A) through (C) of specific situations that Treasury regulations may address is not intended to restrict or limit any other situations that Treasury may address under the general authority of new section 355(g)(5) to carry out, or prevent the avoidance of, the purposes of the disqualified investment corporation provision.

Effective Date

The effective date of the provision that affects transactions involving disqualified investment corporations is the same as that of the Senate amendment provision, except for the conference agreement reduction in the amount of investment assets of a corporation that will cause it to be a disqualified investment corporation, from three-quarters to two thirds of the fair market value of all assets of the corporation. The two-thirds test applies for distributions occurring after one year after the date of enactment.

[¶5026] Section 508. Loan and redemption requirement on pooled financing requirements.

(Code Sec. 148, 149)

[Conference Report]

Present Law

In general

Interest on bonds issued by State and local governments generally is excluded from gross income for Federal income tax purposes if the proceeds of such bonds are used to finance direct activities of governmental units or if such bonds are repaid with revenues of governmental units. These bonds are called "governmental bonds." Interest on State or local government bonds issued to finance activities of private persons is taxable unless a specific exception applies. These bonds are called "private activity bonds." The exclusion from income for State and local bonds does not apply to private activity bonds, unless the bonds are issued for certain permitted purposes. In addition, the Code imposes qualification requirements that apply to all State and local bonds. Arbitrage restrictions, for example, limit the ability of issuers to profit from investment of tax-exempt bond proceeds. The Code also imposes requirements that only apply to specific types of bond issues. For instance, pooled financing bonds (defined below) are not tax-exempt unless the issuer meets certain requirements regarding the expected use of proceeds.

Pooled financing bond restrictions

State or local governments also issue bonds to provide financing for the benefit of a third party (a "conduit borrower"). Pooled financing bonds are bond issues that are used to make or finance loans to two or more conduit borrowers, unless the conduit loans are to be used to finance a single project.[469] The Code imposes several requirements on pooled financing bonds if more than $5 million of proceeds are expected to be used to make loans to conduit borrowers. For purposes of these rules, a pooled financing bond does not include certain private activity bonds.[470]

A pooled financing bond is not tax-exempt unless the issuer reasonably expects that at least 95 percent of the net proceeds will be lent to ultimate borrowers by the end of the third year after the date of issue. The term "net proceeds" is defined to mean the proceeds of the issue less the following amounts: 1) proceeds used to finance issuance costs; 2) proceeds necessary to pay interest on the bonds during a three-year period; and 3) amounts in reasonably required reserves.[471]

An issuer's past experience regarding loan origination is a criterion upon which the reasonableness of the issuer's expectations can be based. As an additional requirement for tax exemption, all legal and underwriting costs associated with the issuance of pooled financing bonds may not be contingent and must be substantially paid within 180 days of the date of issuance.

Arbitrage restrictions on tax-exempt bonds

To prevent the issuance of more Federally subsidized tax-exempt bonds than necessary; the tax exemption for State and local bonds does not apply to any arbitrage bond.[472] An arbitrage bond is defined as any bond that is part of an issue if any proceeds of the issue are reasonably expected to be used (or intentionally are used) to acquire higher yielding investments or to replace funds that are used to acquire higher yielding investments. In general, arbitrage profits may be earned only during specified

469. Treas. Reg. sec. 1.150-1(b).
470. Sec. 149(f)(4)(B).
471. Sec. 149(f)(2)(C).
472. Secs. 103(a) and (b)(2).

periods (e.g., defined "temporary periods") before funds are needed for the purpose of the borrowing or on specified types of investments (e.g., "reasonably required reserve or replacement funds"). Subject to limited exceptions, investment profits that are earned during these periods or on such investments must be rebated to the Federal Government ("arbitrage rebate").

The Code contains several exceptions to the arbitrage rebate requirement, including an exception for bonds issued by small governments (the "small issuer exception"). For this purpose, small governments are defined as general purpose governmental units that issue no more than $5 million of tax-exempt governmental bonds in a calendar year.[473]

Pooled financing bonds are subject to the arbitrage restrictions that apply to all tax-exempt bonds, including arbitrage rebate. Under certain circumstances, however, small governments may issue pooled financing bonds without those bonds counting towards the determination of whether the issuer qualifies for the small issuer exception to arbitrage rebate. In the case of a pooled financing bond where the ultimate borrowers are governmental units with general taxing powers not subordinate to the issuer of the pooled bond, the pooled bond does not count against the issuer's $5 million limitation, provided the issuer is not a borrower from the pooled bond.[474] However, the issuer of the pooled financing bond remains subject to the arbitrage rebate requirement for unloaned proceeds.[475]

House Bill

No provision.

Senate Amendment

In general

The provision imposes new requirements on pooled financing bonds as a condition of tax-exemption. First, the provision imposes a written loan commitment requirement to restrict the issuance of pooled bonds where potential borrowers have not been identified ("blind pools"). Second, in addition to the current three-year expectations requirement, the issuer must reasonably expect that at least 50 percent of the net proceeds of the pooled bond will be lent to borrowers one year after the date of issue. Third, the provision requires the redemption of outstanding bonds with proceeds that are not loaned to borrowers within the expected loan origination periods. Finally, the provision eliminates the rule allowing an issuer of pooled financing bonds to disregard the pooled bonds for purposes of determining whether the issuer qualifies for the small issuer exception to rebate.

Borrower identification

Under the provision, interest on a pooled financing bond is tax exempt only if the issuer obtains written commitments with ultimate borrowers for loans equal to at least 50 percent of the net proceeds of the pooled bond prior to issuance. The loan commitment requirement does not apply to bonds issued by States (or an integral part of a State) to provide loans to subordinate governmental units or State entities created to provide financing for water-infrastructure projects through the federally-sponsored State revolving fund program.

[Joint Committee on Taxation Report [JCX-77-05]]

For purposes of the proposal, a loan commitment exists only if: (a) the issuer is committed to lend bond proceeds to the borrower identified in the commitment, and (b) the borrower has applied for, and agreed to execute, a loan in an amount certain to finance a

473. The $5 million limit is increased to $15 million if at least $10 million of the bonds are used to finance public schools.
474. Sec. 148(f)(4)(D)(ii)(II).
475. Treas. Reg. sec. 1.148-8(d)(1).

specifically identified project and, as part of that application, has paid a nonrefundable commitment fee in an amount that is commensurate with fees customarily paid for similar loan commitments.

[Conference Report]

Loan origination expectations

The provision imposes new reasonable expectations requirements for loan originations. The issuer must expect that at least 50 percent of the net proceeds of a pooled financing bond will be lent to ultimate borrowers one year after the date of issue. This is in addition to the present-law requirement that at least 95 percent of the net proceeds will be lent to ultimate borrowers by the end of the third year after the date of issue.

Redemption requirement

Under the provision, if bond proceeds are not loaned to borrowers within prescribed periods, outstanding bonds equal to the amount of proceeds that were not loaned within the required period must be redeemed with 90 days. The bond redemption requirement applies with respect to proceeds that are unloaned as of expiration of the one-year and three-year loan origination periods. For example, if an amount equal to 45 percent of the net proceeds of an issue are used to make loans to ultimate borrowers as of one year after the bonds are issued, an amount equal to five percent of the net proceeds of the issue is no longer available for lending and must be used to redeem bonds within the following six-month period. Similarly, if only 85 percent of the net proceeds of the issue are used to make qualifying loans (or to redeem bonds) as of three years after the bonds are issued, 10 percent of the remaining net proceeds is no longer available for lending and must be used to redeem bonds within the following six months.

Small issuer exception

The provision eliminates the rule disregarding pooled financing bonds from the issuer's $5,000,000 annual limitation for purposes of the small issuer exception to arbitrage rebate.

Conference Agreement

The conference agreement includes the Senate amendment provision, with the following modifications.

Under the conference agreement, issuers of pooled financing bonds must reasonably expect that at least 30 percent of the net proceeds of such bonds will be loaned to ultimate borrowers one year after the date of issue. The present-law requirement that issuers must reasonably expect to loan at least 95 percent of the net proceeds of a pooled financing bond to ultimate borrowers three years after the date of issue is unchanged. Bond proceeds that are not loaned to borrowers as required under the one- and three-year rules must be used to redeem outstanding bonds within 90 days of the expiration of such one- and three-year periods.

The conference agreement requires issuers of pooled financing bonds to obtain, prior to issuance, written commitments from borrowers equal to at least 30 percent of the net proceeds of the pooled financing bond. The conference agreement includes the Senate amendment's exception to the written loan commitment requirement. Thus, the loan commitment requirement does not apply to pooled financing bonds issued by States (or an integral part of a State) to provide loans to subordinate governmental units or State entities created to provide financing for water-infrastructure projects through the federally-sponsored State revolving fund program.

Effective Date

The provision is effective for bonds issued after the date of enactment.

[¶5027] Section 509. Partial payments required with submission of offers-in-compromise.

(Code Sec. 7122)

[Conference Report]

Present Law

The IRS has the authority to compromise any civil or criminal case arising under the internal revenue laws.[401] In general, taxpayers initiate this process by making an offer-in-compromise, which is an offer by the taxpayer to settle an outstanding tax liability for less than the total amount due. The IRS currently imposes a user fee of $150 on most offers, payable upon submission of the offer to the IRS. Taxpayers may justify their offers on the basis of doubt as to collectibility or liability or on the basis of effective tax administration. In general, enforcement action is suspended during the period that the IRS evaluates an offer. In some instances, it may take the IRS 12 to 18 months to evaluate an offer.[402] Taxpayers are permitted (but not required) to make a deposit with their offer; if the offer is rejected, the deposit is generally returned to the taxpayer. There are two general categories[403] of offers-in-compromise, lump-sum offers and periodic payment offers. Taxpayers making lump-sum offers propose to make one lump-sum payment of a specified dollar amount in settlement of their outstanding liability. Taxpayers making periodic payment offers propose to make a series of payments over time (either short-term or long-term) in settlement of their outstanding liability.

House Bill

No provision.

Senate Amendment

The provision requires a taxpayer to make partial payments to the IRS while the taxpayer's offer is being considered by the IRS. For lump-sum offers, taxpayers must make a down payment of 20 percent of the amount of the offer with any application. For purposes of this provision, a lump-sum offer includes single payments as well as payments made in five or fewer installments. For periodic payment offers, the provision requires the taxpayer to comply with the taxpayer's own proposed payment schedule while the offer is being considered. Offers submitted to the IRS that do not comport with these payment requirements are returned to the taxpayer as unprocessable and immediate enforcement action is permitted. The provision eliminates the user fee requirement for offers submitted with the appropriate partial payment.

The provision also provides that an offer is deemed accepted if the IRS does not make a decision with respect to the offer within two years from the date the offer was submitted.

The Senate amendment authorizes the Secretary to issue regulations providing exceptions to the partial payment requirements in the case of offers from certain low-income taxpayers and offers based on doubt as to liability.

Conference Agreement

The conference agreement includes the Senate amendment provision, with the following modifications. Under the conference agreement, any user fee imposed by the IRS for participation in the offer-in-compromise program must be submitted with the appropriate partial payment. The user fee is applied to the taxpayer's outstanding tax liability. In ad-

401. Sec. 7122.
402. Olsen v. United States, 326 F. Supp. 2d 184 (D. Mass. 2004).
403. The IRS categorizes payment plans with more specificity, which is generally not significant for purposes of the provision. See Form 656, Offer in Compromise, page 6 of instruction booklet (revised July 2004).

dition, under the conference agreement, offers submitted to the IRS that do not comport with the payment requirements may be returned to the taxpayer as unprocessable.

Effective Date

The provision is effective for offers-in-compromise submitted on and after the date which is 60 days after the date of enactment.

[¶5028] Section 510. Increase in age of minor children whose unearned income is taxed as if parent's income.

(Code Sec. 1)

[Conference Report]

Present Law

Filing requirements for children

A single unmarried individual eligible to be claimed as a dependent on another taxpayer's return generally must file an individual income tax return if he or she has: (1) earned income only over $5,150 (for 2006); (2) unearned income only over the minimum standard deduction amount for dependents ($850 in 2006); or (3) both earned income and unearned income totaling more than the smaller of (a) $5,150 (for 2006) or (b) the larger of (i) $850 (for 2006), or (ii) earned income plus $300.[455] Thus, if a dependent child has less than $850 in gross income, the child does not have to file an individual income tax return for 2006.[456]

A child who cannot be claimed as a dependent on another person's tax return is subject to the generally applicable filing requirements. Such a child generally must file a return if the individual's gross income exceeds the sum of the standard deduction and the personal exemption amount ($3,300 for 2006).

Taxation of unearned income under section 1(g)

Special rules (generally referred to as the "kiddie tax") apply to the unearned income of a child who is under age 14.[457] The kiddie tax applies if: (1) the child has not reached the age of 14 by the close of the taxable year; (2) the child's unearned income was more than $1,700 (for 2006); and (3) the child is required to file a return for the year. The kiddie tax applies regardless of whether the child may be claimed as a dependent on the parent's return.

For these purposes, unearned income is income other than wages, salaries, professional fees, or other amounts received as compensation for personal services actually rendered.[458] For children under age 14, net unearned income (for 2006, generally unearned income over $1,700) is taxed at the parent's rate if the parent's rate is higher than the child's rate. The remainder of a child's taxable income (i.e., earned income, plus unearned income up to $1,700 (for 2006), less the child's standard deduction) is taxed at the child's rates, regardless of whether the kiddie tax applies to the child. In general, a child is eligible to use the preferential tax rates for qualified dividends and capital gains.[459]

455. Sec. 6012(a)(1)(C). Other filing requirements apply to dependents who are married, elderly, or blind. See, Internal Revenue Service, Publication 929, Tax Rules for Children and Dependents, at 2, Table 1 (2005).
456. A taxpayer generally need not file a return if he or she has gross income in an amount less than the standard deduction (and, if allowable to the taxpayer, the personal exemption amount). An individual who may be claimed as a dependent of another taxpayer is not eligible to claim the dependency exemption relating to that individual. Sec. 151(d)(2). For taxable years beginning in 2006, the standard deduction amount for an individual who may be claimed as a dependent by another taxpayer may not exceed the greater of $850 or the sum of $300 and the individual's earned income.
457. Sec. 1(g).
458. Sec. 1(g)(4) and sec. 911(d)(2).
459. Sec. 1(h).

The kiddie tax is calculated by computing the "allocable parental tax." This involves adding the net unearned income of the child to the parent's income and then applying the parent's tax rate. A child's "net unearned income" is the child's unearned income less the sum of (1) the minimum standard deduction allowed to dependents ($850 for 2006), and (2) the greater of (a) such minimum standard deduction amount or (b) the amount of allowable itemized deductions that are directly connected with the production of the unearned income.[460] A child's net unearned income cannot exceed the child's taxable income.

The allocable parental tax equals the hypothetical increase in tax to the parent that results from adding the child's net unearned income to the parent's taxable income. If the child has net capital gains or qualified dividends, these items are allocated to the parent's hypothetical taxable income according to the ratio of net unearned income to the child's total unearned income. If a parent has more than one child subject to the kiddie tax, the net unearned income of all children is combined, and a single kiddie tax is calculated. Each child is then allocated a proportionate share of the hypothetical increase, based upon the child's net unearned income relative to the aggregate net unearned income of all of the parent's children subject to the tax.

Special rules apply to determine which parent's tax return and rate is used to calculate the kiddie tax. If the parents file a joint return, the allocable parental tax is calculated using the income reported on the joint return. In the case of parents who are married but file separate returns, the allocable parental tax is calculated using the income of the parent with the greater amount of taxable income. In the case of unmarried parents, the child's custodial parent is the parent whose taxable income is taken into account in determining the child's liability. If the custodial parent has remarried, the stepparent is treated as the child's other parent. Thus, if the custodial parent and stepparent file a joint return, the kiddie tax is calculated using that joint return. If the custodial parent and stepparent file separate returns, the return of the one with the greater taxable income is used. If the parents are unmarried but lived together all year, the return of the parent with the greater taxable income is used.[461]

Unless the parent elects to include the child's income on the parent's return (as described below) the child files a separate return to report the child's income.[462] In this case, items on the parent's return are not affected by the child's income. The total tax due from a child is the greater of:

(1.) the sum of (a) the tax payable by the child on the child's earned income and unearned income up to $1,700 (for 2006), plus (b) the allocable parental tax on the child's unearned income, or

(2.) the tax on the child's income without regard to the kiddie tax provisions.

Parental election to include child's dividends and interest on parent's return

Under certain circumstances, a parent may elect to report a child's dividends and interest on the parent's return. If the election is made, the child is treated as having no income for the year and the child does not have to file a return. The parent makes the election on Form 8814, Parents' Election to Report Child's Interest and Dividends. The requirements for the parent's election are that:

(1.) the child has gross income only from interest and dividends (including capital gains distributions and Alaska Permanent Fund Dividends);[463]

(2.) such income is more than the minimum standard deduction amount for dependents ($850 in 2006) and less than 10 times that amount ($8500 in 2006);

460. Sec. 1(g)(4).
461. Sec. 1(g)(5); Internal Revenue Service, Publication 929, Tax Rules for Children and Dependents, at 6 (2005).
462. The child must attach to the return Form 8615, Tax for Children Under Age 14 With Investment Income of More Than $1,700 (2006).
463. Internal Revenue Service, Publication 929, Tax Rules for Children and Dependents, at 6 (2005).

(3.) no estimated tax payments for the year were made in the child's name and taxpayer identification number;

(4.) no backup withholding occurred; and

(5.) the child is required to file a return if the parent does not make the election.

Only the parent whose return must be used when calculating the kiddie tax may make the election. The parent includes in income the child's gross income in excess of twice the minimum standard deduction amount for dependents (i.e., the child's gross income in excess of $1,700 for 2007). This amount is taxed at the parent's rate. The parent also must report an additional tax liability equal to the lesser of: (1) $85 (in 2006), or (2) 10 percent of the child's gross income exceeding the child's standard deduction ($850 in 2006).

Including the child's income on the parent's return can affect the parent's deductions and credits that are based on adjusted gross income, as well as income-based phaseouts, limitations, and floors.[464] In addition, certain deductions that the child would have been entitled to take on his or her own return are lost.[465] Further, if the child received tax-exempt interest from a private activity bond, that item is considered a tax preference of the parent for alternative minimum tax purposes.[466]

Taxation of compensation for services under section 1(g)

Compensation for a child's services is considered the gross income of the child, not the parent, even if the compensation is not received or retained by the child (e.g. is the parent's income under local law).[467] If the child's income tax is not paid, however, an assessment against the child will be considered as also made against the parent to the extent the assessment is attributable to amounts received for the child's services.[468]

House Bill

No provision.

Senate Amendment

The provision increases the age to which the kiddie tax provisions apply from under 14 to under 18 years of age. The provision also creates an exception to the kiddie tax for distributions from certain qualified disability trusts, defined by cross-reference to sections 1917 and 1614(a)(3) of the Social Security Act.

Conference Agreement

The conference agreement includes the Senate amendment provision with one modification. This modification provides that the kiddie tax does not apply to a child who is married and files a joint return for the taxable year.

Effective Date

The provision applies to taxable years beginning after December 31, 2005.

464. Internal Revenue Service, Publication 929, Tax Rules for Children and Dependents, at 7 (2005).
465. Internal Revenue Service, Publication 929, Tax Rules for Children and Dependents, at 7 (2005).
466. Sec. 1(g)(7)(B).
467. Sec. 73(a).
468. Sec. 6201(c).

[¶5029] Section 511. Imposition of withholding on certain payments made by government entities.

(Code Sec. 3402)

[Conference Report]

Present Law

Withholding requirements

Employers are required to withhold income tax on wages paid to employees, including wages and salaries of employees or elected officials of Federal, State, and local government units. Withholding rates vary depending on the amount of wages paid, the length of the payroll period, and the number of withholding allowances claimed by the employee.

Certain non-wage payments also are subject to mandatory or voluntary withholding. For example:

- Employers are required to withhold FICA and Railroad Retirement taxes from wages paid to their employees. Withholding rates are generally uniform.
- Payors of pensions are required to withhold from payments made to payees, unless the payee elects no withholding.[540] Withholding from periodic payments is at variable rates, parallel to income tax withholding from wages, whereas withholding from nonperiodic payments is at a flat 10-percent rate.
- A variety of payments (such as interest and dividends) are subject to backup withholding if the payee has not provided a valid taxpayer identification number (TIN). Withholding is at a flat rate based on the fourth lowest rate of tax applicable to single taxpayers.
- Certain gambling proceeds are subject to withholding. Withholding is at a flat rate based on the third lowest rate of tax applicable to single taxpayers.
- Voluntary withholding applies to certain Federal payments, such as Social Security payments. Withholding is at rates specified by Treasury regulations.
- Voluntary withholding applies to unemployment compensation benefits. Withholding is at a flat 10-percent rate.
- Foreign taxpayers are generally subject to withholding on certain U.S.-source income which is not effectively connected with the conduct of a U.S. trade or business. Withholding is at a flat 30-percent rate (14-percent for certain items of income).

Many payments, including payments made by government entities, are not subject to withholding under present law. For example, no tax is generally withheld from payments made to workers who are not classified as employees (i.e., independent contractors).

Information reporting

Present law imposes numerous information reporting requirements that enable the Internal Revenue Service ("IRS") to verify the correctness of taxpayers' returns. For example, every person engaged in a trade or business generally is required to file information returns for each calendar year for payments of $600 or more made in the course of the payor's trade or business. Special information reporting requirements exist for employers required to deduct and withhold tax from employees' income. In addition, any service recipient engaged in a trade or business and paying for services is required to make a return according to regulations when the aggregate of payments is $600 or more. Government entities are specifically required to make an information return, reporting certain payments to corporations as well as individuals. Moreover, the head of every

540. Withholding at a rate of 20 percent is required in the case of an eligible rollover distribution that is not directly rolled over.

Federal executive agency that enters into certain contracts must file an information return reporting the contractor's name, address, TIN, date of contract action, amount to be paid to the contractor, and any other information required by Forms 8596 (Information Return for Federal Contracts) and 8596A (Quarterly Transmittal of Information Returns for Federal Contracts).

House Bill

No provision.

Senate Amendment

No provision.

Conference Agreement

The conference agreement requires withholding on certain payments to persons providing property or services made by the Government of the United States, every State, every political subdivision thereof, and every instrumentality of the foregoing (including multi-State agencies). The withholding requirement applies regardless of whether the government entity making such payment is the recipient of the property or services. Political subdivisions of States (or any instrumentality thereof) with less than $100 million of annual expenditures for property or services that would otherwise be subject to withholding under this provision are exempt from the withholding requirement.

The rate of withholding is three percent on all payments regardless of whether the payments are for property or services. Payments subject to withholding under the provision include any payment made in connection with a government voucher or certificate program which functions as a payment for property or services. For example, payments to a commodity producer under a government commodity support program are subject to the withholding requirement. The provision imposes information reporting requirements on the payments that are subject to withholding under the provision.

The provision does not apply to any payments made through a Federal, State, or local government public assistance or public welfare program for which eligibility is determined by a needs or income test. For example, payments under government programs providing food vouchers or medical assistance to low-income individuals are not subject to withholding under the provision. However, payments under government programs to provide health care or other services that are not based on the needs or income of the recipients are subject to withholding, including programs where eligibility is based on the age of the beneficiary.

The provision does not apply to payments of wages or to any other payment with respect to which mandatory (e.g., U.S.-source income of foreign taxpayers) or voluntary (e.g., unemployment benefits) withholding applies under present law. The provision does not exclude payments that are potentially subject to backup withholding under section 3406. If, however, payments are actually being withheld under backup withholding, withholding under the provision does not apply.

The provision also does not apply to the following: payments of interest; payments for real property; payments to tax-exempt entities or foreign governments; intra-governmental payments; payments made pursuant to a classified or confidential contract (as defined in section 6050M(e)(3)); and payments to government employees that are not otherwise excludable from the new withholding provision with respect to the employees' services as an employees.

Effective Date

The provision applies to payments made after December 31, 2010.

[¶5030] Section 512. Conversions to Roth IRAs.

(Code Sec. 408A)

[Conference Report]

Present Law

There are two general types of individual retirement arrangements ("IRAs"): traditional IRAs and Roth IRAs. The total amount that an individual may contribute to one or more IRAs for a year is generally limited to the lesser of: (1) a dollar amount ($4,000 for 2006); and (2) the amount of the individual's compensation that is includible in gross income for the year. In the case of an individual who has attained age 50 before the end of the year, the dollar amount is increased by an additional amount ($1,000 for 2006). In the case of a married couple, contributions can be made up to the dollar limit for each spouse if the combined compensation of the spouses that is includible in gross income is at least equal to the contributed amount. IRA contributions in excess of the applicable limit are generally subject to an excise tax of six percent per year until withdrawn.

Contributions to a traditional IRA may or may not be deductible. The extent to which contributions to a traditional IRA are deductible depends on whether or not the individual (or the individual's spouse) is an active participant in an employer-sponsored retirement plan and the taxpayer's AGI. An individual may deduct his or her contributions to a traditional IRA if neither the individual nor the individual's spouse is an active participant in an employer-sponsored retirement plan. If an individual or the individual's spouse is an active participant in an employer-sponsored retirement plan, the deduction is phased out for taxpayers with AGI over certain levels. To the extent an individual does not or cannot make deductible contributions, the individual may make nondeductible contributions to a traditional IRA, subject to the maximum contribution limit. Distributions from a traditional IRA are includible in gross income to the extent not attributable to a return of nondeductible contributions.

Individuals with adjusted gross income ("AGI") below certain levels may make contributions to a Roth IRA (up to the maximum IRA contribution limit). The maximum Roth IRA contribution is phased out between $150,000 to $160,000 of AGI in the case of married taxpayers filing a joint return and between $95,000 to $105,000 in the case of all other returns (except a separate return of a married individual).[541] Contributions to a Roth IRA are not deductible. Qualified distributions from a Roth IRA are excludable from gross income. Distributions from a Roth IRA that are not qualified distributions are includible in gross income to the extent attributable to earnings. In general, a qualified distribution is a distribution that is made on or after the individual attains age 59-½, death, or disability or which is a qualified special purpose distribution. A distribution is not a qualified distribution if it is made within the five-taxable year period beginning with the taxable year for which an individual first made a contribution to a Roth IRA.

A taxpayer with AGI of $100,000 or less may convert all or a portion of a traditional IRA to a Roth IRA.[542] The amount converted is treated as a distribution from the traditional IRA for income tax purposes, except that the 10-percent additional tax on early withdrawals does not apply.

In the case of a distribution from a Roth IRA that is not a qualified distribution, certain ordering rules apply in determining the amount of the distribution that is includible in income. For this purpose, a distribution that is not a qualified distribution is treated as made in the following order: (1) regular Roth IRA contributions; (2) conversion contributions (on a first in, first out basis); and (3) earnings. To the extent a distribution is treated as made from a conversion contribution, it is treated as made first from the por-

541. In the case of a married taxpayer filing a separate return, the phaseout range is $0 to $10,000 of AGI.
542. Married taxpayers filing a separate return may not convert amounts in a traditional IRA into a Roth IRA.

tion, if any, of the conversion contribution that was required to be included in income as a result of the conversion.

Includible amounts withdrawn from a traditional IRA or a Roth IRA before attainment of age 59-½, death, or disability are subject to an additional 10-percent early withdrawal tax, unless an exception applies.

House Bill

No provision.

Senate Amendment

No provision.

Conference Agreement

The conference agreement eliminates the income limits on conversions of traditional IRAs to Roth IRAs.[543] Thus, taxpayers may make such conversions without regard to their AGI.

For conversions occurring in 2010, unless a taxpayer elects otherwise, the amount includible in gross income as a result of the conversion is included ratably in 2011 and 2012. That is, unless a taxpayer elects otherwise, none of the amount includible in gross income as a result of a conversion occurring in 2010 is included in income in 2010, and half of the income resulting from the conversion is includible in gross income in 2011 and half in 2012. However, income inclusion is accelerated if converted amounts are distributed before 2012.[544] In that case, the amount included in income in the year of the distribution is increased by the amount distributed, and the amount included in income in 2012 (or 2011 and 2012 in the case of a distribution in 2010) is the lesser of: (1) half of the amount includible in income as a result of the conversion; and (2) the remaining portion of such amount not already included in income. The following example illustrates the application of the accelerated inclusion rule.

Example.—Taxpayer A has a traditional IRA with a value of $100, consisting of deductible contributions and earnings. A does not have a Roth IRA. A converts the traditional IRA to a Roth IRA in 2010, and, as a result of the conversion, $100 is includible in gross income. Unless A elects otherwise, $50 of the income resulting from the conversion is included in income in 2011 and $50 in 2012. Later in 2010, A takes a $20 distribution, which is not a qualified distribution and all of which, under the ordering rules, is attributable to amounts includible in gross income as a result of the conversion. Under the accelerated inclusion rule, $20 is included in income in 2010. The amount included in income in 2011 is the lesser of (1) $50 (half of the income resulting from the conversion) or (2) $70 (the remaining income from the conversion), or $50. The amount included in income in 2012 is the lesser of (1) $50 (half of the income resulting from the conversion) or (2) $30 (the remaining income from the conversion, i.e., $100 - $70 ($20 included in income in 2010 and $50 included in income in 2011)), or $30.

Effective Date

The provision is effective for taxable years beginning after December 31, 2009.

---

543. Under the conference agreement, married taxpayers filing a separate return may convert amounts in a traditional IRA into a Roth IRA.

544. Whether a distribution consists of converted amounts is determined under the present-law ordering rules.

[¶5031] Section 513. Repeal of FSC/ETI binding contract relief.

(Code Sec. None)

[Conference Report]

Prior and Present Law

For most of the last two decades, the United States provided export-related tax benefits under the foreign sales corporation ("FSC") regime. In 2000, the World Trade Organization ("WTO") held that the FSC regime constituted a prohibited export subsidy under the relevant trade agreements. In response to this WTO finding, the United States repealed the FSC rules and enacted a new regime, under the FSC Repeal and Extraterritorial Income ("ETI") Exclusion Act of 2000. Transition rules delayed the repeal of the FSC rules and the effective date of ETI for transactions in the ordinary course of a trade or business occurring before January 1, 2002, or after December 31, 2001 pursuant to a binding contract between the taxpayer and an unrelated person which was in effect on September 30, 2000 and at all times thereafter (the "FSC binding contract relief").[545] In 2002, the WTO held that the ETI regime also constituted a prohibited export subsidy.

In general, under the ETI regime, an exclusion from gross income applied with respect to "extraterritorial income," which was a taxpayer's gross income attributable to "foreign trading gross receipts." This income was eligible for the exclusion to the extent that it was "qualifying foreign trade income." Qualifying foreign trade income was the amount of gross income that, if excluded, would result in a reduction of taxable income by the greatest of: (1) 1.2 percent of the foreign trading gross receipts derived by the taxpayer from the transaction; (2) 15 percent of the "foreign trade income" derived by the taxpayer from the transaction;[546] or (3) 30 percent of the "foreign sale and leasing income" derived by the taxpayer from the transaction.[547]

Foreign trading gross receipts were gross receipts derived from certain activities in connection with "qualifying foreign trade property" with respect to which certain economic processes had taken place outside of the United States. Specifically, the gross receipts must have been: (1) from the sale, exchange, or other disposition of qualifying foreign trade property; (2) from the lease or rental of qualifying foreign trade property for use by the lessee outside the United States; (3) for services which were related and subsidiary to the sale, exchange, disposition, lease, or rental of qualifying foreign trade property (as described above); (4) for engineering or architectural services for construction projects located outside the United States; or (5) for the performance of certain managerial services for unrelated persons. A taxpayer could elect to treat gross receipts from a transaction as not being foreign trading gross receipts. As a result of such an election, a taxpayer could use any related foreign tax credits in lieu of the exclusion.

Qualifying foreign trade property generally was property manufactured, produced, grown, or extracted within or outside the United States that was held primarily for sale, lease, or rental in the ordinary course of a trade or business for direct use, consumption, or disposition outside the United States. No more than 50 percent of the fair market value of such property could be attributable to the sum of: (1) the fair market value of articles manufactured outside the United States; and (2) the direct costs of labor performed outside the United States. With respect to property that was manufactured

545. An election was provided, however, under which taxpayers could adopt ETI at an earlier date for transactions after September 30, 2000. This election allowed the ETI rules to apply to transactions after September 30, 2000, including transactions occurring pursuant to pre-existing binding contracts.

546. "Foreign trade income" was the taxable income of the taxpayer (determined without regard to the exclusion of qualifying foreign trade income) attributable to foreign trading gross receipts.

547. "Foreign sale and leasing income" was the amount of the taxpayer's foreign trade income (with respect to a transaction) that was properly allocable to activities constituting foreign economic processes. Foreign sale and leasing income also included foreign trade income derived by the taxpayer in connection with the lease or rental of qualifying foreign trade property for use by the lessee outside the United States.

outside the United States, certain rules were provided to ensure consistent U.S. tax treatment with respect to manufacturers.

The American Jobs Creation Act of 2004 ("AJCA") repealed the ETI exclusion,[548] generally effective for transactions after December 31, 2004. AJCA provides a general transition rule under which taxpayers retain 100 percent of their ETI benefits for transactions prior to 2005, 80 percent of their otherwise-applicable ETI benefits for transactions during 2005, and 60 percent of their otherwise-applicable ETI benefits for transactions during 2006.

In addition to the general transition rule, AJCA provides that the ETI exclusion provisions remain in effect for transactions in the ordinary course of a trade or business if such transactions are pursuant to a binding contract[549] between the taxpayer and an unrelated person and such contract is in effect on September 17, 2003, and at all times thereafter (the "ETI binding contract relief").

In early 2006, the WTO Appellate Body held that the ETI general transition rule and the FSC and ETI binding contract relief measures are prohibited export subsidies.

House Bill

No provision.

Senate Amendment

No provision.

Conference Agreement

The conference agreement repeals both the FSC binding contract relief and the ETI binding contract relief. The general transition rule remains in effect.

Effective Date

The provision is effective for taxable years beginning after date of enactment.

[¶ 5032] Section 514. Only wages attributable to domestic production taken into account in determining deduction for domestic production.

(Code Sec. 199)

[Conference Report]

Present Law

In general

Present law provides a deduction from taxable income (or, in the case of an individual, adjusted gross income) that is equal to a portion of the taxpayer's qualified production activities income. For taxable years beginning after 2009, the deduction is nine percent of such income. For taxable years beginning in 2005 and 2006, the deduction is three percent of income and, for taxable years beginning in 2007, 2008 and 2009, the deduction is six percent of income. However, the deduction for a taxable year is limited

548. Pub. L. No. 108-357, sec. 101. In addition, foreign corporations that elected to be treated for all Federal tax purposes as domestic corporations in order to facilitate the claiming of ETI benefits were allowed to revoke such elections within one year of the date of enactment of the repeal without recognition of gain or loss, subject to anti-abuse rules.

549. This rule also applies to a purchase option, renewal option, or replacement option that is included in such contract. For this purpose, a replacement option is considered enforceable against a lessor notwithstanding the fact that a lessor retained approval of the replacement lessee.

to 50 percent of the wages paid by the taxpayer during the calendar year that ends in such taxable year.[550]

Qualified production activities income

In general, "qualified production activities income" is equal to domestic production gross receipts (defined by section 199(c)(4)), reduced by the sum of: (1) the costs of goods sold that are allocable to such receipts; and (2) other expenses, losses, or deductions which are properly allocable to such receipts.

Application of wage limitation to passthrough entities

For purposes of applying the wage limitation, a shareholder, partner, or similar person who is allocated components of qualified production activities income from a passthrough entity also is treated as having been allocated wages from such entity in an amount that is equal to the lesser of: (1) such person's allocable share of wages, as determined under regulations prescribed by the Secretary; or (2) twice the qualified production activities income that actually is allocated to such person for the taxable year.

House Bill

No provision.

Senate Amendment

No provision.

Conference Agreement

Under the conference agreement, the wage limitation is modified such that taxpayers may only include amounts which are properly allocable to domestic production gross receipts.[551] Thus, the wage limitation is 50 percent of those wages which are deducted in arriving at qualified production activities income.

In addition, the conference agreement repeals the special limitation on wages treated as allocated to partners or shareholders of passthrough entities. Accordingly, for purposes of the wage limitation, a shareholder, partner, or similar person who is allocated components of qualified production activities income from a passthrough entity is treated as having been allocated wages from such entity in an amount that is equal to such person's allocable share of wages as determined under regulations prescribed by the Secretary, even if such amount is more than twice the qualified production activities income that actually is allocated to such person for the taxable year. The shareholder, partner, or similar person will then include in its wage limitation only those wages which are deducted in arriving at qualified production activities income.

Effective Date

The conference agreement is effective with respect to taxable years beginning after the date of enactment.

550. For purposes of the provision, "wages" include the sum of the amounts of wages as defined in section 3401(a) and elective deferrals that the taxpayer properly reports to the Social Security Administration with respect to the employment of employees of the taxpayer during the calendar year ending during the taxpayer's taxable year. Elective deferrals include elective deferrals as defined in section 402(g)(3), amounts deferred under section 457, and, for taxable years beginning after December 31, 2005, designated Roth contributions (as defined in section 402A).

551. As under present law, the Secretary shall provide rules for the proper allocation of items (including wages) in determining qualified production activities income. Section 199(c)(2).

[¶5033] Section 515. Modification of exclusion for citizens living abroad.

(Code Sec. 911)

[Conference Report]

Present Law

In general

U.S. citizens generally are subject to U.S. income tax on all their income, whether derived in the United States or elsewhere. A U.S. citizen who earns income in a foreign country also may be taxed on that income by the foreign country. The United States generally cedes the primary right to tax a U.S. citizen's non-U.S. source income to the foreign country in which the income is derived. This concession is effected by the allowance of a credit against the U.S. income tax imposed on foreign-source income for foreign taxes paid on that income. The amount of the credit for foreign income tax paid on foreign-source income generally is limited to the amount of U.S. tax otherwise owed on that income. Accordingly, if the amount of foreign tax paid on foreign-source income is less than the amount of U.S. tax owed on that income, a foreign tax credit generally is allowed in an amount not exceeding the amount of the foreign tax, and a residual U.S. tax liability remains.

A U.S. citizen or resident living abroad may be eligible to exclude from U.S. taxable income certain foreign earned income and foreign housing costs.[552] This exclusion applies regardless of whether any foreign tax is paid on the foreign earned income or housing costs. To qualify for these exclusions, an individual (a "qualified individual") must have his or her tax home in a foreign country and must be either (1) a U.S. citizen[553] who is a bona fide resident of a foreign country or countries for an uninterrupted period that includes an entire taxable year, or (2) a U.S. citizen or resident present in a foreign country or countries for at least 330 full days in any 12-consecutive-month period.

Exclusion for compensation

The foreign earned income exclusion generally is available for a qualified individual's non-U.S. source earned income attributable to personal services performed by that individual during the period of foreign residence or presence described above. The maximum exclusion amount for any calendar year is $80,000 in 2002 through 2007 and is indexed for inflation after 2007.

Exclusion for housing costs

A qualified individual is allowed an exclusion from gross income (or, as described below, a deduction) for certain foreign housing costs paid or incurred by or on behalf of the individual. The amount of this housing cost exclusion is equal to the excess of a taxpayer's "housing expenses" over a base housing amount. The term "housing expenses" means the reasonable expenses paid or incurred during the taxable year for a taxpayer's housing (and, if they live with the taxpayer, for the housing of the taxpayer's spouse and dependents) in a foreign country. The term includes expenses attributable to housing such as utilities and insurance, but it does not include separately deductible interest and taxes. If the taxpayer maintains a second household outside the United States for a spouse or dependents who do not reside with the taxpayer because of dangerous, unhealthful, or otherwise adverse living conditions, the housing expenses of the second household also are eligible for exclusion. The base housing amount above which costs are eligible for exclusion in a taxable year is 16 percent of the annual salary (computed

552. Sec. 911.

553. Generally, only U.S. citizens may qualify under the bona fide residence test. A U.S. resident alien who is a citizen of a country with which the United States has a tax treaty may, however, qualify for the section 911 exclusions under the bona fide residence test by application of a nondiscrimination provision of the treaty.

on a daily basis) of a grade GS-14, step 1, U.S. government employee, multiplied by the number of days of foreign residence or presence (as described above) in the taxable year. For 2006 this salary is $77,793; the current base housing amount therefore is $12,447 (assuming the taxpayer is a bona fide resident of or is present in a foreign country every day during the year).

To the extent otherwise excludable housing costs are not paid or reimbursed by a taxpayer's employer, these costs generally are allowed as a deduction in computing adjusted gross income.

Exclusion limitation amounts

The combined foreign earned income exclusion and housing cost exclusion (including the amount of any deductible housing costs) may not exceed the taxpayer's total foreign earned income for the taxable year. The taxpayer's foreign tax credit is reduced by the amount of the credit that is attributable to excluded income.

Tax brackets

A taxpayer with excludable income under section 911 is subject to tax on the taxpayer's other income, after deductions, starting in the lowest tax rate bracket.

House Bill

No provision.

Senate Amendment

No provision.

Conference Agreement

Exclusion for compensation

The conference agreement provision adjusts for inflation the maximum amount of the foreign earned income exclusion in taxable years beginning in calendar years after 2005 (rather than, as under present law, after 2007). The limitation in 2006 therefore is $82,400.[554]

Exclusion for housing costs

Under the conference agreement, the base housing amount used in calculating the foreign housing cost exclusion in a taxable year is 16 percent of the amount (computed on a daily basis) of the foreign earned income exclusion limitation (instead of the present law 16 percent of the grade GS-14, step 1 amount), multiplied by the number of days of foreign residence or presence (as previously described) in that year.

Reasonable foreign housing expenses in excess of the base housing amount remain excluded from gross income (or, if paid by the taxpayer, are deductible) under the conference agreement, but the amount of the exclusion is limited to 30 percent of the maximum amount of a taxpayer's foreign earned income exclusion.[555] The Secretary is given authority to issue regulations or other guidance providing for the adjustment of this 30-percent housing cost limitation based on geographic differences in housing costs relative to housing costs in the United States. The conferees intend that the Secretary be permitted to use publicly available data, such as the Quarterly Report Indexes published by the U.S. Department of State or any other information deemed reliable by the Secretary, in making adjustments. The conferees also intend that the Secretary may adjust the 30-per-

554. The $82,400 amount is calculated under section 911(b)(2)(D)(ii) as amended by the conference agreement provision, using current U.S. Bureau of Labor Statistics ("BLS") Consumer Price Index Data.

555. In certain programs including grant-making to subsidize rents, the U.S. Department of Housing and Urban Development considers maximum affordable housing costs to be 30 percent of a household's income. See, e.g., United States Housing Act of 1937, 42 U.S.C. sec. 1437a (a)(1)(A), as amended.

cent amount upward or downward. The conferees intend that the Secretary make adjustments annually.

Under the 30-percent rule described above, the maximum amount of the foreign housing cost exclusion in 2006 is (assuming foreign residence or presence on all days in the year) $11,536 (= ($82,400 × 30 percent) – ($82,400 × 16 percent)).[556]

Tax brackets

Under the conference agreement, if an individual excludes an amount from income under section 911, any income in excess of the exclusion amount determined under section 911 is taxed (under the regular tax and alternative minimum tax) by applying to that income the tax rates that would have been applicable had the individual not elected the section 911 exclusion. For example, an individual with $80,000 of foreign earned income that is excluded under section 911 and with $20,000 in other taxable income (after deductions) would be subject to tax on that $20,000 at the rate or rates applicable to taxable income in the range of $80,000 to $100,000.

Effective Date

The conference agreement provision is effective for taxable years beginning after December 31, 2005.

[¶ 5034] Section 516. Tax involvement of accommodation parties in tax shelter transactions.

(Code Sec. 4965)

[Conference Report]

Present Law

Disclosure of listed and other reportable transactions by taxpayers

Present law provides that a taxpayer that participates in a reportable transaction (including a listed transaction) and that is required to file a tax return must attach to its return a disclosure statement in the form prescribed by the Secretary.[97] For this purpose, the term taxpayer includes any person, including an individual, trust, estate, partnership, association, company, or corporation.[98]

Under present Treasury regulations, a reportable transaction includes a listed transaction and five other categories of transactions: (1) confidential transactions, which are transactions offered to a taxpayer under conditions of confidentiality and for which the taxpayer has paid an advisor a minimum fee; (2) transactions with contractual protection, which include transactions for which the taxpayer or a related party has the right to a full or partial refund of fees if all or part of the intended tax consequences from the transaction are not sustained, or for which fees are contingent on the taxpayer's realization of tax benefits from the transaction; (3) loss transactions, which are transactions resulting in the taxpayer claiming a loss under section 165 that exceeds certain thresholds, depending upon the type of taxpayer; (4) transactions with a significant book-tax difference; and (5) transactions involving a brief asset holding period.[99] A listed transaction means a reportable transaction which is the same as, or substantially similar to, a transaction specifically identified by the Secretary as a tax avoidance transaction for purposes of section 6011 (relating to the filing of returns and statements), and identified by no-

556. The $11,536 amount is based on a calculation under section 911(b)(2)(D)(ii), as amended by the conference agreement, using the BLS data described above.
97. Treas. Reg. sec. 1.6011-4(a).
98. Sec. 7701(a)(1); Treas. Reg. sec. 1.6011-4(c)(1).
99. Treas. Reg. sec. 1.6011-4(b). In Notice 2006-6 (January 6, 2006), the Service indicated that it was removing transactions with a significant book-tax difference from the categories of reportable transactions.

tice, regulation, or other form of published guidance as a listed transaction.[100] The fact that a transaction is a reportable transaction does not affect the legal determination of whether the taxpayer's treatment of the transaction is proper.[101] Present law authorizes the Secretary to define a reportable transaction on the basis of such transaction being of a type which the Secretary determines as having a potential for tax avoidance or evasion.[102]

Treasury regulations provide guidance regarding the determination of when a taxpayer participates in a transaction for these purposes.[103] A taxpayer has participated in a listed transaction if the taxpayer's tax return reflects tax consequences or a tax strategy described in the published guidance that lists the transaction, or if the taxpayer knows or has reason to know that the taxpayer's tax benefits are derived directly or indirectly from tax consequences of a tax strategy described in published guidance that lists a transaction. A taxpayer has participated in a confidential transaction if the taxpayer's tax return reflects a tax benefit from the transaction and the taxpayer's disclosure of the tax treatment or tax structure of the transaction is limited under conditions of confidentiality. A taxpayer has participated in a transaction with contractual protection if the taxpayer's tax return reflects a tax benefit from the transaction, and the taxpayer has the right to the full or partial refund of fees or the fees are contingent.

Present law provides a penalty for any person who fails to include on any return or statement any required information with respect to a reportable transaction.[104] The penalty applies without regard to whether the transaction ultimately results in an understatement of tax, and applies in addition to any other penalty that may be imposed.

The penalty for failing to disclose a reportable transaction is $10,000 in the case of a natural person and $50,000 in any other case. The amount is increased to $100,000 and $200,000, respectively, if the failure is with respect to a listed transaction. The penalty cannot be waived with respect to a listed transaction. As to reportable transactions, the IRS Commissioner may rescind all or a portion of the penalty if rescission would promote compliance with the tax laws and effective tax administration.

Disclosure of listed and other reportable transactions by material advisors

Present law requires each material advisor with respect to any reportable transaction (including any listed transaction) to timely file an information return with the Secretary (in such form and manner as the Secretary may prescribe).[105] The information return must include (1) information identifying and describing the transaction, (2) information describing any potential tax benefits expected to result from the transaction, and (3) such other information as the Secretary may prescribe. The return must be filed by the date specified by the Secretary.

A "material advisor" means any person (1) who provides material aid, assistance, or advice with respect to organizing, managing, promoting, selling, implementing, insuring, or carrying out any reportable transaction, and (2) who directly or indirectly derives gross income in excess of $250,000 ($50,000 in the case of a reportable transaction substantially all of the tax benefits from which are provided to natural persons) or such other amount as may be prescribed by the Secretary for such advice or assistance.[106]

The Secretary may prescribe regulations which provide (1) that only one material advisor is required to file an information return in cases in which two or more material advisors would otherwise be required to file information returns with respect to a particular reportable transaction, (2) exemptions from the requirements of this section, and (3)

100. Sec. 6707A(c)(2); Treas. Reg. sec. 1.6011-4(b)(2).
101. Treas. Reg. sec. 1.6011-4(a).
102. Sec. 6707A(c)(1).
103. Treas. Reg. sec. 1.6011-4(c)(3).
104. Sec. 6707A.
105. Sec. 6707(a), as added by the American Jobs Creation Act of 2004, Pub. L. No. 108-357, sec. 816(a).
106. Sec. 6707(b)(1).

other rules as may be necessary or appropriate to carry out the purposes of this section.[107]

Present law imposes a penalty on any material advisor who fails to timely file an information return, or who files a false or incomplete information return, with respect to a reportable transaction (including a listed transaction).[108] The amount of the penalty is $50,000. If the penalty is with respect to a listed transaction, the amount of the penalty is increased to the greater of (1) $200,000, or (2) 50 percent of the gross income derived by such person with respect to aid, assistance, or advice which is provided with respect to the transaction before the date the information return that includes the transaction is filed. An intentional failure or act by a material advisor with respect to the requirement to disclose a listed transaction increases the penalty to 75 percent of the gross income derived from the transaction.

The penalty cannot be waived with respect to a listed transaction. As to reportable transactions, the IRS Commissioner can rescind all or a portion of the penalty if rescission would promote compliance with the tax laws and effective tax administration.

House Bill

No provision.

Senate Amendment

In general

In general, under the provision, certain tax-exempt entities are subject to penalties for being a party to a prohibited tax shelter transaction. A prohibited tax shelter transaction is a transaction that the Secretary determines is a listed transaction (as defined in section 6707A(c)(2)) or a prohibited transaction. A prohibited reportable transaction is a confidential transaction or a transaction with contractual protection (as defined by the Secretary in regulations) which is a reportable transaction as defined in sec. 6707A(c)(1). Under the provision, a tax-exempt entity is an entity that is described in section 501(c), 501(d), or 170(c) (not including the United States), Indian tribal governments, and tax qualified pension plans, individual retirement arrangements ("IRAs"), and similar tax-favored savings arrangements (such as Coverdell education savings accounts, health savings accounts, and qualified tuition plans).

Entity level tax

Under the provision, if a tax-exempt entity is a party at any time to a transaction during a taxable year and knows or has reason to know that the transaction is a prohibited tax shelter transaction, the entity is subject to a tax for such year equal to the greater of (1) 100 percent of the entity's net income (after taking into account any tax imposed with respect to the transaction) for such year that is attributable to the transaction or (2) 75 percent of the proceeds received by the entity that are attributable to the transaction.

In addition, if a transaction is not a listed transaction at the time a tax-exempt entity enters into the transaction (and is not otherwise a prohibited tax shelter transaction), but the transaction subsequently is determined by the Secretary to be a listed transaction (a "subsequently listed transaction"), the entity must pay each taxable year an excise tax at the highest unrelated business taxable income rate times the greater of (1) the entity's net income (after taking into account any tax imposed) that is attributable to the subsequently listed transaction and that is properly allocable to the period beginning on the later of the date such transaction is listed by the Secretary or the first day of the taxable year or (2) 75 percent of the proceeds received by the entity that are attributable to the subsequently listed transaction and that are properly allocable to the period beginning on the later of the date such transaction is listed by the Secretary or the first day of the tax-

107. Sec. 6707(c).
108. Sec. 6707(b).

able year. The Secretary has the authority to promulgate regulations that provide guidance regarding the determination of the allocation of net income of a tax-exempt entity that is attributable to a transaction to various periods, including before and after the listing of the transaction or the date which is 90 days after the date of enactment of the provision.

The entity level tax does not apply if the entity's participation is not willful and is due to reasonable cause, except that the willful and reasonable cause exception does not apply to the tax imposed for subsequently listed transactions. The entity level taxes do not apply to tax qualified pension plans, IRAs, and similar tax-favored savings arrangements (such as Coverdell education savings accounts, health savings accounts, and qualified tuition plans).

Disclosure of participation in prohibited tax shelter transactions

The provision requires that a taxable party to a prohibited tax shelter transaction disclose to the tax-exempt entity that the transaction is a prohibited tax shelter transaction. Failure to make such disclosure is subject to the present-law penalty for failure to include reportable transaction information under section 6707A. Thus, the penalty is $10,000 in the case of a natural person or $50,000 in any other case, except that if the transaction is a listed transaction, the penalty is $100,000 in the case of a natural person and $200,000 in any other case.[109]

The provision requires disclosure by a tax-exempt entity to the IRS of each participation in a prohibited tax shelter transaction and disclosure of other known parties to the transaction. The penalty for failure to disclose is imposed on the entity (or entity manager, in the case of qualified pension plans and similar tax favored retirement arrangements) at $100 per day the failure continues, not to exceed $50,000. If any person fails to comply with a demand on the tax-exempt entity by the Secretary for disclosure, such person or persons shall pay a penalty of $100 per day (beginning on the date of the failure to comply) not to exceed $10,000 per prohibited tax shelter transaction. As under present-law section 6552, no penalty is imposed with respect to any failure if it is shown that the failure is due to reasonable cause.

Penalty on entity managers

A tax of $20,000 is imposed on an entity manager that approves or otherwise causes a tax-exempt entity to be a party to a prohibited tax shelter transaction at any time during the taxable year, knowing or with reason to know that the transaction is a prohibited tax shelter transaction. An entity manager is defined as a person with authority or responsibility similar to that exercised by an officer, director, or trustee of an organization, except: (1) in the case of an entity described in section 501(c)(3) or (c)(4) (other than a private foundation), an entity manager is an organization manager as defined in section 4958(f)(2); and (2) in the case of a private foundation, an entity manager is a foundation manager as defined in section 4946(b). The reasonable cause (or no willful participation) exception applies to this tax.

Conference Agreement

The conference agreement includes the Senate amendment provision, with modifications.

The conference agreement does not include the provision that the entity level or entity manager tax does not apply if the entity's participation is not willful and is due to reasonable cause.

109. The IRS Commissioner may rescind all or any portion of any such penalty if the violation is with respect to a prohibited tax shelter transaction other than a listed transaction and doing so would promote compliance with the requirements of the Code and effective tax administration. See sec. 6707A(d).

In addition, the conference agreement adds a tax in the event that a tax-exempt entity becomes a party to a prohibited tax shelter transaction without knowing or having reason to know that the transaction is a prohibited tax shelter transaction. In that case, the tax-exempt entity is subject to a tax in the taxable year the entity becomes a party and any subsequent taxable year of the highest unrelated business taxable income rate times the greater of (1) the entity's net income (after taking into account any tax imposed with respect to the transaction) for such year that is attributable to the transaction or (2) 75 percent of the proceeds received by the entity that are attributable to the transaction for such year.[110]

The conference agreement clarifies that the entity level tax rate that applies if the entity knows or has reason to know that a transaction is a prohibited tax shelter transaction does not apply to subsequently listed transactions.

The conference agreement modifies the definition of an entity manager to provide that: (1) in the case of tax qualified pension plans, IRAs, and similar tax-favored savings arrangements (such as Coverdell education savings accounts, health savings accounts, and qualified tuition plans) an entity manager is the person that approves or otherwise causes the entity to be a party to a prohibited tax shelter transaction, and (2) in all other cases the entity manager is the person with authority or responsibility similar to that exercised by an officer, director, or trustee of an organization, and with respect to any act, the person having authority or responsibility with respect to such act.

In the case of a qualified pension plan, IRA, or similar tax-favored savings arrangement (such as a Coverdell education savings account, health savings account, or qualified tuition plan), the conferees intend that, in general, a person who decides that assets of the plan, IRA, or other savings arrangement are to be invested in a prohibited tax shelter transaction is the entity manager under the provision. Except in the case of a fully self-directed plan or other savings arrangement with respect to which a participant or beneficiary decides to invest in the prohibited tax shelter transaction, a participant or beneficiary generally is not an entity manager under the provision. Thus, for example, a participant or beneficiary is not an entity manager merely by reason of choosing among pre-selected investment options (as is typically the case if a qualified retirement plan provides for participant-directed investments).[111] Similarly, if an individual has an IRA and may choose among various mutual funds offered by the IRA trustee, but has no control over the investments held in the mutual funds, the individual is not an entity manager under the provision.

Under the provision, certain taxes are imposed if the entity or entity manager knows or has reason to know that a transaction is a prohibited tax shelter transaction. In general, the conferees intend that in order for an entity or entity manager to have reason to know that a transaction is a prohibited tax shelter transaction, the entity or entity manager must have knowledge of sufficient facts that would lead a reasonable person to conclude that the transaction is a prohibited tax shelter transaction. If there is justifiable reliance on a reasoned written opinion of legal counsel (including in-house counsel) or of an independent accountant with expertise in tax matters, after making full disclosure of relevant facts about a transaction to such counsel or accountant, that a transaction is not a prohibited tax shelter transaction, then absent knowledge of facts not considered in the reasoned written opinion that would lead a reasonable person to conclude that the transaction is a prohibited tax shelter transaction, the reason to know standard is not met.

Not obtaining a reasoned written opinion of legal counsel does not alone indicate whether a person has reason to know. However, if a transaction is extraordinary for the

110. The conference agreement clarifies that in all cases the 75 percent of proceeds received by the entity that are attributable to the transaction are with respect to the taxable year.

111. Depending on the circumstances, the person who is responsible for determining the pre-selected investment options may be an entity manager under the provision.

entity, promises a return for the organization that is exceptional considering the amount invested by, the participation of, or the absence of risk to the organization, or the transaction is of significant size, either in an absolute sense or relative to the receipts of the entity, then, in general, the presence of such factors may indicate that the entity or entity manager has a responsibility to inquire further about whether a transaction is a prohibited tax shelter transaction, or, absent such inquiry, that the reason to know standard is satisfied. For example, if a tax-exempt entity's investment in a transaction is $1,000, and the entity is promised or expects to receive $10,000 in the near term, in general, the rate of return would be considered exceptional and the entity should make inquiries with respect to the transaction. As another example, if a tax-exempt entity's expected income from a transaction is greater than five percent of the entity's annual receipts, or is in excess of $1,000,000, and the entity fails to make appropriate inquiries with respect to its participation in such transaction, such failure is a factor tending to show that the reason to know standard is met. Appropriate inquiries need not involve obtaining a reasoned written opinion. In general, if a transaction does not present the factors described above and the organization is small (measured by receipts and assets) and described in section 501(c)(3), it is expected that the reason to know standard will not be met.

In general, the conferees intend that in determining whether a tax-exempt entity is a "party" to a prohibited tax shelter transaction all the facts and circumstances should be taken into account. Absence of a written agreement is not determinative. Certain indirect involvement in a prohibited tax shelter transaction would not result in an entity being considered a party to the transaction. For example, investment by a tax-exempt entity in a mutual fund that in turn invests in or participates in a prohibited tax shelter transaction does not, in general, make the tax-exempt entity a party to such transaction, absent facts or circumstances that indicate that the purpose of the tax exempt entity's investment in the mutual fund was specifically to participate in such a transaction. However, whether a tax-exempt entity is a party to such a transaction will be informed by whether the entity or entity manager knew or had reason to know that an investment of the entity would be used in a prohibited tax shelter transaction. Presence of such knowledge or reason to know may indicate that that the purpose of the investment was to participate in the prohibited tax shelter transaction and that the tax-exempt entity is a party to such transaction.

The conference agreement clarifies that a subsequently listed transaction means any transaction to which a tax-exempt entity is a party and which is determined by the Secretary to be a listed transaction at any time after the entity has "become a party to" the transaction, and not, as under the Senate amendment, when the entity "entered into" the transaction. The conference agreement provides that a subsequently listed transaction does not include a transaction that is a prohibited reportable transaction. The conference agreement provides that the Secretary has the authority to allocate proceeds as well as income of a tax-exempt entity to various periods. The conference agreement also provides that the disclosure by tax-exempt entities to the Internal Revenue Service required under the provision is based on an entity's being a party to a prohibited tax shelter transaction and not, as under the Senate amendment, on an entity's "participation" in a prohibited tax shelter transaction. The conference agreement further provides that the Secretary may make a demand for disclosure on any entity manager subject to the tax, as well as on any tax exempt entity, and also provides that such managers and entities and not, as under the Senate amendment, "persons" are subject to the penalty for failure to comply with the demand.

Effective Date

In general, the provision is effective for taxable years ending after the date of enactment, with respect to transactions before, on, or after such date, except that no tax shall apply with respect to income or proceeds that are properly allocable to any period ending on or before the date that is 90 days after the date of enactment. The tax on certain knowing transactions does not apply to any prohibited tax shelter transaction to which a tax-exempt entity became a party on or before the date of enactment. The disclosure provisions apply to disclosures the due date for which are after the date of enactment.

¶ 6000. Act Section Cross Reference Table

Act §	Code §	Topic	Generally effective date	Analysis ¶	Com Rep ¶
101	179(b)(1)	The $100,000 Code Sec. 179 expense election limit, $400,000 phaseout threshold, and inflation adjustments are extended for two years to tax years beginning before Jan. 1, 2010	Tax years beginning after 2007 and before 2010	401	5001
101	179(b)(2)	The $100,000 Code Sec. 179 expense election limit, $400,000 phaseout threshold, and inflation adjustments are extended for two years to tax years beginning before Jan. 1, 2010	Tax years beginning after 2007 and before 2010	401	5001
101	179(b)(5)(A)	The $100,000 Code Sec. 179 expense election limit, $400,000 phaseout threshold, and inflation adjustments are extended for two years to tax years beginning before Jan. 1, 2010	Tax years beginning after 2007 and before 2010	401	5001
101	179(c)(2)	Right to revoke or change the Code Sec. 179 expense election without IRS consent is extended for two years to tax years beginning before Jan. 1, 2010	Tax years beginning after 2007 and before 2010	402	5001
101	179(d)(1)(A)(ii)	Inclusion of off-the-shelf computer software as "section 179 property" eligible for the expensing election is extended for two years to tax years beginning before Jan. 1, 2010	Tax years beginning after 2007 and before 2010	403	5001
102	1(h)(1)(B)	5% and 15% tax rates on adjusted net capital gain are extended for two years	Tax years beginning after Dec. 31, 2008 and before Jan. 1, 2011	101	5002

Act §	Code §	Topic	Generally effective date	Analysis ¶	Com Rep ¶
102	1(h)(1)(B)	Post-2007 0% tax rate on adjusted net capital gains is extended for two years	Tax years beginning after Dec. 31, 2008 and before Jan. 1, 2011	102	5002
102	1(h)(1)(C)	5% and 15% tax rates on adjusted net capital gain are extended for two years	Tax years beginning after Dec. 31, 2008 and before Jan. 1, 2011	101	5002
102	1(h)(11)	5% and 15% adjusted capital gains rates on noncorporate taxpayers' qualified dividend income are extended for two years	Tax years beginning after Dec. 31, 2008 and before Jan. 1, 2011	107	5002
102	1(h)(11)(D)(ii)	Long-term capital loss treatment for individuals' losses on stock to the extent extraordinary dividends were taxed as capital gains is extended for two years	Tax years beginning after Dec. 31, 2008 and before Jan. 1, 2011	108	5002
102	1(h)(3)(B)	5% and 15% adjusted capital gains rates on noncorporate taxpayers' qualified dividend income are extended for two years	Tax years beginning after Dec. 31, 2008 and before Jan. 1, 2011	107	5002
102	1445(e)(1)	15% withholding rate that IRS may impose on USRPI gains passed through to foreign persons by U.S. partnerships, trusts or estates is extended for two years	Tax years beginning after Dec. 31, 2008 and before Jan. 1, 2011	105	5002
102	163(d)(4)(B)	Exclusion of qualified dividend income from investment income for investment interest deduction limit purposes (unless taxpayer elects to include it) is extended for two years	Tax years beginning after Dec. 31, 2008 and before Jan. 1, 2011	109	5002
102	306(a)(1)(D)	Qualified dividend income treatment for ordinary income on disposition of Code Sec. 306 stock extended for two years	Tax years beginning after Dec. 31, 2008 and before Jan. 1, 2011	113	5002

Act §	Code §	Topic	Generally effective date	Analysis ¶	Com Rep ¶
102	55(b)(3)(B)	5% (0% in 2008) and 15% maximum AMT rates on adjusted net capital gain are extended for two years	Tax years beginning after Dec. 31, 2008 and before Jan. 1, 2011	103	5002
102	55(b)(3)(C)	5% (0% in 2008) and 15% maximum AMT rates on adjusted net capital gain are extended for two years	Tax years beginning after Dec. 31, 2008 and before Jan. 1, 2011	103	5002
102	57(a)(7)	7% AMT preference percentage for excluded gain on sale of qualified small business stock is extended for two years	Tax years beginning after Dec. 31, 2008 and before Jan. 1, 2011	104	5002
102	584(c)	Passthrough of qualified dividend income by common trust funds is extended for two years	Tax years beginning after Dec. 31, 2008 and before Jan. 1, 2011	111	5002
102	702(a)(5)	Passthrough of qualified dividend income by partnerships is extended for two years	Tax years beginning after Dec. 31, 2008 and before Jan. 1, 2011	112	5002
102	7518(g)(6)(A)	15% maximum tax rate on individuals' nonqualifying withdrawals from Merchant Marine capital gain accounts of capital construction funds (CCFs) is extended for two years	Tax years beginning after Dec. 31, 2008 and before Jan. 1, 2011	106	5002
102	854(a)	Passthrough of qualified dividend income by RICs and REITs is extended for two years	Tax years beginning after Dec. 31, 2008 and before Jan. 1, 2011	110	5002
102	854(b)(1)(B)	Passthrough of qualified dividend income by RICs and REITs is extended for two years	Tax years beginning after Dec. 31, 2008 and before Jan. 1, 2011	110	5002

Act §	Code §	Topic	Generally effective date	Analysis ¶	Com Rep ¶
102	854(b)(1)(C)	Passthrough of qualified dividend income by RICs and REITs is extended for two years	Tax years beginning after Dec. 31, 2008 and before Jan. 1, 2011	110	5002
102	854(b)(2)	Passthrough of qualified dividend income by RICs and REITs is extended for two years	Tax years beginning after Dec. 31, 2008 and before Jan. 1, 2011	110	5002
102	854(b)(5)	Passthrough of qualified dividend income by RICs and REITs is extended for two years	Tax years beginning after Dec. 31, 2008 and before Jan. 1, 2011	110	5002
102	857(c)(2)	Passthrough of qualified dividend income by RICs and REITs is extended for two years	Tax years beginning after Dec. 31, 2008 and before Jan. 1, 2011	110	5002
102	None	15% maximum tax rate on individuals' nonqualifying withdrawals from Merchant Marine capital gain accounts of capital construction funds (CCFs) is extended for two years	Tax years beginning after Dec. 31, 2008 and before Jan. 1, 2011	106	5002
102	None	15% withholding rate that IRS may impose on USRPI gains passed through to foreign persons by U.S. partnerships, trusts or estates is extended for two years	Tax years beginning after Dec. 31, 2008 and before Jan. 1, 2011	105	5002
102	None	5% (0% in 2008) and 15% maximum AMT rates on adjusted net capital gain are extended for two years	Tax years beginning after Dec. 31, 2008 and before Jan. 1, 2011	103	5002
102	None	5% and 15% adjusted capital gains rates on noncorporate taxpayers' qualified dividend income are extended for two years	Tax years beginning after Dec. 31, 2008 and before Jan. 1, 2011	107	5002

Act §	Code §	Topic	Generally effective date	Analysis ¶	Com Rep ¶
102	None	5% and 15% tax rates on adjusted net capital gain are extended for two years	Tax years beginning after Dec. 31, 2008 and before Jan. 1, 2011	101	5002
102	None	7% AMT preference percentage for excluded gain on sale of qualified small business stock is extended for two years	Tax years beginning after Dec. 31, 2008 and before Jan. 1, 2011	104	5002
102	None	Exclusion of qualified dividend income from investment income for investment interest deduction limit purposes (unless taxpayer elects to include it) is extended for two years	Tax years beginning after Dec. 31, 2008 and before Jan. 1, 2011	109	5002
102	None	Long-term capital loss treatment for individuals' losses on stock to the extent extraordinary dividends were taxed as capital gains is extended for two years	Tax years beginning after Dec. 31, 2008 and before Jan. 1, 2011	108	5002
102	None	Passthrough of qualified dividend income by RICs and REITs is extended for two years	Tax years beginning after Dec. 31, 2008 and before Jan. 1, 2011	110	5002
102	None	Passthrough of qualified dividend income by common trust funds is extended for two years	Tax years beginning after Dec. 31, 2008 and before Jan. 1, 2011	111	5002
102	None	Passthrough of qualified dividend income by partnerships is extended for two years	Tax years beginning after Dec. 31, 2008 and before Jan. 1, 2011	112	5002
102	None	Post-2007 0% tax rate on adjusted net capital gains is extended for two years	Tax years beginning after Dec. 31, 2008 and before Jan. 1, 2011	102	5002

Act §	Code §	Topic	Generally effective date	Analysis ¶	Com Rep ¶
102	None	Qualified dividend income treatment for ordinary income on disposition of Code Sec. 306 stock extended for two years	Tax years beginning after Dec. 31, 2008 and before Jan. 1, 2011	113	5002
103(a)(1)	953(e)(10)	Exceptions under Subpart F for active banking, financing and insurance income expiring in 2007 extended through tax years beginning before 2009	May 17, 2006	601	5003
103(a)(2)	954(h)(9)	Exceptions under Subpart F for active banking, financing and insurance income expiring in 2007 extended through tax years beginning before 2009	May 17, 2006	601	5003
103(b)	954(c)(6)	Payments between related controlled foreign corporations under foreign personal holding company income rules subject to look-through treatment for tax years beginning before 2009	Tax years of foreign corporations beginning after Dec. 31, 2005 and before Jan. 1, 2009 and tax years of U.S. shareholders with or within which such tax years of foreign corporations end	602	5004
201(a)	468B(g)	Certain CERCLA environmental settlement funds established before Jan. 1, 2011 are treated as not subject to federal income tax	Accounts and funds established after May 17, 2006	303	5005
202	355(b)(3)	Code Section 355 definition of active conduct of a trade or business made less restrictive for certain controlled groups—pre-Jan. 1, 2011 distributions	Distributions made after May 17, 2006 and before Jan. 1, 2011	501	5006

Act §	Code §	Topic	Generally effective date	Analysis ¶	Com Rep ¶
203(a)(1)	143(l)(4)	Loans financed with veterans' mortgage bonds issued by Alaska, Oregon, and Wisconsin made available to post-1976 veterans for 25 years after leaving active service	Bonds issued on or after May 17, 2006	904	5007
203(b)(1)	143(l)(3)(B)	New $25 million volume limits on qualified veterans' mortgage bonds issued by Alaska, Oregon, and Wisconsin will be phased in from 2006 to 2009; issuance will terminate after 2010	Allocations of state volume limit after Apr. 5, 2006	903	5007
204(a)	1221(b)(3)	Capital gain treatment is permitted for certain self-created musical works sold or exchanged before Jan. 1, 2011	Sales and exchanges in tax years beginning after May 17, 2006 and before Jan. 1, 2011	208	5008
204(b)	170(e)(1)(A)	Capital gain treatment is permitted for certain self-created musical works sold or exchanged before Jan. 1, 2011	Sales and exchanges in tax years beginning after May 17, 2006 and before Jan. 1, 2011	208	5008
205(a)	1355(a)(4)	Weight limit for qualifying vessels in alternative tonnage tax regime lowered for 2006 through 2010	Tax years beginning after Dec. 31, 2005	305	5009
207(a)	167(g)(8)	Five-year amortization election for expenses of creating or acquiring musical compositions or music copyrights for property placed in service in tax years beginning after Dec. 31, 2005, and before Jan. 1, 2011	Expenses paid or incurred for property placed in service in tax years beginning after Dec. 31, 2005, and before Jan. 1, 2011	405	5011

Act §	Code §	Topic	Generally effective date	Analysis ¶	Com Rep ¶
208(a)	144(a)(4)(G)	Allowance of additional $10 million capital expenditures (i.e., $20 million total maximum) for small issue bonds generally is accelerated to bonds issued after 2006 (instead of Sept. 30, 2009)	May 17, 2006 for bonds issued after Dec. 31, 2006	901	5012
208(b)	144(a)(4)(F)	Allowance of additional $10 million capital expenditures (i.e., $20 million total maximum) for small issue bonds generally is accelerated to bonds issued after 2006 (instead of Sept. 30, 2009)	May 17, 2006 for bonds issued after Dec. 31, 2006	901	5012
209(a)	7872(h)	Dollar cap on below-market loans made to qualified continuing care facilities temporarily eliminated, and other rules temporarily eased, for years 2006 through 2010	Calendar years beginning after 2005	207	5013
209(b)(1)	7872(g)(6)	Dollar cap on below-market loans made to qualified continuing care facilities temporarily eliminated, and other rules temporarily eased, for years 2006 through 2010	Calendar years beginning after 2005	207	5013
301(a)(1)	55(d)(1)(A)	AMT exemption amounts for 2006 are increased to $42,500 (from $33,750) for unmarrieds, to $62,550 (from $45,000) for joint filers, and to $31,275 (from $22,500) for marrieds filing separately	Tax years beginning in 2006	201	5015
301(a)(2)	55(d)(1)(B)	AMT exemption amounts for 2006 are increased to $42,500 (from $33,750) for unmarrieds, to $62,550 (from $45,000) for joint filers, and to $31,275 (from $22,500) for marrieds filing separately	Tax years beginning in 2006	201	5015

Act §	Code §	Topic	Generally effective date	Analysis ¶	Com Rep ¶
302(a)(2)	1400C(d)	Nonrefundable personal credits may offset AMT through 2006 (instead of 2005)	Tax years beginning after Dec. 31, 2005 and before Jan. 1, 2007	202	5016
302(a)(2)	23(b)(4)	Nonrefundable personal credits may offset AMT through 2006 (instead of 2005)	Tax years beginning after Dec. 31, 2005 and before Jan. 1, 2007	202	5016
302(a)(2)	24(b)(3)	Nonrefundable personal credits may offset AMT through 2006 (instead of 2005)	Tax years beginning after Dec. 31, 2005 and before Jan. 1, 2007	202	5016
302(a)(2)	25(e)(1)(C)	Nonrefundable personal credits may offset AMT through 2006 (instead of 2005)	Tax years beginning after Dec. 31, 2005 and before Jan. 1, 2007	202	5016
302(a)(2)	25B(g)	Nonrefundable personal credits may offset AMT through 2006 (instead of 2005)	Tax years beginning after Dec. 31, 2005 and before Jan. 1, 2007	202	5016
302(a)(2)	25D(c)(2)	Nonrefundable personal credits may offset AMT through 2006 (instead of 2005)	Tax years beginning after Dec. 31, 2005 and before Jan. 1, 2007	202	5016
302(a)(2)	26(a)(2)	Nonrefundable personal credits may offset AMT through 2006 (instead of 2005)	Tax years beginning after Dec. 31, 2005 and before Jan. 1, 2007	202	5016
302(a)(2)	904(h)	Nonrefundable personal credits may offset AMT through 2006 (instead of 2005)	Tax years beginning after Dec. 31, 2005 and before Jan. 1, 2007	202	5016

Act §	Code §	Topic	Generally effective date	Analysis ¶	Com Rep ¶
401	6655	Percentages and due dates of otherwise required estimated tax payments due from corporations are changed for some installment due dates in 2006, and 2010 to 2013	May 17, 2006	803	5018
501(a)	163(j)(8)	Earnings-stripping rules are applied to corporate partners	Tax years beginning on or after May 17, 2006	503	5020
501(b)	163(j)(9)(D)	Earnings-stripping rules are applied to corporate partners	Tax years beginning on or after May 17, 2006	503	5020
502(a)	6049(b)(2)(B)	Tax-exempt interest is subject to information reporting in the same manner as interest paid on taxable obligations	Interest paid after Dec. 31, 2005	801	5021
503(a)	167(h)(5)	Major integrated oil companies must use 5-year amortization for geological and geophysical expenditures	Amounts paid or incurred after May 17, 2006	404	5022
504(a)	897(h)(4)(A)(i)(II)	Qualified investment entity FIRPTA exclusion is amended	After Dec. 31, 2004	603	5023, 5024
505(a)(1)	897(h)(1)	Qualified investment entity FIRPTA exclusion is amended	Tax years of qualified investment entities beginning after Dec. 31, 2005	603	5023, 5024
505(a)(2)	897(h)(4)(A)(ii)	Qualified investment entity FIRPTA exclusion is amended	Tax years of qualified investment entities beginning after Dec. 31, 2005	603	5023, 5024
505(b)	1445(e)(6)	Qualified investment entity FIRPTA exclusion is amended	Tax years of qualified investment entities beginning after Dec. 31, 2005	603	5023, 5024

Act §	Code §	Topic	Generally effective date	Analysis ¶	Com Rep ¶
505(c)(1)	852(b)(3)(E)	Qualified investment entity FIRPTA exclusion is amended	Tax years of qualified investment entities beginning after Dec. 31, 2005	603	5023, 5024
505(c)(2)	871(k)(2)(E)	Qualified investment entity FIRPTA exclusion is amended	Tax years of qualified investment entities beginning after Dec. 31, 2005	603	5023, 5024
506(a)	897(h)(5)	Certain wash sales of interests in domestically controlled qualified investment entities result in gain recognition under FIRPTA	Tax years beginning after Dec. 31, 2005	604	5024
506(b)	1445(b)(8)	Certain wash sales of interests in domestically controlled qualified investment entities result in gain recognition under FIRPTA	Tax years beginning after Dec. 31, 2005	604	5024
507(a)	355(g)	Distribution can't qualify as a Code Sec. 355 corporate division if the distributing corporation or the controlled corporation is a disqualified investment corporation	Distributions after May 17, 2006	502	5025
508(a)	149(f)(2)(A)	Pooled financing bonds must meet requirements relating to loan origination, written loan commitments, and redemptions, and are counted in applying small issuer exception to arbitrage rebate requirements	Bonds issued after May 17, 2006	902	5026

Act §	Code §	Topic	Generally effective date	Analysis ¶	Com Rep ¶
508(b)	149(f)(4)	Pooled financing bonds must meet requirements relating to loan origination, written loan commitments, and redemptions, and are counted in applying small issuer exception to arbitrage rebate requirements	Bonds issued after May 17, 2006	902	5026
508(b)	149(f)(5)	Pooled financing bonds must meet requirements relating to loan origination, written loan commitments, and redemptions, and are counted in applying small issuer exception to arbitrage rebate requirements	Bonds issued after May 17, 2006	902	5026
508(c)	148(f)(4)(D)(ii)	Pooled financing bonds must meet requirements relating to loan origination, written loan commitments, and redemptions, and are counted in applying small issuer exception to arbitrage rebate requirements	Bonds issued after May 17, 2006	902	5026
508(d)(1)	149(f)(1)	Pooled financing bonds must meet requirements relating to loan origination, written loan commitments, and redemptions, and are counted in applying small issuer exception to arbitrage rebate requirements	Bonds issued after May 17, 2006	902	5026
509	7122(c)(3)	Partial payments are required with submissions of offers in compromise; offers are deemed accepted if not rejected within a certain period	Offers in compromise submitted on and after the date that is 60 days after May 17, 2006	804	5027

Act §	Code §	Topic	Generally effective date	Analysis ¶	Com Rep ¶
509(a)	7122(c)	Partial payments are required with submissions of offers in compromise; offers are deemed accepted if not rejected within a certain period	Offers in compromise submitted on and after the date that is 60 days after May 17, 2006	804	5027
509(b)(2)	7122(f)	Partial payments are required with submissions of offers in compromise; offers are deemed accepted if not rejected within a certain period	Offers in compromise submitted on and after the date that is 60 days after May 17, 2006	804	5027
510(a)	1(g)(2)(A)	Unearned income of children under age 18 (instead of under age 14) is subject to kiddie tax	Tax years beginning after Dec. 31, 2005	204	5028
510(b)	1(g)(4)(C)	Distributions from certain qualified disability trusts are excepted from kiddie tax	Tax years beginning after Dec. 31, 2005	205	5028
510(c)	1(g)(2)(C)	Unearned income of children under age 18 (instead of under age 14) is subject to kiddie tax	Tax years beginning after Dec. 31, 2005	204	5028
511(a)	3402(t)	Government entities will have to report and withhold income tax on certain payments made after 2010	For payments made after Dec. 31, 2010	802	5029
512(a)(1)	408A(c)(3)(B)	AGI limit on conversion of non-Roth IRAs to Roth IRAs is eliminated; income from conversion can be deferred and spread over two years—after 2009	For tax years beginning after Dec. 31, 2009	203	5030
512(b)(1)	408A(d)(3)(A)(iii)	AGI limit on conversion of non-Roth IRAs to Roth IRAs is eliminated; income from conversion can be deferred and spread over two years—after 2009	For tax years beginning after Dec. 31, 2009	203	5030

Act §	Code §	Topic	Generally effective date	Analysis ¶	Com Rep ¶
512(b)(2)(A)	408A(d)(3)(E)(i)	AGI limit on conversion of non-Roth IRAs to Roth IRAs is eliminated; income from conversion can be deferred and spread over two years—after 2009	For tax years beginning after Dec. 31, 2009	203	5030
513	None	FSC and ETI binding contract transition rules repealed	Tax years beginning after May 17, 2006	304	5031
514(a)	199(b)(2)(B)	Only wages allocable to domestic production gross receipts may be taken into account in determining 50%-of-W-2-wages limitation on U.S. production activities deduction	Tax years beginning after May 17, 2006	301	5032
514(b)(1)	199(d)(1)(A)(iii)	Special rule for computing a partner's or S corporation shareholder's W-2 wages for purposes of the 50%-of-W-2-wages limitation on U.S. production activities deduction is repealed	Tax years beginning after May 17, 2006	302	5032
515(a)	911(b)(2)(D)(ii)	Foreign earned income exclusion amended	Tax years beginning after Dec. 31, 2005	206	5033
515(b)(1)	911(c)(1)(B)(i)	Foreign earned income exclusion amended	Tax years beginning after Dec. 31, 2005	206	5033
515(b)(2)(A)	911(c)(1)(A)	Foreign earned income exclusion amended	Tax years beginning after Dec. 31, 2005	206	5033
515(b)(2)(B)	911(c)(2)	Foreign earned income exclusion amended	Tax years beginning after Dec. 31, 2005	206	5033
515(c)	911(f)	Foreign earned income exclusion amended	Tax years beginning after Dec. 31, 2005	206	5033

Act §	Code §	Topic	Generally effective date	Analysis ¶	Com Rep ¶
516(a)	4965	Excise tax is imposed on tax-exempt entities that are parties to prohibited tax shelter transactions, and on entity managers who knowingly approve prohibited tax shelter transactions	Tax years ending after May 17, 2006	701	5034
516(b)(1)(A)	6033(a)(2)	Tax-exempt entities must disclose participation in prohibited tax shelter transactions to IRS	Disclosures the due date for which is after May 17, 2006	702	5034
516(b)(2)	6011(g)	Taxable parties to a prohibited tax shelter transaction must disclose that tax shelter status to any tax-exempt entity that is a party to the transaction	Disclosures the due date for which is after May 17, 2006	703	5034
516(c)	6652(c)	$100 per day penalties imposed where exempt organizations fail to make required disclosures to IRS relating to prohibited tax shelter transactions	Disclosures the due date for which is after May 17, 2006	704	5034

¶ 6001. Code Section Cross Reference Table

Code §	Act §	Topic	Generally effective date	Analysis ¶	Com Rep ¶
1(g)(2)(A)	510(a)	Unearned income of children under age 18 (instead of under age 14) is subject to kiddie tax	Tax years beginning after Dec. 31, 2005	204	5028
1(g)(2)(C)	510(c)	Unearned income of children under age 18 (instead of under age 14) is subject to kiddie tax	Tax years beginning after Dec. 31, 2005	204	5028
1(g)(4)(C)	510(b)	Distributions from certain qualified disability trusts are excepted from kiddie tax	Tax years beginning after Dec. 31, 2005	205	5028
1(h)(1)(B)	102	5% and 15% tax rates on adjusted net capital gain are extended for two years	Tax years beginning after Dec. 31, 2008 and before Jan. 1, 2011	101	5002
1(h)(1)(B)	102	Post-2007 0% tax rate on adjusted net capital gains is extended for two years	Tax years beginning after Dec. 31, 2008 and before Jan. 1, 2011	102	5002
1(h)(1)(C)	102	5% and 15% tax rates on adjusted net capital gain are extended for two years	Tax years beginning after Dec. 31, 2008 and before Jan. 1, 2011	101	5002
1(h)(3)(B)	102	5% and 15% adjusted capital gains rates on noncorporate taxpayers' qualified dividend income are extended for two years	Tax years beginning after Dec. 31, 2008 and before Jan. 1, 2011	107	5002
1(h)(11)	102	5% and 15% adjusted capital gains rates on noncorporate taxpayers' qualified dividend income are extended for two years	Tax years beginning after Dec. 31, 2008 and before Jan. 1, 2011	107	5002
1(h)(11)(D)(ii)	102	Long-term capital loss treatment for individuals' losses on stock to the extent extraordinary dividends were taxed as capital gains is extended for two years	Tax years beginning after Dec. 31, 2008 and before Jan. 1, 2011	108	5002

Code §	Act §	Topic	Generally effective date	Analysis ¶	Com Rep ¶
23(b)(4)	302(a)(2)	Nonrefundable personal credits may offset AMT through 2006 (instead of 2005)	Tax years beginning after Dec. 31, 2005 and before Jan. 1, 2007	202	5016
24(b)(3)	302(a)(2)	Nonrefundable personal credits may offset AMT through 2006 (instead of 2005)	Tax years beginning after Dec. 31, 2005 and before Jan. 1, 2007	202	5016
25(e)(1)(C)	302(a)(2)	Nonrefundable personal credits may offset AMT through 2006 (instead of 2005)	Tax years beginning after Dec. 31, 2005 and before Jan. 1, 2007	202	5016
25B(g)	302(a)(2)	Nonrefundable personal credits may offset AMT through 2006 (instead of 2005)	Tax years beginning after Dec. 31, 2005 and before Jan. 1, 2007	202	5016
25D(c)(2)	302(a)(2)	Nonrefundable personal credits may offset AMT through 2006 (instead of 2005)	Tax years beginning after Dec. 31, 2005 and before Jan. 1, 2007	202	5016
26(a)(2)	302(a)(2)	Nonrefundable personal credits may offset AMT through 2006 (instead of 2005)	Tax years beginning after Dec. 31, 2005 and before Jan. 1, 2007	202	5016
55(b)(3)(B)	102	5% (0% in 2008) and 15% maximum AMT rates on adjusted net capital gain are extended for two years	Tax years beginning after Dec. 31, 2008 and before Jan. 1, 2011	103	5002
55(b)(3)(C)	102	5% (0% in 2008) and 15% maximum AMT rates on adjusted net capital gain are extended for two years	Tax years beginning after Dec. 31, 2008 and before Jan. 1, 2011	103	5002
55(d)(1)(A)	301(a)(1)	AMT exemption amounts for 2006 are increased to $42,500 (from $33,750) for unmarrieds, to $62,550 (from $45,000) for joint filers, and to $31,275 (from $22,500) for marrieds filing separately	Tax years beginning in 2006	201	5015

Code §	Act §	Topic	Generally effective date	Analysis ¶	Com Rep ¶
55(d)(1)(B)	301(a)(2)	AMT exemption amounts for 2006 are increased to $42,500 (from $33,750) for unmarrieds, to $62,550 (from $45,000) for joint filers, and to $31,275 (from $22,500) for marrieds filing separately	Tax years beginning in 2006	201	5015
57(a)(7)	102	7% AMT preference percentage for excluded gain on sale of qualified small business stock is extended for two years	Tax years beginning after Dec. 31, 2008 and before Jan. 1, 2011	104	5002
143(l)(3)(B)	203(b)(1)	New $25 million volume limits on qualified veterans' mortgage bonds issued by Alaska, Oregon, and Wisconsin will be phased in from 2006 to 2009; issuance will terminate after 2010	Allocations of state volume limit after Apr. 5, 2006	903	5007
143(l)(4)	203(a)(1)	Loans financed with veterans' mortgage bonds issued by Alaska, Oregon, and Wisconsin made available to post-1976 veterans for 25 years after leaving active service	Bonds issued on or after May 17, 2006	904	5007
144(a)(4)(F)	208(b)	Allowance of additional $10 million capital expenditures (i.e., $20 million total maximum) for small issue bonds generally is accelerated to bonds issued after 2006 (instead of Sept. 30, 2009)	May 17, 2006 for bonds issued after Dec. 31, 2006	901	5012
144(a)(4)(G)	208(a)	Allowance of additional $10 million capital expenditures (i.e., $20 million total maximum) for small issue bonds generally is accelerated to bonds issued after 2006 (instead of Sept. 30, 2009)	May 17, 2006 for bonds issued after Dec. 31, 2006	901	5012

Code §	Act §	Topic	Generally effective date	Analysis ¶	Com Rep ¶
148(f)(4)(D)(ii)	508(c)	Pooled financing bonds must meet requirements relating to loan origination, written loan commitments, and redemptions, and are counted in applying small issuer exception to arbitrage rebate requirements	Bonds issued after May 17, 2006	902	5026
149(f)(1)	508(d)(1)	Pooled financing bonds must meet requirements relating to loan origination, written loan commitments, and redemptions, and are counted in applying small issuer exception to arbitrage rebate requirements	Bonds issued after May 17, 2006	902	5026
149(f)(2)(A)	508(a)	Pooled financing bonds must meet requirements relating to loan origination, written loan commitments, and redemptions, and are counted in applying small issuer exception to arbitrage rebate requirements	Bonds issued after May 17, 2006	902	5026
149(f)(4)	508(b)	Pooled financing bonds must meet requirements relating to loan origination, written loan commitments, and redemptions, and are counted in applying small issuer exception to arbitrage rebate requirements	Bonds issued after May 17, 2006	902	5026
149(f)(5)	508(b)	Pooled financing bonds must meet requirements relating to loan origination, written loan commitments, and redemptions, and are counted in applying small issuer exception to arbitrage rebate requirements	Bonds issued after May 17, 2006	902	5026

Code §	Act §	Topic	Generally effective date	Analysis ¶	Com Rep ¶
163(d)(4)(B)	102	Exclusion of qualified dividend income from investment income for investment interest deduction limit purposes (unless taxpayer elects to include it) is extended for two years	Tax years beginning after Dec. 31, 2008 and before Jan. 1, 2011	109	5002
163(j)(8)	501(a)	Earnings-stripping rules are applied to corporate partners	Tax years beginning on or after May 17, 2006	503	5020
163(j)(9)(D)	501(b)	Earnings-stripping rules are applied to corporate partners	Tax years beginning on or after May 17, 2006	503	5020
167(g)(8)	207(a)	Five-year amortization election for expenses of creating or acquiring musical compositions or music copyrights for property placed in service in tax years beginning after Dec. 31, 2005, and before Jan. 1, 2011	Expenses paid or incurred for property placed in service in tax years beginning after Dec. 31, 2005, and before Jan. 1, 2011	405	5011
167(h)(5)	503(a)	Major integrated oil companies must use 5-year amortization for geological and geophysical expenditures	Amounts paid or incurred after May 17, 2006	404	5022
170(e)(1)(A)	204(b)	Capital gain treatment is permitted for certain self-created musical works sold or exchanged before Jan. 1, 2011	Sales and exchanges in tax years beginning after May 17, 2006 and before Jan. 1, 2011	208	5008
179(b)(1)	101	The $100,000 Code Sec. 179 expense election limit, $400,000 phaseout threshold, and inflation adjustments are extended for two years to tax years beginning before Jan. 1, 2010	Tax years beginning after 2007 and before 2010	401	5001

Code §	Act §	Topic	Generally effective date	Analysis ¶	Com Rep ¶
179(b)(2)	101	The $100,000 Code Sec. 179 expense election limit, $400,000 phaseout threshold, and inflation adjustments are extended for two years to tax years beginning before Jan. 1, 2010	Tax years beginning after 2007 and before 2010	401	5001
179(b)(5)(A)	101	The $100,000 Code Sec. 179 expense election limit, $400,000 phaseout threshold, and inflation adjustments are extended for two years to tax years beginning before Jan. 1, 2010	Tax years beginning after 2007 and before 2010	401	5001
179(c)(2)	101	Right to revoke or change the Code Sec. 179 expense election without IRS consent is extended for two years to tax years beginning before Jan. 1, 2010	Tax years beginning after 2007 and before 2010	402	5001
179(d)(1)(A)(ii)	101	Inclusion of off-the-shelf computer software as "section 179 property" eligible for the expensing election is extended for two years to tax years beginning before Jan. 1, 2010	Tax years beginning after 2007 and before 2010	403	5001
199(b)(2)(B)	514(a)	Only wages allocable to domestic production gross receipts may be taken into account in determining 50%-of-W-2-wages limitation on U.S. production activities deduction	Tax years beginning after May 17, 2006	301	5032
199(d)(1)(A)(iii)	514(b)(1)	Special rule for computing a partner's or S corporation shareholder's W-2 wages for purposes of the 50%-of-W-2-wages limitation on U.S. production activities deduction is repealed	Tax years beginning after May 17, 2006	302	5032

Code §	Act §	Topic	Generally effective date	Analysis ¶	Com Rep ¶
306(a)(1)(D)	102	Qualified dividend income treatment for ordinary income on disposition of Code Sec. 306 stock extended for two years	Tax years beginning after Dec. 31, 2008 and before Jan. 1, 2011	113	5002
355(b)(3)	202	Code Section 355 definition of active conduct of a trade or business made less restrictive for certain controlled groups—pre-Jan. 1, 2011 distributions	Distributions made after May 17, 2006 and before Jan. 1, 2011	501	5006
355(g)	507(a)	Distribution can't qualify as a Code Sec. 355 corporate division if the distributing corporation or the controlled corporation is a disqualified investment corporation	Distributions after May 17, 2006	502	5025
408A(c)(3)(B)	512(a)(1)	AGI limit on conversion of non-Roth IRAs to Roth IRAs is eliminated; income from conversion can be deferred and spread over two years—after 2009	For tax years beginning after Dec. 31, 2009	203	5030
408A(d)(3)(A)(iii)	512(b)(1)	AGI limit on conversion of non-Roth IRAs to Roth IRAs is eliminated; income from conversion can be deferred and spread over two years—after 2009	For tax years beginning after Dec. 31, 2009	203	5030
408A(d)(3)(E)(i)	512(b)(2)(A)	AGI limit on conversion of non-Roth IRAs to Roth IRAs is eliminated; income from conversion can be deferred and spread over two years—after 2009	For tax years beginning after Dec. 31, 2009	203	5030
468B(g)	201(a)	Certain CERCLA environmental settlement funds established before Jan. 1, 2011 are treated as not subject to federal income tax	Accounts and funds established after May 17, 2006	303	5005

Code §	Act §	Topic	Generally effective date	Analysis ¶	Com Rep ¶
584(c)	102	Passthrough of qualified dividend income by common trust funds is extended for two years	Tax years beginning after Dec. 31, 2008 and before Jan. 1, 2011	111	5002
702(a)(5)	102	Passthrough of qualified dividend income by partnerships is extended for two years	Tax years beginning after Dec. 31, 2008 and before Jan. 1, 2011	112	5002
852(b)(3)(E)	505(c)(1)	Qualified investment entity FIRPTA exclusion is amended	Tax years of qualified investment entities beginning after Dec. 31, 2005	603	5023, 5024
854(a)	102	Passthrough of qualified dividend income by RICs and REITs is extended for two years	Tax years beginning after Dec. 31, 2008 and before Jan. 1, 2011	110	5002
854(b)(1)(B)	102	Passthrough of qualified dividend income by RICs and REITs is extended for two years	Tax years beginning after Dec. 31, 2008 and before Jan. 1, 2011	110	5002
854(b)(1)(C)	102	Passthrough of qualified dividend income by RICs and REITs is extended for two years	Tax years beginning after Dec. 31, 2008 and before Jan. 1, 2011	110	5002
854(b)(2)	102	Passthrough of qualified dividend income by RICs and REITs is extended for two years	Tax years beginning after Dec. 31, 2008 and before Jan. 1, 2011	110	5002
854(b)(5)	102	Passthrough of qualified dividend income by RICs and REITs is extended for two years	Tax years beginning after Dec. 31, 2008 and before Jan. 1, 2011	110	5002
857(c)(2)	102	Passthrough of qualified dividend income by RICs and REITs is extended for two years	Tax years beginning after Dec. 31, 2008 and before Jan. 1, 2011	110	5002

Code §	Act §	Topic	Generally effective date	Analysis ¶	Com Rep ¶
871(k)(2)(E)	505(c)(2)	Qualified investment entity FIRPTA exclusion is amended	Tax years of qualified investment entities beginning after Dec. 31, 2005	603	5023, 5024
897(h)(1)	505(a)(1)	Qualified investment entity FIRPTA exclusion is amended	Tax years of qualified investment entities beginning after Dec. 31, 2005	603	5023, 5024
897(h)(4)(A)(i)(II)	504(a)	Qualified investment entity FIRPTA exclusion is amended	After Dec. 31, 2004	603	5023, 5024
897(h)(4)(A)(ii)	505(a)(2)	Qualified investment entity FIRPTA exclusion is amended	Tax years of qualified investment entities beginning after Dec. 31, 2005	603	5023, 5024
897(h)(5)	506(a)	Certain wash sales of interests in domestically controlled qualified investment entities result in gain recognition under FIRPTA	Tax years beginning after Dec. 31, 2005	604	5024
904(h)	302(a)(2)	Nonrefundable personal credits may offset AMT through 2006 (instead of 2005)	Tax years beginning after Dec. 31, 2005 and before Jan. 1, 2007	202	5016
911(b)(2)(D)(ii)	515(a)	Foreign earned income exclusion amended	Tax years beginning after Dec. 31, 2005	206	5033
911(c)(1)(A)	515(b)(2)(A)	Foreign earned income exclusion amended	Tax years beginning after Dec. 31, 2005	206	5033
911(c)(1)(B)(i)	515(b)(1)	Foreign earned income exclusion amended	Tax years beginning after Dec. 31, 2005	206	5033
911(c)(2)	515(b)(2)(B)	Foreign earned income exclusion amended	Tax years beginning after Dec. 31, 2005	206	5033
911(f)	515(c)	Foreign earned income exclusion amended	Tax years beginning after Dec. 31, 2005	206	5033

Code §	Act §	Topic	Generally effective date	Analysis ¶	Com Rep ¶
953(e)(10)	103(a)(1)	Exceptions under Subpart F for active banking, financing and insurance income expiring in 2007 extended through tax years beginning before 2009	May 17, 2006	601	5003
954(c)(6)	103(b)	Payments between related controlled foreign corporations under foreign personal holding company income rules subject to look-through treatment for tax years beginning before 2009	Tax years of foreign corporations beginning after Dec. 31, 2005 and before Jan. 1, 2009 and tax years of U.S. shareholders with or within which such tax years of foreign corporations end	602	5004
954(h)(9)	103(a)(2)	Exceptions under Subpart F for active banking, financing and insurance income expiring in 2007 extended through tax years beginning before 2009	May 17, 2006	601	5003
1221(b)(3)	204(a)	Capital gain treatment is permitted for certain self-created musical works sold or exchanged before Jan. 1, 2011	Sales and exchanges in tax years beginning after May 17, 2006 and before Jan. 1, 2011	208	5008
1355(a)(4)	205(a)	Weight limit for qualifying vessels in alternative tonnage tax regime lowered for 2006 through 2010	Tax years beginning after Dec. 31, 2005	305	5009
1400C(d)	302(a)(2)	Nonrefundable personal credits may offset AMT through 2006 (instead of 2005)	Tax years beginning after Dec. 31, 2005 and before Jan. 1, 2007	202	5016

Code §	Act §	Topic	Generally effective date	Analysis ¶	Com Rep ¶
1445(b)(8)	506(b)	Certain wash sales of interests in domestically controlled qualified investment entities result in gain recognition under FIRPTA	Tax years beginning after Dec. 31, 2005	604	5024
1445(e)(1)	102	15% withholding rate that IRS may impose on USRPI gains passed through to foreign persons by U.S. partnerships, trusts or estates is extended for two years	Tax years beginning after Dec. 31, 2008 and before Jan. 1, 2011	105	5002
1445(e)(6)	505(b)	Qualified investment entity FIRPTA exclusion is amended	Tax years of qualified investment entities beginning after Dec. 31, 2005	603	5023, 5024
3402(t)	511(a)	Government entities will have to report and withhold income tax on certain payments made after 2010	For payments made after Dec. 31, 2010	802	5029
4965	516(a)	Excise tax is imposed on tax-exempt entities that are parties to prohibited tax shelter transactions, and on entity managers who knowingly approve prohibited tax shelter transactions	Tax years ending after May 17, 2006	701	5034
6011(g)	516(b)(2)	Taxable parties to a prohibited tax shelter transaction must disclose that tax shelter status to any tax-exempt entity that is a party to the transaction	Disclosures the due date for which is after May 17, 2006	703	5034
6033(a)(2)	516(b)(1)(A)	Tax-exempt entities must disclose participation in prohibited tax shelter transactions to IRS	Disclosures the due date for which is after May 17, 2006	702	5034
6049(b)(2)(B)	502(a)	Tax-exempt interest is subject to information reporting in the same manner as interest paid on taxable obligations	Interest paid after Dec. 31, 2005	801	5021

Code §	Act §	Topic	Generally effective date	Analysis ¶	Com Rep ¶
6652(c)	516(c)	$100 per day penalties imposed where exempt organizations fail to make required disclosures to IRS relating to prohibited tax shelter transactions	Disclosures the due date for which is after May 17, 2006	704	5034
6655	401	Percentages and due dates of otherwise required estimated tax payments due from corporations are changed for some installment due dates in 2006, and 2010 to 2013	May 17, 2006	803	5018
7122(c)	509(a)	Partial payments are required with submissions of offers in compromise; offers are deemed accepted if not rejected within a certain period	Offers in compromise submitted on and after the date that is 60 days after May 17, 2006	804	5027
7122(c)(3)(C)	509(b)(1)	Partial payments are required with submissions of offers in compromise; offers are deemed accepted if not rejected within a certain period	Offers in compromise submitted on and after the date that is 60 days after May 17, 2006	804	5027
7122(f)	509(b)(2)	Partial payments are required with submissions of offers in compromise; offers are deemed accepted if not rejected within a certain period	Offers in compromise submitted on and after the date that is 60 days after May 17, 2006	804	5027
7518(g)(6)(A)	102	15% maximum tax rate on individuals' nonqualifying withdrawals from Merchant Marine capital gain accounts of capital construction funds (CCFs) is extended for two years	Tax years beginning after Dec. 31, 2008 and before Jan. 1, 2011	106	5002

Code §	Act §	Topic	Generally effective date	Analysis ¶	Com Rep ¶
7872(g)(6)	209(b)(1)	Dollar cap on below-market loans made to qualified continuing care facilities temporarily eliminated, and other rules temporarily eased, for years 2006 through 2010	Calendar years beginning after 2005	207	5013
7872(h)	209(a)	Dollar cap on below-market loans made to qualified continuing care facilities temporarily eliminated, and other rules temporarily eased, for years 2006 through 2010	Calendar years beginning after 2005	207	5013
None	102	15% maximum tax rate on individuals' nonqualifying withdrawals from Merchant Marine capital gain accounts of capital construction funds (CCFs) is extended for two years	Tax years beginning after Dec. 31, 2008 and before Jan. 1, 2011	106	5002
None	102	15% withholding rate that IRS may impose on USRPI gains passed through to foreign persons by U.S. partnerships, trusts or estates is extended for two years	Tax years beginning after Dec. 31, 2008 and before Jan. 1, 2011	105	5002
None	102	5% (0% in 2008) and 15% maximum AMT rates on adjusted net capital gain are extended for two years	Tax years beginning after Dec. 31, 2008 and before Jan. 1, 2011	103	5002
None	102	5% and 15% adjusted capital gains rates on noncorporate taxpayers' qualified dividend income are extended for two years	Tax years beginning after Dec. 31, 2008 and before Jan. 1, 2011	107	5002
None	102	5% and 15% tax rates on adjusted net capital gain are extended for two years	Tax years beginning after Dec. 31, 2008 and before Jan. 1, 2011	101	5002

Code §	Act §	Topic	Generally effective date	Analysis ¶	Com Rep ¶
None	102	7% AMT preference percentage for excluded gain on sale of qualified small business stock is extended for two years	Tax years beginning after Dec. 31, 2008 and before Jan. 1, 2011	104	5002
None	102	Exclusion of qualified dividend income from investment income for investment interest deduction limit purposes (unless taxpayer elects to include it) is extended for two years	Tax years beginning after Dec. 31, 2008 and before Jan. 1, 2011	109	5002
None	102	Long-term capital loss treatment for individuals' losses on stock to the extent extraordinary dividends were taxed as capital gains is extended for two years	Tax years beginning after Dec. 31, 2008 and before Jan. 1, 2011	108	5002
None	102	Passthrough of qualified dividend income by RICs and REITs is extended for two years	Tax years beginning after Dec. 31, 2008 and before Jan. 1, 2011	110	5002
None	102	Passthrough of qualified dividend income by common trust funds is extended for two years	Tax years beginning after Dec. 31, 2008 and before Jan. 1, 2011	111	5002
None	102	Passthrough of qualified dividend income by partnerships is extended for two years	Tax years beginning after Dec. 31, 2008 and before Jan. 1, 2011	112	5002
None	102	Post-2007 0% tax rate on adjusted net capital gains is extended for two years	Tax years beginning after Dec. 31, 2008 and before Jan. 1, 2011	102	5002
None	102	Qualified dividend income treatment for ordinary income on disposition of Code Sec. 306 stock extended for two years	Tax years beginning after Dec. 31, 2008 and before Jan. 1, 2011	113	5002
None	513	FSC and ETI binding contract transition rules repealed	Tax years beginning after May 17, 2006	304	5031

¶ 6002. Code Sections Amended by Act

Code Sec.	Act Sec.	Code Sec.	Act Sec.
1(g)(2)(A)	510(a)	149(f)(7)(B)	508(d)(2)
1(g)(2)(A)	510(c)	163(j)(8)	501(a)
1(g)(2)(B)	510(c)	163(j)(9)	501(a)
1(g)(2)(C)	510(c)	163(j)(9)(B)	501(b)
1(g)(4)(C)	510(b)	163(j)(9)(C)	501(b)
26(a)(2)	302(a)(1)	163(j)(9)(D)	501(b)
26(a)(2)	302(a)(2)	167(h)(5)	503(a)
54(l)(2)	508(d)(3)	170(e)(1)(A)	204(b)
55(d)(1)(A)	301(a)(1)	179(b)(1)	101
55(d)(1)(B)	301(a)(2)	179(b)(2)	101
142(d)(2)(B)	209(b)(2)	179(b)(5)	101
143(l)(3)(B)	203(b)(1)(B)	179(c)(2)	101
143(l)(3)(B)(i)(I)	203(b)(1)(A)	179(d)(1)(A)(ii)	101
143(l)(3)(B)(i)(II)	203(b)(1)(A)	199(a)(2)	514(b)(2)
143(l)(3)(B)(ii)	203(b)(1)(C)	199(b)(2)	514(a)
143(l)(3)(B)(iii)	203(b)(1)(C)	199(d)(1)(A)(iii)	514(b)(1)
143(l)(3)(B)(iv)	203(b)(1)(C)	355(b)(3)	202
143(l)(4)	203(a)(1)	355(g)	507(a)
144(a)(4)(F)	208(b)	408A(c)(3)(B)	512(a)(1)
144(a)(4)(G)	208(a)	408A(c)(3)(B)(i)	512(a)(2)
148(f)(4)(D)(ii)(II)	508(c)	408A(c)(3)(C)	512(a)(1)
148(f)(4)(D)(ii)(III)	508(c)	408A(d)(3)(A)(iii)	512(b)(1)
149(f)(1)	508(d)(1)	408A(d)(3)(E)	512(b)(2)(B)
149(f)(2)(A)	508(a)	408A(d)(3)(E)(i)	512(b)(2)(A)
149(f)(4)	508(b)	468B(g)	201(a)
149(f)(5)	508(b)	852(b)(3)(E)	505(c)(1)
149(f)(6)	508(b)	871(k)(2)(E)	505(c)(2)
149(f)(7)	508(b)	897(h)(1)	505(a)(1)(A)

Code Sec.	Act Sec.	Code Sec.	Act Sec.
897(h)(1)	505(a)(1)(B)	167(g)(8)	207(a)
897(h)(1)	505(a)(1)(C)	3402(t)	511(a)
897(h)(4)(A)(i)(II)	504(a)	4965	516(a)(1)
897(h)(4)(A)(ii)	505(a)(2)	6011(g)	516(b)(2)
897(h)(5)	506(a)	6011(h)	516(b)(2)
911(b)(2)(D)(ii)	515(a)(1)	6033(a)(1)	516(b)(1)(B)
911(b)(2)(D)(ii)	515(a)(2)	6033(a)(2)	516(b)(1)(A)
911(c)(1)(A)	515(b)(2)(A)	6033(a)(3)	516(b)(1)(A)
911(c)(1)(B)(i)	515(b)(1)	6049(b)(2)(B)	502(a)
911(c)(2)	515(b)(2)(B)	6049(b)(2)(C)	502(a)
911(c)(3)	515(b)(2)(B)	6049(b)(2)(C)	502(b)
911(c)(4)	515(b)(2)(B)	6159(f)	509(c)
911(d)(4)	515(b)(2)(C)(i)	6652(c)(1)	516(c)(2)
911(d)(7)	515(b)(2)(C)(ii)	6652(c)(3)	516(c)(1)
911(f)	515(c)	6652(c)(4)	516(c)(1)
911(g)	515(c)	6652(c)(5)	516(c)(1)
953(e)(10)	103(a)(1)(A)	7122(c)	509(a)
953(e)(10)	103(a)(1)(B)	7122(d)	509(a)
954(c)(6)	103(b)(1)	7122(d)(3)(A)	509(b)(1)
954(h)(9)	103(a)(2)	7122(d)(3)(B)	509(b)(1)
1221(b)(3)	204(a)	7122(d)(3)(C)	509(b)(1)
1221(b)(4)	204(a)	7122(e)	509(a)
1355(a)(4)	205(a)	7122(f)	509(b)(2)
1445(b)(8)	506(b)	7872(g)(6)	209(b)(1)
1445(e)(6)	505(b)	7872(h)	209(a)
1445(e)(7)	505(b)	7872(i)	209(a)

¶ 6003. Act Sections Amending Code

Act Sec.	Code Sec.	Act Sec.	Code Sec.
101	179(b)(1)	501(b)	163(j)(9)(D)
101	179(b)(2)	502(a)	6049(b)(2)(B)
101	179(b)(5)	502(a)	6049(b)(2)(C)
101	179(c)(2)	502(b)	6049(b)(2)(C)
101	179(d)(1)(A)(ii)	503(a)	167(h)(5)
103(a)(1)(A)	953(e)(10)	504(a)	897(h)(4)(A)(i)(II)
103(a)(1)(B)	953(e)(10)	505(a)(1)(A)	897(h)(1)
103(a)(2)	954(h)(9)	505(a)(1)(B)	897(h)(1)
103(b)(1)	954(c)(6)	505(a)(1)(C)	897(h)(1)
201(a)	468B(g)	505(a)(2)	897(h)(4)(A)(ii)
202	355(b)(3)	505(b)	1445(e)(6)
203(a)(1)	143(l)(4)	505(b)	1445(e)(7)
203(b)(1)(A)	143(l)(3)(B)(i)(I)	505(c)(1)	852(b)(3)(E)
203(b)(1)(A)	143(l)(3)(B)(i)(II)	505(c)(2)	871(k)(2)(E)
203(b)(1)(B)	143(l)(3)(B)	506(a)	897(h)(5)
203(b)(1)(C)	143(l)(3)(B)(ii)	506(b)	1445(b)(8)
203(b)(1)(C)	143(l)(3)(B)(iii)	507(a)	355(g)
203(b)(1)(C)	143(l)(3)(B)(iv)	508(a)	149(f)(2)(A)
204(a)	1221(b)(3)	508(b)	149(f)(4)
204(a)	1221(b)(4)	508(b)	149(f)(5)
204(b)	170(e)(1)(A)	508(b)	149(f)(6)
205(a)	1355(a)(4)	508(b)	149(f)(7)
207(a)	167(g)(8)	508(c)	148(f)(4)(D)(ii)(II)
208(a)	144(a)(4)(G)	508(c)	148(f)(4)(D)(ii)(III)
208(b)	144(a)(4)(F)	508(d)(1)	149(f)(1)
209(a)	7872(h)	508(d)(2)	149(f)(7)(B)
209(a)	7872(i)	508(d)(3)	54(l)(2)
209(b)(1)	7872(g)(6)	509(a)	7122(c)
209(b)(2)	142(d)(2)(B)	509(a)	7122(d)
301(a)(1)	55(d)(1)(A)	509(a)	7122(e)
301(a)(2)	55(d)(1)(B)	509(b)(1)	7122(d)(3)(A)
302(a)(1)	26(a)(2)	509(b)(1)	7122(d)(3)(B)
302(a)(2)	26(a)(2)	509(b)(1)	7122(d)(3)(C)
501(a)	163(j)(8)	509(b)(2)	7122(f)
501(a)	163(j)(9)	509(c)	6159(f)
501(b)	163(j)(9)(B)	510(a)	1(g)(2)(A)
501(b)	163(j)(9)(C)	510(b)	1(g)(4)(C)

Act Sec.	Code Sec.	Act Sec.	Code Sec.
510(c)	1(g)(2)(A)	515(b)(2)(B)	911(c)(2)
510(c)	1(g)(2)(B)	515(b)(2)(B)	911(c)(3)
510(c)	1(g)(2)(C)	515(b)(2)(B)	911(c)(4)
511(a)	3402(t)	515(b)(2)(C)(i)	911(d)(4)
512(a)(1)	408A(c)(3)(B)	515(b)(2)(C)(ii)	911(d)(7)
512(a)(1)	408A(c)(3)(C)	515(c)	911(f)
512(a)(2)	408A(c)(3)(B)(i)	515(c)	911(g)
512(b)(1)	408A(d)(3)(A)(iii)	516(a)(1)	4965
512(b)(2)(A)	408A(d)(3)(E)(i)	516(b)(1)(A)	6033(a)(2)
512(b)(2)(B)	408A(d)(3)(E)	516(b)(1)(A)	6033(a)(3)
514(a)	199(b)(2)	516(b)(1)(B)	6033(a)(1)
514(b)(1)	199(d)(1)(A)(iii)	516(b)(2)	6011(g)
514(b)(2)	199(a)(2)	516(b)(2)	6011(h)
515(a)(1)	911(b)(2)(D)(ii)	516(c)(1)	6652(c)(3)
515(a)(2)	911(b)(2)(D)(ii)	516(c)(1)	6652(c)(4)
515(b)(1)	911(c)(1)(B)(i)	516(c)(1)	6652(c)(5)
515(b)(2)(A)	911(c)(1)(A)	516(c)(2)	6652(c)(1)

¶ 6004. FTC 2nd ¶ s Affected by Act

FTC 2d ¶	Analysis ¶
A-1301	204
A-1307	205
A-1309	205
A-4010	202
A-4054	202
A-4255	202
A-4405	202
A-4455	202
A-4781	202
A-8102	103
A-8162	201
A-8163	201
A-8304	104
B-1903	112
E-3602	111
E-6163.1	110
E-6617	603
E-6619.1	110
F-4602	502
F-4801	501
F-4802	501
F-4803	501
F-4804	501
F-12101	113
G-2791	303
H-4226 *et seq.*	802
H-4258 *et seq.*	802
H-4475 *et seq.*	802
H-4486 *et seq.*	802
H-12290.11	203
H-12290.16	203
H-12290.20	203
H-12290.41	203
I-5104.1	108
I-5110 *et seq.*	101
I-5110.1	102
I-5110.10	101
I-5115 *et seq.*	107
I-5115.1	109
I-6100	208
I-6601	208
J-1360	106
J-2901	207
J-2917	207
J-2988	207
J-2989	207
J-2990	207
J-2991	207
J-3182	903, 904
J-3233.1	901
J-3233.2	901
J-3462	902
J-3664	902
K-5318.1	109
L-4385 *et seq.*	301
L-4386 *et seq.*	302
L-9907	401
L-9922	403
L-9933	402
L-18101	202
L-18102	202
N-3201	404
O-1101	206
O-1102	206
O-1114	206
O-1161	206
O-1162	206
O-1164	206
O-1166	206
O-1167	206
O-1171	206
O-1201	206
O-1652	304
O-1657	304
O-1658	304
O-1660.1	304
O-2404	601
O-2423.1	601
O-2423.2 *et seq.*	601
O-2448.2	601
O-2480.3 *et seq.*	601
O-2494	601
O-4401	202
O-10701	603, 604
O-10734	603, 604
O-10735	603, 604
O-10753	603, 604
O-10771	603, 604
O-11554	305
O-13000	603
O-13035	105
S-3040	801
S-3151 *et seq.*	802
S-3656 *et seq.*	802
S-3679 *et seq.*	802
S-4427.1	702, 703
S-5353	803
T-9601	804
T-9612	804
T-9618	804
T-9620	804
T-9627	804
T-10024	804
V-1907	704

¶ 6005. USTR ¶s Affected by Act

USTR ¶	Analysis ¶	USTR ¶	Analysis ¶	USTR ¶	Analysis ¶
14.08	101, 102	1994.01	301, 302	12,214.45	208
14.085	107, 109	3064.02	113	13,554	305
14.087	108	3554.01	502	14,00C4	202
14.09	204, 205	3554.02	501	14,454	603
234	202	408A4	203	14,454.02	105
244.01	202	468B4	303	34,014.37 *et seq.*	802
254.01	202	5844	111	34,024 *et seq.*	802
25B4	202	6145.01(20)	404	34,024.25	802
25D4	202	7024.01	112	34,044 *et seq.*	802
264	202	8524.02	110	60,114.02	702, 703
554.01	103, 201	8574.02	110	60,414	802
574	104	8974	603, 604	60,494.03	801
594	201	8974.02	603, 604	60,50M4.01	802
1114	304	9044.01	202	60,514	802
1434.019	903, 904	9114.01	206	66,524	704
1444.01	901	9114.02	206	66,554	803
1484.04	902	9114.11	206	71,224.01	804
1494.05	902	9114.12	206	71,224.03	804
1634.053	109	9214	304	71,224.05	804
1674.126	404	9534.01	601	75,184	106
1794.01	401	9544.02	601	78,724.02	207
1794.02	403	12,214.01	208	78,724.20	207
1794.04	402				

¶ 6006. Tax Desk ¶s Affected by Act

TaxDesk ¶	Analysis ¶	TaxDesk ¶	Analysis ¶	TaxDesk ¶	Analysis ¶
155,001	207	244,401	113	569,205	202
155,020	207	249,500	208	569,505	202
155,056	207	252,501	208	569,551	202
155,057	207	268,410	402	584,003	112
155,058	207	268,411	401	609,201	803
155,059	207	268,424	403	643,001	603, 604
173,002.1	110	271,701	404	643,015	603, 604
173,009	110	283,312	203	643,016	603, 604
191,002	206	283,316	203	643,022	603, 604
191,004	206	283,326	203	644,000	603
191,028	206	283,349	203	644,019	105
191,033	206	307,803	301	644,602	305
191,034	206	315,018.1	109	657,304	111
191,500	206	380,502	202	691,002	103
191,701	304	393,001	202	691,302	201
191,711	304	398,000	202	691,303	201
191,712	304	398,001	202	697,004	104
223,304.1	108	534,001 *et seq.*	802	811,501	801
223,309 *et seq.*	101	535,007 *et seq.*	802	812,001	802
223,310	102	538,001 *et seq.*	802	814,001	802
223,320	101	538,049	802	816,014	802
223,345 *et seq.*	107	568,301	204	842,001	804
223,346	109	568,307	205	842,012	804
237,002	502	568,309	205	842,022	804
237,401	501	568,805	202	842,027	804
237,426	501	569,104	202	901,006	804
237,427	501				

INDEX

References are to paragraph numbers

D

E